RESPLENDENT SYNAGOGUE

RESPLENDENT SYNAGOGUE

Architecture and Worship in an Eighteenth-Century Polish Community

THOMAS C. HUBKA

Brandeis University Press

Waltham, Massachusetts

For Judith

BRANDEIS UNIVERSITY PRESS

© 2003 by Brandeis University Press
Foreword © 2022 by Barbara Kirshenblatt-Gimblett
Preface © 2022 by Thomas C. Hubka
Afterword © 2022 by Sergey R. Kravtsov

Manufactured in the United States of America
Designed by Katherine Kimball
Typeset in Galliard by Passumpsic Publishing

First paperback edition 2022

For permission to reproduce any of the material in this book,
contact Brandeis University Press, 415 South Street, Waltham
MA 02453, or visit brandeisuniversitypress.com

This book was published with the generous support of the
Lucius N. Littauer Foundation, Inc., the Koret Foundation,
and the Samuel H. Kress Foundation.

Library of Congress Control Number: 2022910867
Paperback ISBN: 978-1-68458-133-7
Ebook ISBN: 978-1-68458-134-4

5 4 3 2 1

Frontispiece: *Entrance to the Prayer Hall, West Wall, Gwoździec Synagogue.* A painting by Isidor Kaufmann, *Portal of the Rabbis,* c. 1897–1898, oil on wood, 24 x 34 cm. (Courtesy of the Hungarian National Gallery.)

For the complete list of books available in this series, please see https://brandeisuniversitypress.com/series/tauber

CONTENTS

ILLUSTRATIONS

COLOR PLATES

Color plates begin after page 102.

FIGURES

FOREWORD

Resplendent Synagogue is a transformative volume. Its impact far exceeds the wildest expectations of its author, Thomas C. Hubka, and the historians of the Polish wooden synagogue who preceded him. Of the hundreds of wooden synagogues built between the sixteenth and eighteenth centuries on the territory of the Polish-Lithuanian Commonwealth (today's Poland, Latvia, Lithuania, Belarus, and parts of Ukraine, Estonia, and western Russia), not one was left standing by the end of the Second World War. The Germans had destroyed the last still standing at the time of the invasion.

All that remained was the documentation by architectural historians and artists, starting with the pioneering work of Zygmunt Gloger (1845–1910), a historian and ethnographer, who was documenting wooden synagogues by at least 1870. The rise of interest in vernacular architecture and folk culture during the second half of the nineteenth century played an important role in the construction of national heritage as well as of the heritage of national minorities. It was only after the First World War that the countries we know today (Poland, Lithuania, Belarus, and Ukraine, among others), albeit with different borders, gained or regained their independence. The Polish-Lithuanian Commonwealth had been partitioned in three stages between 1772 and 1795 by the Russian and Austrian Empires and Kingdom of Prussia and disappeared from the map of Europe, but the dream of regained independence lived on, and national culture, rooted in the local and the vernacular, became ever more important in the absence of sovereign territory.

Jewish national awakening took many forms during the second half of the nineteenth century, from Zionism and the Jewish labor movement to Diaspora Nationalism. At the heart of this new awakening was the rise of modern Jewish culture and political movements, and with them the amassing of historical documents and artifacts, ethnographic expeditions, folklore collecting, and the documentation of synagogue architecture and tombstones. These developments continued after the First World War. Despite the losses suffered during the war, Maria and Kazimierz Piechotka led the efforts after the war to recover the documentation and to enrich what could be learned from it.

It is based on these developments that Hubka, who had long been interested in vernacular wooden architecture, albeit in America, turned to the Polish wooden synagogue. He achieved something unprecedented, the most detailed and comprehensive analysis of a single wooden synagogue, the one that once stood in Gwoździec, today in Ukraine. It is by far the best documented of all wooden synagogues, although it was destroyed by fire during the First World War, when the Russian front moved through the town.

The first to document this synagogue was the artist Karol Zyndram Maszkowski (1868–1938). His handwritten manuscript, *Bóżnica drewniana w miasteczku Gwoźdźcu*, describes the building, its exterior and interior, in words and drawings. Dated 1890, this manuscript appears to be his doctoral dissertation, which he submitted a few years later but never published; it can be found today in the Archives of PAU, the Polish Academy of Learning, in Kraków. Maszkowski prepared additional drawings in 1894 and returned to Gwoździec in 1899, commissioned by the Polish Academy of Arts and Sciences to make more drawings of this synagogue.

Isidor Kaufmann (1853–1921), a Jewish artist living in Vienna, documented two wooden synagogue interiors in color. *Portal of the Rabbis* (1897/1898) shows the entrance door and view of the west wall from inside the sanctuary of the Gwoździec wooden synagogue. A second painting, dated 1897, shows the interior of the nearby Jabłonów wooden synagogue from a similar angle. Kaufmann would spend months at a time in

Galicia, the part of the Polish-Lithuanian Commonwealth annexed by the Austrian Empire at the end of the eighteenth century. In an ecstatic letter to his wife, Kaufmann called this region his "promised land." It was here that he found what he considered an authentically Jewish world, one that seemed to have been bypassed by modernity and that was unlike his acculturated Jewish milieu in Vienna.

The most extensive documentation of the Gwoździec wooden synagogue—indeed, of any wooden synagogue—was made by Alois Breyer, also Breier (1885–1948), a Viennese architect, who was inspired by Kaufmann to study wooden synagogues. Between 1910 and 1913, while a student, Breyer made hundreds of drawings, watercolor renderings, and albumen prints of this and other wooden synagogues for his doctoral dissertation at the Vienna University of Technology. He was especially taken with their painted interiors. Together with Max Grunwald and Max Eisler, Breyer published his findings in *Menorah* in installments in 1932 and as a book, *Holzsynagogen in Polen*, in 1934. Grunwald, a rabbi and folklorist, wrote about the origins and nature of the synagogue, deciphered the inscriptions and explained the liturgical aspects, and arranged for the publication of the work. Eisler, a Viennese art historian, placed the construction of these synagogues in the context of wooden construction and synagogue architecture more generally—and praised Breyer, who he noted was not Jewish and therefore, in his view, more objective. Breyer gave his documentation to the Tel Aviv Museum in 1937 and exhibited the material there in 1941. His documentation of the Gwoździec wooden synagogue is of special value, not only because it was so detailed and comprehensive, but also because this synagogue was destroyed during the First World War not long after he had documented it.

Although the first mention of Jews in Gwoździec is in a document dated 1635, around the time that they formed a Jewish community, they must have arrived earlier, likely in the previous century, albeit in small numbers. They built their wooden synagogue sometime between 1640 and 1652. Though magnificent, the synagogue was relatively small, reflecting the size of the Jewish community. When they refurbished the synagogue between 1729 and 1731, there were only between 150 and 250 Jews living in Gwoździec, by Hubka's estimate, and even fewer a century earlier when the synagogue was built. By 1765, the Jewish commu-

nity consisted of only the 541 individuals who lived in Gwoździec, about 60 percent of the town's population, and the 126 Jews residing in smaller localities nearby. Alterations and expansions over the years reflected the Jewish community's growth—and its prosperity and optimism—although the town and its Jewish community always remained relatively small.

This synagogue and thousands of others, both wooden and masonry, challenge the idea that East European Jews lived by words alone, that they inhabited the colorless world of the black-and-white photographs by which we know them, and that they were iconophobic, apparently in keeping with the Second Commandment's prohibition against making and worshiping graven images. These synagogues, as well as illuminated manuscripts and elaborately carved and painted tombstones, among many other examples, are testimony to their rich visual culture. These synagogues were, to paraphrase Moshe Rosman, distinctly local, whether Polish, Ukrainian, Belarusian, or Lithuanian, and categorically Jewish.

Wooden synagogues were the result of a collaboration between local carpenters, who worked on the construction of the building, and Jewish cabinetmakers, who carved the intricate Torah arks, which held parchment scrolls on which a scribe had written the five books of the Hebrew Bible. A prime example of cultural symbiosis, these buildings shared architectural forms, construction techniques, and visual style with local churches and other vernacular wooden buildings. As such, the wooden synagogue was the perfect way to express cultural symbiosis within the Core Exhibition at POLIN Museum of the History of Polish Jews.

POLIN Museum was created from the inside out. The idea for a museum of the history of Polish Jews in Warsaw arose in 1993, just four years after the fall of communism, and was embraced by the Association of the Jewish Historical Institute of Poland, a Jewish charitable organization established in 1951. With neither a collection nor a building, the project took as its starting point the story, the thousand-year history of Polish Jews, and made the multimedia narrative exhibition that would tell that story its first priority. Event Communication, an exhibition design firm in London, was commissioned to develop the master plan for the Core Exhibition, a process that lasted from 2000 to 2004. From the beginning, there was to be a wooden synagogue ceiling element in the eighteenth-century sec-

Reconstruction of the 18th-century painted ceiling and central bimah (raised platform for the public reading from the Torah scroll) that once stood in the Polish wooden synagogue of Gwoździec, today Hvizdets in Ukraine. The installation is the centerpiece of "The Jewish Town" gallery in POLIN Museum of the History of Polish Jews, Warsaw, Poland. Courtesy of POLIN Museum. Photo: Magdalena Starowieyska and Darek Golik.

tion of the exhibition. As visualized in the master plan, it was unpainted, and the budget would cover its construction by a prop maker.

In 2007, Michael Berkowitz, then a member of the North American Council for the Museum of the History of Polish Jews, insisted that I meet Rick and Laura Brown of Handshouse Studio, a nonprofit educational organization in Massachusetts. During a brief visit to New York—I was living in Warsaw at the time—I met with them at a café in Lower Manhattan. They showed me a short video documenting their project to build the wooden bima, the reader's platform, of the Gwoździec wooden synagogue. They had completed the construction with their students in one week using traditional

tools, materials, and techniques. I knew then and there that we had to work together. They yearned to build an entire wooden synagogue in this way. Would that we could have realized that dream. What we could do, within the limits of the Core Exhibition, was to build the timber-frame roof and painted ceiling of a wooden synagogue. But, which one? Gwoździec, thanks to *Resplendent Synagogue*, was the obvious choice. No other synagogue had been as fully documented and analyzed.

However, to build this component in the Handshouse Studio way would take more time, be more complicated, and cost more. Irene Kronhill Pletka immediately understood the value of this project and generously underwrote it. Construction began in the summer of 2011 with three two-week workshops at the open-air Rural Museum of Folk Architecture on the outskirts of Sanok, in the south of Poland. There followed two-week workshops that summer and the next to complete the painted ceiling. In all, more than 300 students, volunteers, and experts took part. In 2013, the parts were brought to Warsaw, lowered into the exhibition space, reassembled, hoisted, and the twenty-five-ton structure suspended from cables. Maria Piechotka (1920–2020), the doyenne of Polish synagogue architecture historians, lived to see the materialization of the documentation she and her husband, Kazimierz, had done so much to bring to light. She got to help hoist the Gwoździec ceiling and roof into place.

I like to think of this project—and Handshouse Studio's approach—as recovering intangible heritage through a process of materialization in the absence of the original object but in the presence of documentation. The mission of Handshouse Studio is to recover lost objects. As the Browns explain, it is not possible to recover the original object, in the sense of the original material. It is however possible to recover the knowledge of how to build that object by constructing it using traditional tools, materials, and techniques, a process based on documentation, comparison with related examples still standing, and reverse engineering.

The object that results is not a reconstruction, recreation, copy, facsimile, simulation, or any other "second-order" version of something "original," but rather the materialization of new knowledge in a new object, a new kind of object, an object that is actual, not a virtual version of something else. The value of this object lies in how it was made and in the knowledge that was re-covered in the process. This approach is in keeping with the Japanese tradition of tearing down the Ise Jingu grand shrine every twenty years and rebuilding it, a tradition that has persisted for about 1,300 years or even longer. In this way, the knowledge of how to build the shrine is transmitted and will outlast the materials. The intangible heritage turns out to be more durable than the tangible heritage, and it is valued more highly.

We made the decision to construct the ceiling and timber-framed roof at about 85 percent scale, given the constraints of the exhibition space, and to create an opening in the gallery's ceiling so that the roof would rise up from the exhibition level to the main floor. Because we decided to shingle only part of the roof, visitors can view the complex internal structure of this architecture. Surrounding the roof on the main floor is a glass ledge. This where we present the construction process and source materials and where we place the Gwoździec wooden synagogue within the wider history of wooden synagogues.

Today, the Gwoździec painted ceiling and timber-frame roof are a centerpiece of POLIN Museum's Core Exhibition. The value of this object is exponentially greater thanks to the way we made it. Without *Resplendent Synagogue*, an inspiration and a manual, it would not have been possible to create this gem. What finer way to honor this splendid book and what it has inspired than to make it available to a new generation of readers.

February 18, 2022

Barbara Kirshenblatt-Gimblett is the Ronald S. Lauder Chief Curator, Core Exhibition, POLIN Museum of the History of Polish Jews.

More than a half century ago, I first read Maria and Kazimierz Piechotka's remarkable book, *Wooden Synagogues*. Like Louis Kahn, who discovered the same book several years earlier, I was captivated by a fascinating, exotic, and unexpectedly Jewish architecture. More than thirty-five years ago, as a young professor of architecture, I began researching the wooden synagogues as an example of Polish vernacular architecture. I primarily studied the details of their construction and building history, but their origins in cultural and religious history were more difficult to decipher. I recall sharing my early enthusiasm for the Polish synagogues with several rabbis and scholars of the synagogue, but their caution and skepticism surprised me. Surely this was significant Jewish architecture, strange looking perhaps, but still the dominant synagogue architecture of the entire Eastern European region.

I have come to recognize this cautious reaction as a commonly shared reluctance to engage Eastern European "shtetl" topics. During the nineteenth century, a negative attitude toward shtetl Jews (the *Ostjuden*) was developed by an urban, German Reform Jewry toward a rural Polish-Russian Orthodox Jewry—attitudes later carried by immigrants to America in the late nineteenth and early twentieth centuries. Consequently, the highly ornate exteriors and densely decorated interiors of the wooden synagogues seemed inexplicable to modern observers, who often attributed this expression to the effects of poverty and persecution within Eastern European shtetl communities—effects accompanied by disdain toward religious mysticism often associated with the Sabbatian movement and the rise of Hasidism.

Many of these misleading and negative attitudes toward the shtetl and its cultural life have changed in the last fifty years as our knowledge of Eastern European Jewish culture and the history of its synagogue architecture has greatly expanded, especially since the fall of communism and the opening of Eastern European archives. Despite the complete destruction of the wooden synagogues, historical and material cultural studies have continued to fill in the history of the small Jewish town. The study of the Eastern European synagogue has also been greatly facilitated by the work of Hebrew University's Center for Jewish Art in Jerusalem, as well as by the completion of a crowning achievement in the documentation and presentation of Polish and Eastern European Jewish history—the POLIN Museum of the History of Polish Jews—to which this republication is a tribute and where a partial replica of the Gwoździec Synagogue takes center stage.

Since the first printing of *Resplendent Synagogue* in 2003, I have averaged about five wooden synagogue lectures per year to both academic and Jewish community audiences. In architectural student lectures, I express genuine unbridled enthusiasm for an architecture that I still find to be fascinating and highly instructive of architectural and cultural history. Yet, to audiences with knowledge of Jewish history and synagogue architecture, I maintain a more restrained approach, for I am accustomed to the surprise and hesitation of those unfamiliar with the exotic shapes of the wooden synagogue exterior and the blaze of discordant interior color, the density of unfamiliar animal imagery, and a cacophony of painted prayer. For those viewers, I pause to emphasize that despite its unfamiliarity, this was authentic Jewish art and architecture both of long duration and spread over a wide area of Eastern Europe. Finally, I stress that the dominant wall-paintings were Jewish art made by Jews, for Jews, and about Jews. I go on to emphasize that these dramatic ensembles were not concocted by fringe congregations or radical elements in their Jewish communities but were commissioned with the full support of the leading rabbinical authorities, members of the *kahal* (the local Jewish governing body), and leading town merchants. And as if these approvals were not enough, they were usually commissioned with the support of Christian municipal authorities and often with contributions from the town's magnate, or ruling Catholic authority. In other words, officially sanctioned, by Jew and ruling gentile alike.

Returning to Jewish traditions, the synagogues' decorative program and architectural elements surrounding the ark and bimah, and especially the wall-paintings covering all interior surfaces, were components of a unified program of Jewish religious art and architectural motifs for which there is no modern equivalent. These artistic elements were not produced or commissioned in the manner of a donor painting or a stained glass for a modern synagogue. Rather they formed part of a highly coherent (but not identical) institutional program of art and architecture uniting hundreds of communities stretching over vast areas of Eastern Europe and developed within these Jewish communities stretching back centuries to late-medieval traditions, particularly from Rhineland German communities. We simply have no modern equivalent to this vast, unified program of art and architecture for the synagogue.

Yet this internal Jewish development of synagogal art and especially its architectural forms are made more complex by the extensive borrowing of styles and motifs from multicultural regional and international sources within the lands Jews settled. Here the well-established traditions of Eastern European monumental, institutional, and church architectures contributed to the underlying vocabulary for the dramatic roof forms, interior domes, and decorative elements surrounding the ark and bimah. Unlike the elaborate wall-paintings that were created solely by Jewish artists in well-established Jewish guilds, the entire architecture of the wooden synagogues' interior and exterior was crafted by non-Jewish regional builders. Because Jews were excluded from the major building trades, these architectural forms were constructed by competent gentile builders serving Jewish clients and their communities.

Despite these well-recognized non-Jewish sources of the architectural style and forms, the totality of a wooden synagogue was still distinctively, unmistakably Jewish. Whether constructed within Polish, Ukrainian, or Russian contexts or borrowing architectural styles from churches or state buildings, the distinctiveness of the Polish wooden synagogue was continuously recog-

nized by observers and foreign travelers for hundreds of years. This distinctively Jewish, Eastern European synagogue architecture is particularly surprising in Jewish diaspora context, where such architectural originality was achieved in no other community worldwide. In all other countries of the diaspora, Jews primarily borrowed the standard architecture styles of their host countries and cultures. In lectures I summarize these characteristic qualities of the Eastern European wooden synagogue as a combination of well-known local and regional architectural forms—but combined in a distinctly Jewish way!

Although this book is primarily an architectural analysis of one Polish synagogue, it is also a study that consistently searches to find and interpret the social, cultural, and religious origins of its art and architecture. Consequently, the book proceeds from a more solidly grounded interpretation of the architecture and paintings of the Gwoździec Synagogue toward a more speculative interpretation of the religious, social, and communal culture that nurtured its creation. To mention just one of several unresolved cultural issues that deserve further study, this book focuses on the early eighteenth-century period when the Gwoździec Synagogue was constructed and expanded—a period for which there is no clear historical consensus about the nature and practices of the popular religious services conducted within synagogues like Gwoździec. In other words, the critical relationship between the documented art and architecture of the common synagogue and the conduct of daily worship has not been adequately studied or understood. To answer this type of question is to speculate about religious traditions of Jewish popular culture in the early eighteenth century—a pre-Hasidic Jewish popular worship that sustained an architecture and artistic culture within hundreds of similar communities of Eastern Europe.

After almost twenty years since publication, I have been pleased by the reception of *Resplendent Synagogue* and the major themes of its research. Some of these themes have been continued and developed by current scholars, as reviewed by Sergey Kravtsov in the afterword to this volume. A lingering regret about this study is that I was unable to explore more deeply the meaning and symbolism of the wall-paintings, particularly the painted prayers that dominate the interior of most synagogues and whose standardization over space and time points to a shared liturgy among the small Jewish towns of Eastern Europe. Such future study must obviously be grounded in a thorough knowledge of the rabbinical and liturgical literature of the early modern period, but also of the popular and ethical literature of the same period, an extremely difficult subject, as outlined for me by scholars such as Zeev Gries. This is the type of complexity that will continue to challenge future researchers of the wooden synagogues.

ACKNOWLEDGMENTS

After nearly fifteen years of research, I find myself indebted to many people who helped me understand the wooden synagogues and the cultures that produced them. While scholarly acknowledgments are the standard introduction to most books, the following acknowledgments are especially heartfelt, for this is a multidisciplinary work that has required collaboration with scholars from many disciplines. Architects do not cultivate an image of themselves as team players, but such collaborative effort, both among ourselves and with clients and builders, has always been essential to our work. So consulting with specialists from many different fields seemed like the obvious approach to this difficult research. Critical to this multidisciplinary approach was the unification of three broad fields of study: Polish (or Eastern-European) historical studies, Jewish cultural and religious studies, and Polish/Jewish art and architectural studies. I am convinced that this book will demonstrate that these three critical components, frequently separated in existing research, must be considered together if we are to understand the complex unity of context, culture, and architecture that is revealed in the wooden synagogues. Many of the ideas in this book have remained undeveloped because expertise sufficient to integrate these fields of study has rarely existed in any one scholar. The collaborative scholarly approach that I have followed is one way to gain access to that expertise. I could have written a more-than-adequate architectural history of the wooden synagogues if I had confined myself to my own discipline. But it would not have told the story of the crucial relationship between the synagogue and its community. It is, therefore, with a great sense of honor and humility that I acknowledge the following scholars, many of them the very finest in their respective fields, who helped create this book. For the flaws in this text, I am fully responsible; for the ways that the synagogue and community of Gwoździec shine through, I thank my collaborators.

To my teachers, with whom my initial contact came through their influential texts, I owe the greatest debt. I was particularly influenced by Elliot Wolfson, *Through a Speculum That Shines*; Henry Glassie, *Folk Housing in Middle Virginia*; Moshe Idel, *Kabbalah: New Perspectives*; Marc Epstein, *Dreams of Subversion in Medieval Jewish Art and Literature*; and Gershom Scholem, *Major Trends in Jewish Mysticism*. In the initial phase of my research, several scholars went out of their way to guide my work and offer encouragement, especially Carol Krinsky, Michael Steinlauf, Adam Miłobędzki, Leo Marx, and Richard Schoenwald.

Many individuals reviewed various drafts of my manuscript and provided critical evaluation and guidance for my research. I am particularly indebted to Avriel Bar-Levav, Carol Krinsky, Michael Steinlauf, Eleonora Bergman, Adam Miłobędzki, Iaroslav Isaievych, Elliot Wolfson, Maria and Kazimierz Piechotka, Moshe Rosman, Boaz Huss, Zeev Gries, Chone Shmeruk, Michael Mikoś, Elliot Ginsburg, Antony Polonsky, Marc Epstein, and Arnold Rosenberg. I would also like to acknowledge the influence of the Piechotkas' seminal works on this book as well as on all research about the Polish wooden synagogues.

Many other scholars and advisors provided invaluable assistance, suggestions, and critical analysis during the extended period of research. They include: Gershon Hundert, Stasys Samalavicius, Israel Bartal, Rachel Elior, Joseph Gutmann, Sergei Kravtsov, Bezalel Narkiss, Iris Fishof, Shalom Sabar, Aliza Cohen-Mushlin, Haviva Pedaya, Pinchas Giller, Chava Weissler, Marvin Herzog, Samuel Gruber, Shaul Stampfer, David Kaufman, Mark Verman, Hillel Levine, Rakhmiel Peltz, Byron Sherwin, Vivian Mann, Edward van Voolen, Alan Corre, James Young, Zachery Baker, Joanna Kilian,

Evelyn Cohen, Steven Fine, Daniel Abrams, Richard Cohen, Mira Friedman, Titus Hewryk, Volodymyr Chornovus, Ida Huberman, Rafi Grafman, Ruth Jacoby, Aharon Kashtan, David Assaf, Vladimir Melamed, Elhanan Reiner, Annette Weber, Jan Jagielski, Jacob Chonigsman, Ivan Mogytych, Ryszard Brykowski, Michall Galas, Ania Kilian, Samuel Heilman, Jacek Purchla, Joachim Russek, William Gross, Rabbi Leonard Mishkin, Dina Abramowicz, Shula Laderman, Rainia Fehl, Henryk Drzewiecki, Aron Lutwak, and David Davidovitch.

Research support for this book has been provided by two major grants. I owe thanks to the National Endowment for the Arts for their support of my research in Poland and Ukraine, and to the National Endowment for the Humanities for their support of my research in Israel. Other organizations that provided generous research support at critical periods include the Wisconsin Society for Jewish Learning, the National Endowment of the Humanities (Summer Stipends Program), and the Department of Architecture, University of Wisconsin–Milwaukee. To my architecture faculty colleagues at the University of Wisconsin–Milwaukee, especially Dean Robert Greenstreet and Jerry Weisman, I offer thanks for their patience and support.

Amy Lewis helped me shape the many drafts of this text. Phyllis Deutsch and Sylvia Fuks-Fried understood the goals of the research and provided just the right amount of editorial carrot and stick to bring the book together. Janet Tibbetts and Paul Olsen helped with secretarial support and media development. Several of my students and research assistants have assisted with preliminary architectural drawings and documentation, including Pao Yang, Cecile Kunznitz, Peter Foerster, and Julie Erickson-Heiberger.

In chapter 4, the "Painted Prayers" section was written collaboratively with Arnold Rosenberg. The prayers in the appendix were translated from Hebrew by Avri Bar-Levav. Parts of chapter 6 have been adapted from an article first published in the *Journal of Jewish Thought and Philosophy*.

My overseas research was immeasurably enriched by two of the finest guides and friends I could have found: Sławek Parfianowicz in Warsaw and Avri Bar-Levav in Jerusalem. Through their expertise and guidance, they helped me to understand their cultures and their histories in ways that would have been inaccessible to even the most diligent researcher. Through their eyes, I learned to see the wooden synagogues and their communities more clearly, and for this I am extremely grateful.

To my family of Hubkas and Kennys, I have appreciated their long-distance support for my project. I hope that my nieces and nephew will find inspiration in these pages. Finally I would like to thank my wife, Judith Kenny, for her support as helpful critic and delightful colleague during the extended period of the book's development. She has allowed me to appreciate the balance between life and scholarship, which has enriched my work, and for this I am very grateful. It is with love and affection that I dedicate this book to her.

In 1916, my paternal grandfather, Anthony Hubka, came to America. He left a tiny Polish village along the Nemen River in what is now Belarus to settle in Perth Amboy, New Jersey. From my childhood, I remember a faded photograph of his family's thatched-roof cottage as well as stories of annual floods and a hard farming life. His own grandfather had been a serf under the Czar, and by the time Anthony left for America, prospects for his family were only marginally better. Many Poles trace their ancestry to the nobility from the local manor house, just as other Americans might imagine a royal family and castle in their past; but the Hubkas trace their family to peasants and serfs as far back as anyone can imagine. It has been a long journey out, and now I return for a closer look. I have never been able to find my grandfather's village, but I have traveled through hundreds of similar tiny, agricultural hamlets, and I have studied the history of these farmers—former serfs, more recently peasants, and now just poor Belarusians. I think grandfather Hubka would have understood the work that this return has entailed, for he certainly understood the nature of hard work, and through him, so do I. Thank you, grandfather.

The return to my Polish roots has involved studying the complex relationships between Poles and Jews in the small towns of prewar Poland. During lectures about the architecture of these towns, I have frequently been asked to identify the designers of Jewish buildings and especially the master builders of the wooden synagogues. Most scholars believe it is unlikely that Jews were directly involved in pre-nineteenth-century Polish construction like the creation of the wooden synagogues. However, my brother's father-in-law, David Scheckman, tells me that his father and grandfather were carpenters and furniture makers from a small town in eastern Poland, Barmichiz (this is probably the Yiddish pronun-

ciation of the Polish name). His stories initially led me to think about Jewish carpenters and woodworkers in Poland. And so, when asked about the possibility of Jews in the building trades, I think of Pop Scheckman's answer to that question—his father was a carpenter when he emigrated from Poland in 1906, his grandfather was a carpenter before him, and as far as we know it was Scheckman carpenters from there on back. So why should it be assumed that Jews were not involved in the building of their own synagogues? If there were Scheckmans in that shtetl, I think they would have been involved. And so, I have begun this research believing that Jews could be involved in the construction of their synagogues. Thank you, Pop Scheckman.

The great-grandfathers of the Hubka and the Scheckman families probably never met each other in Poland, but I like to think they might have. I can even imagine them coming to know each other in a spirit of mutual acceptance between Gentile and Jew, a mutual acceptance that most often defined the relationships between farmer and villager in their separate yet always intertwining worlds. So much has been written about the disunity and antagonism between these worlds that it is sometimes hard to imagine a time of peaceful coexistence. Yet this book describes such a time when the wooden synagogue of Gwoździec was built. This synagogue could not have been constructed without long periods of peaceful coexistence and mutual acceptance among the multi-ethnic and religious communities that lived in these small towns. This book was written about such an era. It was not written to blur or erase the tragedies and hard times that plagued Jewish communities in other times and other regions. It was written as a way of remembering the mutual coexistence and cooperation between Jewish and Gentile worlds that, as we shall see, paved the way for constructing the Gwoździec Synagogue.

RESPLENDENT SYNAGOGUE

FIG. 1. *West Facade, Gwoździec Synagogue, c. 1900.* A small entrance shed covered the main doorway. A stovepipe can be seen on the roof of a masonry addition to the right of the entry. The synagogue was located at the northeast edge of town near a woodland in the background. (Courtesy of the Tel Aviv Museum of Art.)

SYNAGOGUE AND COMMUNITY

Gwoździec (pronounced **Gov-vosz-djets**) was a small but relatively prosperous trading center located on the southeastern edge of the former Polish-Lithuanian Commonwealth, in what is now part of western Ukraine (fig. 2).[1] At the beginning of the eighteenth century, Gwoździec (called Gvozdets in present-day Ukraine) was inhabited by communities of Poles, Ukrainians, and Jews. Following the typical settlement pattern for a small, Eastern-European, commercial town, these communities settled in loosely clustered neighborhoods around an open market square. Beginning in the early 1700s, all these communities, but particularly the Jewish community, experienced an extended period of growth and prosperity that, in retrospect, marks Gwoździec's finest hour.

In the summer of 1731, the Jewish community of Gwoździec had nearly finished remodeling their wooden synagogue (fig. 1). The centerpiece of this construction project was the reconfiguration of the prayer hall's ceiling. What was once a low, barrel-vaulted ceiling was transformed into a towering, tent-like wooden cupola with a curving, undulating surface. This cupola was probably the first of its kind to be built in the region. The interior of the remodeled synagogue was completely covered by elaborate paintings depicting Hebrew inscriptions and vibrant animal figures set against dense, vegetative backgrounds. Compared to the drab daily environment in which most of the town's Jewish community lived, their synagogue was a resplendent space unlike anything they were likely to see in their lifetimes.

FIG. 2. *Central Eastern Europe, 2000.* Dashed lines show current national boundaries. Note the location of the town of Gwoździec in present-day western Ukraine. (Based on P. R. Magocsi, *Historical Atlas of East Central Europe.*)

In these opening pages, we follow members of Gwoź-dziec's Jewish community through a summer evening in 1731, as they journey from their homes to their synagogue for the Friday evening service (fig. 3). The drawings that trace their journey provide views of the town and its synagogue that have been compiled from photographs, maps, and other historical documentation. They are intended both to introduce the community of Gwoździec and to convey the striking contrast between the realm of public life and the realm of spiritual life within the walls of the synagogue. Set in the early eighteenth century, these vignettes of town and synagogue may portray environments unfamiliar to the contemporary reader. Yet for the Jews of Gwoździec, these were the ordinary settings of their day-to-day lives, where the daily activities of life and worship were highly integrated. We begin on a Friday evening during the summer of 1731, when the sun is setting at the end of a warm, clear day.

The Jewish Street

As the sun sets, the residents of Gminna (Village) Street leave their houses to walk to the synagogue for the Friday evening service (fig. 4). Their journey takes them along deserted earthen streets lined with wooden houses that are typical of homes in the Jewish district. The streets they walk along have no sidewalks, vegetation, or lighting. Before the twentieth century, this barren street scene was typical of the small towns in eastern Poland.

The sketch shows the closely packed houses of Gminna Street. Except for their basic shape on a map and the names of their late-nineteenth-century owners, little is known about these houses. At the beginning of the First World War, they, along with a large portion of Gwoździec, were destroyed by fire in a military battle between Russia and Austria-Hungary.

Based on what we know about similar houses found both in Gwoździec and in neighboring towns, we believe that the houses along Gminna Street shared a set of basic physical characteristics. The walls of most houses were made of horizontally stacked hewn logs, and these logs were either left exposed or covered with a white plaster that turned gray over time. Ornamental woodwork surrounded some of the doorways and windows, although most houses had only a few small windows set into each wall. Most houses had roofs covered with wooden shingles, but the poorest residents may have used thatch or lapped boards instead. Inside, most houses had plaster or whitewashed walls and wood-plank floors. Of course, there was neither plumbing nor electricity. Judged by current standards, the interiors of most residences on Gminna Street would seem dark and sparsely furnished. A masonry heating and cooking stove made of crude brick and covered with stucco served as the central focal point of a typical dwelling. Unlike the open fires used in American Colonial houses during the same period, these masonry stoves concealed their flames in brick chambers. Unlike the drafty American fireplaces, these Eastern-European stoves were reasonably well designed for fuel efficiency and home heating.

When seen in early photographs and period drawings, the houses in small Polish towns appear to be joined together (see fig. 13). But most of the houses, like the ones along Gminna Street, were separate structures. Typically, houses were constructed perpendicular to the road with their modestly ornamented gable ends and

FIG. 3. *Aerial Diagram, Town of Gwoździec.* The dotted line traces the route to the synagogue taken by the residents of Gminna Street. The numbers indicate the various locations shown in the nine sketches (figures 4–12) that follow. The arrows indicate the direction of the view depicted in each sketch.

porches facing the street. In the early twentieth century, Polish artists and historians sketched and photographed the picturesque porches, gables, and balconies of the most elaborate houses in these small towns. Many observers saw these structures as romantic examples of an ancient Polish/Jewish architecture. They were, in fact, seventeenth-, eighteenth-, and nineteenth-century examples of mixed commercial and residential architecture that their small-town occupants had maintained and preserved for long periods. Because these more ornate buildings were popular subjects for early-twentieth-century artists, they came to be seen as typical of small-town Jewish architecture, although most Jewish residents of these small towns lived in more modest structures.

In 1731, Gwoździec was not a utopian environment for its Jewish population; but, measured by the standards of its period, neither was it an impoverished or declining community. Elements of the town's physical environment like housing were probably similar to those found in other expanding small towns in Eastern Europe, and the overall quality of town life certainly surpassed that of the agricultural Ukrainian peasantry living in the surrounding countryside. The Jewish district of Gwoździec was concentrated in the northeast quarter of the town, but this area was neither a segregated district nor an isolated, walled ghetto. Although ethnic and religious groups tended to live together, there were some Polish and Ukrainian families living in the Jewish district as well as some Jewish families living in the Polish and Ukrainian districts. In 1731, the cohesiveness of the Jewish district was created as much by its own customs and traditions of settlement as by any acts of exclusion or persecution. If there were restrictions placed on Jewish residency, as was sometimes the case in town settlement, these restrictions did not inhibit the steady expansion of the Jewish community. By the middle of the nineteenth century, the Jewish community formed the majority population of Gwoździec.

FIG. 4. *The Jewish Street.*

The Town Square

As they walk to the synagogue, the residents of Gminna Street pass through the Town Square (Rynek) (fig. 5). Gwoździec's town square is the secular and commercial center for both the town and its surrounding agricultural region. Market activities conducted here are the central reason for the town's existence. As the worshipers walk through the square, the setting sun casts its last rays upon the pediment of the large structure near the center of the square. This building is the Town Hall (Ratusz), from which the town council governs under the supervision of Ludwik Kalinowski, the local ruler or magnate. The Kalinowski/Puzyna family owns a considerable portion of Gwoździec as well as much of the surrounding agricultural land and farming villages. It is extremely important for members of the Jewish community to maintain good relations with Ludwik Kalinowski, because he controls many aspects of their lives. At the same time, the Kalinowski/Puzyna family often supports and protects the town's Jewish residents because they play an important role in the town's economic prosperity.

Although it has since been destroyed, the Town Hall was once one of Gwoździec's most impressive monumental buildings. Surviving plans for the building show that it was a large structure with wall buttresses and an elaborate porch. This is enough to suggest that it was one of the finest masonry buildings in the town. Perhaps, like Gwoździec's Bernardine Catholic Church, under construction in 1731, it was designed by architects who followed the late-Baroque Italian styles that dominated Polish architecture until the modern period.

In 1731, the town square may already have been bordered by a row of connected masonry buildings on the northern edge of the square (fig. 5). These commercial buildings, also destroyed in 1916, had an exterior masonry arcade, ground-floor shops, and upper-story residences for the town's wealthiest merchants and traders. In the provinces of eastern Poland, such commercial arcades, modeled on those found in larger towns like Lviv, signified a prosperous trading town. On a Friday evening in 1731, the normal business activities on the square would already have ceased in preparation for the Sabbath, as many of the town's principal merchants and traders were Jewish.

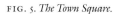

FIG. 5. *The Town Square.*

The Synagogue Courtyard

Beyond the market square, there are several streets and alleyways that lead to the synagogue courtyard (fig. 6). The synagogue courtyard is surrounded by buildings, most of which are owned by the Jewish community. These buildings include the Rabbi's house just behind the synagogue and two small ritual bath houses, one for men and one for women, just beyond the fenced courtyard to the east. The residents of Gminna Street enter the courtyard from an alley to the south. As they walk down the alley, they see the doorway to their synagogue straight ahead. They have finally arrived at the spatial and spiritual center of their community.

In most towns, the main courtyard of the synagogue was not a formally organized, geometric square like the Polish rynek. Instead, it was a loosely organized space with no predetermined shape. This private, residential courtyard was defined by the mass of the synagogue and bordered by buildings associated with religious activi-ties. Study houses, schools, and perhaps a yeshiva (Tal-mudic academy), as well as the residences of the princi-pal members of the Jewish community, lined the court-yard. In 1731, there were probably only 30 to 50 Jewish families, or approximately 150 to 250 Jews, living in Gwoździec.

Over the years, both the synagogue and its surround-ing buildings were altered and added to many times. Beginning in the seventeenth century, this additive, nonuniform quality of the typical Jewish district was criticized by Polish authorities who disapproved of its disorganized appearance. They saw the irregular appear-ance of Jewish districts as a sign of separateness and alienation from Polish national culture and its neoclas-sical institutional styles. Other minority communities were also singled out for such criticism, but the distinct architecture of the small-town Jewish community be-came a long-term symbol of their separation from the Polish national culture.

FIG. 6. *The Jewish Courtyard.*

The Synagogue

Emerging from darkening streets and alleys into the synagogue courtyard, the residents of Gminna Street and their neighbors gather in front of the synagogue (fig. 7). The entire courtyard is dominated by the synagogue's towering, pyramidal roof, now bathed in the last light of the setting sun. For those worshiping at the Gwoździec Synagogue, it is a transforming moment of equipoise between profane and sacred worlds.

Like many of the region's monumental buildings—manor houses, commercial buildings, and churches—the synagogue was built entirely of wood and followed many of the same stylistic practices. Yet, although the Gwoździec Synagogue shared many standard components with other regional monumental buildings, it also had a distinctive style drawn from a specifically Jewish architecture. For those living in the other ethnic and religious communities of Gwoździec and its region, there was no mistaking this distinctively Jewish style for any other type of regional architecture.

If we could stand in the Gwoździec town square looking north and east, the sunlit roof of the synagogue would be clearly visible. Although the exterior was relatively plain, the height and volume of the synagogue made a bold statement in the midst of Gwoździec's other buildings. The only other structure that might also attract our attention would be the rising spires of the Bernardine Monastery Church, which was then under construction just 200 yards north of the synagogue. For contemporary observers, the juxtaposition of a synagogue and a large Catholic church is startling. The long, acrimonious relationship between Catholics and Jews in Poland would seem to discourage such proximity. Yet the Gwoździec Synagogue was built alongside the monastery's garden wall, and just as the rising spires of the church were clearly visible to the Jews gathering in the synagogue's courtyard, so the towering roof of the synagogue was also visible to those in the churchyard and monastery dwellings. Settlement records from similar towns in eastern Poland also indicate that such close proximity was not unusual in the multiethnic and religious communities of Poland. As far as can be determined, there were no outbreaks of persecution or violence initiated by the Bernardines against the Jews of Gwoździec. This complex cultural relationship is further explored in chapter 5.

FIG. 7. *The Synagogue.*

The Entrance

As the worshipers approach the main entrance, the men and women take separate paths. The women and small children proceed to a low doorway on the left, and the men pass through a small entrance porch that leads to the central doorway. To provide protection from inclement weather, this entrance porch does not open directly onto the courtyard, but it is turned toward the south. As the men enter the outer doorway and turn right, twenty feet of darkening foyer lead to the doorway of the inner prayer hall (fig. 8). As they advance toward the heavy inner door, they can already glimpse the changing colors of the prayer hall, balanced between the sun's last rays and the newly lighted candles in brass chandeliers.

The foyer was a sparsely furnished room with exposed structural beams, one that gave no hint of the brilliance beyond the far threshold. This dimly lit passageway offered a cool respite from the summer's heat, but in winter, neither the entry nor the synagogue itself offered much relief from the cold that accompanied services for almost half the year. Although fireplaces and stoves were available, they were never used in wooden synagogues like Gwoździec before the modern period, probably because of the danger of fire.

FIG. 8. *The Entrance.*

The Prayer Hall

Stepping across the wide threshold, the men of the congregation enter a prayer hall glowing with the last rays of sunlight. As the light fades from the twelve upper windows, uneven candlelight transforms the decorated walls in the prayer hall into a deep, carpet-like texture. Directly ahead stands the pavilion-like bimah with its open, crown-shaped top and ornate wood carvings. This is the place where the Torah scroll is read. Beyond the bimah, the ark's towering cabinetry rises in the center of the far eastern wall. At its summit, the ark's wooden canopy projects inward, following the sloping ceiling until it finally dissolves in a profusion of swirling painted forms. In 1731, the highly ornamented ark had just been completed. It was the final element in a remodeling campaign that transformed the entire prayer hall into a brilliantly painted space topped by the unique pyramid-shaped cupola (fig. 9).

For the Gwoździec congregation, moving from the outside world into the prayer hall's swirling vortex of form and color must have been an intense spatial transition. Their day-to-day lives were set in a muted environment dominated by the dull browns and smoky grays of earthen streets and untreated wooden structures, broken only rarely by points of color and texture. Against this muted backdrop, the prayer hall had a visceral intensity that was literally not of their everyday world.

The prayer hall's richly colored images often startle contemporary viewers, who may see the ornate interior as chaotic. But the wall-paintings were actually highly organized both geometrically and artistically. The artists who painted the synagogue walls and ceiling organized the entire interior within a grid-like pattern and filled this grid with carefully articulated frames and decorative surrounds. Even more significantly, the paintings were not merely a decorative background for worship, but, as we shall see, the entire composition was associated with Jewish prayer, legends, and ethical stories and it formed a context for liturgy that was characteristic of the synagogues in the Gwoździec region of eastern Poland.

For the Jews of Gwoździec, the beginning of the Friday evening service marked the arrival of the Sabbath (Shabbat). From the sixteenth through the eighteenth centuries, the traditional importance of the Sabbath for Polish Ashkenazi communities like Gwoździec was magnified by the almost universal adoption of rituals associated with the practices of "Kabbalat Shabbat" (reception of the Sabbath). One of the primary goals of this book is to explore the connection between this re-intensification of Sabbath worship and the art and architecture of Gwoździec's newly remodeled synagogue.

FIG. 9. *The Prayer Hall.*

The Cupola

As the rising cadences of preliminary prayer signal the beginning of the Friday evening service, the worshipers' attention moves toward the base of the ark where the cantor (hazzan) is about to begin the service. Perhaps on this summer evening in 1731, the newly appointed Rabbi Isaac Schor attended his first Sabbath service beneath the remodeled and freshly painted cupola (fig. 10). During the past few years, the Jews of Gwoździec had followed the progress of the ceiling construction. Some worshipers may even have become acquainted with the two principal painters who worked on the ceiling: Isaac, son of Judah Leib ha-Cohen, and Israel, son of Mordecai. These gifted artists came from the community of Jarychów, a hundred miles to the northwest, near the regional center, Lviv. Both artists probably lived within the Gwoździec community for many months while they painted the synagogue's interior. In 1729, when they finally signed their names in prominent ceiling medallions, Isaac and Israel had completed a masterwork of Jewish art that combined characteristics of design, calligraphy, and painting into a unified ensemble.

The ceiling that Isaac and Israel painted was shaped like an elaborate Polish tent, and they painted many tent motifs on the ceiling to reinforce the tent-like atmosphere. We do not know if most worshipers recognized the ceiling's distinctive shape or if they noticed the many trompe l'oeil details that evoked a tent interior. Most congregants would certainly have known about the most famous tent in Judaism—the Tent of the Tabernacle—but we do not know whether they associated this famous tent with the shape of the ceiling and its painted details. We consider this issue in chapters 4 and 7.

For a variety of reasons, twentieth-century scholars have found the wall-paintings in the Polish wooden synagogues extremely difficult to interpret. For some, they represent an abandonment of the Second Commandment's apparent prohibition against visualization. For others, accustomed to sparse decoration in modern synagogues, the dense, colorful patterns, especially the animal figures, seem inappropriate for a synagogue. However, as we will see in chapter 4, the density of the paintings was typical of the region and period, and such paintings were used in wooden synagogues to communicate Jewish legends, ethical teachings, and liturgical themes.

FIG. 10. *The Cupola.*

The Women's Section

The women enter the synagogue through a separate doorway located to the left of the men's entrance and gather in a small foyer that leads to the women's section. The women's section is a low, narrow room extending along the north side of the prayer hall. This room has two narrow, horizontal slits that run along the wall separating the women's section from the prayer hall. The slits were made by removing portions of a single horizontal log from the prayer hall wall. The resultant openings were only four to five inches tall and six to eight feet long. From a seated position, the women could look in upon the evening service through these narrow slits (fig. 11). Unlike their contemporaries from the larger towns, who sit behind large lattice screens in the upper galleries of masonry synagogues, the women of Gwoździec have a very restricted view of the prayer hall.

While we have some information about how worship was conducted in the men's prayer hall, little is known about the practice of women's worship. It is not even known how the women's section developed in Eastern-European synagogues. We suspect that the construction and expansion of women's galleries in Polish synagogues during the seventeenth and eighteenth centuries reflected the rise in women's status and synagogue attendance. But apparently the women of Gwoździec were not affected by these developments, since early-twentieth-century photographs show that the Gwoździec women's section had only the narrow viewing slits opening into the men's prayer hall. Although limited in their ability to view the service, the women of Gwoździec may have developed their own traditions of Yiddish prayer and pietistic worship. We explore these issues in chapter 3.

FIG. 11. *The Women's Section.*

The Lattice Window

At the beginning of the Friday evening service, the congregation sings the prayer "Lekhah Dodi": "Come my beloved friend let us welcome the (Sabbath) Bride." The intensity of this prayer builds toward its conclusion. As they begin to recite the last stanza, the entire congregation turns to face the doorway on the synagogue's western wall (fig. 12). Together, they sing the last stanza of the prayer, symbolically welcoming the Shekhinah (Divine presence) into the synagogue.

By 1731, the singing of "Lekhah Dodi" may have been the only way of beginning the Friday service that most of the Jews of Gwoździec knew, though some worshipers may have known that previous generations did not begin the Sabbath service with this prayer. At the beginning of the eighteenth century, "Lekhah Dodi" was a relatively new prayer. First used in Safed, Palestine, during the second half of the sixteenth century, "Lekhah Dodi" appears to have spread throughout eastern Polish communities during the seventeenth century, accompanied by other refinements to the liturgy associated with the practices of Kabbalat Shabbat. By 1731, the practice of beginning the service with "Lekhah Dodi" may have

been in place for fifty years. In chapter 7, we explore how the "Lekhah Dodi" prayer came to be adopted during this period and how the ideas associated with this prayer may have inspired the construction of Gwoździec Synagogue's cupola.

As the congregation turned to the western wall to welcome the Sabbath Bride, they would have faced a circular, lattice window set above the door (fig. 12). This small window stood alone, high on the western wall. Unlike the twelve paired windows on the other three walls, it gave no light to the room and was, in fact, a blind window that opened into an unlighted attic above the entry. But even though it gave no light, it served an important purpose for the Gwoździec community. There is considerable evidence to suggest that this lattice window symbolized both a passageway for prayers to ascend to God and a portal through which the Divine presence (Shekhinah) might look in on the congregation at prayer. The window's dual purpose had much to do with the Gwoździec ceiling being raised. But before we can establish the meaning of the lattice window for its congregation, we must first look more closely at the history and architecture of the Gwoździec Synagogue.

FIG. 12. *The Lattice Window.*

FIG. 13. *Market Street, Krzemieniec, Poland.* (Courtesy of YIVO Institute for Jewish Research.)

2

CONCEPTIONS AND MISCONCEPTIONS

This book tells the architectural story of one synagogue, and it also tells the story of how one community built its synagogue. These overlapping stories form a cultural history of one Jewish community told primarily through the evidence of the synagogue itself.[1] For some, accustomed to histories that rely on written sources, this is a surprising way to research a community's social and religious traditions. In the case of the Gwoździec community, however, the most reliable surviving historical sources are the comprehensive architectural documents that describe the Gwoździec Synagogue.

Competing Interpretations

Before examining the history of the Gwoździec Synagogue and its community, it is important to address some misconceptions about Polish wooden synagogues that have shaped contemporary attitudes toward these buildings and their communities. Several well-known images from the 1964 Broadway play and the 1971 film *Fiddler on the Roof*, as well as images from the influential book *Life Is with People*, both inspired by the works of the author Sholem Aleichem, highlight these misconceptions of the prewar, Eastern-European Jewish experience.[2] It is not my purpose to uncover any shortcomings in these two popular works. Rather, I emphasize that works such as these generally draw on images of Jewish life after the late eighteenth century, that is, after the period in which the Gwoździec Synagogue was built.

Unfortunately, the portrayal of Jewish life found in these influential texts has become the standard applied to all periods and regions of Eastern Europe. Such relatively modern images have obscured our understanding of earlier periods when, for example, conditions in many Jewish communities were not uniformly oppressive. During the fifteen years of researching this subject, I have found that these preconceived ideas inhibit a full and objective discussion of wooden synagogues' development. By concentrating on the late seventeenth and early eighteenth centuries, the period during which the Gwoździec Synagogue was constructed, my goal has been to uncover the initial inspirations and motivations that led to its design and construction. This strategy requires that the synagogue be examined from within its contemporary Eastern-European historical context, rather than from the perspective of later periods on which many popular texts about Eastern Europe are based. We can only appreciate how and why the Gwoździec Synagogue was built through an understanding of the premodern historical context in which the community of Gwoździec lived and worshiped.[3]

To understand why such contextual historical study can be so difficult, we examine five misconceptions that have consistently inhibited the study of Polish wooden synagogues like Gwoździec.

Shtetl Poverty and Impoverishment

The Polish communities that built the wooden synagogues have often been portrayed as blighted by poverty

FIG. 14. *Wooden Bridge, Maciejowice, Poland.* (Courtesy of YIVO Institute for Jewish Research.)

(figs. 13, 14, 15). This negative image developed over a long period of time, but for many Americans it was crystallized in the play and film, *Fiddler on the Roof.*[4] For both Jewish and Gentile audiences, this musical created a compelling, and soon to become mythic image of the poor Eastern-European small town—the shtetl. The uncritical popular acceptance of such imagery has created a powerful account of the Eastern-European Jewish Diaspora, one that poses special problems for any research focusing on a period of relative Jewish prosperity in the small towns of eastern Poland. For example, no matter how I might attempt to describe the sophistication of the wooden synagogues, no matter how I stress that these structures are evidence of excellence in architectural development, the fact that they were the product of small Jewish towns of Eastern Europe will, for many readers, consign them to a very low order of technical and architectural merit.[5]

The image of the impoverished shtetl is, of course, not a fabrication. It is an appropriate description of many nineteenth- and early-twentieth-century, Eastern-European Jewish communities, whose declining towns and dilapidated wooden synagogues have been well documented. Clearly poverty did exist in small-town Eastern Europe, and the persecutions of Jewish communities that accompanied this poverty are neither fictional nor insignificant. However, these negative depictions rely primarily on the experiences of nineteenth- and early-twentieth-century emigrants whom poverty and persecution drove in large numbers to America. Their memories, like the accounts of Jewish experiences in the Russian "Pale of (Jewish) Settlement," vividly recall the declining shtetl.

In the seventeenth and eighteen centuries, when the wooden synagogues were first built in eastern Poland, these structures and their sponsoring communities were not, by any standard, poor. They were not even bordering on poverty. Wooden synagogues like that at Gwoździec were built by relatively affluent communities who could afford to build a synagogue using the highest

community longevity and growth in Poland than about community decline and emigration. This book tells one such story, a story not about placelessness and exile but about permanence and growth. It is a story about a very particular place and time, a story about the Jewish community in the town of Gwoździec, in the Lviv region, Podolia province of the Polish-Lithuanian Commonwealth during the year 1731. In comparison to many other small Jewish towns of the Podolian region, it is a typical story, not an unusual story, about how one Jewish community built its wooden synagogue.

Shtetl Romanticism

Images of the Eastern-European shtetl evoke complex reactions for contemporary American audiences. Preconceptions about poverty and backwardness are certainly not the only factor in these reactions. Popular myths also nostalgically recall a romanticized ideal of the shtetl (figs. 16, 17). In this romantic view, the poor shtetl is, paradoxically, envisioned as a twilight golden era of small-town Jewish life, when communities were homo-

regional standards of construction and craftsmanship. Despite restrictions placed on Jewish communities, despite acts of persecution against them, and despite the well-documented reversals of the Chmielnicki massacres that occurred in the middle of the seventeenth century, the overall climate in this region of eastern Poland was still quite favorable to Jewish settlement and growth. Although they were never unrestricted environments, small towns like Gwoździec did allow extensive Jewish cultural development wherein Jewish populations increased and many remarkable wooden synagogues were built.

The dominant image of shtetl poverty also reinforces the myth of Jewish impermanence and placelessness in Eastern Europe. Even before the Holocaust, post-immigration discourse about the experience of the shtetl generally emphasized the impermanence of Jewish populations.[6] In *Fiddler on the Roof*, the location of Tevye's shtetl, Annatevka, is not so much a particular place in Russia as it is all the displaced locations of a wandering Eastern-European Jewry. Without discounting the factual basis for these stories, it should be emphasized that before the Polish partitions at the end of the eighteenth century, many more stories could be told about Jewish

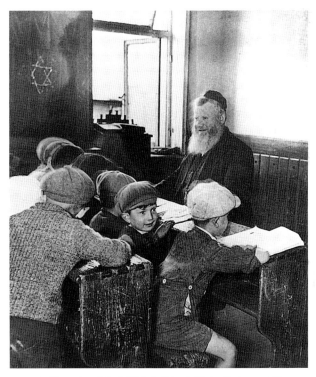

Conceptions and Misconceptions 15

FIG. 17. *Yeshiva Student, Ukraine.* (*Yeshiva Student, Mukachevo*, 1938. Photograph by Roman Vishniac. Collection of the International Center of Photography. © Mara Vishniac Kohn, reprinted courtesy of the International Center of Photography.)

geneous and unified, before the ravages of persecutions and pogroms caused widespread displacement and emigration.[7]

Beginning in the late nineteenth century, a romantic image of shtetl life began to be cultivated despite the negative assessments of popular and scholarly sources. Martin Buber, Sholom Aleichem, and Abraham Joshua Heschel were authors whose early revisionist work emphasizes the positive aspects of the Ashkenazi historical experience in Eastern Europe. These revisionist ideas and sentiments were later popularized in photographic collections that recalled bittersweet memories of pre-Holocaust Eastern Europe. These "vanished world" books often included photographs by Roman Vishniac and Alter Kacyzne, whose depiction of the shtetl provided wistful views of the heder (children's school) and revealed the worship of pious scholars (figs. 16, 17). Such images helped crystallize modern nostalgia for a mythic golden era of Yiddish culture, represented by the shtetl. Although highly selective, these nostalgic images acted

as a counterforce to the generally negative perceptions of small-town Jewish communities that dominated pre-Holocaust attitudes in the United States. This romantic reappraisal of the shtetl, reinforced by such influential books as *Life Is with People*, helped to create an image of small-town Jewish homogeneity, a world largely detached from its surrounding Eastern-European cultures.[8]

While the religious and family life of premodern Polish Jews in most small towns remained separate from outside cultural influences, this book emphasizes how Jewish communities like Gwoździec were also fully integrated into their Polish economic and cultural milieus.[9] As we shall see, this participation was a necessary component in the construction of their synagogue. For example, because most aspects of building construction were not controlled by Jews, a close cooperation among Christian builders, municipal authorities, and Jewish community representatives was necessary in the building of a typical synagogue.

In order to understand this integrated Jewish cultural

milieu, it is important to separate historical fact from popular fiction, especially with regard to the extremes of either shtetl romanticism or shtetl negativism. To understand the story of the Gwoździec Synagogue, we must shift our focus from these popular images of later periods to a time when the stable, relatively prosperous, economically integrated Jewish community of Gwoździec prepared to remodel its synagogue in the early eighteenth century.

Eastern-European Jewry

Just as popular ideas about the poverty and romance of the shtetl have obscured the history behind the wooden synagogue, so have long-term perceptions of Eastern-European Jewry. One of the most decisive cultural dividing lines in the history of European and American Jewry has been the distinction between Western-European (German) and Eastern-European (Polish/Russian) Jewry. The resulting rift between eastern and western cultures defined many aspects of inter-Jewish relationships well into the twentieth century. This division has taken many forms, but from an American-Jewish perspective, it can best be summarized historically as the skepticism or prejudice that a more prosperous, better educated, reform German Jewry held toward a poorer, initially Orthodox, Eastern-European Jewry—the Ostjuden (Figs. 18, 19).[10]

A bias against Eastern-European Jewry was nurtured by late-nineteenth- and early-twentieth-century European historians of Judaism, such as Heinrich Graetz and S. M. Dubnow. Profoundly influenced by the ideas of the Jewish Enlightenment (Haskalah), these influential historians were often highly critical of traditional, Orthodox, Eastern-European Jewry. While much of this history has since been revised or rejected, a lingering skepticism toward the merits of the Eastern-European shtetl culture, and especially its material culture, remains. For example, the elaborate art forms and animal iconography of the wooden synagogues have often been interpreted as signs of Eastern-European shtetl mysticism. In this interpretation, desperation and hopeless-

FIG. 18. *Three Hasidim, Warsaw, Poland.* (*Three Hasidim, Warsaw,* 1938. Collection of the International Center of Photography. © Mara Vishniac Kohn, courtesy of the International Center of Photography.)

FIG. 19. *Zelig the Tailor, Wolomin, Poland.* (Courtesy of YIVO Institute for Jewish Research.)

ness in the pre-modern Ostjuden, brought about by poverty and pogroms, reinforced a preference for mystical (usually meaning irrational) liturgical art forms in Eastern-European synagogues. In this book, however, the wall-paintings are interpreted as authentic artistic traditions developed alongside and in support of Eastern-European Jewish worship. The synagogues and their wall-paintings were certainly not a response to desperate or hopeless conditions.[11] Without ignoring the harsh realities of eighteenth-century, Eastern-European Jewish life, this book aims to correct such misrepresentations of the Ostjuden, misrepresentations that have led to a general devaluation of the art and architecture of the wooden synagogue.

Issues in Jewish Art and Architecture

Locating documentation of the art and architecture of a destroyed seventeenth-century Polish synagogue is difficult at best, and this difficulty is compounded by the lack of detailed artistic studies in Jewish historiography. The study of Jewish art and architecture is a relatively new discipline in comparison, for example, with the extraordinary depth of Jewish social and religious historical scholarship. Many reasons have been offered to explain the relative lack of Jewish artistic studies before the modern period, the most frequently cited being the Second Commandment's prohibition against the making and worshiping of idols. An extensive commentary found in all periods of Jewish scholarship interprets the commandment's possible restraint of artistic endeavors —a commentary that, despite a current blossoming of Jewish art scholarship, has generally served to limit both the potential importance of Jewish art and the depth and range of Jewish artistic study.[12]

The prohibition of the Second Commandment and the problems this raises for the study of Jewish art lead directly to the issue of art and artistic expression in the synagogue. The degree to which decorative expression and material splendor may be used in the synagogue has been debated since the building of the original Temple.[13] As a general rule, Diaspora communities borrowed architectural forms and artistic styles from the regions in which they settled and then integrated these foreign elements into long-standing synagogue building traditions and liturgical requirements. The architectural forms of their host countries, therefore, usually determined the external style of Diaspora synagogues. Seen in historical perspective, the architectural and decorative styles of Diaspora synagogues have oscillated between periods of sparse and ornate artistic expression, but the motivations that determine one form of aesthetic expression or another have not been clearly articulated.[14] A central goal of this study is to interpret the inspirations and motivations for the period of intense architectural and artistic expression that influenced the remodeling of the Gwoździec Synagogue.

Issues in Jewish History

Some eras, regions, and events in Jewish history, like the late-fifteenth-century Spanish expulsions, have received extraordinary attention, while others, like the early-eighteenth-century development of wooden synagogues in eastern Poland, received relatively little attention. For much of the twentieth century, Eastern-European Jewish historical scholarship has emphasized two critical eras before the Holocaust: the late-medieval "Golden Age," c. 1400–1650, and the developments of the modern era, including the advent of Haskalah and Hassidism, c. 1750–1939. This emphasis has produced a scholarly gap between the medieval and modern periods, a gap that spans the late seventeenth and early eighteenth centuries when the Gwoździec Synagogue was designed, built, and remodeled.[15] The term "early modern," a phrase frequently used in recent Eastern-European, Jewish historical studies, has become a necessary corrective intended to address this under-explored historical era.

While recent Eastern-European scholarship addresses the early modern period, many studies of this era focus on either the earlier "seeds" of the modern period or the lingering "ashes" of the late-medieval period. Only rarely have they investigated the realities of pre-1800 daily life in the small towns of Eastern Europe. For example, little attention has been given to the pre-Hasidic Jewish popular culture that shaped the wooden synagogues in the small towns of eastern Poland.[16] It is not only the destruction of historical data that has curtailed this type of investigation. For many historians, it is difficult to imagine a popular Jewish culture before the rise of Hasidism (c. 1750), or to imagine relatively prosperous shtetl communities after the Chmielnicki massacres (1648), or to imagine the content of normative worship during the period after the false messianism of Sabbatai Sevi (1666) and before the rise of Hasidism. Yet imagining a late-seventeenth- and early-eighteenth-century, pre-Hasidic, Jewish popular culture in the eastern provinces of Poland is precisely what must be done if we are to understand the development of the wooden synagogues and their Jewish communities.[17] Close study of the Gwoździec Synagogue is one step toward addressing this difficult-to-conceptualize topic.

Issues in Eastern European History

Before the Second World War, the major works of Eastern-European national and religious history generally emphasized the lives of their ruling classes. Consequently, developments in popular cultural history were often overlooked. Later works written during and after communism have addressed topics of popular culture, but because they were written under the influence of either communist or nationalist perspectives, they have not, until quite recently, addressed territorial minorities like the Jewish populations in eastern Poland.[18]

Because the Jews who built the Gwoździec Synagogue lived under Polish rule, Polish history is a critical component of this research. Like Jewish historical studies, Polish studies often concentrate on a late-medieval "Golden Age" (1300–1400). Although Polish scholarship has given careful attention to the eighteenth century, most histories emphasize national, political history, especially the causes and consequences of the partitions and the dismantling of the Polish state.[19] In their efforts to interpret and sometimes to justify the economic declines and territorial losses that led to the partitioning of Poland, many studies devote insufficient attention to the modest economic prosperity and social cohesion of the eastern provinces in the disintegrating Polish territory.[20] Such an oversight is important to this study because it was in these prospering and expanding towns of the Podolia region that Jewish communities like Gwoździec constructed their wooden synagogues.

Relations Between Jews and Eastern Europeans

This study analyzes late-seventeenth- and early-eighteenth-century Jewish architecture and culture within its historic Eastern-European context, frequently interweaving Jewish, Polish, and Ukrainian perspectives. It is a task made difficult by the long and often acrimonious relations between various Eastern-European cultures and their Jewish minorities. As one might expect, differences exist between the conclusions reached in the works

of Jewish religious and cultural history and those drawn from Eastern-European religious and cultural history. In the last twenty-five years, however, considerable progress has been made toward achieving a meaningful consensus between Jewish and Eastern-European perspectives. Today, the finest works addressing pre-1900 topics of Eastern-European Jewish history have been written by scholars who strive to integrate both Jewish and Eastern-European sources.[21]

Considering the differences between Jewish and Eastern-European perspectives, I wish to portray the Gwoździec community as I believe it saw itself in 1731—as a Jewish community in a Diaspora place called Poland, both separate from and integrated with Polish society and culture.[22] If only it could be so simple. The intervening developments of nineteenth-century nationalism, the tragedies of the Second World War and especially the Holocaust, and the founding of the Jewish State have all contributed to the redefinition of the Jewish historical experience in Poland.[23] We cannot ignore the impact of these more recent historical events in fundamentally altering and restructuring our perception of the past. Yet, the later events should not be allowed to overwhelm or distort our understanding of the seventeenth- and eighteenth-century period in which Polish wooden synagogues were constructed. My goal, therefore, is to interpret the building of the Gwoździec Synagogue, not as it is seen through the filters of the more recent past, but from the perspective of the Gwoździec community that remodeled its synagogue in 1731.[24]

Interpreting the Gwoździec Synagogue

Identifying the misconceptions of others is far easier than outlining the steps needed to correct them. This section introduces the major hypotheses of the book. In a sense, I am giving away the conclusion at the beginning of the story. But it is a story with so many complicated subplots that I think it best to begin by revealing the framework that holds them together. The development of the Gwoździec Synagogue can be explained through the following six interrelated arguments.[25]

Unique and Integrated Jewish Architecture

Buildings like the Gwoździec Synagogue were unique structures, yet they were also significantly influenced by regional building traditions. Separating the unique characteristics of Jewish minority architecture from the borrowed characteristics of Polish and Eastern-European architecture is a difficult task, requiring detailed analysis of design and construction. It is important to note that while the construction vocabularies used in regional buildings such as wooden churches and manor houses resemble those used in wooden synagogues, the total ensemble of the wooden synagogues is fundamentally different from other regional buildings. The wooden synagogues, therefore, constitute a unique form of Polish-Jewish architecture.

Jewish Community Support

Support for the remodeling of the Gwoździec Synagogue would have come from all segments of the Jewish community—from rabbis and influential citizens as well as from less influential tradesmen and laborers. Unified community sponsorship was essential for any synagogue construction project because it was always vulnerable to church, burgher, and magnate scrutiny and disapproval. The similarities among synagogues of its region also indicate that the Gwoździec Synagogue was not produced by isolated, peripheral, or radical elements within its community. The entire architectural and artistic ensemble of the Gwoździec Synagogue should, therefore, be seen as the expression of a discrete type of Judaism popularly practiced in the small towns of eighteenth-century Poland.

Multicultural Design Development

The architectural and artistic traditions underlying the development of wooden synagogues like Gwoździec reflect the integration of several design sources. Three primary sources will be emphasized. One source is the Eastern-European vernacular or folk building techniques drawn from the various regions of Jewish settlement. In the case of Gwoździec, Ukrainian folk building traditions were the principal source for the synagogue's basic wood construction. Another source, high-style Baroque influences of the Polish nobility and the Catholic Church, influenced the more elaborate features of construction such as the synagogue's complex cupola. The third source is Jewish design traditions that stressed ancient patterns of synagogue construction and decoration. These traditions were maintained through oral and literary sources of the period, including Kabbalistic literature such as the *Zohar*. Together, these three different sources combined to create a unique hybrid building, one unlike any other building in its region.

Wall-Paintings as Liturgical Art

The wall-paintings are probably the most distinctively Jewish element in the art and architecture of the Gwoździec Synagogue. Although they are often attributed to Eastern-European vernacular influences, the paintings have a variety of internal Jewish sources. Perhaps the most important were medieval Ashkenazi traditions, which contributed, for example, to the distinctive animal figures in the paintings. These medieval artistic traditions probably came to Poland with Ashkenazi settlers and were developed by Jewish artists working in relative isolation from other Eastern-European artistic influences. This book interprets the wall-paintings as primarily a Jewish liturgical art, one created to visually communicate the legends and stories that accompanied worship in the prayer halls of the Polish synagogues.

Cupola and Tent of the Tabernacle

In 1729, the ceiling of the Gwoździec Synagogue was remodeled into an elaborate, multitiered, wooden cupola, requiring the reconfiguration of the existing ceiling. While the overall form of the new ceiling was influenced by Eastern-European building precedents, the Gwoździec wooden cupola, like the cupolas of similar wooden synagogues, was a hybrid design unique to its region. The particular shape of Gwoździec's wooden cupola was modeled after a Polish/Ottoman tent and was intended by its Jewish designers to symbolize the Tent of the Tabernacle. In chapters 6 and 7, the many liturgical and cultural reasons that may have motivated the community of Gwoździec to design such a cupola are explored.

Decline of the Wooden Synagogue Traditions

The Gwoździec Synagogue and similar eighteenth-century synagogues of the Podolian region represent the material expression of a largely undocumented, pre-Hasidic, Jewish popular culture. By the beginning of the nineteenth century, this popular culture from which wooden synagogues emerged was transformed by the rapid changes of the modern period. These changes include the rise of the Haskalah and Hasidic movements. During the rise of Hasidism, wooden synagogues such as that at Gwoździec were usually maintained, but their Hasidic communities did not continue to build in this earlier tradition. After about 1800, many of the oldest, most elaborate art and architectural traditions, as represented by the Gwoździec Synagogue, were largely abandoned. Although later Polish communities continued to build synagogues, they discontinued the most elaborate features of the earlier period.

FIG. 20. *West Facade, Gwoździec Synagogue, c. 1910.* Note the repaired roof shingles and metal roofing added to the meeting room. It is not known why rocks are piled in the synagogue courtyard. (Courtesy of the Tel Aviv Museum of Art.)

ARCHITECTURE

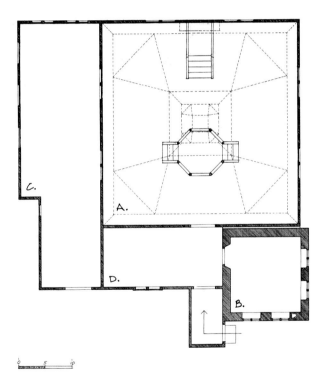

FIG. 21. *Floor Plan, Gwoździec Synagogue.* A. Prayer Hall, B. House of Study, C. Women's Section, D. Entrance Room. The dashed lines represent the reflected ceiling. (Based on Piechotka, *Wooden Synagogues.*)

Chapter 1 described the Gwoździec Synagogue and its Jewish community as they were in 1731, the year the synagogue remodeling was completed. In this chapter, the entire synagogue will be examined from an architectural perspective (figs. 20, 21, 22, 23). The analysis of the synagogue begins with the interior space of worship, then proceeds outward, addressing the construction system and the architectural style of the building. As we move from the inside to the outside of the synagogue, the description of architectural design and artistic qualities shifts from an emphasis on Jewish influences to an emphasis on Polish or Eastern-European influences. In essence, the interior was informed by Jewish culture while the exterior was influenced by non-Jewish, regional cultures, although, as we will see, there is also considerable overlap between regional and Jewish influence. The contrast between the interior and exterior has been a consistent feature of synagogue architecture in Diaspora communities worldwide. In Eastern Europe, regional influences on the synagogue's construction were inevitable given that Jews were a minority culture living within dominant Christian cultures that largely controlled the building trades.[1] Nevertheless, the integration of Jewish and Polish influences produced distinctive and original works of art and architecture on both the inside and the outside of the Polish synagogues.

FIG. 22A. *West Elevation, Gwoździec Synagogue.* (Based on Piechotka, *Bramy Nieba*.)

FIG. 22B. *South Elevation, Gwoździec Synagogue.* (Based on Piechotka, *Bramy Nieba*.)

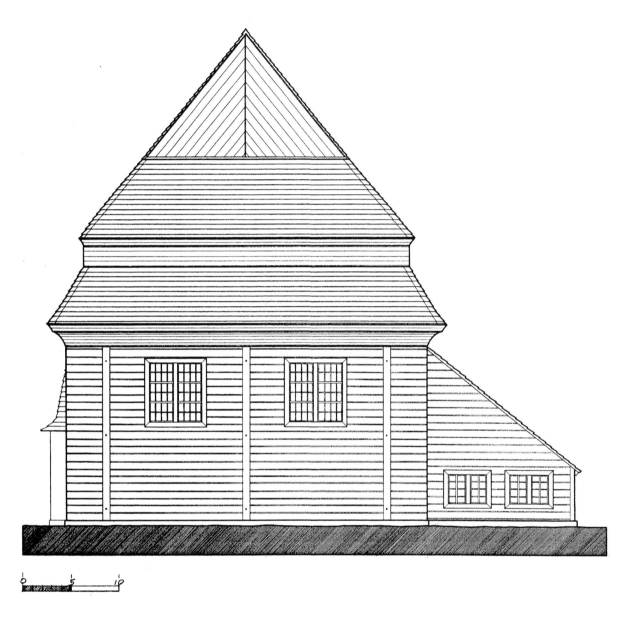

FIG. 22C. *East Elevation, Gwoździec Synagogue.* (Based on Piechotka, *Bramy Nieba*.)

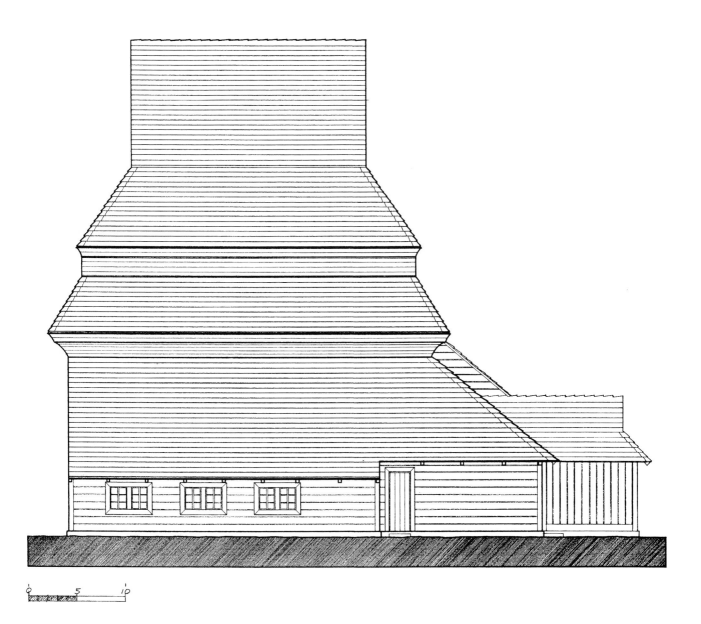

FIG. 22D. *North Elevation, Gwoździec Synagogue.* (Based on Piechotka, *Bramy Nieba.*)

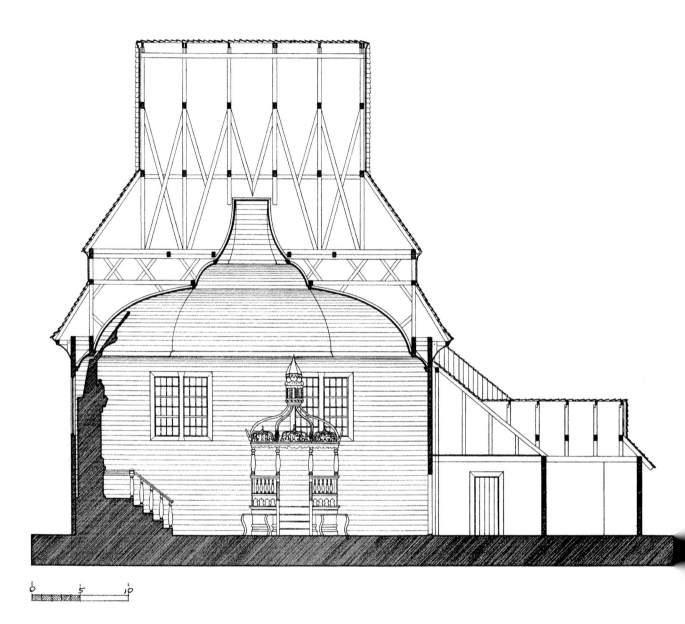

FIG. 23. *Section, Looking South, Gwoździec Synagogue.* Note the central bimah, the ark attached to the east wall, and the reverse-curve, S-shaped profile of the cupola. (Based on Piechotka, *Bramy Nieba.*)

Organization and Function

Over the course of approximately five centuries following the destruction of the Second Temple in 70 C.E., a uniform design for synagogues was gradually developed. In Roman communities throughout the Mediterranean basin, the sacred temple was replaced by a nonsacred house of meeting or synagogue (Beit Kenesset). The basic plan for the Gwoździec Synagogue was brought to Eastern Europe by migrating Jewish communities whose understanding of the synagogue derived from these Roman Mediterranean communities.[2]

Ark and Bimah

The prayer hall at the Gwoździec Synagogue was organized around a central axis that linked the two principle elements of worship: the ark (Aron ha-kodesh) containing the Torah scrolls and the bimah (raised platform) from which the Torah was read (fig. 24). The entrance to the prayer hall was aligned with the central axis that began in the middle of the western wall and continued through the bimah to the ark.[3] If you were to stand at the main entrance looking straight ahead, you would see past the open bimah to the ark towering against the far eastern wall. The raised octagonal bimah occupied the center of the room midway between the steps to the ark and the entrance door (fig. 25). The ark was set within an elaborate, double-tiered cabinet attached to the middle of the eastern wall (fig. 26).[4] The towering ark and the raised, central bimah dominated the space of the prayer hall. The entire room was only thirty-six feet square, although the pyramidal, tent-like cupola, with its dimly lit upper regions, made the prayer hall appear much larger.

The eastern-facing central axial alignment of ark and bimah has defined the space of Jewish worship since the third to sixth centuries C.E.[5] Worship was uniformly directed eastward toward the ark, just as symbolically it was directed toward Jerusalem.[6] Jerusalem was located almost directly south of Gwoździec, and the eighteenth-century Jewish community certainly knew the location of Jerusalem relative to Gwoździec. Yet, an eastern orientation of worship was maintained in Gwoździec, just as it was in most communities throughout the Diaspora.

The bimah in the Gwoździec Synagogue had an open-ribbed, crown-shaped canopy in a regional version of the Italian Baroque style. Its profile also loosely followed the contours of the undulating ceiling above (see

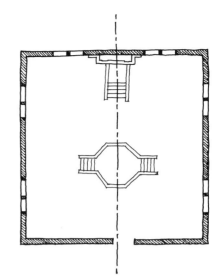

A.

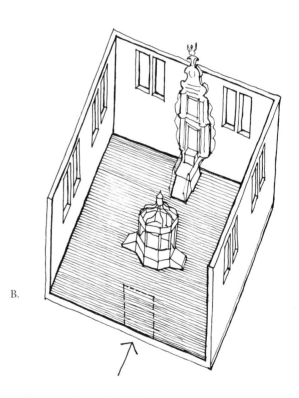

B.

FIG. 24. *Plan Organization, Gwoździec Synagogue.* A. Floor Plan, B. Aerial View. Both diagrams show the axial arrangement of entrance, bimah, and ark.

FIG. 25. *Bimah, Gwoździec Synagogue.* A photograph, looking northeast, shows the Torah reading table at the top of the stairs. At the cornice of the bimah, slender wooden ribs spring from a richly carved wooden frieze to support an ornamental wooden lantern. Note the Hebrew inscriptions (translated in the appendix) painted on the inside of the bimah. Note also the built-in benches at its base. (Courtesy of the Tel Aviv Museum of Art.)

fig. 25). As in similar wooden synagogues of the eighteenth century, the bimah was placed along the east-west axis, but slightly off center. With respect to the spatial center of the prayer hall, it was often set closer to the doorway on the western wall than to the ark on the eastern wall (see fig. 23). A table was then placed on the eastern side of the bimah's platform in a spot nearest the ark. This spot where the table stood was very near to the spatial center of the synagogue. Therefore when the Torah was placed on this table to be read, it was located at or near the exact center of the synagogue (fig. 27). Similar placement of bimahs and reading tables in other Polish synagogues suggests that the designers of the Gwoździec interior clearly intended the Torah to be placed and read at the spatial center of the synagogue.[7]

The ark and its highly ornamental architectural surround dominated the synagogue's eastern wall (fig. 26). Although originally only a cabinet used to store the Torah scrolls, the ark grew to be an architectural element of massive size and elaborate ornamentation in the synagogues of the Polish Ashkenazi communities. The cabinets of these arks were attached to the eastern wall and usually surrounded by a two-tiered architectural facade featuring pairs of neoclassical columns and entablatures. At Gwoździec, the entire facade of the ark rose into the ceiling of the synagogue, bending inward as it touched the ceiling at the top. In 1731, when Gwoździec's ark was built, most Polish synagogues followed a standardized format for composing and decorating the ark. Although the compositions were based on church altars and Baroque cabinetry, the addition of Jewish motifs and symbols, such as the Tablets of Law, the Three Crowns of Torah, paired lions, and Hebrew inscription transformed this standard format into a unique showplace for Jewish liturgical and decorative arts (see fig. 70).[8]

The spatial relationship between the ark and the bimah can be understood as serving two purposes, one functional and one symbolic (fig. 28). The functional purpose of the ark and bimah is straightforward. The Torah scroll is stored in the ark, then it is removed and carried to the bimah platform, from which it is read and returned to the ark. The symbolic purpose for the ark and bimah gives clarity to two levels of pre- and post-Temple worship. On the one hand, the ark, located on the eastern-oriented axis, is the focus of the post-Second Temple, synagogue-oriented worship. Thus the ark and its eastern wall are the spatial focus for most daily and

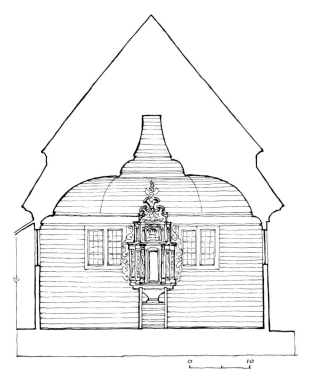

FIG. 26. *Ark, Gwoździec Synagogue.* An elevation drawing, looking east, shows the cabinet-like ark with a narrow flight of stairs. Note how the ark is positioned between the paired windows of the east wall. (Based on Piechotka, *Bramy Nieba.*)

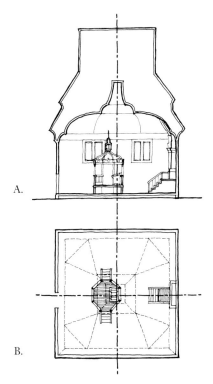

FIG. 27. *Centering the Torah Reading Table.* A. Section, B. Plan. Note that the Torah reading table is located near the spatial center of the synagogue, and this centering of the table forces the bimah slightly off-center in the middle of the prayer hall.

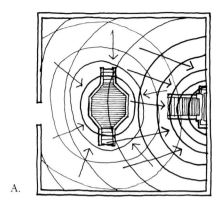

A.

B.

FIG. 28. *Ark and Bimah.* A. Plan, B. Interior Perspective. Note the difference between the bimah in the center and the ark along the outer wall.

festival prayer of the rabbinical liturgy. On the other hand, it is the bimah, not the ark, that is the central architectural focus of the prayer hall. The bimah represents an earlier, Second Temple period of worship, when the platform was used to deliver the Priestly Blessing as well as for reading the Torah. These practices recall the oldest forms of Jewish worship and the former rituals of the Temple.

The alternating directionality of worship between the ark and bimah is also uniquely balanced. Though the bimah is located at the spatial center of the synagogue, the dominance of this position is reduced by its lesser role in the daily liturgy. It is the ark, located along the eastern wall of the prayer hall, that is the spatial focus for the vast majority of the daily and festival prayer. This alternating focus expresses a dialectical relationship between two contrasting orientations to worship — between an earlier, Temple-based, priest-directed orientation represented by the central bimah, and a later, synagogue-based, rabbi-directed orientation toward the ark.[9] In the final chapter, we shall return to the issue of emphasis between ark and bimah to explore why the reading of the Torah at the bimah was given renewed ritual emphasis in the early-modern liturgies of Eastern Europe.

Axis and Procession

Although their interiors were organized along a central axis, wooden synagogues like that at Gwoździec did not use this axis for ceremonial entry into or processional movement through the prayer hall. This lack of ceremonial movement sharply contrasts with the almost universal use of processional movement in Christian worship from outside to inside toward a sacred precinct (fig. 29).[10] In the synagogue, the central bimah prevents forward movement along the central axis. Ceremonial procession is further restricted by the placement of the bimah's stairs, which are aligned sideways to the entry and lead away from both the entry and the ark. Therefore, although most Polish synagogues aligned the principal spatial elements of ark, bimah, and doorway along a central axis, the spatial organization and function of the prayer hall did not encourage formal, processional entry.

In Judaism, there is no requirement for outside-to-inside processional movement (although there is a circumambulatory procession with the Torah around the bimah), because the synagogue does not symbolize the home of a divine being or the precinct of a priestly class. The post–Second Temple synagogue, a communal house of meeting, was a nonsacred environment for a new, nonauthoritarian, participatory form of worship. Following the destruction of the Temple, the spatial order of worship was not focused on the central axis that led to God's symbolic presence in the Holy of Holies; rather it was focused on knowledge of Torah and on community-oriented worship. The architectural result of this move away from a sacred precinct was the creation of a new type of space for worship, one with no need for a monumental axial entry.

Square Plan and Central Cupola

The space of worship at the Gwoździec Synagogue was defined by the towering central cupola that funneled upward and inward toward a dramatic central peak. The cupola's pyramidal volume transformed the four-sided log walls into the eight-sided undulating surfaces of the cupola. This transition was accomplished through the use of a vaulting device called a pendentive. A pendentive is a minor wooden vault that bridges across each of the four corners of the square log walls to produce an eight-sided volume (fig. 30). As these pendentives arch upward and inward, they produce an eight-sided canopy, which gradually tapers inward until it reforms into a four-sided cupola at the very top (see fig. 23).

The exotic curving shape of the cupola and its dazzling paintings may obscure the underlying regularity of the synagogue's interior plan. Most seventeenth- and eighteenth-century Polish wooden synagogues consistently followed a rectangular, nearly square plan (with width-to-length ratios of approximately 9 to 10).[11] The designers of Gwoździec's prayer hall had, for unknown reasons, altered this standard proportion to produce an exactly square plan, slightly more than 36 feet (10.5 meters) on each side (see fig. 21). The spatial volume was defined by stacked log walls, smoothly jointed and finished, which rose vertically to a height of 17 feet (almost 5 meters). At the junction of roof and wall, the tent-like cupola arched gradually inward before reversing itself and funneling sharply upward toward a flat, truncated top that rose to a height of 36 feet above the floor (see fig. 23).

The 36-foot height of the cupola matched the 36-foot sides of the square plan. If the corners of the square plan were projected upward 36 feet, they would produce

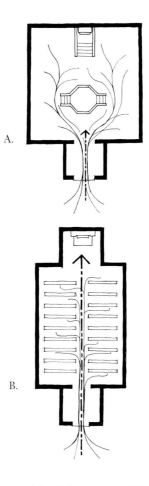

FIG. 29. *Entrances and Axes in Synagogues and Churches.* A. Synagogue, B. Church. Note the contrasting patterns of entry and directionality of worship in synagogues compared to Catholic and Orthodox churches of the Gwoździec region.

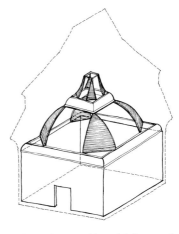

FIG. 30. *Cupola Pendentives.* This aerial diagram shows how the pendentives create a transition between the four-sided lower walls and the eight-sided upper cupola.

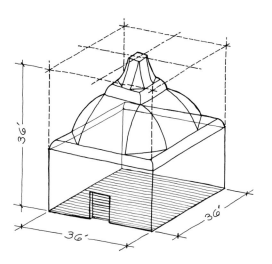

FIG. 31. *Cubic Measurement of the Prayer Hall, Gwoździec Synagogue.* This aerial diagram shows the same thirty-six-foot length, width, and height of the prayer hall.

a conceptual cubic square with a height, width, and length of 36 feet (fig. 31). Detailed measured drawings and photographs allow us to see that, because there was a vast amount of interior space in the attic, the top of the remodeled cupola could have been placed either higher or lower than 36 feet (see figs. 59, 60). This suggests that the 36-feet height was purposely selected by the designers of the remodeled cupola to match the sides of the square plan below. The decision to construct this conceptual 36-foot cubic volume was based, most likely, on the one completely symmetrical space in Judaism, the Holy of Holies in the Temple and, by extension, the Holy of Holies in the Tabernacle.[12] However, the equality of height, width, and length could only have been appreciated by its designers or builders because it was not readily discernible from the floor of the synagogue. In other words, the Gwoździec designers may have created the outlines of a perfect cube, but the pyramidal shape of the ceiling obscured this cubic relationship.

Such abstract conceptualization in the design process suggests that professional regional specialists, such as Italian and Polish architects, served knowledgeable Jewish clients in the design of the Gwoździec Synagogue. These specialists routinely employed similar conceptual strategies in Eastern-European, neoclassical, Baroque buildings constructed during the seventeenth and eighteenth centuries.[13] The mastery of this design tradition was vividly displayed just two hundred yards away from the Gwoździec Synagogue in the ongoing construction of the Bernardine Monastery and Church, a sophisticated example of the late Italian Baroque. Because this church was constructed between 1728 and 1734 (with the

FIG. 32. *Middle-Eastern and European Tents.* Compare A., the flat or gently sloping Middle-Eastern tent, and B., the conical European tent.

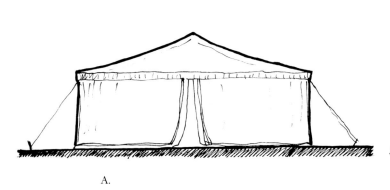

A.

B.

interior completed in later stages), it is possible that its architects may have participated in the design of the synagogue's cupola. For some, this transfer of skills between a Christian and a Jewish construction project may seem highly unlikely, but magnate Ludwik Kalinowski and his wife, Zofia Puzyna, owners of the town, were major contributors to both church and synagogue construction projects.[14]

The possible contribution of professional architects to the design of the cupola does not mean, however, that the design for the synagogue's ceiling was entirely the product of professional designers. Architects may have been involved only in an advisory role. For example, they may only have fashioned the shape of the unique ceiling, or they may only have advised the regional builders about the problems of adapting a traditional roof structure to the new demands of a central vaulted space (see below). Lacking further evidence, we cannot be sure whether talented regional builders or professional architects solved the new design problems of the Gwoździec Synagogue's cupola.[15]

Tent Imagery

Most analysts agree that the complex shape of the Gwoździec ceiling was meant to suggest the interior of a tent (see figs. 23, 87). Although there is no written documentation to confirm this symbolic intent, there are many reasons to suppose that the image of a tent was important to both the designers and the painters of the ceiling. The tent is a potent, multifaceted symbol found in all periods of Jewish history, and tent imagery often alludes to the Tent of the Tabernacle, Judaism's sacred first tent. From the sixteenth to eighteenth centuries, both before and during the period that wooden synagogues like Gwoździec were developed, the Tabernacle and the associated imagery of the marriage canopy gained increasing significance in the liturgy and popular culture of Ashkenazi Jewry. In the final chapter, we return to the question of why the Tent of the Tabernacle was an appropriate symbol for the ceiling of the Gwoździec Synagogue. Here we will delineate the tent imagery found in the Gwoździec cupola.

When attempting to depict the tents of the Israelites, the early-seventeenth-century artists and designers of the Gwoździec Synagogue did not picture Middle-Eastern tents or authentic biblical tents that had flat or gently sloping roofs (fig. 32). Instead they imagined biblical tents to be like the Eastern-European tents with which they were familiar, borrowed from European and Turkish models with steeply sloping, pyramidal roofs and vertical walls. Therefore, when Polish Jews of the early modern period recalled the Tent of the Tabernacle, they pictured not a flat, Middle-Eastern tent, but a steep-roofed European or Turkish tent.[16] This appropriation of regional forms to represent biblical precedents is quite common in the history of European art where, for example, Jerusalem is often portrayed as a European city.[17]

The details of the tent-like ceiling were further influenced by the tents of the Polish aristocracy. Tents were potent symbols for Polish nobleman, whose militaristic traditions included considerable attention paid to pageantry and tent encampments. These traditions were crystallized in a widely influential "Sarmatian" ideology that romanticized the alleged Cossack and "Eastern" heritage of the Polish nobility. In their real or imagined nomadic exploits, the nobles' exotic, oriental-inspired tents figure prominently.[18] In the fifty years prior to the remodeling of the Gwoździec ceiling, the grand Ottoman tent became a unifying image for the nobility and citizens of Poland. In 1683, the forces of Polish King Jan III Sobieski (1629–1696) assisted in lifting the Turkish siege of Vienna. The dramatic breakthrough of the Polish forces resulted in the capture of Ottoman camps, including the Ottoman Grand Vizier's personal tents. When they were removed to Poland, these finely crafted Ottoman tents with conical tops, ornamental cresting, and vertical walls, became potent symbols of Polish national culture (fig. 33).[19] In a complex blending of Ottoman and orientalist imagery with Polish national and Sarmatian ideology, these Ottoman tents served as an inspiration for the artistic portrayal of Polish culture—an inspiration that has continued to the present day.

The Jewish appropriation and adaptation of Ottoman tent symbolism for the Gwoździec Synagogue may or may not have been based on the same national or Sarmatian associations. There were, however, many other reasons for the use of this tent symbol by the Jewish community. By 1725, the image of the Ottoman tent had become current and meaningful in all spheres of Polish society, including the Jewish community. In addition, as we will see in chapter 4, Polish Ashkenazi Jews had long maintained cultural contacts with Sephardic communities and thus were familiar with various Ottoman motifs and symbolism that pervaded Sephardic culture. Furthermore, Lviv, the regional capital and leading trading

FIG. 33. *Ottoman Tent.* Captured by Polish forces in 1683 during the siege of Vienna, this tent has repeating arabesque motifs similar to those on the upper cupola of the Gwoździec synagogue. (Courtesy of the Royal Castle at Wawel, Cracow.)

city, was also an important center for the production and sale of Ottoman tapestries and tents, a trade largely facilitated by Jewish merchants. Hence, Ottoman-style tents could have influenced synagogue design simply because members of the Jewish community in eastern Poland were involved in trading such tents.[20] Given such wide exposure, it is therefore not surprising that, even in a provincial town like Gwoździec, Jewish artists, designers, and synagogue authorities should have selected this seemingly exotic motif for their synagogue.

While the specific shape of the Ottoman tent used for the Gwoździec ceiling was not reproduced in detail at other Polish synagogues, the centralized wooden cupola rising above the prayer hall was soon to become the dominant pattern for Polish wooden synagogues. Remodeled in 1729, the Gwoździec cupola was one of several early, experimental precursors of this general pattern. What makes the early development of these small-town wooden cupolas of eastern Poland more than just a minor stylistic phenomenon is the fact that before the nineteenth century, there were few if any other syna-

gogues with central cupolas or domes. Even the masonry synagogues built in larger towns did not employ a centralized cupola.[21] In the final chapter, we return to the question of why such a dramatic, experimental form of spatial expression became the dominant type of synagogue design in small-town Poland. We ask whether these dramatic centralized cupolas merely reflected popular regional styles of architecture or were motivated by significant religious changes that took place within Jewish communities of seventeenth- and eighteenth-century Poland.

Worship and Usage

Little is known about the spatial patterns of daily use and worship in the Gwoździec Synagogue and in similar eighteenth-century Polish synagogues.[22] We have already seen how the placement of the ark and bimah structured the overall organization of worship. Here the plan and furnishing of the synagogue are examined for insights into the spatial order of usage and worship.

A ring of built-in benches, interrupted only by the ark and the doorway, once lined the four log walls of the prayer hall (fig. 34). Several benches appear to have been removed before the synagogue was photographed in 1900. On the walls behind these benches, painted decorative arches marked individual seating locations (fig. 35). Many of the arches were inscribed with a name, presumably that of a community member, and a religious proverb (see figs. 89, 116).[23] Whether the approximately fifty personalized inscriptions in the Gwoździec Synagogue were largely honorific and used to acknowledge donor contributions, or whether they were also intended to mark purchased or ceremonial seating locations for individual worshipers cannot be determined.[24] Nor is it known how often individual worshipers actually used these seats during services or meetings. It is likely, moreover, that the original intended usage may have changed over time. Tradition suggests that the seats nearest the ark along the eastern wall were reserved for privileged individuals, but again, at Gwoździec, this practice cannot be confirmed.[25] In addition to the built-in benches along the walls, fixed benches surrounded the bimah on four of its six sides (see fig. 25). Together the fixed benches of the synagogue could have provided seating for fifty to sixty worshipers, and it is reasonable to assume that in 1731 there were other moveable seats and benches used in the prayer hall.

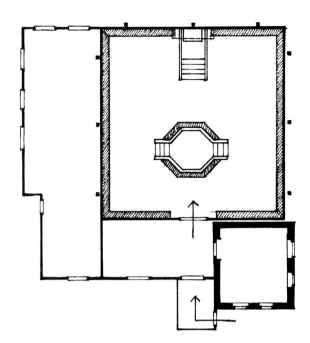

FIG. 34. *Benches in the Prayer Hall, Gwoździec Synagogue.* The benches are shaded in the diagram.

FIG. 35. *Inscriptions Behind the Benches, Gwoździec Synagogue.* Individual names were painted within arches behind the fixed benches. The names may have marked reserved seats or acknowledged donors.

Surviving photographs show that uniform furniture types—individual prayer stands, benches of varying lengths, and a variety of table sizes—were used in wooden synagogues similar to Gwoździec (fig. 36). The loosely structured arrangement of furniture in early photographs may reflect a fluid spatial order for prayer, or it may suggest that the synagogue was used for multiple activities. In photographs of other wooden synagogues, built-in bookshelves line the side walls, and piles of books on tables suggest that the synagogue was used as a house of study (beit midrash). It must be emphasized, however, that these photographs date from the late nineteenth and early twentieth centuries, when a far greater number of books would have been available. Thus, during this earlier period, fewer prayer and study books would have been found in the synagogue, with perhaps only a few books or manuscripts available to the entire congregation. In 1731, most worshipers from a small town like Gwoździec would not have had access to individual prayer books, and perhaps only a few owned prayer books during the early eighteenth century.[26]

In order to imagine the interior of the Gwoździec prayer hall in 1731, we must modify the scenes depicted in early-twentieth-century photographs in at least two ways. First, the value and scarcity of books would eliminate open bookshelves and piles of unattended books. Second, the individual prayer stand, probably one of the most common pieces of synagogue furniture shown in early photographs, would have been less frequently observed. In 1731, before the common availability of printed prayer books, only a few such stands would have been used at Gwoździec (fig. 37).[27] Moreover, it is important to remember that photographic evidence drawn from the early twentieth century may or may not reveal patterns of daily usage from the early eighteenth century.[28]

FIG. 36. *(Above left) Prayer Stands and Benches, Peczenizyn Synagogue, Peczenizyn, Poland.* Moveable prayer stands are clustered next to fixed benches along the wall. The wall-paintings seen here are similar in composition to the Gwoździec wall-paintings and were probably completed in the second half of the eighteenth century. (Courtesy of the Tel Aviv Museum of Art.)

FIG. 37. *Wooden Prayer Stand.* This eighteenth-century prayer stand or lectern from Jabłonów, Poland, has elaborate carvings. Note the Sephardic/Islamic motif on the upper side panel. (Courtesy of the Museum of Ethnography and Crafts, Lviv, Ukraine.)

Support Rooms and Spaces

On two of its four sides, the prayer hall of the Gwoź-dziec Synagogue was bordered by a string of one-story sheds, probably added at different times (fig. 38, and see figs. 1, 20). A low shed containing the women's section stood along the northern wall of the prayer hall. Site documentation reveals an irregularity in the outer wall of this shed, which suggests that it may have been constructed in two phases. Perhaps the second phase indicates an expansion of the women's section (see fig. 20). Located along the western wall was the entrance to the women's section, the main entrance vestibule (fig. 39) with an enclosed porch, and a large masonry addition, possibly added during the nineteenth century. This masonry room was described by early researchers as a school, but it may also have been used as a place for religious study or for meetings of community groups, such as the Kahal council (community governing body) or a burial society. It is likely, however, that all the additions served different purposes over time.[29]

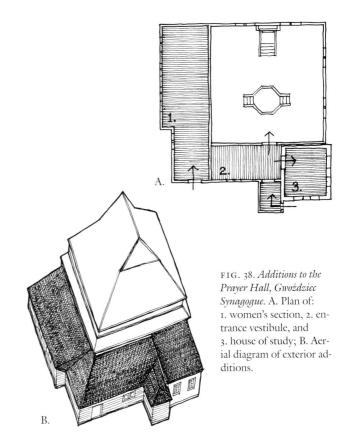

FIG. 38. *Additions to the Prayer Hall, Gwoździec Synagogue.* A. Plan of: 1. women's section, 2. entrance vestibule, and 3. house of study; B. Aerial diagram of exterior additions.

FIG. 39. *Entrance Room, Wołpa Synagogue, Wołpa, Poland.* A rare photograph records the wooden interior of an entrance room. On the left is the exterior entrance, and on the far right is the door to the prayer hall. The floor of the entry is packed earth, but the prayer hall had a wooden floor. (Photo: S. Zajczyk, Courtesy of the Instytut Sztuki PAN, Warsaw, Poland.)

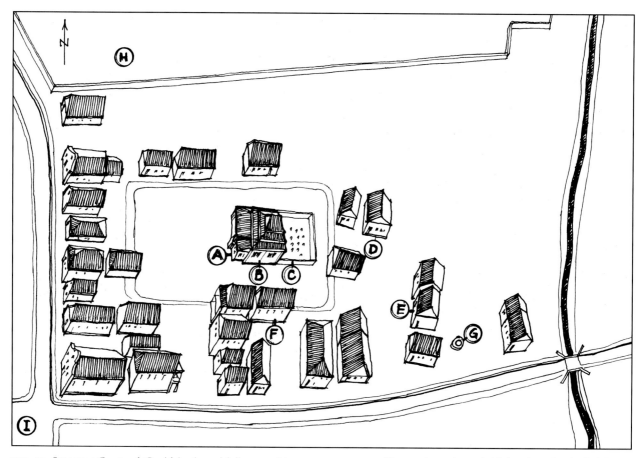

FIG. 40. *Synagogue Courtyard, Gwoździec.* An aerial diagram of the synagogue courtyard in 1731 shows the probable location of major buildings associated with the Jewish community: A. house of study, B. prayer hall, C. old cemetery, D. Rabbi's house, E. mikva, F. school, G. well, H. monastery garden, I. market square.

Surrounding the synagogue and its courtyard were buildings used for religious and community functions. Typically, these buildings contained schools, perhaps a yeshiva (Talmudic academy), ritual bath houses for men and women, and, in later periods, a hospital or poorhouse. The homes of the community's major religious functionaries—the rabbi, cantor, and shamash (synagogue caretaker)—were also frequently located on or near the synagogue courtyard (fig. 40).[30] In a typical sequence of development, religious functions that had been located within or next door to the synagogue in earlier periods were moved to separate buildings within the Jewish district during later periods as the congregation grew. By the late nineteenth century, multiple houses of study, schools, and yeshivas were generally located outside the synagogue in separate buildings.

Women's Section

The women's section in the Gwoździec Synagogue was located in an adjoining structure on the north side of the prayer hall. As described in chapter 1, a low doorway to the north of the men's entry served as a separate entrance for women (see figs. 1, 22A). Women observed the prayer service through a narrow horizontal slit, approximately four inches high, that stretched across half of the prayer hall's northern wall (fig. 41). Unlike the lattice screens typically used to separate the women's balcony from the prayer hall in other synagogues, this opening provided an extremely limited view (see fig. 11). Even before 1700, women's sections in larger masonry synagogues commonly had more generous openings. We have no way of knowing whether the restricted viewing conditions at

FIG. 41. *Women's Viewing Slot, Gwoździec Synagogue. (Left)* The narrow viewing slot—the black stripe near the bottom of the wall—as seen near the north wall of the prayer hall. Note the faded wall-painting of a shew-bread table at the center of the photograph. (Courtesy of the Tel Aviv Museum of Art.) *(Below)* A sectional diagram showing the location of the women's section next to the prayer hall. The viewing slot is approximately three feet above the floor, so it may have been designed to allow seated women to see into the prayer hall.

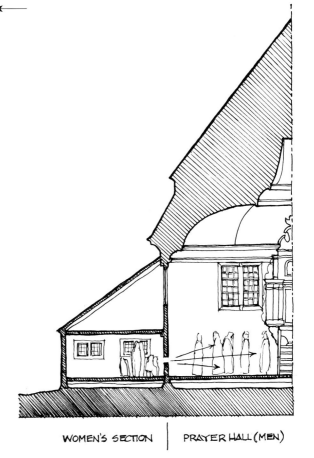

WOMEN'S SECTION | PRAYER HALL (MEN)

Gwoździec reflect conditions unique to Gwoździec or were based on unchanging older traditions. Perhaps by restricting the size of this opening, the religious authorities of Gwoździec hoped to solve the problem of women distracting men during service.[31]

Later in the eighteenth century, in other wooden synagogues of the Podolia region, women's balconies were frequently added above the entry foyers of existing prayer halls. By the beginning of the nineteenth century, an exterior staircase added to the front facade of a synagogue was the conspicuous mark of a second-floor women's gallery. This stairway often served as an entry to the women's gallery, separate from the men's entry to the prayer hall below (see fig. 62). The increasing frequency and larger size of such additions to synagogues in the eighteenth century may be evidence of a gradual increase in women's attendance at the services of small-town Polish synagogues.[32]

FIG. 42. *House of Study*. Isidor Kaufmann's painting, *Beth Hamidrash* (House of study), c. 1895, depicts a study room similar in scale to the Gwoździec meeting room. Watercolor and distemper on cardboard, 35 x 40 cm. (Private collection; reprinted by permission.)

Schools and Houses of Study

A masonry addition that contained the house of study (beit midrash) was probably added to the Gwoździec Synagogue after the ceiling was remodeled in 1731. In the small towns of eastern Poland, a masonry structure added to a log structure was usually indicative of a nineteenth-century improvement. Previous to the masonry addition, congregants would have studied either in a similar wooden addition, in a separate wooden structure, or within the prayer hall itself. Several twentieth-century photographs show a metal stovepipe protruding from the roof of this masonry addition (see figs. 1, 20), but a stove would certainly have been a nineteenth-

century addition. The threat of fire was so serious in earlier periods that fireplaces or stoves were not used in wooden synagogues before the middle of the nineteenth century. Even in the twentieth century, most wooden synagogues remained unheated.[33] No information is available on the interior of the Gwoździec house of study, but it is similar in scale to another study room depicted by Viennese artist Isidor Kaufmann (1853–1921) (fig. 42). Kaufmann had visited the Gwoździec Synagogue in 1897 and painted a picture of its western wall. His watercolor sketch is a romantic but probably physically accurate depiction of a well-organized house of study.[34]

In 1731, Gwoździec's Jewish community may have

conducted all daily services, community meetings, and religious study in the main prayer hall of the synagogue. While small-town Jewish histories from later periods frequently describe multiple Hasidic houses of prayer (competing minyan), in pre-Hasidic Gwoździec separate houses of prayer or study probably did not exist.[35] It is my belief that before 1750, in small communities like Gwoździec, a single synagogue with a single house of study (or the prayer hall also serving as a house of study) was probably the norm. In 1731, the Gwoździec prayer hall and adjacent rooms would have served as a multifunctional community center, accommodating many of the Jewish community's religious and secular activities.[36] By the late nineteenth century, this centralized pattern of worship was altered by the broad effects of modern social and reform movements, the dispersal of Jewish community functions in expanding communities, and the decentralized traditions of Hasidic worship (fig. 43).

Courtyard and Community

The town map of Gwoździec locates the Jewish district, the synagogue, and its courtyard as they were probably organized in the early eighteenth century (fig. 44).[37] The diagram (fig. 45) shows the location of Gwoździec's Polish, Jewish, Ukrainian, and German communities. The communities of Gwoździec appear to be spatially distinct, yet there was also considerable overlap of residency and property ownership among them.[38]

While each town in the Podolian region contained unique features, common patterns of settlement and development created an underlying geographical similarity among Jewish communities in the small towns of eastern Poland. In hundreds of small-to-mid-sized communities, the main courtyard or street of the Jewish community was located in a district close to, but separate from, the central market square (fig. 46). In a typical pattern, Jews found themselves relegated to marginal,

FIG. 43. *Synagogue Yard, Brzozdowce, Poland.* This photograph shows the town's wooden synagogue and the homes of the Jewish community. The entrance to the synagogue is located in a small gabled shed on the west wall. The synagogue itself was located at the edge of town, and this boundary is marked by a small stream and the beginning of pasture land. (Courtesy of the Museum of Ethnography and Crafts, Lviv, Ukraine.)

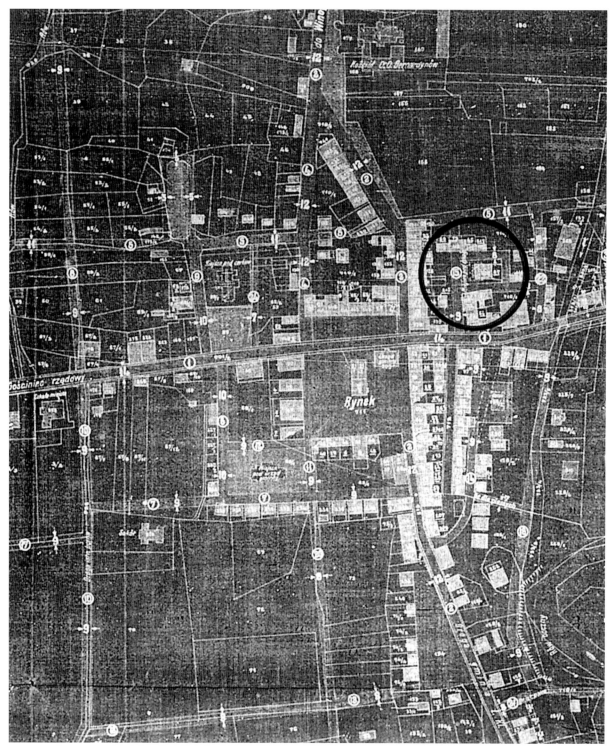

FIG. 44. *Plan of Gwoździec.* A map of roads and buildings c. 1920. The circle marks the location of the synagogue and its courtyard. Many of the town's buildings, including the synagogue, were destroyed in 1916 during military action between Austria-Hungary and Russia. This twentieth-century map shows the location of both intact and destroyed buildings. In 1731, the town was less than half this size. (Courtesy of the Bernardine Monastery Library, Lviv, Ukraine.)

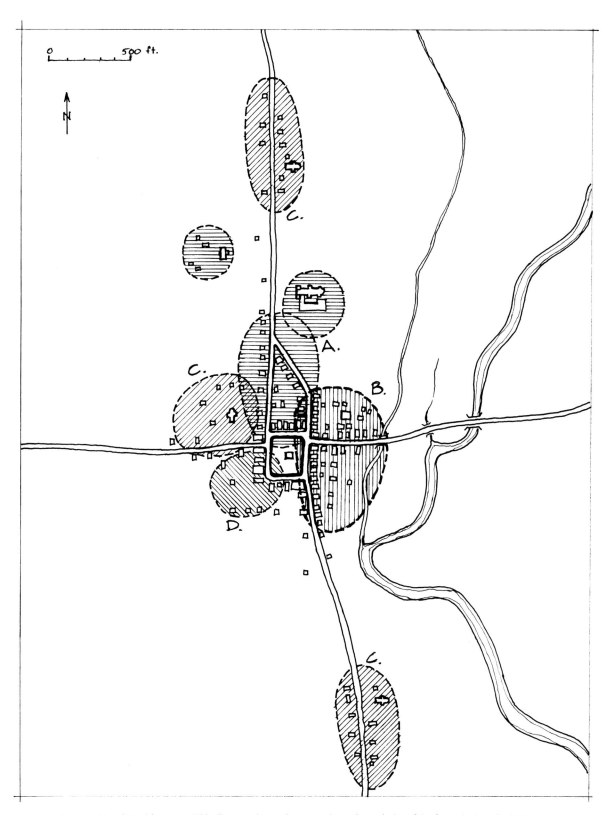

FIG. 45. *Communities of Gwoździec, 1731.* This diagram shows the approximate boundaries of the four ethnic and religious communities: A. Polish, B. Jewish, C. Ukrainian, and D. German. The town square joins the communities at the center of the town.

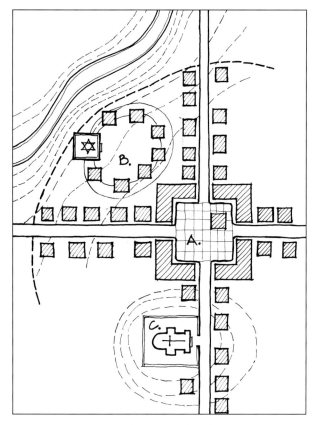

FIG. 46. *Town Square, Jewish District, and Catholic Church.* A diagram of the typical spatial relationship of A. town square, B. Jewish district, and C. Catholic church. Note how the communities come together at the square in the center of the town.

nonagricultural parcels of land. While such areas were generally considered less desirable, this location did satisfy one important Jewish community requirement—a source of water for the ritual bath (mikva).[39] At Gwoź-dziec, the community's ritual bathhouses were located on the eastern edge of the synagogue courtyard, close to a small stream (see fig. 40). In this way, Jewish ritual needs were fulfilled by the marginal, leftover lands usually available for Jewish settlement. Thus, the Jewish district was often located between the established town square and the nearest low-lying area, usually adjoining a stream or source of water.[40] Whenever I arrive in the market square of a small Polish town and wish to know the location of the former Jewish district, I look for the nearest source of water or the lowest adjoining lands. At Gwoździec, even though I arrived for the first time after dark, this technique led me directly to the district I was seeking.

From its initial settlement near the synagogue court-yard, the Jewish community of Gwoździec appears

to have expanded to the south and west, bringing it into greater contact with other ethnic communities. In Poland's eastern regions during the seventeenth and eighteenth centuries, land ownership and development practices created considerable overlap among ethnic and religious groups, so we should not be surprised to find families from other ethnic communities living among the Jewish community. We should certainly not imagine Gwoździec's Jews within a space of exclusive segregation, like a walled medieval ghetto. Such ghettos were not familiar to Gwoździec's Jewish community nor were they found in small-town, Eastern-European communities.[41] If there were restrictions placed on Jewish residency and trading activities in 1731, they did not prevent the continued expansion of the Jewish community to become, by around 1750, Gwoździec's majority population.[42]

Designers of the Synagogue

Who designed the Gwoździec Synagogue, and how was it designed? Given the subsequent destruction of the synagogue and its community, it is not surprising that these questions have remained unanswered. Yet even before it was destroyed, those who visited the synagogue and interviewed members of the Gwoździec community could find little concrete information about the synagogue.[43] While there has been considerable speculation about the identity of the designers or architects, especially about whether or not they were Jewish, there is still no precise information about their identities, where they came from, or how they designed the building. Yet even without standard historical sources, there are other ways to determine how the synagogue was built. Let us begin by examining the standard method of seventeenth- and eighteenth-century synagogue design.

The search for an architect or an original source for design ideas is frequently skewed by current assumptions about the role of architects and designers. These assumptions need to be reexamined because designers played a very different role during the eighteenth century in Eastern Europe.[44] Based on what we know about the design of equivalent vernacular buildings in pre-modern Eastern Europe, we should not assume that the Gwoździec Synagogue was "designed" by a single designer, architect, or builder. Instead, we should imagine an extended process of design decision-making that developed over many years, a process based on precedents set by previous synagogue designers, all of whom worked within well-established building traditions. This "vernacular" design method is chiefly characterized by the maintenance of tradition and the containment of experimentation to limited, but not inconsequential, aspects of the building.[45] The design decisions actually made by the builders of the Gwoździec Synagogue were significant, but they were limited to new or experimental portions of the design, such as the tent-like shape of the cupola. Most design decisions, like the organization of the floor plan and the log wall assembly, would have been based on precedent. These decisions had already been made by previous generations of synagogue designers and builders.

For those unfamiliar with Eastern-European construction methods, wooden buildings like the Gwoździec Synagogue may seem to require only minimal design and construction skill, such as that of an unskilled shtetl carpenter. Nothing could be farther from the truth. Considerable design and construction skills were required to build wooden synagogues like that at Gwoździec, and workers with such skills were seldom found in one rural region. Thus it is likely that a group of skilled itinerant builders was employed.[46]

Many have asked if these designers and builders were Jewish or Gentile. Although most scholars with an understanding of Eastern-European building construction say that local Christian builders probably designed and built the wooden synagogues, still the influence of Jewish architects or designers cannot be entirely discounted. Before the nineteenth century, however, there is no mention of Jewish architects, designers, or builders in written documents, donor inscriptions, or oral histories, a lack of recognition that is surprising if indeed Jewish artisans and craftsmen were involved. Such men would have had high social status, and they would have been employed and recognized by many communities in the region. Given the lack of information about such men, it seems only remotely possible that Jewish architects, designers, or builders played any central role in the creation of the Gwoździec Synagogue or similar synagogues in its region. There is the possibility, however, that amateur consultants or professional advisors from the Jewish community made contributions, and this possibility is explored in chapter 6. It is far more likely that Gentile architects, designers, and builders who had built other buildings for the Jewish community

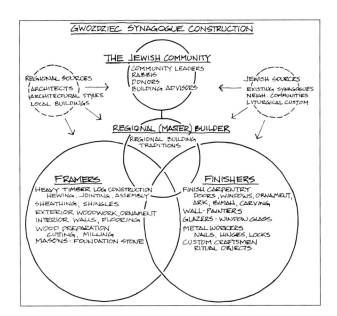

FIG. 47. *Building Trades.* This chart illustrates the typical division of labor in the building trades during the construction of the Gwoździec Synagogue.

and who were accepted by the Jewish communities of their region built the Gwoździec Synagogue. If such Gentiles designed and constructed synagogues like Gwoździec, it would explain the lack of documentation. They would have been respected by the Jewish community for their accomplishments, but they would not have been awarded formal, long-term recognition, as was given, for example, to the two Jewish painters who decorated the Gwoździec ceiling.[47]

In most aspects of its construction, the Gwoździec Synagogue followed standard seventeenth- and eighteenth-century Eastern-European regional practices. Although no detailed, pre-1800 construction documents for wooden synagogues have been found, detailed accounts of similarly scaled buildings—inns, manor houses, and churches—provide documentation that outlines the probable course of the synagogue's construction.[48] Early-modern construction systems often divided labor between the rough and the finished portions of a building (fig. 47). Typically two types of construction workers were involved: framers were responsible for general carpentry like hewing and squaring logs, log jointing, structural framing, and roofing, while finishers were responsible for tasks requiring advanced carpentry skills like making and installing doors and windows and creating decorative woodwork and furniture. Specialty craftsmen would also have contributed to the building project. Glaziers would have made and installed glass panes; masons would have constructed foundations; iron workers would have made nails and tools; specialty cabinetmakers and carvers would have constructed the ark and bimah; and painters would have decorated the interior.

While some of these craftsman may have lived in Gwoździec, most would have come from larger towns in the Podolian region. Local craftsmen had the skills needed to construct standard wooden houses, shops, and agricultural structures in Gwoździec. They may even have possessed the skills necessary to construct the elaborate log walls of the synagogue. But to construct such a unique, once-in-a-generation building as the synagogue, local craftsmen would have been supplemented by itinerant, professional craftsmen, usually from the larger towns, who, before the late eighteenth century, belonged to Christian carpentry guilds.[49] These experienced professionals may have employed local workers to supply labor for the project. But it was the technical expertise of the professional carpenters that made the many atypical features of the synagogue's design possible. Only they could have solved advanced carpentry problems like the complex cove jointing of the ceiling and the atypical unbraced length of the synagogue's walls.

Given what is known about the design and building of similar-sized parish churches in the region, we can envision a small network of regional builders who were capable of undertaking a demanding project like the Gwoździec Synagogue. These professional builders would not have consulted plans or written documentation (like those likely produced by the architects for the neighboring Bernardine Monastery Church), but they would have followed an oral tradition based on incremental design development and trial-and-error testing. Such a tradition was passed from master to apprentice within a guild or guild-like association. These regional builders would also have worked within a late medieval style of timber construction that was heavily influenced by Germanic traditions of design and building construction. Many of the craftsmen who built the Gwoździec Synagogue may even have had a distant German heritage or possessed technical skills derived from Germanic approaches to building construction.[50]

Professional builders employing traditional building techniques and working with local laborers could have produced most of the Gwoździec Synagogue. But even

they did not have the expertise needed to create three critical, nontraditional portions of the synagogue design: the engineering for the timber-framed roof, the design for the unique cupola, and the liturgical understanding necessary for the plan and decoration of the synagogue. These three critical components of the synagogue's design were all shaped by designers and design traditions that were not a part of the standard building expertise from the Podolian region. Each of these areas of design development is addressed in the following sections.

Synagogue Construction

The exterior of the Gwoździec Synagogue may appear exotic to modern observers, but it resembled other wooden buildings found in the small towns of seventeenth- and eighteenth-century Eastern Europe. Manor houses, town halls, churches, and inns were all built in a similar fashion utilizing standard construction techniques. These buildings typically had multitiered roofs, stacked-log walls, and ornamental decorative woodwork interpreted in various local styles. In this section, we examine the material and construction systems used to build the Gwoździec Synagogue, emphasizing their relationship to regional traditions of Eastern-European construction.

Exterior

The exterior surfaces of the Gwoździec Synagogue were covered by fir shingles, exposed larch or pine log walls, and small amounts of decorative trimming (fig. 48).[51] Without paints or preservatives, the log walls and shingled roofs eventually weathered to a uniformly dark, black/brown color. Ornamentation on the synagogue's exterior was confined to the cornice edges, window and door surrounds, and upper gable ends. Gwoździec's upper gables were sheathed in a simple version of a herringbone and diamond pattern that was typically used to cover prominent wall surfaces on important community buildings in the region (fig. 49).[52] In almost all cases, even on the most elaborately decorated synagogues, exterior ornamentation was restrained in comparison to other large or monumental buildings such as manor houses, town halls, and churches.

Most observers have linked the synagogues' mini-

FIG. 48. *East Facade, Gwoździec Synagogue.* The photograph, looking northwest, shows the back, eastern side of the synagogue with its shingled roofs and log walls. The six vertical posts, covered by shingles, were used to stabilize the log walls. The synagogue's fenced courtyard, extending to the right, contained an old cemetery. The twin towers of the Bernardine Monastery Church are on the far right. (Courtesy of the Tel Aviv Museum of Art.)

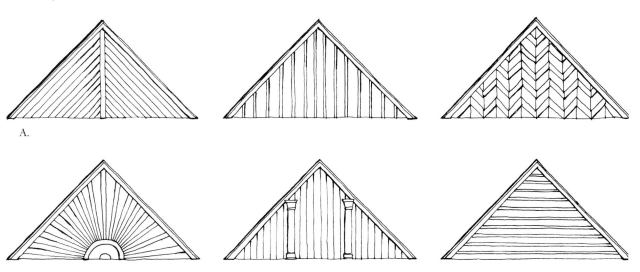

FIG. 49. *Ornamental Woodwork.* The woodwork on the gable end of the Gwoździec Synagogue (A.) was one of many patterns of decorative boarding found on wooden synagogues in the region. (Based on Piechotka, *Wooden Synagogues*.)

mal exterior decoration to the persecutions of Jewish communities, both in Poland and throughout the Diaspora, seeing it as an effort to avoid the attention that ostentatious architecture might invite. Because we have no evidence of Jewish community intentions, we assume that the negative pressures of the Eastern-European environment encouraged minimal exterior ornamentation. Yet other factors internal to the community may also have influenced this design decision.

Before the nineteenth century, few synagogues in any Diaspora environment had ornate exteriors, perhaps as the result of long-standing traditions of synagogue building developed by Jewish communities in southern climates and Islamic cultures. Monumental buildings in these communities, including mosques and synagogues, usually had plain exteriors—in sharp contrast to their interiors, which had extensive architectural articulation and decoration. Therefore the plain exterior of the Gwoździec Synagogue might be understood as a southern-climate or Islamic regional approach to building design—

a deeply ingrained cultural bias reserving the most elaborate decoration for a building's interior, thereby minimizing exterior architectural expression. I believe Polish-Jewish communities were indeed conditioned by these long-term Islamic/Sephardic traditions of minimum exterior expression.[53] Despite intermittent disruptions, communication and travel between Ashkenazi communities in Polish lands and Sephardic communities in Islamic lands remained constant into the modern period. As we shall see, artistic exchange was one component of this communication, a component that was to influence the multicultural artistic and architectural expression of Polish synagogues like the Gwoździec Synagogue.

The fact that the Gwoździec Synagogue did not have an ornate exterior does not mean that it was meant to blend into its surroundings. Exterior ornamentation is only one component of distinctive and powerful architectural expression. Even with minimum exterior ornament, the size and height of most wooden synagogues

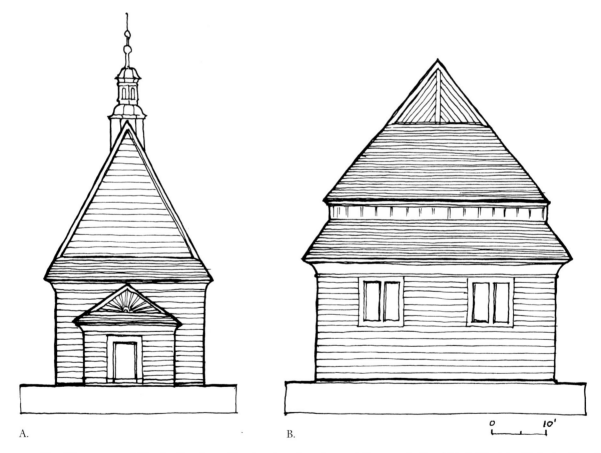

A.   B.   0   10'

FIG. 50. *Size of Synagogues and Churches.* Exterior and interior views *(opposite page).* Compare A. Gwoździec's Ukrainian Orthodox Church and B. the Gwoździec Synagogue.

would have had considerable visual impact. In many towns like Gwoździec, the community's wooden synagogue was often larger, even two to three times larger, than local wooden churches (fig. 50).[54] Therefore, synagogues such as Gwoździec, often the largest buildings in their towns, had a considerable presence in their local environments. This effect was achieved not by powerful axial entrances, excessive Baroque ornamentation (often associated with the Catholic Church), or tall bell towers (either attached or separate), but simply by their massive size and modest adornment. Thus synagogues often stood out as respectful but forceful indicators of a major Jewish presence in their expanding Polish communities (figs. 51, 52).

Recognition of the synagogue's physical prominence does not ignore the many attempts that church and municipal authorities made to curb Jewish visibility and presence. Many restrictions were imposed on synagogue construction, just as they were on Jewish commercial and domestic building practices in general. For example,

many scholars cite the typical municipal requirement that the synagogue's height not rival the height of the Catholic Church as the town's tallest building.[55] With respect to this restriction, Jewish communities obeyed the letter of the law: the roofs of most synagogues did not rise above the steeples of even the most modest of churches. But if the height of the church bell towers is discounted, synagogue roofs were generally taller than those of equivalent-sized churches (see figs. 50, 52). Even while following such restrictive requirements, Jewish communities still produced a strong, undisguised architecture that, in balance, created some of the most conspicuous buildings in many small towns.

Walls

Stacked log walls are probably the most widely recognized indigenous feature of Eastern-European vernacular architecture (see fig. 131). Log structures were found in some of the earliest Slavic settlements of Eastern

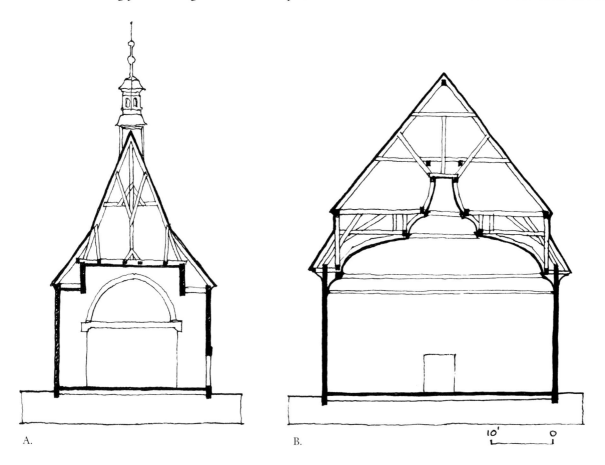

A.   B.   10'   0

FIG. 51. *Synagogue Visibility and Presence.* The Snaidowo Synagogue was built on the edge of its community along a road bordering agricultural fields. (Photo: K. Klos, Courtesy of the Instytut Sztuki PAN, Warsaw, Poland.)

FIG. 52. *Synagogue and Church Visibility and Presence.* A photograph of Druja, Poland, shows the typical spatial relationship of church and synagogue in small towns of eastern Poland. The church is located on high ground at one end of town, and the synagogue is located on the outer edge of the Jewish district at the other end. The church towers were always the tallest structures in town, but the roof of the synagogue may have been taller than the roof of the church. Frequently, the spatial volume of the synagogue was larger than that of the church. (Courtesy of the Institute of Art at the Polish Academy of Sciences, Warsaw, Poland.)

Europe, and log buildings were still being constructed well into the modern era. In 1731, perhaps more than 95 percent of the buildings in small towns like Gwoździec were built of such logs. (The least substantial buildings of any town may have been built only partially of logs with clay or rubble infill.) Only a few masonry buildings were constructed for the ruling nobility, wealthy merchants, and the Catholic Church.[56] Like the majority of American log buildings of the same era, Polish wooden synagogues were built with square hewn logs joined at squared corners by concealed notched joints (fig. 53).[57] These logs were stacked with minimum spacing between the horizontal joints, so that patching and sheathing were not always required. On the exterior surfaces, the logs were either left exposed or covered with wooden boards and shingles. Like most log construction systems, the exposed horizontal joint required protection against water penetration and subsequent decay, so wide roof overhangs and stone foundations were important features of these wooden structures.

Log walls are quite stable unless they are weakened by openings cut for doors and windows. Consequently, openings are typically strengthened by wide framing members. Such wide frames were used on the door and windows of the Gwoździec Synagogue prayer hall (fig. 54, and see fig. 97). In Eastern-European vernacular

FIG. 53. *Log Wall Corner Joints.* This diagram shows the corner joints typically used in wooden buildings of the Gwoździec region. The specific method of corner joining used at the Gwoździec Synagogue is unknown. (Based on T. Hewryk, *Masterpieces in Wood*.)

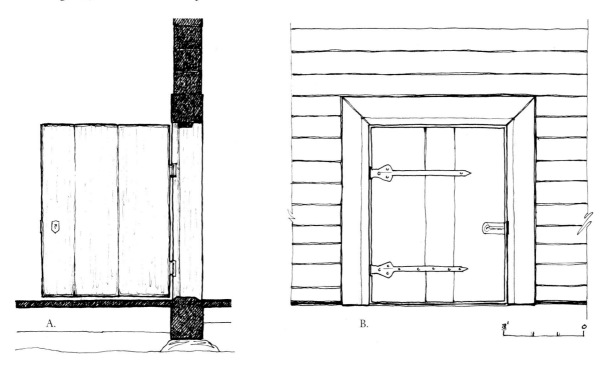

A.

B.

FIG. 54. *Door Frame, Gwoździec Synagogue.* A. Elevation and B. Section. The date 1717 was carved into the lintel above the door.

building traditions, these thick door and window frames were used for ornamental, decorative woodwork. For example, over the doorway to the Gwoździec prayer hall, the lintel was painted with Hebrew inscriptions and carved with the date 1718 (see fig. 97).[58] The log walls of large buildings like the Gwoździec Synagogue were sometimes strengthened by vertical post stiffeners that stabilized the stacked logs with vertical support. Photographs and plans show nine vertical posts on three of the prayer hall's exterior walls. We do not know whether these posts were original components of the structural system or whether they were added later to stabilize an aging building (see figs. 22, 48).[59] In other wooden synagogues, similar posts appear to have been added later for structural support.

Log construction was common, but it was not cheap. Although no financial records for the building of synagogues have survived, documents describing the cost of materials for similar buildings are available. In most cases prior to 1800, hewn logs were one of the most expensive items used in the construction of Eastern-European wooden buildings.[60] In the eastern provinces of the Polish Commonwealth, local magnates often owned the forests and controlled any milling facilities, a monopoly that could easily raise the cost of this already valuable resource. Fortunately for many eighteenth-century Jewish communities in eastern Poland, magnates generally found that it was in their best interest to support their local Jewish populations. Magnates demonstrated their support by granting the necessary municipal approval for synagogue construction, and frequently they would even provide financial support for synagogue construction through the donation of logs or other building materials.[61] These stories of magnate support for the Jewish community have been noted in a perfunctory manner by some scholars, perhaps because they did not realize the significance of such gifts. But the high cost of logs, the major material component of the wooden synagogues, indicates a significant level of magnate support. Apart from the financial savings, the donations signified support from the single most powerful individual in the lives of a town's Jewish community. This is exactly the case in the construction and remodeling of the Gwoździec Synagogue where, as we have seen, the magnate rulers Ludwik Kalinowski and Zofia Puyzna donated funds and construction materials to underwrite the remodeling of the Gwoździec Synagogue.

Roof, Structure, and Cupola

The unique combination of roof, structure, and cupola gives wooden synagogues like Gwoździec their most distinctive characteristics (fig. 55). The first component is the roof. Viewed from the outside, the roof cascades downward in a three-tiered, pagoda-like fashion (fig. 56). Within its late-seventeenth-century, eastern-Polish context, the synagogue's roof was an elaborate version of a common, two-tiered, gambrel roof.[62] Throughout the small towns of eastern Poland, versions of this roof featuring multiple tiers and decorative cornice banding were found on prominent buildings such as town halls and manor houses. In modest or elaborate forms, they signaled the presence of a significant building in rural regions of premodern Poland.

The second component is the roof structure, serving as a foundation to which the roof shingles were attached on the outside and from which the cupola was hung on the inside (fig. 55). Although most roof structures combine both roof and ceiling support, it is the special relationship between the structure and the internal cupola ceiling that sets it apart. In similarly scaled Polish buildings such as manor houses and wooden churches, a massive triangulation of wooden beams filled the entire attic space with structural members that supported the roof and the ceiling. At Gwoździec and at other wooden synagogues, this triangular structural system had to be modified because the cupola projected upward into the attic space and consequently broke the typical triangulation of the roof structure (fig. 57). In order to solve the structural problems created by this new type of cupola, the designers of the Gwoździec cupola devised other ways of transferring the weight of the roof outward to the log walls. In later periods, other synagogue designers developed more advanced types of scissors trusses and upper wall reinforcements to transfer the outward thrusting weight of the roof to the log wall below (see fig. 69).[63]

The third component is the wooden cupola or raised ceiling that was designed to hang from the roof structure (fig. 55). Examining this cupola from a cultural perspective, we have already established that it resembled a pyramidal Ottoman tent and was intended to symbolize the Tent of the Tabernacle. From an architectural perspective, the cupola's most unique characteristic is its double-curving profile, which, as we will see below, was built in two stages. The finished surface of the cupola

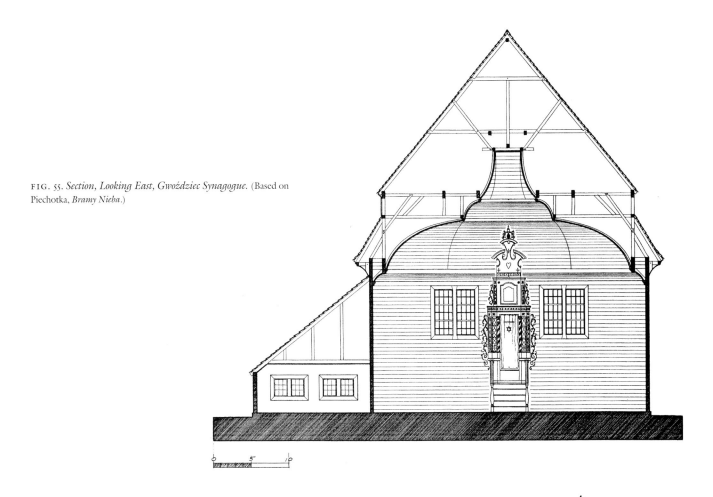

FIG. 55. *Section, Looking East, Gwoździec Synagogue.* (Based on Piechotka, *Bramy Nieba*.)

FIG. 56. *Roof Massing.* Three diagrams analyze the shape and volume of Gwoź-dziec's multi-tiered roof: A. roof plan, B. roof elevation, and C. roof components.

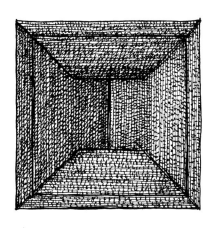

A.

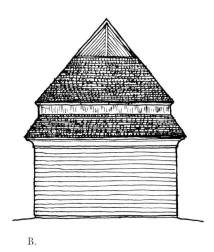

B.

C.

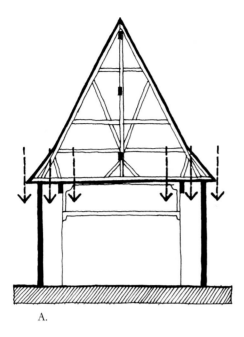

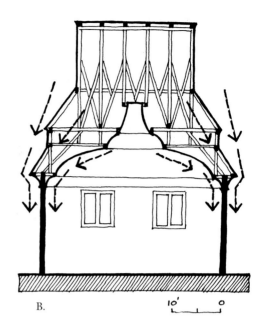

A.   B.

FIG. 57. *Roof Structural Systems.* A comparison of the structural systems: A. a typical wooden Orthodox church of the Gwoździec region; B. the Gwoździec Synagogue. (Based on Piechotka, *Wooden Synagogues.*)

FIG. 58. *Exterior-Interior Relationships.* Eastern-European vernacular design shaped the exterior, while Jewish/Polish Baroque ideas influenced the interior.

was made of carefully jointed boards that followed a lightweight frame that hung from the structural roof trusses. Significantly, the shape of the cupola did not follow the shape of the roof structure, but instead followed the shape of a tent. Clearly the designers and builders went to considerable trouble to create this tent-like shape.

The juxtaposition of the exterior roof and the interior cupola suggests two fundamentally different sources for the design of the synagogue (fig. 58). Seen from the exterior, the roof primarily suggests Polish and Eastern-European sources; seen from the interior, the cupola primarily suggests the influence of Baroque stylistic and Jewish community traditions. Although the roof and the cupola are joined together and supported by the same structural frame, they do not function together as a unified design ensemble. In other words, there is no unity between the shape and purpose of the cupola and the shape and purpose of the roof. In modern usage, a shape-function unity of outside and inside has become a commonly accepted principle, but the designers of the Gwoździec ceiling, following late-Baroque preferences, subordinated structural expression to the expression of form and surface.[64] Consequently, the shape of the cupola follows an independent logic, dictated by the form of an Ottoman tent and the stylistic language of the Baroque period. Together, the hybrid combination of roof and cupola creates a complex juxtaposition of distinctly different influences, influences that symbolize how Ashkenazi Jewish culture was simultaneously separate from and integrated into its Eastern-European cultural context.

History of Construction

When analyzing the particular construction history of the Gwoździec Synagogue, it is important to stress that this history represents just one type of Eastern-European synagogue drawn from a vast array of previous, contemporary, and later structures. For over six hundred years before their destruction began in 1939, communities of Ashkenazi Jews built synagogues over a wide expanse of Eastern Europe. Many such communities had complex building histories wherein synagogues were continuously remodeled or replaced and new congregations emerged from older congregations to build their own synagogues. Over time, hundreds of communities across Eastern Europe produced many different types of synagogues.[65] As we investigate the history of the Gwoździec Synagogue, we will attempt to place this particular synagogue among the many types of synagogues built in Eastern Europe.

The Gwoździec Synagogue was closely related to a group of wooden synagogues built throughout the Polish-Lithuanian Commonwealth in the seventeenth and eighteenth centuries. This group of synagogues was extensively documented during the fifty years prior to 1939, when the Nazis destroyed almost all wooden synagogues and most masonry synagogues in Poland and Eastern Europe.[66] When these wooden synagogues are seen in the context of all Polish synagogues and similarly scaled vernacular buildings such as manor houses and churches, the interior, tent-like cupolas of wooden synagogues like Gwoździec stand out.[67] As we shall see, the Gwoździec Synagogue was an important catalyst in the development of this unique form of the synagogue. In the following sections, the specific history of the Gwoździec Synagogue is examined, and then this history is placed within the larger context of Polish synagogue and Polish architectural development.

Gwoździec Synagogue

All modern researchers who visited the Gwoździec Synagogue between about 1890 and 1914 identified this building as one of the oldest surviving synagogues in Poland. The pre-1640 date for its construction was based on paintings dated 1640 and 1652. However, both paintings were assigned these dates by one observer whose findings were neither verified by other investigators nor confirmed in extensive photographic documentation of the interior.[68] While the synagogue may have been built before 1640, it is also possible that it was built later in the seventeenth century, and perhaps as late as 1700. Wooden vernacular buildings like the Gwoździec Synagogue can rarely be dated with complete accuracy, often because there are no written records, but also because remodeling and additions to the original structure make a fixed date of origin extremely difficult to assign. Often a recorded date might refer to the initial Jewish settlement (as I think is the case in Gwoździec) or to an original building, one that may or may not be the same structure that survived to be recorded and photographed in the twentieth century. In the case of the Gwoździec Synagogue, several such scenarios are possible, so the commonly accepted dates for the early wall-paintings, 1640 and 1652, should be cautiously evaluated.[69] Regardless of the initial construction date, however, the most important data for this research illuminate the events that led to the construction of the tent-like cupola of the Gwoździec Synagogue. Fortunately, all modern researchers agree about how and when the cupola was constructed.

At the Gwoździec Synagogue, an earlier ceiling, most likely a barrel vault of unspecified height, was replaced by the centralized, tent-like cupola before the ceiling paintings were completed in 1729 (fig. 59). With its original ceiling in place, the Gwoździec Synagogue would have closely resembled other monumental and religious buildings of its region. Prior to 1729, however, the barrel-vaulted ceiling was totally or partially removed and replaced by the tent-like cupola subsequently recorded in twentieth-century photographs and measured drawings (fig. 60). The entire ceiling remodeling process probably took place between 1725 and 1729. Modern researchers were careful to note that the remodeled ceiling was inserted in trial-and-error fashion within an older, preexisting roof structure, one that was not originally designed to accommodate the new ceiling. Consequently, a portion of the original structure had to be cut away to create a space for the new cupola, which extended into the attic. Later the new ceiling sagged and required repair because these beams had been removed.[70]

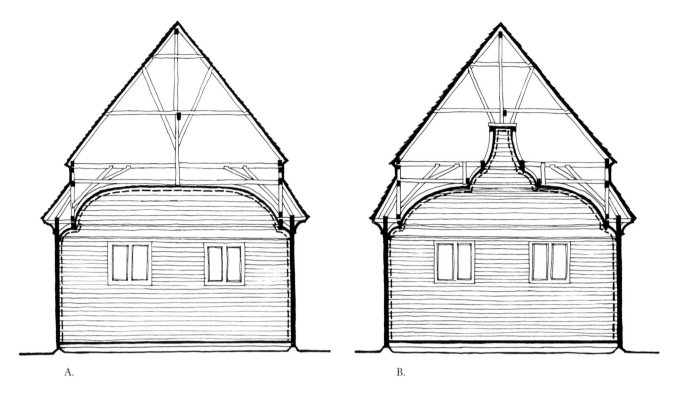

A.   B.

FIG. 59. *Ceiling Remodeling, Gwoździec Synagogue, c. 1720–1728.* The ceiling changed from A. the original barrel vault (exact shape unknown) to B. the pyramid-shaped cupola. (Based on Piechotka, *Bramy Nieba.*)

Based on stylistic evidence alone, the Gwoździec cupola could not have been constructed before about 1700–1725. Stylistically, the Gwoździec cupola draws on Baroque architectural experimentation that occurred in larger cities and in the homes of the Polish upper classes throughout the second half of the seventeenth century. Specifically, the Gwoździec cupola's reverse curving elliptical shape (see fig. 55) is loosely modeled after Italian Baroque precedents that were widely used in Polish cities and estates only after the middle of the seventeenth century.[71] The independent development of such an advanced style of Baroque architecture in Gwoździec, a small town on the periphery of the Polish-Lithuanian Commonwealth, before 1700, would have been a dazzling, unprecedented event, but it is highly unlikely.

Based on the construction records and stylistic evidence, the Gwoździec Synagogue's wooden cupola was

FIG. 60. *Cupola Structure and Roof Framing, Gwoździec Synagogue.* A rare photograph shows the upper portion of the central cupola from within the attic. The photograph looks upward into a complex assemblage of structural members hidden within the vast barn-like space of the roof. (Courtesy of the Tel Aviv Museum of Art.)

probably constructed between 1725 and 1728, in the period immediately preceding the painting of the ceiling. Because there are no known precedents for this ceiling, and because it was developed in a trial-and-error fashion, Gwoździec's cupola may have been an experimental model that inspired later designers to incorporate centralized vaults or cupolas into wooden synagogues. These centralized cupolas were to become the major, characteristic feature of wooden synagogues throughout the small towns of eighteenth-century Poland.

This conclusion is based in part on the documentation provided by late-nineteenth- and early-twentieth-century scholars who examined wooden synagogues throughout Poland before their destruction in 1939. All agreed that the Gwoździec Synagogue was one of oldest, if not the oldest, wooden synagogue to have survived into the twentieth century. More important for this research, the same scholarship confirmed that Gwoździec's remodeled cupola, completed in 1729, was one of the oldest wooden cupolas. Although synagogue documentation for earlier periods and for other regions of Poland is incomplete, Gwoździec's Podolian region is commonly viewed as a center for the early development of the centralized wooden cupola, which spread throughout Poland during the second half of the eighteenth century.

Many details of the design and construction of the Gwoździec Synagogue remain unknown. For example, we know little about previous wooden synagogues that influenced the designers and builders of the Gwoździec Synagogue. The following short construction histories of four wooden synagogues from the same region will provide some added information about the design of the Gwoździec Synagogue.

Lviv Synagogue

One of the earliest recorded wooden synagogues in the Podolian region was a synagogue in Lviv. A German diarist, Martin Greenewegs, drew this synagogue in 1578 (fig. 61). His sketch shows a log structure with a double-sloped hip roof similar to the roofs of secular and religious buildings constructed in all periods of Polish history.[72]

By the beginning of the fifteenth century, Lviv had become one of the principal trading centers of Eastern Poland with a large and well-established Jewish community. The synagogue pictured in the diarist's sketch was

FIG. 61. *Wooden Synagogue Sketch, Lviv, Ukraine.* This sixteenth-century drawing from Martin Greenewegs's travel diary shows a wooden synagogue in the city of Lviv. (Diary of Martin Greenewegs, Gdańsk Library.)

built in a Jewish district located outside the walls of the city. The destruction of this synagogue by fire in 1624 led to the construction in 1632–1633 of the famous Suburban Synagogue. This new masonry synagogue had a nine-vault plan with four central columns and was constructed on the same site as the previous wooden synagogue. Because Lviv was a center of Jewish wealth and rabbinical authority, and because this affluent congregation originally built a wooden synagogue, it is reasonable to assume that most towns of the region, including Gwoździec, built similar, but more modest, wooden structures.

Jabłonów Synagogue

The synagogue in Jabłonów, twenty miles southeast of Gwoździec, is another example of a wooden synagogue that was built before the beginning of the eighteenth century (fig. 62). Similar in appearance to the wooden synagogue in Lviv, the Jabłonów Synagogue was one of the three oldest, substantially documented wooden synagogues to survive into the twentieth century.[73] Built between 1674 and 1700, the almost square plan of the prayer hall was similar to that of the Gwoździec Synagogue, with an ark, a bimah, and an entrance all organized along a central east-west axis. The exterior shape of the prayer hall is partially obscured by later additions

FIG. 62. *West Elevation, Jabłonów Synagogue, Jabłonów, Poland.* The main entry is below the porch of the women's gallery. The metal roofing was a twentieth-century replacement for wooden shingles. (Courtesy of the Tel Aviv Museum of Art.)

FIG. 63. *West Wall, Jabłonów Synagogue.* The entrance to the prayer hall is adorned with a circular lattice window above the doorway. The wall-paintings seen here are similar but not identical to the Gwoździec wall-paintings. (Courtesy of the Tel Aviv Museum of Art.)

such as an assembly room, an entrance vestibule, and a second floor women's gallery.

Both the Jabłonów and Gwoździec synagogues had wall-paintings that completely covered their interior walls (fig. 63; see fig. 116). Both interiors exhibit an overall aesthetic unity with exact duplicates of many animal figures and inscriptions, marked with early-eighteenth-century dates. These shared features suggest that the same artists or school of artists painted both synagogues. But more important for this study, these similarities strongly suggest that a uniform grammar of liturgical art for the synagogue circulated among the communities of Gwoździec's Podolian region. Because all the Jabłonów wall-paintings were done by the same artists at one time, they create a more homogeneous style of liturgical art for the entire synagogue (see fig. 116).[74] At Gwoździec, the lower walls were painted in a more piecemeal fashion, probably by several different artists over a longer period of time (see figs. 97, 113).

The Jabłonów Synagogue was similar to Gwoździec in almost every major aspect of construction and decoration except for one critical difference—it had a flat ceiling (fig. 64). Unlike most communities in the region of Gwoździec, the Jabłonów congregation never built a cupola above their prayer hall, so this synagogue was likely built before the popularization of the interior vaulted cupola. The flat ceiling in the Jabłonów Synagogue is especially important for this study because it allows us to establish a time frame for an earlier style of wooden synagogue. Without an interior cupola rising above the prayer hall, the Jabłonów Synagogue was much more closely aligned with the traditional architecture of eastern Poland, including wooden churches with flat ceilings, than later wooden synagogues built or remodeled to create vaulted cupolas.

Chodorów Synagogue

The synagogue at Chodorów also resembled the Gwoździec Synagogue and shared many of its most important features (fig. 65). It contained an almost square plan organized around a central east-west axis aligning the ark, bimah, and entrance. It was surrounded on three sides by auxiliary rooms, and the ground floor women's section had a narrow viewing slit similar to that at Gwoździec.[75] The initial construction date of the Chodorów Synagogue was recorded as 1642 or 1652, making it one

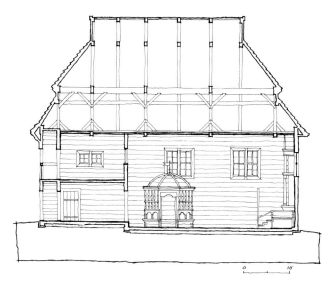

FIG. 64. *Section, Looking North, Jabłonów Synagogue.* Drawing showing the flat ceiling above the prayer hall and the women's gallery above the entrance. (Based on Piechotka, *Bramy Nieba*.)

FIG. 65. *North Facade, Chodorów Synagogue, Chodorów, Ukraine.* Additions to the prayer hall. The women's section is to the left and the main entrance room is to the right. As in the Gwoździec Synagogue, the Chodorów women's section was connected to the prayer hall by a narrow viewing slot. (Courtesy of the Tel Aviv Museum of Art.)

of the earliest wooden synagogues of the Podolian region.

The ceiling of the Chodorów Synagogue was a magnificent example of a centralized vaulted wooden cupola. This cupola combined two types of vaulting with an upper barrel vault supported by a lower cove vaulting. Joined together, these vaults produced a dramatic two-tiered arrangement (fig. 66). The ceiling was probably built between 1700 and 1714, making it one of the oldest documented cupolas of its kind, even older than the remodeled cupola at Gwoździec. While Gwoździec's unique pyramidal vaulting was not known to have been copied in later synagogues, Chodorów's rounded cupola was widely copied in wooden synagogues throughout eighteenth-century Poland. The originality of the Chodorów Synagogue ceiling cannot be established, but it is likely that this ceiling set the precedent in a region that appears to have been a hotbed of art and architectural experimentation for Polish wooden synagogues.

Like Gwoździec and Jabłonów, the interior of Chodorów's prayer hall was completely covered with wall-paintings that were extensively documented (fig. 67).[76] The combination of painted imagery and prayer that covers the Chodorów prayer hall directly parallels the style and content of the wall-paintings found at Jabłonów and Gwoździec. When seen together, the many similarities among the wall-paintings of these three

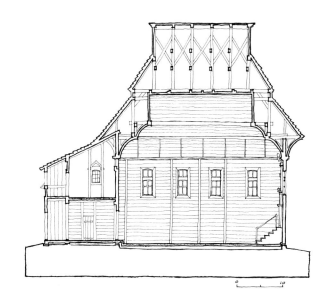

FIG. 66. *Section, Looking North, Chodorów Synagogue.* The central barrel vault was mounted atop double projecting coves. (Based on Piechotka, *Bramy Nieba*.)

FIG. 67. *East Wall, Chodorów Synagogue.* The ark and elaborate wall-paintings are depicted in this photograph. Note that the wall-paintings include Hebrew prayer panels, animals in medallions, and floral backgrounds similar to those in the Gwoździec Synagogue. (Courtesy of the Tel Aviv Museum of Art.)

neighboring synagogues make a convincing case for a highly unified liturgical art that circulated in the small towns of the Podolian region during the first quarter of the eighteenth century.

When the three synagogues at Jabłonów, Gwoździec,

and Chodorów are viewed together, the dynamic central cupolas at Gwoździec and Chodorów make a striking contrast to the flat ceiling of the Jabłonów Synagogue. Although all three synagogues were built in the same region and decorated by the same school of artists, the raised cupolas of the Gwoździec and Chodorów synagogues represent a significant and dramatic change in the architectural development of the Eastern-European synagogue. The Chodorów cupola represents the style that was to become popular throughout the small towns of Poland during the eighteenth century. The Gwoździec Synagogue cupola, completed a short time later, represents a parallel spatial exploration of the form of the prayer hall, one whose meaning and symbolism are explored in the final chapter.

Wołpa Synagogue

As I have argued, a style of vaulted cupolas, probably initiated in the Podolian region, spread throughout the small towns of the Polish-Lithuanian Commonwealth during the eighteenth century. The apex of this style's popularity can be seen in the late-eighteenth-century synagogues built in the economically expanding Grodno-Białystok region, located between present-day Poland and Belarus. The wooden synagogues of this region have long been recognized as the apex of the vaulted cupola synagogue design, and the Wołpa Synagogue is usually considered to be a masterwork among these wooden synagogues (fig. 68).[77]

When the Wołpa Synagogue was completed, in the second half of the eighteenth century, one of its most distinctive features was the combination of a multitiered cupola, characteristic of wooden synagogues, with a four-column, clustered-column plan, characteristic of masonry synagogues. The most original feature of the Wołpa Synagogue was the dramatic three-tiered cupola

FIG. 68. *West Facade, Wołpa Synagogue, Wołpa, Poland.* The central entry is set between twin helmeted pavilions with upper porches. Similar pavilions were a standard component of monumental buildings found throughout Poland in the eighteenth century. (Courtesy of the Tel Aviv Museum of Art.)

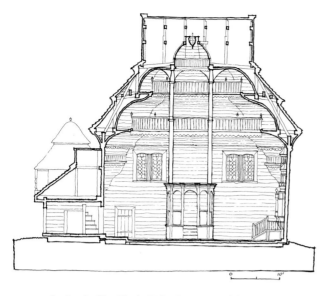

FIG. 69. *Section, Looking North, Wołpa Synagogue.* Elaborate interior vaulting unites a three-tiered cupola with a central, four-column plan. (Based on Piechotka, *Wooden Synagogues.*)

with deep recesses—a powerful and original expression of Baroque spatial principles adapted to regional vernacular traditions of wooden construction (fig. 69). The spectacular bimah also combined many decorative styles and traditions of Baroque wooden cabinetry and reflected the overall distillation of church altar motifs into an elaborate conception of the bimah (fig. 70).

Many of the architectural characteristics of the Wołpa Synagogue, although more elaborate than those found in most wooden synagogues, are clearly related to the earlier synagogues of the Gwoździec region. However, there was a fundamental change from the synagogues of the Gwoździec region to the synagogues of the Wołpa region: the Jewish community of Wołpa did not continue the tradition of elaborate wall-paintings so fundamental to the earlier synagogues. The walls of the Wołpa synagogue were painted to imitate stone or marble, a technique unrelated to the liturgical painting traditions found at Gwoździec, Jabłonów, and Chodorów synagogues.

Abandonment of Tradition

Although many types of synagogues were built on the partitioned lands of the former Polish Commonwealth during the nineteenth and early twentieth centuries, the most elaborate characteristics of the eighteenth-century wooden synagogues, including the wall-paintings and vaulted cupolas, were either severely modified or completely eliminated.[78] Many historical factors contributed to this change in architectural and artistic traditions. The spread of Hasidism, the advent of reform (Haskalah) movements, and the broad economic and social changes of the early-modern period in Eastern Europe all affected the design and construction of synagogues.[79] Here we briefly examine the abandonment of the wall-paintings as representative of changes made to wooden synagogues during the early-modern period.

The wall-paintings that decorated the interiors of seventeenth- and eighteenth-century synagogues like Gwoździec survived into the modern period. Their communities, many of which had become partially or completely Hasidic by 1900, usually did not alter a synagogue's paintings. This maintenance of an older syna-

FIG. 70. *Ark, Wołpa Synagogue.* Note the large, elaborate ark with flanking turrets. (Courtesy of the Tel Aviv Museum of Art.)

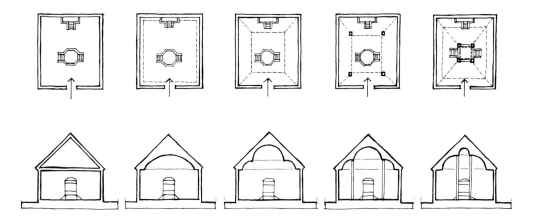

FIG. 71. *Typology of Wooden Synagogues.* A diagram of the plans and sections for the major types of premodern Polish wooden synagogues. (Based on Piechotka, *Bramy Nieba.*)

gogue art in the small towns may seem unremarkable, until it is compared to the removal of synagogue wall-paintings that occurred in the larger cities of Poland and in other European countries. In regions of Jewish Enlightenment outside of Poland, rabbinical responsa (rulings on Jewish law), always cautious about the use of imagery and decoration in the synagogue, increasingly recommended the removal of wall-paintings and other decorative art. There is reason to believe that wall-paintings were also removed from synagogues throughout Poland, especially from the synagogues in larger towns.[80] More research is needed to determine the precise reasons for these rabbinically sanctioned removals, although the general Enlightenment-era condemnation of traditional forms of Orthodox worship, presumably including the elaborate imagery in small-town synagogues, appears to be the primary motivation. It is important to recognize that the effort to eradicate the tradition of wall-paintings, as preserved in synagogues like Gwoździec, suggests that the tradition of synagogue art was far more widespread than has commonly been appreciated. While it may be easy to dismiss the wall-paintings of a few synagogues in a rural region of eastern Poland, there is the possibility that they were typical of synagogues from a much broader spectrum of Ashkenazi Jewry. If so, we would need to consider these paintings as far more representative of mainstream popular Jewish culture from eighteenth-century eastern Poland than we have previously assumed.

While smaller Polish congregations generally did not remove the wall-paintings from existing synagogues, neither did they continue the tradition of elaborate wall-

painting they had inherited.[81] By 1800, fewer than seventy-five years after the Gwoździec Synagogue's cupola was painted, the tradition of liturgical wall-painting had almost completely disappeared.[82] It is a principal argument of this study that the Gwoździec Synagogue's wall-paintings should be seen as a visible record of a now-vanished Jewish popular culture that once characterized the late seventeenth and early eighteenth centuries but was radically changed by the beginning of the nineteenth century.

Wooden and Masonry Synagogue Precedents

Wooden synagogues, usually built in small towns, and masonry synagogues, usually built in larger towns, represent two parallel and frequently intersecting traditions of synagogue construction. By comparing and contrasting these two traditions, we can better appreciate both the overall qualities of wooden synagogues and the reasons why small-town communities chose to build them.

Wooden Synagogues

As previously noted, the vast majority of Eastern-European synagogues built before 1800 were made of wood. Most of them were built with hewn logs, as were the vast majority of buildings in the small towns of Poland. Wooden synagogues with vaulted cupolas like the Gwoździec Synagogue were the grandest, most sophisticated examples of this type of building (fig. 71). Although masonry buildings had represented the highest standard of building construction since the medieval period, wood was the accepted material for most structures built in all but the largest cities before the nineteenth century. During the eighteenth century, when many of the finest wooden synagogues were constructed, wood was also used to build some of the most elaborate palaces, churches, and government buildings. Before 1800, in a typical Eastern-European small town like Gwoździec, probably only the Catholic Church, the town's defensive fortifications, and the residences of the local nobility were built in masonry. In these towns, wooden structures were the norm and not the exception.[83] Throughout the nineteenth century, masonry construction gradually supplanted wood construction for major public buildings in all but the smallest towns. The increase in nineteenth-century masonry synagogue construction and the subsequent decline in wooden synagogue construction generally reflects the advent of modern construction and city planning practices.

Masonry Synagogues

The first masonry synagogues in Poland followed a medieval, two-aisle plan that was brought to Eastern Europe during Ashkenazi immigration to Poland (fig. 72). In Poland, this medieval plan was later replaced in masonry synagogues that used square instead of rectangular plans (fig. 73). These new synagogue prototypes were all established by the middle of the seventeenth

FIG. 72. *Interior, Old Synagogue, Cracow, Poland.* Note the location of the bimah along the central axis between the two central columns. (Courtesy of the Instytut Sztuki PAN, Warsaw, Poland.)

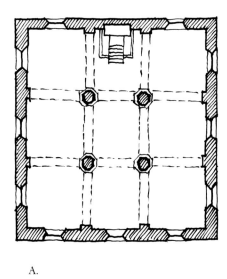

A.

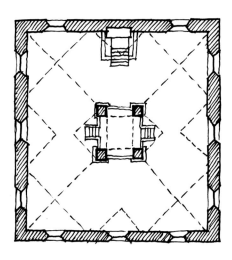

B.

FIG. 73. *Square Synagogue Plans.* A. Nine-vault plan with four columns; B. Clustered-column plan with four columns. (Based on Piechotka, *Bramy Nieba.*)

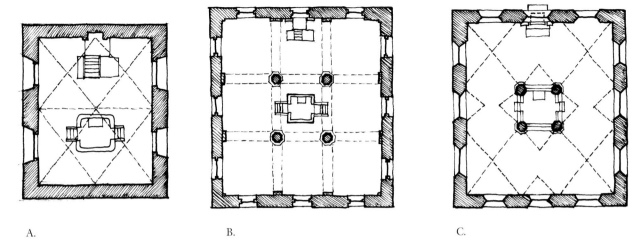

FIG. 74. *Masonry Synagogue Plans*. A. Single-vault plan; B. Nine-vault plan with four columns; C. Clustered-column plan with four columns. (Based on Piechotka, *Bramy Nieba*.)

century, and they were refined, but not substantively altered, during the eighteenth century.[84]

The three dominant types of Polish masonry synagogues were the masonry vault plan, the nine-vault plan, and the clustered-column plan (fig. 74). All three types shared a basic floor plan similar to that used in the wooden synagogues. They had an almost square, centralized plan and an axial arrangement of the entrance,

bimah, and ark. Between 1500 and 1700, square and almost square plans were used in most masonry synagogues built in Poland and, later, in Russia.[85]

Three synagogues from Gwoździec's Lviv region are representative of these dominant masonry types. The TaZ or Golden Rose Synagogue of Lviv had a single masonry vault composed of four groin vaults (fig. 75).[86] The Suburban Synagogue of Lviv, built in 1632–33, had a

FIG. 75. *Single Masonry Vault, TaZ or Golden Rose Synagogue, Lviv, Ukraine, 1582*. A. Plan, B. Section. (Based on Krinsky, *Synagogues of Europe*.)

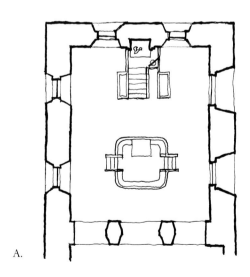

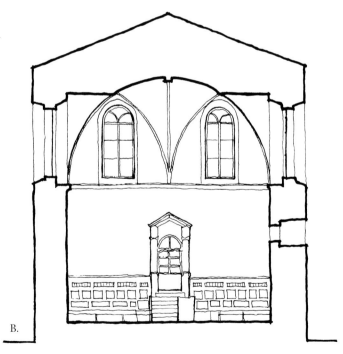

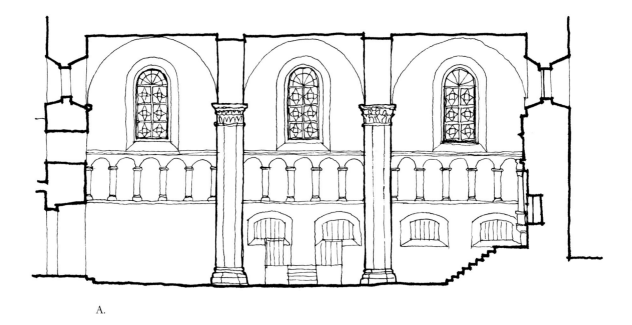

A.

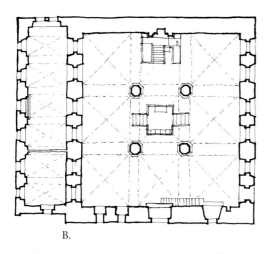

B.

FIG. 76. *Nine-Vault Plan, Suburban Synagogue, Lviv, Ukraine, 1632.*
A. Section, B. Plan. (Based on Krinsky, *Synagogues of Europe*.)

nine-vault plan and four central columns (fig. 76).[87] The Pińsk synagogue, built in 1640, had a clustered-column plan with four central columns tightly grouped about the central bimah (fig. 77).[88] The centralized plans of the Suburban Synagogue and the Pińsk Synagogue have both been attributed to the influence of Italian Renaissance architectural sources, but, as we shall see in chapter 6, they may also have been influenced by regional Jewish sources.

Wooden and Masonry Synagogues

When comparing wooden and masonry synagogues, most researchers either call attention to the different traditions of design and construction used to build these synagogues or, when focusing on their similarities, conclude that wooden synagogues were derivative of or secondary to masonry synagogues.[89] Both types of synagogue, however, date back to the earliest period of Jewish settlement, and both types have valid claims to originality and distinctiveness within their long period of intertwined development. Although documented masonry synagogues were far older than any documented wooden synagogues, these same masonry synagogues were often preceded by wooden structures that have since been destroyed. In the typical incremental process of Jewish community growth, wooden synagogues were often built first, then replaced by masonry

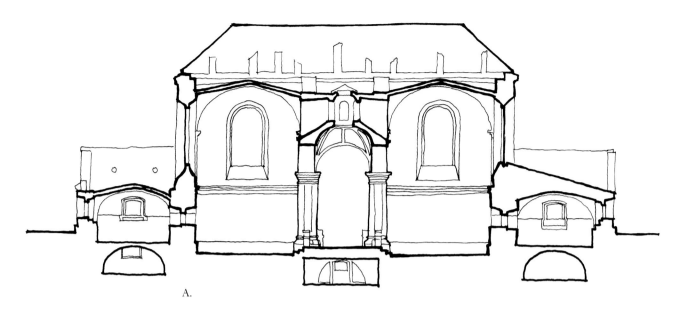

A.

synagogues. For example, the oldest masonry synagogues in large cities like Cracow, Lviv, and Łańcut were
all built after wooden structures had been destroyed or
removed from the same or adjacent sites.[90] Although the
number of documented examples is not large, whenever
sufficient records do document the type of synagogue
that preceded a pre-1800 masonry synagogue, it is often
a wooden synagogue. Therefore, wooden synagogues
preceding masonry synagogues may have been a far
more typical pattern of development then was previously believed.

Comparisons between wooden and masonry synagogues also reveal two strikingly dissimilar conceptions
of the spatial quality of the synagogue. It is generally
true that the interior wooden vaulting in synagogues
like Gwoździec was inspired by earlier masonry structures, including both synagogues and churches. However, the vaulted cupola found in eighteenth-century
wooden synagogues drew on many divergent sources for
its unique design, and this design was not essentially derivative of masonry prototypes. The differences between
masonry and wooden vaulting are clearly demonstrated
in sectional analysis, where the smooth, continuous contours of the typical masonry vault are fundamentally different from the irregularly stepped, multitiered vaulting
of a typical wooden synagogue (fig. 78). Wooden vaulting and masonry vaulting, therefore, produced different types of interior spaces and reveal different attitudes

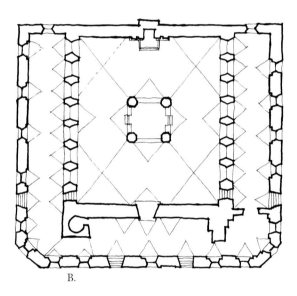

B.

FIG. 77. *Clustered-Column Plan, Pińsk Synagogue, Pińsk, Belarus, 1640.*
A. Section, B. Plan. (Based on Piechotka, *Bramy Nieba.*)

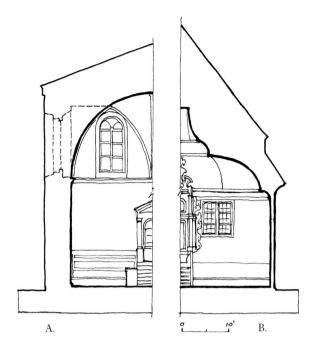

FIG. 78. *Wooden and Masonry Synagogue Ceilings.* Compare A. the masonry ceiling at TaZ Synagogue, Lviv, and B. the wooden ceiling at Gwoździec Synagogue. (Based on Piechotka, *Wooden Synagogues.*)

toward the space of worship. On the one hand, masonry synagogue vaulting typically conveyed a uniform structural rationality, while on the other hand, wooden synagogue vaulting typically conveyed a vibrant, nonstructural complexity. We should resist simplistic analysis of this contrast—for example, one that attributes rationality to masonry synagogues and irrationality or mysticism to wooden synagogues. Yet we should not disregard the implications of these two fundamentally different approaches to the space of worship. In an unusually clear separation of synagogue types, the eighteenth-century space of worship in larger towns differed sharply from the eighteenth-century space of worship in smaller towns (or shtetls).

The differences between wooden and masonry synagogues are especially significant for this study, because they suggest that during the eighteenth century there existed two parallel yet frequently intersecting architectural traditions that shaped the prayer halls in Polish synagogues: a masonry tradition from the larger towns, which culminated in the nine-vault plan during the seventeenth century, and a wooden tradition from small towns, which culminated in the wooden cupola design during the eighteenth century.[91] In the final chapters of this book, we return to the question of whether the architectural differences between large- and small-town

synagogues merely reflected stylistic and aesthetic factors or whether they represented deeper liturgical and cultural differences.

Whatever the meaning of these differences in architectural expression, the defining characteristic of the wooden synagogue, the centralized vaulted cupola, was definitely not simply copied from masonry synagogues. Therefore, the idea that the wooden synagogues were derivative of and subordinate to the masonry synagogues must be abandoned. Instead we should assume a theory of parallel development in which two synagogue types shared some mutual influences while still developing separate and distinct traditions.[92]

Eastern-European Building Precedents

The wooden synagogues of the Gwoździec region were built within an architectural context that included many types of non-Jewish and nonreligious buildings. Together, these buildings constituted a regional genre that affected the style, materials, and construction of the wooden synagogues. Palaces and manor houses (dwóry) of the nobility, as well as a wide range of monumental religious structures, such as churches and monasteries, and various commercial buildings, including inns and taverns, had some degree of influence on the design of wooden synagogues of the Gwoździec region.

Polish institutional and religious architecture after 1600 is dominated by late-Baroque architectural styles associated with the Catholic Counter-Reformation. In Poland's eastern provinces, Baroque motifs were initially used in masonry buildings and continued to affect regional vernacular styles well into the nineteenth century. Although frequently criticized by architectural historians as eclectic and lacking the discipline of the classical precedents from which they borrowed, these regional vernacular traditions produced vibrant, hybrid mixtures of classical and regional motifs that ultimately defined the architecture in their Eastern-European regions. The wooden synagogues built in Poland's eastern provinces drew on a similar aesthetic mix of regional traditions and imported Baroque styles.

Manor Houses and Civic Architecture

The Polish manor house influenced the Polish synagogues in many direct and indirect ways (fig. 79) The

FIG. 79. *Manor House, Ożarów, Poland.* Note the typical double-sloped roof and helmeted pavilions. (Courtesy of the Instytut Sztuki PAN, Warsaw, Poland.)

magnates' extraordinary wealth and political power in the small towns of eastern Poland ensured that their principal residences would exert considerable aesthetic influence on the architecture of their regions. This impact on regional buildings included a degree of influence on the architecture of the Jewish community and its synagogue.[93] Specific features of the Polish manor house such as the two-tiered, gambrel roof and exterior detailing that combined neo-Classical and vernacular elements influenced the design of many synagogues.[94] These architectural features were not, however, exclusive to the manor house. Instead they formed a common regional vocabulary used in most major buildings in Poland's eastern provinces, including commercial buildings and inns or taverns of the eighteenth century (fig. 80).[95]

Another way Baroque styles of manor houses may have come to the attention of the Jewish community was through business contact with local magnates, who often employed Jews to manage their estates. The Polish

nobles' lavish entertainments, which included plays and pageants performed at their country houses, introduced into the remote provinces and towns spatial and decorative ideas from the royal courts of Europe. The Jewish employees of a magnate would have witnessed this elaborate court pageantry, which, unlike the ceremonies of the Baroque church, was open to their observation.[96] Thus, various elements of the court theater, such as concealed lighting techniques, lunette windows, and late-Baroque and Rococo interior styles and textile patterns, may have influenced the aesthetic vocabulary of synagogue design, just as they influenced seventeenth- and eighteenth-century monumental architecture in Poland.[97]

Catholic Churches and Baroque Style

Some scholars have identified similarities between wooden synagogues and wooden churches built in various regions of Poland. Although many construction

FIG. 80. *Eighteenth-Century Inn/Tavern, Spytkowice (village), near Żywiec, Poland.* (Courtesy of the Instytut Sztuki PAN, Warsaw, Poland.)

details are shared by wooden synagogues and wooden churches, they remain fundamentally different structures (fig. 81).[98] The larger, plainer, centralized mass of the typical wooden synagogue contrasts sharply with the smaller, more ornate, elongated mass of a typical wooden church. For example, the exotic towers and complex forms of the Church of St. George (1659–60) in Drohobycz, fifty miles west of Gwoździec, are characteristic of Greek and Russian Orthodox church architecture found in the Podolian region (fig. 82). Even though the builders of wooden churches like St. George and the builders of wooden synagogues like Gwoździec used a similar vocabulary of architectural styles and construction techniques, the individual buildings were quite distinct.[99]

While the design of wooden churches had a mini-

mal impact on the wooden synagogues, masonry church design was quite influential. Most scholars agree that wooden synagogues like Gwoździec were deeply influenced by the Italian and European Baroque styles as they were used in Polish masonry churches (fig. 83). In most wooden and masonry synagogues, the furniture-like elements of the ark and bimah closely follow the spatial and technical woodworking practices of the Baroque style. These were the same woodworking practices used to produce church altars and furnishings in seventeenth- and eighteenth-century Poland.[100] But perhaps the most important influence of the Baroque style on synagogues like Gwoździec can be seen in the shape of their undulating wooden cupolas. While inspired by the Tent of the Tabernacle and based on the Ottoman tent, the Gwoździec Synagogue cupola was created in a climate of spa-

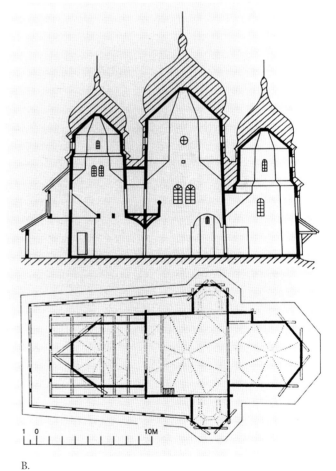

FIG. 81. *Wooden Church of St. Paraskeva, Krekhiv, Ukraine, 1658.* The three-part massing is typical of Ukrainian and Russian Orthodox wooden churches in the Gwoździec region. Note the separate bell tower in the far left of the photograph. (From *Masterpieces in Wood: Houses of Worship in Ukraine*, Titus Hewryk, Guest Curator, The Ukrainian Museum, New York, 1987.)

FIG. 82. *Church of Saint George, Drohobyc, Ukraine, 1659–1666.* A. Photograph showing the elaborate triple domes of this regional Orthodox church; B. Section and plan. (From *Masterpieces in Wood: Houses of Worship in Ukraine*, Titus Hewryk, Guest Curator, The Ukrainian Museum, New York, 1987.)

A.

B.

FIG. 83. *Jesuit Church of Saints Peter and Paul, Cracow, Poland, 1596–1633*. This church was closely modeled after the Jesuit Church of the Gesu, Rome, built between 1568–1583. (Photo: S. Kolowca, Courtesy of the Instytut Sztuki PAN, Warsaw.)

tial experimentation generated by the new spatial plasticity of Polish Baroque architecture. While we do not know the specific influences of the Baroque style on the design of the Gwoździec ceiling, we can place its development within the same seventeenth- and eighteenth-century era of spatial experimentation that transformed the ceilings and walls of equivalent monumental and religious buildings throughout Poland and Eastern Europe.

The Baroque influence on wooden synagogues like Gwoździec is a specific instance of the profound impact Baroque architecture had on all levels of Polish culture. During the seventeenth and eighteenth centuries, in the period when wooden synagogues were built, Polish culture was fundamentally transformed by a Counter-Reformation movement that precipitated an influx of Italian-Catholic institutions into Poland. This movement was led by newly founded religious orders, such as the Jesuits, who imported Italian Baroque artists and architects. These artisans brought with them advanced ideas on architecture, art, and city planning.[101] When the Bernardines built their large monastic church next door to the Gwoździec Synagogue, the Jewish community experienced, first-hand, the powerful impact of this sophisticated Baroque artistic style (figs. 84, 85). We do not know if this church or its architects directly influ-

FIG. 84. *Church of the Immaculate Conception at the Bernardine Monastery, Gwoździec, c. 1715–1750*. A twentieth-century photograph shows the twin towers and entrance arch. The wooden steeples were replaced in 1888 and the gateway was added in 1890. (Courtesy of the National Museum in Lviv.)

FIG. 85. *Nave and Main Altar, Bernardine Monastery Church, Gwoź-dziec*. This church is a powerful example of the late-Baroque architectural style in Eastern Europe. (Courtesy of the National Museum in Lviv.)

enced the remodeling of the Gwoździec Synagogue. We can be sure, however, that the Baroque style of architecture and decoration, so pervasive in Polish culture of the period, did have a significant impact on the development of the Gwoździec Synagogue, and especially its remodeled cupola.[102]

Derivative and Unique

As the previous examples make clear, Polish wooden synagogues were influenced by the non-Jewish architecture of their regions. These varied influences included the houses of the magnates, regional architecture in the small towns, and the architectural styles of the late Baroque period. Yet the necessarily derivative nature of regional building vocabularies did not prevent Jewish communities from producing highly distinctive synagogues with vaulted wooden cupolas that were their most original feature.

The synagogues' wooden cupolas, however, do not at first appear to originate in Jewish building traditions.

This is primarily because precedents for the vaulted cupola can be found in most Eastern-European religious and secular buildings. The wooden domes and vaulted ceilings of regional churches, especially the log cupolas of Ukrainian Uniate and Russian Orthodox folk churches, are cited by most scholars as regional precedents for the vaulted cupolas of the synagogues. Elaborate Baroque domes and vaulting were found in Catholic churches and in monumental secular buildings of Eastern Europe during the seventeenth and eighteenth centuries, and these structures did indeed influence the wooden synagogue builders.[103] Furthermore, as scholars have consistently emphasized, the vaulting of masonry synagogues was a likely precedent for the vaulting found in wooden synagogues.[104] In other words, there was no shortage of raised ceilings nor of vaulted cupolas for the eighteenth-century wooden synagogue builders to copy.

Yet, even with these precedents, vaulted cupolas in wooden synagogues like Gwoździec still represent a unique synthesis of all these sources. In the most sophisticated examples of the late eighteenth century, the wooden synagogue combined several Baroque spatial devices to produce a novel, telescoping cupola. By accentuated blind balconies and deep recesses, synagogue designers employed techniques of spatial foreshortening to exaggerate the apparent height of the cupola. This technique of spatial foreshortening in the vaulted cupola, begun at Gwoździec and culminating at Wołpa, was perhaps the single most original architectural feature of the wooden synagogues (see fig. 69).[105]

FIG. 86. *Entrance to the Prayer Hall, West Wall, Gwoździec Synagogue.* This painting depicts the synagogue's west wall covered with Hebrew prayer panels, inscriptions, and decorative motifs. Beyond the threshold to the prayer hall, sunlight comes through the main entry to illuminate the entrance room. Isidor Kaufmann, *Portal of the Rabbis*, c. 1897–1898, oil on wood, 24 x 34 cm. (Courtesy of the Hungarian National Gallery.)

WALL-PAINTINGS

If we could still enter the Gwoździec Synagogue, we would step into a prayer hall covered with a vibrant tapestry of wall-paintings.[1] Looking upward, the ceiling ascends in richly bordered tiers toward a steeply sloping, pyramidal top (fig. 87). Looking to either side, ribbons of swirling vegetation and architectural fragments frame brilliant white panels inscribed with Hebrew texts. Animals, both familiar and strange, are prominently located throughout the prayer hall. Especially noticeable are a band of animal figures set in large medallions that ring the lower edge of the ceiling. The entire interior composition radiates a palate of deep, intense colors that saturate the prayer hall with intricate designs like those found in an oriental carpet (fig. 86, and see color plates 1, 3, 4). It is an interior unlike anything most readers have ever seen. Even when pictured in faded, early-twentieth-century black and white photographs, the visual intensity of the synagogue's wall-paintings can be overwhelming. Yet these elaborate wall-paintings lack neither organization nor clarity. Upon closer inspection, one sees that the wall surfaces are subdivided into geometric units that frame various images and inscriptions, and an underlying visual unity becomes apparent (fig. 88).

The paintings that covered the walls and the ceiling of the Gwoździec Synagogue can be divided into two artistic and historic periods (figs. 89, 90, 91, 92). The walls were painted between about 1700 and 1725 by a group or guild of artists who worked in similar, but not identical, styles. The paintings on these walls were a

series of panels containing the text of Hebrew prayers set in elaborate architectural frames and surrounded by arches and columns similar to those found on the title pages of manuscripts and early printed books.[2] As they were arranged around the prayer hall, the vertically framed prayer panels appeared linked together in one continuous band as if the pages of a gigantic book lined the synagogue walls.

The paintings on the ceiling vaulting were also uniformly organized. These paintings were completed in 1729 by a pair of artists from the town of Jarychów, one hundred miles northwest of Gwoździec, near Lviv.[3] Together they created an elaborate geometric composition that subdivided the ceiling into a series of framed panels, often containing realistically drawn and vividly colored animal figures. These panels followed the curving and narrowing sides of the ceiling as it sloped upward and inward to the top of the tent-like cupola. There, an illustrated zodiac circled the uppermost tier of the ceiling (see fig. 87).

The Gwoździec wall-paintings contain a density of inscriptions, figures, and motifs that has proven extremely difficult to interpret. The paintings defy traditional stylistic and thematic categories because they combine inscriptions of prayers and ethical expressions with images of domestic and exotic animals. Both inscriptions and images are framed by decorative borders that divide the entire surface of walls and ceiling with strongly articulated borders and edge motifs. The artistic sources for the paintings reflect the complex artistic

FIG. 87. *Wall-Paintings, Central Cupola, Gwoździec Synagogue.* A photograph looking directly up into the peak of the cupola shows a ring of twelve zodiac figures circling the center. At the peak, four arabesques face each other. The dark vertical lines on the left side of the photograph are ropes that supported the hanging candelabra. (Courtesy of the Tel Aviv Museum of Art.)

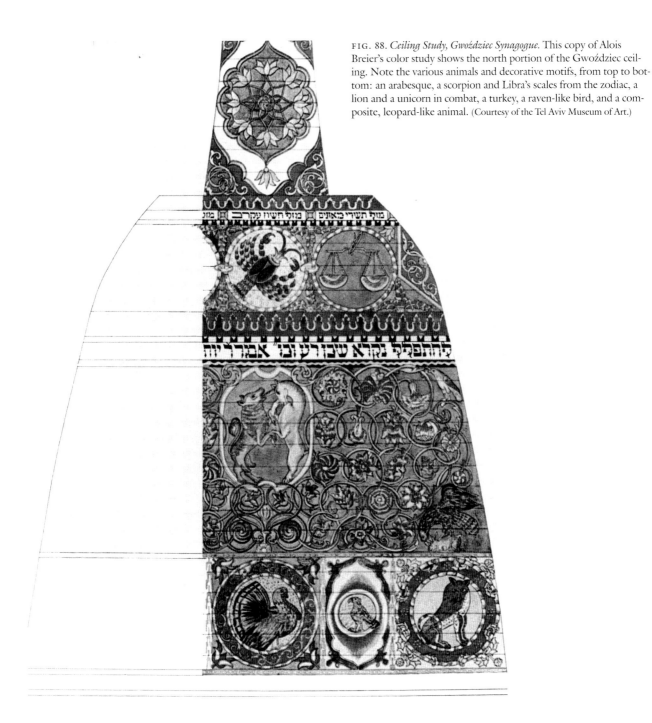

FIG. 88. *Ceiling Study, Gwoździec Synagogue.* This copy of Alois Breier's color study shows the north portion of the Gwoździec ceiling. Note the various animals and decorative motifs, from top to bottom: an arabesque, a scorpion and Libra's scales from the zodiac, a lion and a unicorn in combat, a turkey, a raven-like bird, and a composite, leopard-like animal. (Courtesy of the Tel Aviv Museum of Art.)

and liturgical background of the Gwoździec community, which draws on sources both Jewish and Gentile, contemporary and archaic, local and foreign, folk and fine art.[4] As we shall see, these diverse artistic sources reflect the multinational, cosmopolitan nature of this Jewish community, a community simultaneously integrated into and distinctly separated from its seventeenth- and eighteenth-century Polish context.

Interpretation

For over one hundred years, historians of art and architecture have struggled to interpret the Polish wooden synagogues and their elaborate wall-paintings. Before the destruction of the synagogues began in 1939, these paintings were observed in situ by researchers who emphasized their combination of Jewish artistic traditions

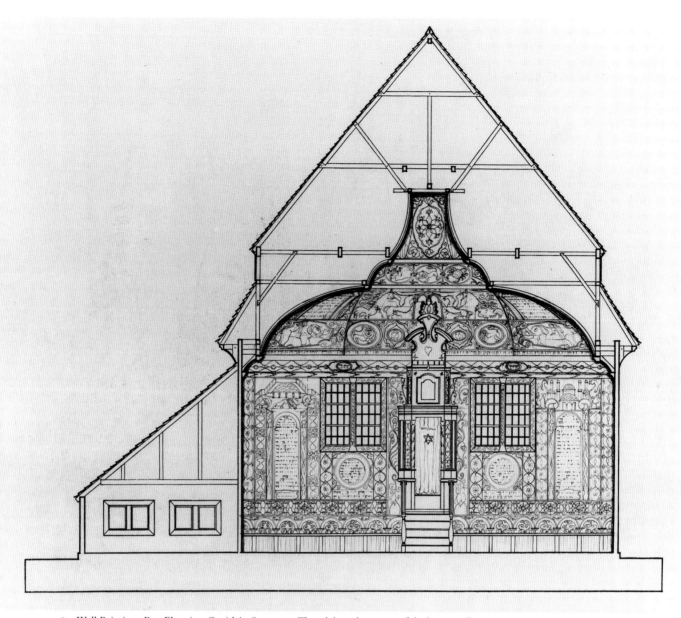

FIG. 89. *Wall-Paintings, East Elevation, Gwoździec Synagogue.* The ark is at the center of the lower wall.

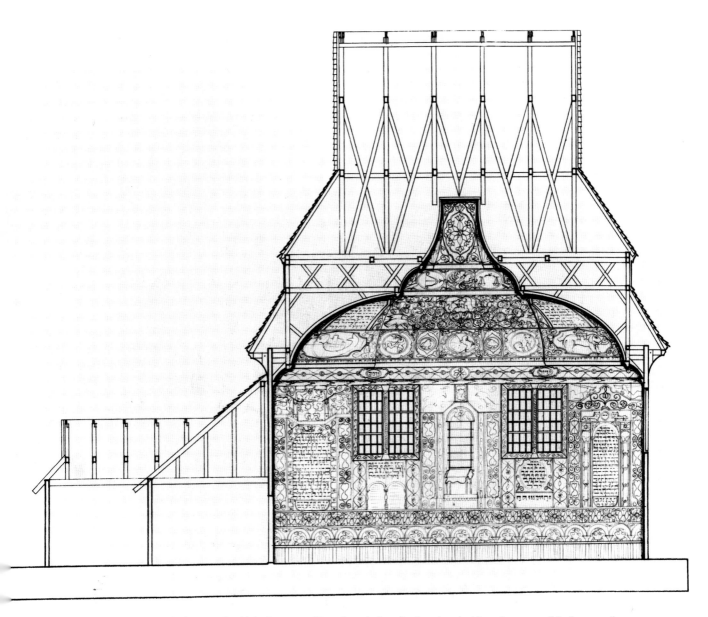

FIG. 90. *Wall-Paintings, North Elevation, Gwoździec Synagogue.* Note the painting of a shew-bread table at the center of the lower wall.

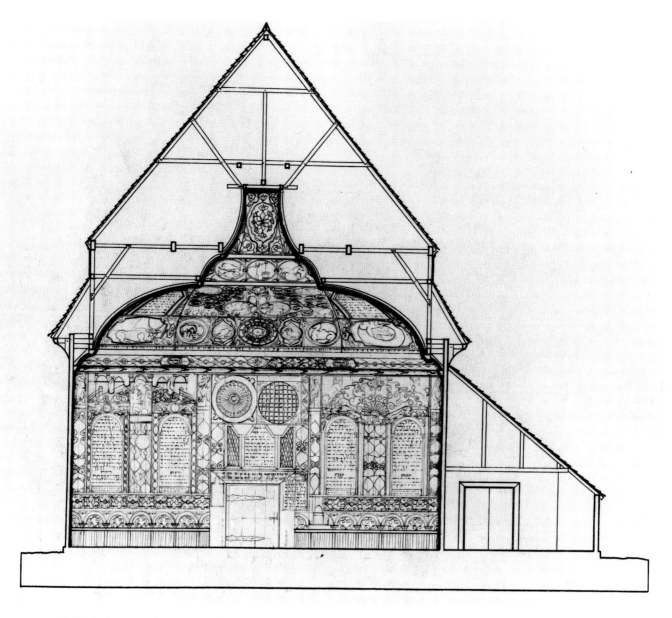

FIG. 91. *Wall-Paintings, West Elevation, Gwoździec Synagogue.* Note the entrance door and lattice window near the center of the lower wall.

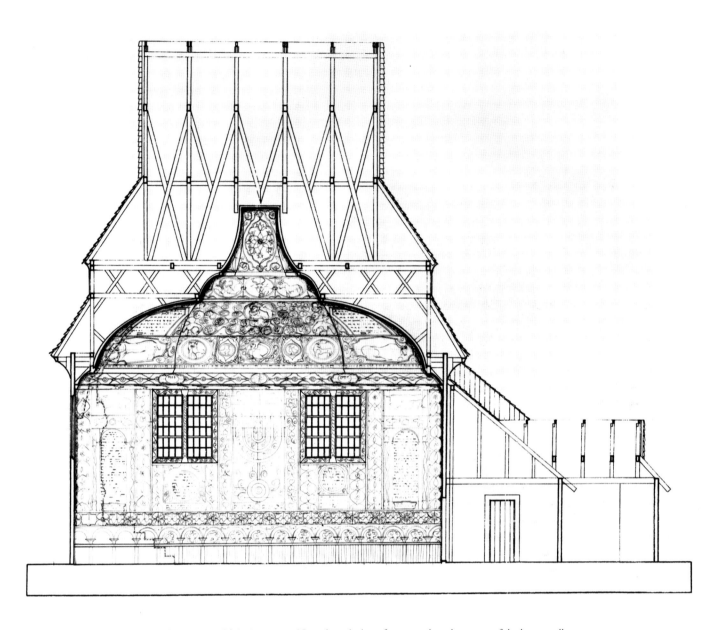

FIG. 92. *Wall-Paintings, South Elevation, Gwoździec Synagogue.* Note the painting of a menorah at the center of the lower wall.

and Eastern-European, vernacular, aesthetic influences.[5] Most often the wall-paintings were described as a form of Eastern-European folk art that was practiced by small-town, Jewish communities.

Following the Second World War, scholarly interpretation of the wall-paintings could be divided into two schools of thought. One approach continued to emphasize the influence of regional, non-Jewish precedents, while the other interpreted the paintings as an indigenous Jewish art form, often with messianic overtones. Scholars who emphasized regional influences stressed the influence Eastern-European art had on synagogue art and tended to delimit the religious importance such paintings had for their Jewish communities. In this first approach, the wall-paintings were seen as a minor folk art that was a direct product of its Eastern-European cultural context. On the other hand, those who emphasized messianic influences saw the wall-paintings less as a contextually derived art form and more as a distinctively Jewish art produced by preemancipated, Ostjuden, shtetl Jewry. The inspiration for these distinctively Jewish paintings was often attributed to the negative pressures of impoverishment, pogroms, and exile, which were in turn linked to messianic themes in Judaism. In

this second approach, the development of the wall-paintings, especially their extensive use of animal symbolism, was seen as a messianism of desperation, one generated by an increasingly impoverished shtetl Jewry (fig. 93).[6]

While both approaches provide some insight into the meaning of the wall-paintings, both are also based on inaccurate assumptions about their meaning and symbolism. Most contemporary scholars have escaped the limitations of these earlier views and recognize the importance of both Jewish artistic and religious sources, but there is still little agreement on the meaning and symbolism of the wall-paintings. Although general themes related to Jewish art and legends are clearly discernible, the specific contextual meaning of the vast majority of images in the wall-paintings found at Gwoździec remains largely unexplained.

Because the destruction of the wooden synagogues and their communities was so thorough, there is little or no substantive documentation concerning the historic periods in which these paintings were produced. Before the synagogues were destroyed, however, researchers surveyed the wooden synagogues, analyzed the wall-paintings, and interviewed residents of the local com-

FIG. 93. *Evening Worship.* A painting by Jan Kanty Hruzik, *Yom Kippur in the Old Synagogue in Cracow,* 1870–1875, oil on canvas, 72 x 57 cm. (Courtesy of the Historical Museum of the City of Cracow.)

FIG. 94. *Artist's Signature, Gwoździec Synagogue.* On the west wall of the ceiling, the artist's signature, "Israel, son of Mordecai," and a short dedication were painted in a large medallion. A unicorn and a bird labeled "ostrich" were painted in neighboring medallions. (Courtesy of the Tel Aviv Museum of Art.)

munities. Yet even these efforts yielded little concrete information about the wall-paintings. At Gwoździec, the first documentation and interviews were done in the early 1890s, 170 years after the ceiling was remodeled and painted. Despite the passage of so much time, it was possible that the meaning of these paintings had been passed on through oral histories, but even among long-time residents, their history and meaning were largely forgotten.[7] As I will show, these paintings were the last examples of a premodern or late-medieval tradition of synagogue art that was already rapidly vanishing at the end of the eighteenth century. Seen in this light, it is not so surprising that, when scholars came to document these paintings at the beginning of the twentieth century, their meanings and sources were only vaguely remembered by the Gwoździec community. We are, therefore, left with limited information on the contextual meaning these paintings had for their congregants

in 1731. Fortunately, there are other ways to unravel their meaning. We will begin by examining the artists.

Artists

The artists who painted the Gwoździec cupola each signed their names and wrote brief passages in large oval medallions set on opposite sides of the ceiling's western wall (fig. 94, and see fig. 106).

The signature on the northwest side reads:

"See, all this was made by my hand [Isaiah 66:2], for the glory of the place and the glory of the community, [said?] the artist Isaac son of Rabbi Judah Leib ha Cohen from the Holy community of Jarychów. In the year (1729) 'This is my handiwork, in which I glory'" [Isaiah 60:21]. [The date is calculated by Hebrew letter-number equivalents identified by marks above selected letters.]

The signature on the southwest side reads:

"By the worker, engaged in the holy labor, [said?] the artist Israel, son of the venerable Rabbi Mordecai from the Holy community of Jarychów, district of the Holy community of Lviv." [In both cases, the title "Rabbi" was a standard convention of the period and did not indicate rabbinical parentage of the painters.[8]]

The two artists set their signatures within symmetrical medallions and integrated these medallions into the artistic pattern of the overall composition. Their prominent placement indicates that the painters were important, regionally known artists. The fact that their signatures were symmetrically composed probably indicates that they shared equal status. Whatever their professional status, these were not untutored folk or shtetl artisans. They were skillful artists who had considerable status within the Jewish communities they served.

When the Gwoździec wall-paintings are compared to the wall-paintings from neighboring synagogues in the Lviv region, it is clear that all the painters of the Gwoździec Synagogue worked within a commonly accepted, regional tradition. Like other contemporary artists of their region, they would have worked within a guild, or guild-like association, where artistic, technical, and, most likely, liturgical knowledge was handed down orally from master to apprentice.[9] I stress their late-seventeenth- and early-eighteenth-century context because, as we contemplate these artists, we should not imagine independent artists working outside the rabbinical establishment. Rather we should picture a guild of established artists working within highly developed, and in some ways standardized, artistic and liturgical traditions.

The tradition of synagogue painting as it was practiced throughout the Polish-Lithuanian Commonwealth is of considerable importance to this research. Although only limited documentation survives, there is enough information drawn from scattered communities to suggest that the artistic traditions from Gwoździec were practiced throughout the eastern provinces of Poland and probably had been for hundreds of years. There is even evidence to suggest that these traditions extended beyond eastern Poland. The well-documented synagogue wall-paintings of Eliezer Sussman, a Jewish painter from Brody, Ukraine, one hundred miles north of Gwoździec, are a leading example. Between 1732 and 1742, Sussman painted at least seven synagogues in southern Germany, and his work closely follows the artistic style and liturgical symbolism used in the wooden synagogues of the Podolian region surrounding Gwoździec. Sussman's work has many of the same decorative motifs, animal figures, and prayer inscriptions that we

find at the Gwoździec Synagogue (fig. 95, and color plate 6). Although today his work is only an isolated example, I believe that Sussman's paintings illuminate a unified tradition of synagogue art that once flourished among Ashkenazi communities in regions of Eastern and Central Europe.[10]

The unity of small-town synagogue art found throughout Gwoździec's Podolian region suggests that the wall-paintings were not commissioned by individuals or groups acting outside the hierarchy of religious and secular authority within their communities. In other words, these wall-paintings were not the whimsical decision of one community leader, but probably reflect mainstream institutional values of the towns and regions that commissioned them. I stress this point to emphasize the necessity for institutional support behind the wall-paintings—support for synagogue art that has no contemporary equivalent. We should not imagine that the commissioning of the wall-paintings was a process similar to obtaining an artwork or donor portrait for a contemporary synagogue. As we shall see, these wall-paintings functioned as a visual layer of artistic liturgy reflective of the rabbinic establishment.

FIG. 95. *Painted Ceiling, Horb Synagogue, Horb, Germany.* The eastern portion of the barrel-vaulted ceiling, painted by Eliezer Sussman in 1735, closely resembles the wall-paintings in the Gwoździec Synagogue. Many of the same inscriptions and motifs were used in each synagogue, and the overall composition of the wall-paintings is similar. (Photo: © The Israel Museum, Jerusalem.)

Composition

As I have emphasized above, the densely interwoven forms and colors of the wall-paintings may give the initial impression of disorder or randomness, but they are highly organized compositions. Their artistic and compositional order, however, is one that has few if any direct parallels in contemporary synagogues or contemporary art. As twenty-first-century viewers, we must be prepared to adjust our eyes in order to see and appreciate an artistic ensemble that has few equivalents in our own time.

Organization

The paintings on the walls and the ceiling of the Gwoździec Synagogue were set within geometric frames that divided the entire surface of the interior into richly bordered grids (fig. 96). In order to create such a grid, the overall composition had to be laid out by an artist with a clear conception of the entire interior space. Although segments of the lower walls may have been painted by different artists over time, the Gwoździec interior was a carefully planned and meticulously executed creation that closely followed a well-established, regional tradition of synagogue art.

The geometric composition of the wall-paintings was directly influenced by the architectural organization of the prayer hall. The basic composition was formed by a system of grids aligned with such architectural features of the interior as the doorway, windows, cornice lines, and ceiling joints. For example, the spacing of the large windows on three of the four walls determined the major geometric rhythm of the interior grid. The large panels inscribed with prayers were evenly spaced between these large windows. Then the spaces between the windows and the panels were subdivided into smaller geometric panels with decorative borders (see figs. 89–92). Although we do not know if there was any contact between the painters and the architects, the skillful alignment of the paintings within the architectural features of the interior, an alignment that is especially evident in the layout of the ceiling, suggests that the painters were very aware of the architectural elements that defined the interior space of the prayer hall.

Nowhere is the geometric order of the paintings more apparent than in the composition of the western wall (fig. 97). The asymmetrical placement of the doorway beneath the symmetrical placement of the circular lattice window would have challenged the painters' creation of a unified, symmetrical composition. In a creative response to this challenge, the painters integrated

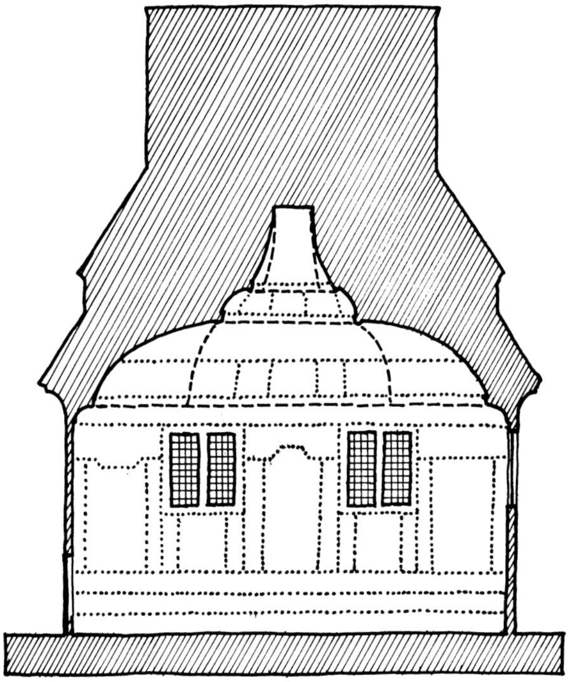

FIG. 96. *Composition, Wall-Paintings, Gwoździec Synagogue.* This diagram shows the compositional outline for the wall-paintings on the south wall.

FIG. 97. *West Wall, Gwoździec Synagogue.* Note how the doorway and the Gate of Heaven lattice window are not aligned. At the bottom left of the photograph is the railing for a staircase that leads to the central bimah. (Courtesy of the Tel Aviv Museum of Art.)

the door into the overall symmetry of the painted grids by subtly realigning their composition (fig. 98). To enhance the expression of symmetry, they painted a duplicate circular medallion next to the original circular window and widened one side of the doorway's decorative border. These aesthetic adjustments to the composition of the western wall provide rare insight into the painters' methods. We observe how they adjusted their standard pattern of geometric composition, one they had used throughout the synagogue, to address the problem of the asymmetrical doorway.[11] Other design decisions shed less light on the painters' aesthetic intentions, but this type of rigorous ordering clearly reflects the sort of compositional thinking the artists brought to the interior of the Gwoździec Synagogue.

Not enough is known about the meaning and symbolism of most figures and inscriptions in the wall-paintings to know whether they were designed for specific locations in the synagogue. A few paintings, however, did have specific spatial meaning within the overall composition. At the Gwoździec Synagogue, four such paintings were set in the middle of each of the four walls (fig. 99). A Tablets of Law was painted above the ark on the eastern wall (see fig. 157), a Menorah was painted on the southern wall (see fig. 117), a Shew-bread table was painted on the northern wall (see fig. 41), and a lattice window or "Gate of Heaven" window was painted on the western wall (see fig. 97). Three of these images, the Menorah, Tablets, and Shew-bread table, were the holy vessels from the Tent of the Tabernacle. Each was painted in the same ritual position it occupied in the Tent of the Tabernacle (Exodus 25:23–40). (The meaning of the fourth object, the "Gate of Heaven" window, is analyzed in the last chapter.) The painting of the holy vessels in their ritual locations supports the theory that the Tabernacle served as an influential model for the remodeling of the Gwoździec Synagogue interior.[12] As we will see in chapter 6, the image of the Tabernacle's holy vessels set in a square plan is repeatedly referred to in the *Zohar*. The *Zohar* uses this Tabernacle image as a symbol of Divine perfection. The fact that the four painted images were also found in the same locations in other synagogues of the Gwoździec region further suggests that allusions to the Tabernacle were meaningful throughout the small-town congregations of eastern Poland.[13]

The vibrant combination of intense colors is another surprising element of the wall-paintings (see color plates 1, 3, 4). The colors most often used in the Gwoździec

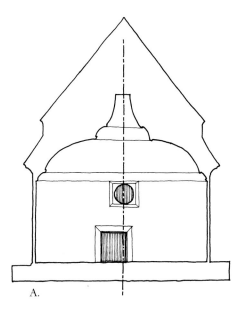

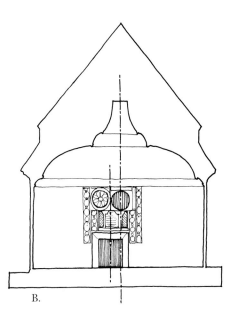

FIG. 98. *Composition, Wall-Paintings, West Wall, Gwoździec Synagogue.* Diagrams showing A. the asymmetrical alignment of the door and the lattice window and B. the adjustments the painters made to reinforce the symmetrical composition.

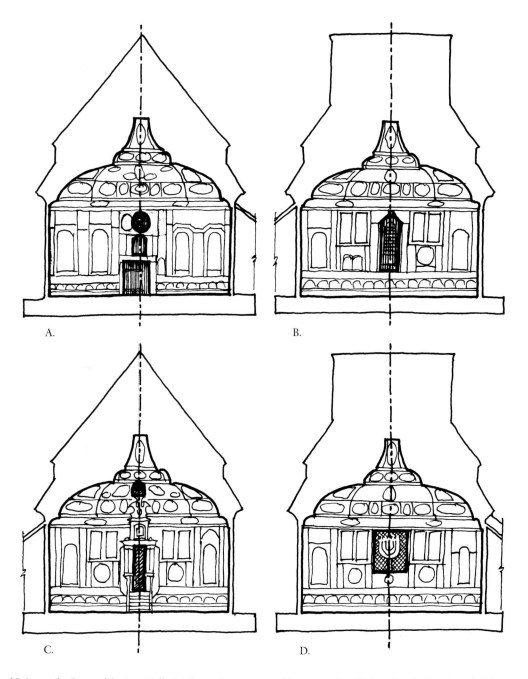

FIG. 99. *Focal Points at the Center of the Four Walls*. A. West wall: entrance and lattice window; B. North wall: shew-bread table; C. East wall: ark with Tablets of Law above; and D. South wall: menorah.

Synagogue were deep red, pastel blue, white, and black.[14] This spectrum of deep colors forcefully juxtaposed was typical of early-eighteenth-century interiors in Eastern-European monumental buildings. Writing in 1899, Karol Maszkowski, an early researcher, described their overall impact: "All the surfaces are covered with drawings and ornaments of various colors; the back-

ground is usually dark but always colored. No detail is glaring except for the white tables with inscriptions. All the paintings are subordinate, one to another; they flow together like areas of various colors and many shapes with the effect of one entity. The entire interior gives the impression of a carpet. There are sometimes very bright colors, even glaring, but they are well composed and they adapt themselves to the general tone, [being] deep and quite dark."[15] Here Maszkowski attempted to describe the unified intensity of these unique painted compositions, which, even by the end of the eighteenth century, were already considered highly unusual. Along with other observers, Maszkowski used the image of a densely colored oriental rug to describe the overall composition of the Gwoździec interior.

The paintings' actual colors may also have had specific or symbolic meaning in the legends and liturgy of the Gwoździec community. Since only a few scattered samples of the synagogue's original interior colors have survived, and the total record of premodern wooden and masonry Polish synagogues is so incomplete, we cannot follow this line of inquiry.[16] This is unfortunate, because the intense colors may have had many meanings for their eighteenth-century viewers. For example, the choice of color may have been related to techniques of ecstatic prayer, as described by Moshe Idel and elaborately detailed in the *Zohar*.[17] In any case, there is much that we do not know about Gwoździec's vibrant colors. They may represent a former mode of artistic expression related to liturgy, a mode of thinking and worship for which there is little contemporary equivalent.[18]

Prayer Panels

The geometric composition of the interior surfaces and the use of vibrant colors are two dynamic aspects of the painters' work, but the most striking feature of the wall-paintings was a series of large framed panels containing Hebrew prayer inscriptions that lined the lower walls (fig. 100). These inscriptions were set against a brilliant white background in vertical panels with arched tops. Bright white contrasting sharply with the generally dark backgrounds of the remaining surfaces, the painted prayer panels ringing the interior became the dominant visual feature of the prayer hall (see fig. 97).

The inscriptions on these panels were portions of weekly and festival prayers written in letters large enough to be read from any location in the room. Some prayers may have been painted on particular walls so that they could be used as aids to daily worship. For example, in the neighboring Chodorów Synagogue, the prayer "Lekhah Dodi" (Come my beloved friend let us welcome the [Sabbath] Bride) was painted near the doorway on the western wall (see fig. 115).[19] For the last stanza of this prayer, the congregation turns toward the doorway on the western wall to symbolically welcome the Shekhinah (Divine presence) into the synagogue.

The prayer panels were framed by architectural surrounds composed of columns and arches. The architectural frame or gate is one of the most common motifs found in Jewish art of all periods, and it was particularly common in art created from the sixteenth to the eighteenth centuries.[20] Similar motifs can be found on most examples of Jewish decorative art such as gravestones, ritual and decorative objects, and textiles made during the early modern period. The place where the architectural gate motif is most often found, however, is in Jewish manuscripts and printed books. In the most typical pattern, the title and colophon were inscribed within an architectural surround featuring an arch or lintel supported by two or four flanking columns (see figs. 124,

FIG. 100. *Painted Prayer Panel.* A typical prayer panel is framed by an architectural surround composed of a rounded arch and flanking columns. At the bottom of the panel, the donor inscription is separated from the prayer text. (Courtesy of the Tel Aviv Museum of Art.)

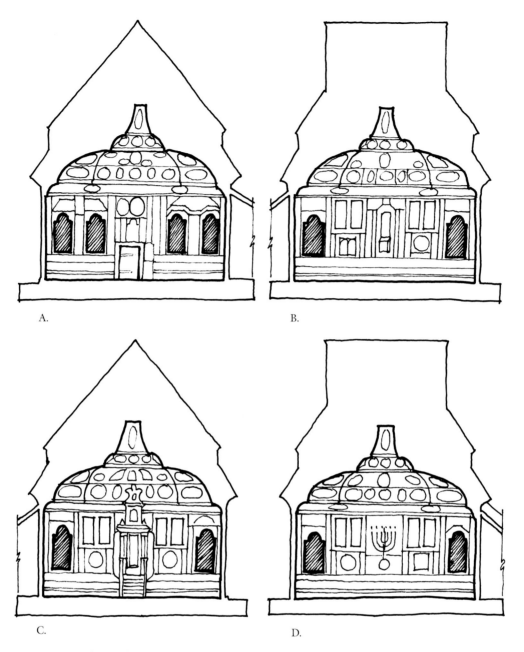

A.   B.

C.   D.

FIG. 101. *Ten Major Prayer Panels, Gwoździec Synagogue.* This diagram shows the locations of the prayer panels on the interior elevations: A. west, B. north, C. east, and D. south.

125). While recognizing the wide use of this motif both inside and outside Jewish art, I believe that the most influential source for it among the painters and commissioners of the Gwoździec wall-paintings was Ashkenazi book art from both Polish and Germanic sources.

At Gwoździec, a total of ten prayer panels were spaced between the windows, the corners, and the door, with four panels on the western wall and two panels on each of the three remaining walls (fig. 101). The fact that other synagogues in the Gwoździec region also had ten large prayer panels arranged in the same locations within their prayer halls further suggests that the selection of ten panels for the synagogue was not arbitrary but deliberate. One explanation for the selection of ten prayer panels is that they were associated with the ten tapestries of the Tabernacle, as described in Exodus 26:1. In

FIG. 102. *Scallop Motif.* A portion of the north ceiling with a scallop motif similar to ornamental tent edging. The drawing shows the scallop motif in the photograph. (Courtesy of the Tel Aviv Museum of Art.)

the *Zohar*, the precedent for ten tapestries of the Tabernacle is cited in an extended passage related to prayer in the synagogue: "Therefore, concerning the Tabernacle, it says: 'and thou shalt make the Tabernacle with ten pieces of tapestry' (Exodus 26:1), ten being the number required for the full perfection of the Tabernacle" (II: 164b).[21] While this specific influence of the Tabernacle cannot be proved, the ten prayer panels reinforce the many other aspects of the Gwoździec Synagogue that specifically evoked the imagery of the Tabernacle.

Tent Symbolism

In chapter 3, we saw how the image of the tent literally shaped the interior cupola of the Gwoździec Synagogue, uniting the biblical ideal of the Tabernacle's tent with regional and national images of the Ottoman tent (see fig. 33). Several painted motifs on the ceiling reinforce the cupola's allusion to tents, and some motifs specifically refer to the Tent of the Tabernacle.

Elaborate decorative borders closely resembling the scalloped edging of Ottoman tents lined the lower edges of two prominent ceiling cornices in the Gwoździec Synagogue (fig. 102). Similar borders are found both in Polish folk architecture and in European textiles, but the elongated, double-curved shapes used in the synagogue's painted borders most closely resemble the highly ornate borders of the Ottoman/Polish tents. As we saw in chapter 3, similar motifs were found in the Ottoman tents captured by King Sobieski, and these tents had a significant impact on Polish decorative art during the era in which the Gwoździec ceiling was painted.[22] For painter and viewer, with or without these historical associations, the scalloped edges reinforced the tent-like appearance of the prayer hall.

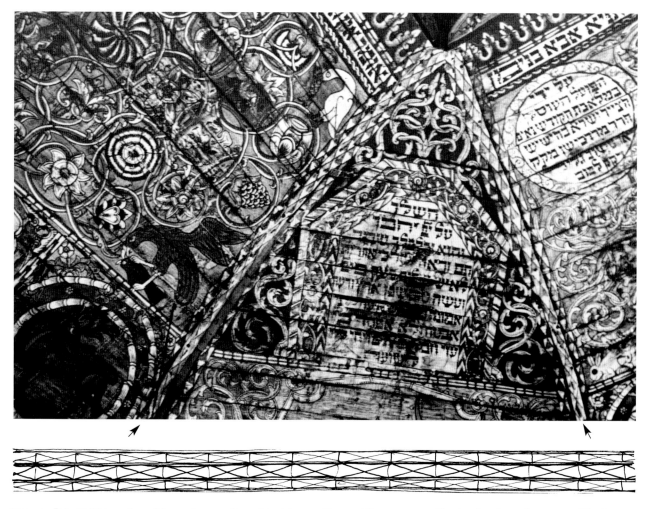

FIG. 103. *Rope Motif.* A portion of the northwest ceiling with edging motifs resembling tent ropes. The drawing shows the rope motif in the photograph. (Courtesy of the Tel Aviv Museum of Art.)

Another painterly device that enhanced the tent-like appearance of the ceiling was the exaggerated depiction of tent cords and ropes commonly used as tent supports. At the eight junctions of the ceiling's pendentive vaults, the artists painted masses of tent cords so that they appeared to hang from the upper levels of the cupola (fig. 103). These rope cords, painted in a simple repeating diamond pattern, were also used as an edging and border device throughout the interior. Although the rope motif appears in decorative arts traditions worldwide, the Gwoździec ceiling paintings emphasize ropes bunched at the upper corners of the cupola in just the way that ropes were actually used in Polish tents of the early modern period.[23] Together the painted symbols of tent ropes and the tent-like shape of the ceiling reinforced the overall idea of the prayer hall as a tent of worship.

Close examination of the geometric borders of the ceiling shows an unusual dot-dash pattern that resembles a stitched fabric. I feel this unusual border pattern is another tent motif, representing fabric seams where tent cloth was sewn together (fig. 104). Since this motif was only used on the ceiling, it may have been selected to reinforce the overall tent imagery of Gwoździec's remodeled ceiling.[24]

A final motif that may have been used to create tent imagery was a horizontal band of interlocking chevrons (V-shaped patterns) painted on a cove that circled the prayer hall where the walls and the cupola met (fig. 105). The interlocking chevron pattern was one commonly found in Polish textiles and carpets manufactured in the Lviv region during the same period (see fig. 129).[25] However, it is my opinion that this band referred to a

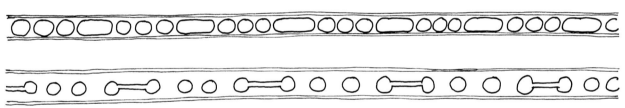

FIG. 104. *Stitching Motif.* A portion of the north ceiling with edging motifs resembling stitching on tent fabric. The drawing shows the stitching motif in the photograph. (Courtesy of the Tel Aviv Museum of Art.)

band of "clasps" that God directed the Israelites to construct for the original Tabernacle. A passage in Exodus reads: "And he made fifty golden clasps, and coupled the curtains one to another with the clasps; so that the Tabernacle was one [bound together]" (Exodus 36:13).

Animal Figures

While the painted prayer panels were the most prominent feature of the walls, what for many observers is most striking about the ceiling is the abundance of animal figures (figs. 106, 107). If these figures were minor

decorative elements, as some researchers suggest, they could be dismissed as insignificant features of the interior. However, the animal figures were not minor decorative elements. Animal scenes account for almost half of the ceiling's surface and are clearly the central vehicle of artistic expression in the overall composition of the ceiling. Even on the walls, where fewer animals are used, animal figures still play an important supportive role, surrounding many of the framed prayer panels. Altogether, the painted interior walls and ceiling of the Gwoździec Synagogue contained over eighty individual animal figures in the major panels. In addition, numerous minor animal figures found their way into decora-

FIG. 105. *Clasp-like Motif.* A portion of the north ceiling with a chevron or V-shaped motif, possibly related to the Tabernacle's fifty clasps. The clasp-like border motif is shown in the drawing. (Courtesy of the Tel Aviv Museum of Art.)

tive borders and floral backgrounds. The major animal figures included lions, bears, storks, camels, eagles, birds, snakes, as well as imaginary animals such as griffins, unicorns, and serpents. Within its late-seventeenth- and early-eighteenth-century Eastern-European context, there was no comparable artistic tradition that actively embraced this kind of dense and sophisticated animal imagery. Previous research has not emphasized the distinctive nature of this animal iconography in relation to the typical art forms, both elite and vernacular, of its time and place.[26] Consequently, neither its artistic isolation from contextual sources nor its independent development within Jewish sources has been sufficiently acknowledged.

Historians have long noted the aesthetic unity in the Jewish animal iconography found in the Polish wooden synagogues. Although several attempts have been made to list and interpret the figures using the commonly accepted canons of Jewish art, these studies have generally lacked sufficient contextual grounding to move interpretation beyond unconvincing generalizations about the meanings of similar animal imagery found in Jewish folklore and literature.[27] Recently, Marc Epstein has advanced the study of animal iconography in Jewish art by insisting that some of these animal figures can best be explained when considered in their regional context of Christian symbolism and culture. Epstein demonstrates the many ways in which minority Jewish communities

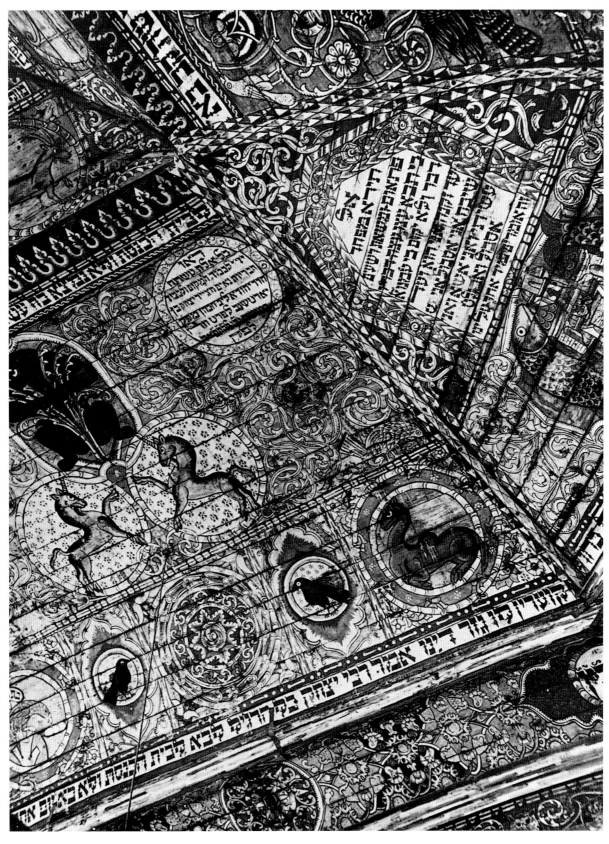

FIG. 106. *Animal Figures, West Ceiling, Gwoździec Synagogue.* Various animals are set within medallions: heraldic unicorns, raven-like birds, and a camel. There are also partial views of a seated bear holding vegetation, far left, and a Leviathan, far right. The signature of the artist, "Isaac, son of Judah Leib ha Cohen," is located in a small circular medallion in the upper center of the photograph. (Courtesy of the Tel Aviv Museum of Art.)

FIG. 107. *Animal Figures, Northeast Ceiling, Gwoździec Synagogue.* Note the various painted animals: in the center, a large elephant; on the left, a composite leopard-like animal sits below an eagle or hawk attacking a rabbit; and on the right, a lion stands below a dark rooster. (Courtesy of the Tel Aviv Museum of Art.)

appropriated such symbols from the dominant Christian culture in order to tell overt and covert Jewish stories.[28] As we shall see, Jewish artists frequently appropriated standard Christian images like the unicorn and the elephant and used them to tell Jewish legends and stories to Jewish audiences.

Although I have emphasized the many ways that the architecture of the Gwoździec Synagogue reflects the complexity of its Eastern-European cultural context, external sources do not appear to have significantly influenced the art of the wall-paintings and particularly the central animal figures. In the following sections, the internal Jewish influences that shaped the animal figures are emphasized, especially their meaning within the context of Jewish legend and liturgy. But the initial question to consider is why these animal images were created, developed, and maintained within Polish Ashkenazi Jewry in the first place.

Several unique factors in the Polish Ashkenazi experience help to explain the presence of the animal figures. Various sources confirm that, even after many centuries of living in Eastern Europe, Polish Jews consistently honored the memory of their medieval Ashkenazi homeland.[29] Maintaining a traditional system of animal symbolism associated with that homeland is one way they might have honored and preserved that past. More important, the maintenance of an archaic symbolic system in the synagogue may have facilitated an internal Jewish dialogue, allowing a symbolic conversation to take place in the public realm beyond the grasp of Christian censors. Perhaps by employing an archaic vocabulary of shared symbols drawn from a revered past, Eastern-European Jews sought to avoid Christian scrutiny and censorship. The animal iconography may, therefore, have served as a symbolic vehicle for covert Jewish communication. This visual strategy would have been especially useful to seventeenth- and eighteenth-century Jewish communities living within a Counter-Reformation environment that was saturated with the Baroque symbolism of the Catholic Church.[30] For the Jews of Gwoździec, powerful Christian symbolism was not a distant theoretical issue, but a constant presence in their daily lives, as they literally lived in the shadow of the Bernardine Monastery Church.

The realization that Polish Jews valued the heritage of their former Germanic homelands, despite the persecutions they suffered there, may also answer questions about the sources for the animal iconography used in their synagogues. Though to most researchers, as we have seen, these animal figures seem strangely isolated from the aesthetic context of Eastern-European art, they can also be seen as the logical continuation of late-medieval Ashkenazi artistic traditions, and especially as a direct extension of a decorative arts tradition of animal figures preserved in medieval illuminated manuscripts of Jewish and Christian cultures.[31] The influence of late-medieval artistic motifs is particularly evident in the use of imaginary creatures like unicorns, serpents, and griffins, as well as Jewish eschatological creatures such as the Leviathan, Behemoth, and Ziz in the artwork of the Gwoździec prayer hall. All these creatures can be traced through a long period of artistic development in both Jewish and Christian medieval and late-medieval manuscripts and decorative art.[32] Unfortunately, because so few Jewish medieval artistic sources have survived, it is difficult to trace an aesthetic continuity between Polish and earlier Ashkenazi sources. Nonetheless, I will attempt to find these artistic motifs and animal imagery in earlier Ashkenazi literary sources.

We find an extensive use of visual imagery in the religious writings of the medieval German Pietists (Hasidei Ashkenaz) and especially in the writings of Eleazar ben Judah of Worms (c. 1165–1230). Eleazar of Worms was one of the leading religious figures in the German Pietism movement. Although most scholars, prominent among them Gershom Scholem, have certainly alluded to his long-term influence on Polish Jewry, Eleazar's writings and the works of his contemporaries have not been analyzed for their practical influence on Ashkenazi culture in Poland, including its artistic culture.[33] In Eleazar of Worms's vast corpus of writings, there is an abundance of vibrant imagery, including animal imagery, which he used as a vehicle for metaphoric expression. Even lacking much physical evidence of medieval Ashkenazi visual culture, we can still see the extraordinary richness of the medieval Ashkenazi visual imagination in Eleazar's literary works.[34]

In Eleazar's writings, we find the interweaving of anthropomorphic and zoomorphic images. For example, the multileveled symbolism of the well-known nut and "nut garden" images weaves in and out of Eleazar's writings in many variations.[35] Alexander Altmann traces the nut image in Eleazar's writings as a central symbol of his mystical vocabulary. In Eleazar's *Hokhmath ha-Nefesh* (Wisdom of the Soul), Altmann quotes a typical example of Eleazar's nut imagery:

> I went down into the nut garden: A nut has four segments and a ridge in its center. Likewise, there are four camps of Israel and one of the mixed multitude. And the entire subject of the Torah is like the nut. . . . Even as the nut has an external bitter shell surrounding it, so were the Scroll of Torah and the sword handed down wrapped together. . . . The kernel is shaped like four double columns corresponding to the four camps; and the four double columns of the kernel are round about its stalk, and the stalk is in the center.[36]

Perhaps only the *Zohar* develops a visual imagery of comparable metaphoric complexity, one that uses plant and animal imagery as a major vehicle for metaphoric expression.

The interior of the Gwoździec Synagogue was painted more than five hundred years after Eleazar's writings, so that specific plant and animal images from Eleazar's writings should not be expected to appear on the synagogue's walls. I have referred to Eleazar's writings, however, to demonstrate the existence of a genre of medieval Jewish writing, rich in naturalistic metaphoric associations, that may have nourished a tradition of Jewish visual imagery. It is the importation of this now vanished tradition that may have influenced the animal iconography in the wall-paintings of the Polish wooden synagogues.

The *Zohar* is another influential literary text that may explain the animal iconography of the wall-paintings. Like the writings of Eleazar of Worms, the *Zohar* probably did not provide specific animal imagery for the artists of Gwoździec Synagogue, but it did help to create a climate in which such visual imagery was seen as appropriate and meaningful for the prayer hall of a synagogue.[37] In the final chapters, we will see how issues of visual imagery and visualization in worship relate to the

Zohar's sanction for visual inquiry. Here, I analyze five animal figures—the deer, the ostrich, the wolf, the goat, and the turkey—animals that figure prominently in the Gwoździec wall-paintings.

Deer

The figures of two identical antlered deer were set in circular medallions on the north and south faces of the cupola (fig. 108, and see fig. 103). Each deer is turning its head to look backward, while it lifts one hind leg. The image of the deer has been used in Jewish art since antiquity,[38] but I believe the deer turning and looking backward is directly related to a group of stories from early-modern Ashkenazi literature, stories that were emphasized in the *Zohar*. In a beautiful passage from the *Zohar*, beginning with a verse from the Song of Songs, the author dwells on the image of a fleeing, turning deer:

> "Flee away, my beloved, like a gazelle, or a young hart on the mountains of spices" (Song of Songs 7:14). This signifies the longing of Israel for the Holy One, blessed be He: she [Israel] implores Him not to depart from her to a distance, but to be even as a gazelle and a young hart. These animals, unlike all the others, do when running go but a little way, and then look back, turning their faces toward the place from which they came, then running on, do again turn round and look back. So the Israelites say to the Holy One, blessed be He: "If our sins have caused Thee to flee from us, may it be Thy pleasure to run like a gazelle or a young hart, and look back on us." (II: 14a).

FIG. 108. *Deer, Gwoździec Synagogue.* Identical deer were painted on the north and south sides of the ceiling.

Here the author of the *Zohar* uses the deer as a metaphor for Divine mercy, comparing the love of God to a turning deer, constantly looking back at the Israelites who, by their sin, drive the deer away.

There are other sources for the image of a backward-turning deer in Jewish literature, although many of these sources were directly influenced by the *Zohar*. The image of the deer is found in a group of similar stories based on the *Zohar* that were widely disseminated in Eastern Europe during the early modern era. These stories mention a returning deer (II: 138b), the hind of the morning (II: 10a), the serpent biting the deer (II: 219b), and the watchful (never-sleeping) deer/gazelle (II: 14a).[39] In most of these stories, the deer represents the Shekhinah (Divine presence), who is also driven away but, like the watchful deer, looks backward.[40] For congregants familiar with these stories from the *Zohar*, the backward-turning deer on Gwoździec's ceiling may have been a familiar, meaningful image.

Ostrich

In another circular medallion on the ceiling above the entrance, an eagle-like bird is shown landing on the top of a tree trunk, looking directly down at three eggs in its nest (fig. 109, and see fig. 94). Although it looks like an eagle, the artist labeled the figure as "ostrich" in Hebrew. This figure is the only animal in the entire synagogue that was given a label. The artist painted other animals very realistically, so the fact that he labeled the painting "ostrich" probably indicates that he did not know what an ostrich looked like, but wanted his viewers to imagine an ostrich looking down at eggs in a nest.[41]

Most Northern-European, Polish Jews would never have seen an ostrich, so it would not be surprising if the painter did not know how to paint this exotic bird. But most congregants would have been familiar with the term "ostrich" because it was used in biblical legends and ethical stories of the early modern period. For example, the story of the ostrich's ability to hatch its own eggs through the power of its vision is told in Zwi Hirsch Kaidanover's popular *Kav ha-Yasher* (The Honest Measure). Kaidanover writes: "Important evidence that the sense of sight can be damaging to oneself and others can be deduced from a bird named the ostrich. While the eggs are laid in front of her, she looks at them, and with her gaze she makes a hole in the egg, and from

FIG. 109. *Ostrich, Gwoździec Synagogue.* A bird, labeled "ostrich" in Hebrew, was painted on the west side of the ceiling.

every egg a chick comes out." Kaidanover uses this story as a moral lesson about the importance of looking at good things and refraining from looking at evil things. The power of vision to accomplish good or evil was a popular theme in the ethical literature of the period, one that already had a long history in Jewish literature.[42] Kaidanover's book, itself deeply influenced by the *Zohar*, was one of the most influential books on conduct and ethics of the early modern era. Although only one of several possible sources for the ostrich story, *Kav ha-Yashar* was in 1731 one of the sources most widely available to the community of Gwoździec.[43]

The ostrich label on the ceiling of the Gwoździec Synagogue is a small but significant indicator of the meaning behind its animal iconography. Although an isolated incident, it provides specific evidence that the animals alluded to Jewish legends and ethical stories. Although conclusive proof about the meaning of most of Gwoździec's many animal figures has yet to be found, I believe that the animal iconography was largely intended to communicate moral and ethical teachings and to reinforce the liturgy used within the prayer hall of the synagogue.

Wolf and Goat

Five scenes on the ceiling and walls show wolves/foxes or eagles attacking small domestic animals like goats, geese, and rabbits (see fig. 104). Similar scenes of predators attacking small prey were standard components of Eastern-European synagogue paintings. Many observers have assumed that these scenes allude to the persecu-

tion of the Jewish people by restrictions, pogroms, and repressive governments.[44] It is certainly possible that these predator paintings came to represent Jewish persecution for nineteenth- and twentieth-century communities, but to the Gwoździec community in 1731, there is reason to believe that they communicated other meanings.

In the *Zohar*, the persecution of Jews by the Gentile nations, particularly by Rome, is frequently described. But these accounts are not typically accompanied by images of animals devouring other animals (II: 8a, 8b). In fact, the *Zohar* reserves its most vivid imagery of animals attacking both animals and humans, not for references to Jewish persecution, but as a warning to the righteous about the dangers that await those who fail to keep God's commandments.

One frequently cited warning reminds the faithful that God placed human beings above the animals, going on to say that, through the effects of sin, humans risk losing their divinely given human qualities. Once these qualities are lost, humans may thus fall victim to animal predators. The author(s) of the *Zohar* warns: "But when men transgress the precepts of the Torah, their visages change, and they fear the other creatures and tremble before them; the beasts of the field obtain dominion over men because they do not see any more in them the true supernal image" (I: 71a, I: 191a). Here the faithful are told that their own "supernal image" is changeable. Those who break God's laws risk losing both their dominion over animals and their Divine image. This "loss of the Divine image" is an ancient theme in Jewish literature, one that is dramatically recast through animal imagery in the *Zohar*.[45]

This basic tenet of the *Zohar*'s ethical teaching is alluded to in many stories and is fully developed in a passage that warns the righteous to keep the dietary laws. The *Zohar* warns: "'Ye shall not make yourselves unclean . . . that ye shall be defiled' (Leviticus 11:43). . . . This [not keeping dietary laws] is an impurity which is exceedingly gross, and which cannot be done away with by means of purification as can other defilement. Besides, such a person [who breaks dietary law], having come to look, even in outer [form] seeming, like a goat —as we have said—goes in constant fear of wild animals, for the human image has disappeared from both his inner and his outer aspects" (II: 125b). On the western wall of the Gwoździec Synagogue, a painting depicts a wolf or fox carrying off a goat in its teeth (fig. 110, and see fig.

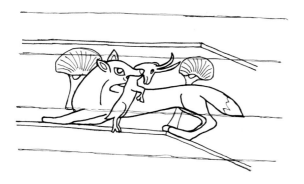

FIG. 110. *Wolf Carrying off Goat, Gwoździec Synagogue.* A wolf or fox-like predator with a goat in its jaws was painted on the west wall.

FIG. 111. *Wolf Carrying off Kid, Chodorów Synagogue.* (Based on a photograph of the Chodorów Synagogue ceiling. Courtesy of the Tel Aviv Museum of Art.)

97). We do not know if this painting was intended to remind the Gwoździec congregation to keep the kosher dietary laws, but it is my hypothesis that similar predator scenes found in the synagogues of the Gwoździec region were intended to communicate ethical teachings to their viewers.[46] For example, a similar predator scene is shown on the ceiling of the Chodorów Synagogue in a finely executed painting of a fox carrying off a goat (fig. 111).[47]

These predator scenes found in the Polish synagogues are not typical of synagogue art from other eras. The symbolic presence of evil or evildoers in the synagogue is completely foreign to the nature of liturgical worship and synagogue art of all periods.[48] Yet the predator scenes found in Polish synagogues are too numerous to be dismissed as minor, accidental, or inconsequential representations.[49] To resolve this dilemma, the predator scenes from the Polish synagogues should not be seen as representations of evil or evil acts. Rather they should be seen as ethical teachings related to an extensive literature of good conduct that circulated within the Jewish communities of Eastern Europe.[50]

Turkey

At least one, and possibly two, turkeys are painted in the prominent lower band of animal figures at the base of the cupola (fig. 112, and see fig. 158). (The second turkey is only partially visible in a blurred photograph of the ceiling's south wall.) The painted turkey we can see shows a zoologically correct North American turkey with particular attention given by the artist to the

PLATE I. *Entrance to the Prayer Hall, West Wall, Gwoździec Synagogue.* A painting by Isidor Kaufmann, *Portal of the Rabbis*, c. 1897–1898, oil on wood, 24 x 34 cm. (Courtesy of the Hungarian National Gallery.)

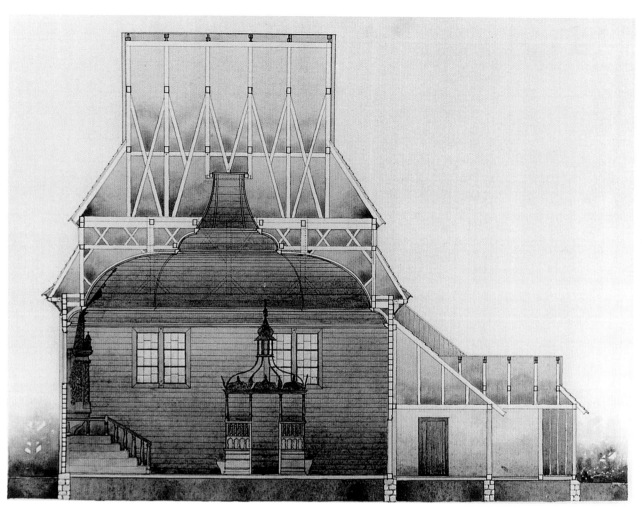

PLATE 2. *Section, Looking South, Gwoździec Synagogue.* (Courtesy of the Tel Aviv Museum of Art.)

PLATE 3. *North Ceiling Study, Gwoździec Synagogue*. A color rendering of the original pre-1914 study by Alois Breier. (Courtesy of the Tel Aviv Museum of Art.)

PLATE 4. *Wall-Painting Study, North Wall, Gwoździec Synagogue.* A copy of a pre-1914 color study of decorative motifs. Location of original source unknown. (Courtesy of the Tel Aviv Museum of Art.)

PLATE 5. *Medieval Hebrew Illuminated Manuscript*, Worms Mahzor, *Worms, Middle Rhine region, Germany, 1272.* JNUL ms. Heb. 4°781/I, fol. 151r. (Courtesy of the Jewish National and University Library in Jerusalem.)

PLATE 6. *Ceiling Paintings, Horb Synagogue, Horb, Germany.* (Currently displayed at the Israel Museum, Jerusalem.) The photograph shows the east portion of the barrel-vaulted ceiling painted by Eleazar Sussman in 1735. (Photo: © The Israel Museum, Jerusalem.)

PLATE 7. *Ashkenazi Book Art,* Sefer Evronot, *1664.* (Courtesy of the Hebrew Union College–Jewish Institute of Religion. Klau Library, Cincinnati. Ms. no. 906.)

PLATE 8. Rabbi at the wooden synagogue of Jablonów, *1897–1898*. A painting by Isidor Kaufmann, oil on wood, 28 x 26 cm. (Courtesy of the Sussi Collection.)

FIG. 112. *American Turkey, Gwoździec Synagogue.* Identical turkeys were painted in the center of the north and south sides of the ceiling.

turkey's distinctive wattle. Such accuracy could not have been the product of the artist's imagination. At first, it is difficult to imagine how the North American turkey could have been painted in an early-eighteenth-century Polish synagogue, but books depicting the exotic flora and fauna from beyond the European world were widely available in eighteenth-century Europe.[51] The illustrated *Perek Shira* (Chapter of Song) was a popular "exotic creature" book specifically written for a Jewish audience. The book was a collection of hymnic sayings in praise of the Creator placed in the mouths of various animals, especially exotic animals. Many animals and their sayings emphasized the wonder and incomprehensibility of God's creations. For example, written next to a drawing of a dragon: "What does the dragon say? Sing unto Him, sing psalms unto Him: talk ye of all His wondrous works" (Psalm 105:2). As a measure of its popularity and ethical function, *Perek Shira* was included in some of the earliest printed prayer books in Eastern Europe.[52]

The "exotic" turkey was, therefore, an appropriate animal for depiction in the synagogue because it represented one of the splendors of God's creation. Thus the unknown turkey was to be contemplated by pious Jews as an example of the unfathomable variety of God's creatures. As they did with the exotic ostrich and unicorn, the artists of the Gwoździec Synagogue may have placed the turkey in a prominent central location so that the congregation would "Lift up [its] eyes . . . to obtain a

knowledge of the works of the Holy One" (II: 231b). By placing exotic animals on the walls of the synagogue, the Gwoździec artists would have been inviting the congregation to contemplate God's majesty through images of His wondrous creations.[53]

The five animals discussed above were selected for interpretation because, for a variety of reasons, more is known about their particular religious and cultural meaning for the Gwoździec congregation. Other animals, like the lion, Leviathan, and eagle, while frequently analyzed in Jewish art and legend, could not be interpreted here because we do not know what they meant to the Gwoździec congregation in 1731. Some animals, like the camel, squirrel, and (sitting) bear have defied analysis. It is my belief, however, that all the animals depicted in the Gwoździec Synagogue, like the ostrich, had specific meaning (or meanings) in Jewish liturgy and legend for the Gwoździec congregation that commissioned them. It is only our ability to recover these meanings, not the meanings themselves, that is in question.

Painted Prayers

This section was written jointly with Arnold S. Rosenberg.

On the ceiling of the Gwoździec Synagogue, animal figures were the central vehicle for artistic and symbolic expression. On the walls, however, Hebrew prayers, written in large black letters set on white panels with elaborate architectural surrounds, were the dominant features. Ten prayer panels ringed the prayer hall, forming an imposing boundary of architectural gates and Hebrew script (see fig. 101). Each panel contained a portion of daily, Sabbath, or festival prayer (fig. 113). For example, one of the panels on the eastern wall contains the "Modim d'Rabbanan" (Thanksgiving prayer of the Rabbis), a prayer that is read silently by the congregation during the repetition of the Amidah (Standing Prayer). (See appendix for translations of the prayers and inscriptions from the Gwoździec Synagogue.)[54]

Hebrew inscriptions have been a component of the synagogue's interior since the earliest period of development. There have been variations in the use of inscriptions, however, among synagogues in different Diaspora regions and eras, probably reflecting local customs. Before the early modern era, historical sources are extremely limited and scattered, so that larger patterns revealing

FIG. 113. *Painted Prayer Panels, Gwoździec Synagogue.* On the west wall, architectural frames surround large Hebrew prayer panels. On the left are the prayers recited by the priests before and after the blessing of the congregation, and on the right is the "Prelude to the Thirteen Attributes." Centered above the prayers is the popular image of bears attempting to climb a tree for a hive full of honey. The bears' quest for honey is usually interpreted as a scholar's quest for knowledge of the Torah. (Courtesy of the Tel Aviv Museum of Art.)

FIG. 114. *Painted Prayer Panel, Gwoździec Synagogue.* On the west wall, the prayer "Sovereign of the universe, I am Yours, and my dreams are Yours" is set within an architectural surround. (Courtesy of the Tel Aviv Museum of Art.)

the frequency and purpose of such inscriptions and prayers in the synagogue are not presently discernible.[55]

At the Gwoździec Synagogue, no single unifying theme or purpose has been identified for the selection of the prayers that cover its walls. Many of the prayers painted in the major panels are common liturgical texts, such as "Modim d'Rabbanan" and prayers associated with the Torah Service, such as "Berirkh Shemei" (Blessed Is His Name). Another prayer "Ribono shel olam, ani shelakh vehalomatai shelakh" (Sovereign of the universe, I am Yours and my dreams are Yours), a Talmudic prayer (B. T. Brachot 55b) painted prominently on the western wall, was recited during the Priestly Blessing to nullify a bad dream (hatavat halom, fig. 114). Other prayers indicate a mystical influence. For example, "Ribono shel olam, malei misheloti" (Master of the world, fulfill my wishes), a prayer that first appeared in the mystical *Sha'arey Zion* (Gates of Zion) prayer book in 1662, is painted on the northern wall at Gwoździec, and the Kabbalistic motif of Psalm 67, painted on the seven branches of a Menorah (candelabrum), is found on the synagogue's southern wall (fig. 117).

In addition to the ten major prayer panels there are numerous nonliturgical inscriptions such as rabbinic verses, proverbs, and ethical writings. For example, the upper ceiling contains Talmudic and midrashic verses about the benefits of coming to synagogue and saying "Amen." Several prayer inscriptions are followed by dedications that include the names of donors. As described earlier in this chapter, two inscriptions on the ceiling were dedicated by the artists themselves, honoring God and acknowledging their own artistic work. Various other inscriptions contain excerpts from the Prophets, astrological sayings, and Kabbalistic references.

It might be assumed that the prayers and inscriptions were independently selected by their congregations or rabbis. Many of the same prayers painted at Gwoździec, however, were also found in synagogues across eastern Poland. This partial consistency in painted prayer selection suggests that some prayers were consciously chosen as part of a common, but not strictly uniform, liturgical repertoire. Such a repertoire may have reflected shared communal and liturgical practices that extended over a wide region of eastern Poland. The possibilty of a shared repertoire of wall-painted prayers is suggested by an account from Deutze, Germany, where a scholar who died in 1728 left money to paint prayers on the walls of his synagogue, including the Modim d'Rabbanan and Berirkh Shemei, both also found at the Gwoździec Synagogue.[56]

Any interpretation of the painted prayers must also consider the introduction of printed prayer books ito the common liturgy. When prayers were painted on the walls of the Gwoździec Synagogue in the early eighteenth century, printed prayer books with standardized liturgies were only beginning to be commonly used in the small towns of eastern Poland.[57] Some tension may thus have existed between the oral liturgical tradition of the small Polish congregations and the new printed prayer books that were more prevalent in the larger towns and cities. Hasidism, which developed in the half-century after the final painting of the Gwoździec ceiling, adopted a liturgy, the Nusah Sfard (Sephardic version), based largely on the Sephardic tradition, that was at odds with many of the printed Polish and Eastern-European liturgical texts.[58] The tension between printed and oral liturgies and the practical changes caused by the introduction of printed prayer books in the small towns of eastern Poland have not been adequately explored.[59] It can be assumed, however, that many or most of the Gwoździec congregation prayed without the aid of a written prayer book. It is within this context of transition from an oral-based to a text-based liturgy that one must consider how and why these prayers were chosen for the walls of the Gwoździec Synagogue.

Listed below are some of the reasons scholars have given to explain the selection and meaning of the painted prayers. Because there are still so many unanswered questions, no single explanation for their selection and overall meaning appears adequate. Rather, several different factors appear to be at work.

Aids to Prayer

The most common explanation offered for the selection of the painted prayers suggests that they were intended to aid members of the congregation who may have needed help in remembering the prayers. Therefore prayers may have been selected for display because they were not widely known, because they were frequently misquoted, or because they reflected adjustments or changes in the liturgy. In each case, the painted prayers would have assisted prayer recitation for worshipers, especially those lacking adequate Hebrew reading skills or those lacking a prayer book.[60]

For example, verses from a prayer such as "Al tira mi 'fahad" (Do not recoil in fear) painted on the northwest ceiling may have been selected to promote better recitation by the congregation or to assist visitors. Thus, the painter followed the "Al tira mi 'fahad" prayer with the painted admonition, "We always say this after Aleinu" (a concluding prayer recited while standing), suggesting either that some congregants were unfamiliar with it or tended to recite it at the wrong point in the service. (It seems unlikely that the painter added this admonition independently or inadvertently, given the importance and visual prominence of the prayers.[61])

Other prayers, such as "U'v'nuho yomar" (When [the ark] was set down [Moses said]) (Num. 10:36), recited when returning the Torah to the ark and painted on the northeast ceiling, may have been displayed on the walls, even though they would have been familiar to the well-schooled and regular worshipers, in order to avoid inadvertent mistakes in recitation. Other painted prayers may have directly aided recitation. For example, the prayers said before and after the recital of Birkat ha-Cohanim (Blessing of the Priests) by the Cohanim (Priests' descendants), appeared on the western wall, which the Cohanim would be facing during their recitation. It is plausible that these prayers were deemed sufficiently important to provide the Cohanim with the prayer texts to read from the wall during their word-by-word recitation. Another prayer, "Va'ani b'rov hasdecha" (And as for me, in the abundance of Your kindness) (Psalms 5:8), a verse of ten words recited upon entering the synagogue and used to count the minyan (quorum of ten men required for public prayer), appeared on the eastern wall, perhaps as a reminder to attend weekly services so that a minyan could be achieved.

While these are reasonable explanations, there are also weaknesses in such "aid-to-worship" explanations. First, there is no historical precedent for remedial instruction or prompting to dominate the prayer hall of a synagogue.[62] Second, the lighting conditions in wooden synagogues were generally uneven or poor, especially during the evening services, so that it would be difficult to read the prayers under many conditions. (Given sufficient lighting, however, the three-inch letters of the prayer panels were large enough to be read from any location in the synagogue.) Third, and most significantly, many of the painted inscriptions were only excerpts of longer prayers, and as a whole, the painted inscriptions encompass only a tiny fraction of the liturgy. Therefore, if aid to common worship was the primary goal for selecting prayers, much more assistance would have been required to significantly influence the performance of the liturgy.

Although some prayers may at first seem to have been

Donor Influences

Donor contributions may have had some influence on prayer selection. The names of donors are inscribed at the bottom of many of the prayer panels. For example, the prayers said before and after the Priestly Blessing are followed by "donation of the Katz brothers."[63] As "Katz" is a common surname for a Cohen, it can be inferred that, while the prayers might have been selected as an aid to their recitation by the *Cohanim*, the donor's wishes may also have played a role in selection. Diminishing the possibility of donor influence, however, are the numerous parallels in the selection of the painted prayers appearing on the walls of wooden synagogues over a wide area of eastern Poland. Extensive donor influence might be expected to create greater diversity of prayer selection. The possibility of donor influence on the selection of the prayers is also lessened if the donors' names were added after the completion of the prayers, as appears to be the case in some inscriptions. But even in these cases, it is possible that the donors' names were matched with a previously selected prayer that was related in some way to the donor, as may have been the case with the Katz brothers' donation.

FIG. 115. *"Lekhah Dodi" Prayer.* On the west wall of the Chodorów Synagogue, the prayer is set in an architectural panel (left center) next to the synagogue entrance (far right, bottom). (Courtesy of the Tel Aviv Museum of Art.)

Liturgical Symbols

Instead of a practical function, the painted prayers may have served a more symbolic function, either as iconic symbols of prayers or as symbols of broader themes associated with particular prayers. A prayer such as "Modim d'Rabbanan" would have been memorized at an early age by most Jewish men. Few worshipers would, therefore, have needed to read the prayer from the wall, so it might have been placed on the wall to emphasize its importance. In these cases, a symbolic rather than a remedial purpose may have been intended.[64] Similarly, prayers such as "U'v'nuho yomar" and "Va'ani b'rov hasdecha" might have been selected, respectively, to underscore the importance of Torah reading and the importance of attending daily synagogue service.

Another possible explanation for the painted prayers is that the written Hebrew script served a primarily iconic rather than a didactic purpose in the synagogue. The letters of the Hebrew prayers have been ascribed symbolic and mystical significance since at least the Hasidei Ashkenazi movement of twelfth-century Germany, and this tendency is known to have flourished in

chosen to aid recitation, they were probably selected for other reasons. The location of the prayer, "Lekhah Dodi" (Come my beloved let us welcome the [Sabbath] Bride) on the western wall of the neighboring Chodorów Synagogue would at first appear to be an example of a prayer's placement to aid recitation (fig. 115). For example, in the Friday evening Kabbalat Shabbat service, it is customary for the congregation to rise, turn, and face the entrance at the back, western wall of the synagogue, before reciting the final stanza of "Lekhah Dodi." However, it does not follow that the prayer was placed on the synagogue's western wall to aid recitation, because the congregation would have been facing the eastern wall until the final stanza. Rather, placement of "Lekhah Dodi" probably reflects the association of the prayer with the symbolic advent of the "Sabbath bride" (the Shekhinah or Divine presence) through the synagogue entrance.

FIG. 116. *Painted Prayer Panels, North Wall, Jablonów Synagogue.* Ludwik Wierzbicki's 1891 drawing shows the composition of Jablonów Synagogue's wall-paintings, which closely resembles the composition of those at Gwoździec Synagogue. (Courtesy of the Polish Academy of Sciences, Warsaw, Poland.)

Poland during the early modern period.[65] There is also precedent for displaying the enlarged Hebrew script, including prayers, on the walls of the synagogue. In Islamic countries, such as pre-Christian Spain, the symbolic and decorative use of Hebrew script was a widespread and commonly accepted tradition of synagogue decoration.[66] It is, therefore, possible that the large size and visual importance awarded these painted prayers at Gwoździec was intended to serve, at least in part, a visual/symbolic purpose. This symbolic interpretation of the painted prayers does not overlook the fact that some members of the congregation may also have read these prayers for a variety of reasons during worship. For most of the congregation, however, especially for the well-educated, these prayers would have been "read" symbolically, as representations of themes related to worship.

Thematic Emphasis

Although no obvious theme unites the prayers in the ten large panels, three of the prayer panels in the Gwoździec

Synagogue are related to the Torah service. These include two prayers, "Berirkh Shemei" and "Ribono shel Olam, malei misheloti" (Master of the Universe, fulfill my wishes), recited by the congregation during the liturgy for removing the Torah on festivals and on the Sabbath, and one prayer, "U'v'nuho yomar" (When [the ark] was set down), recited by the congregation when returning the Torah to the ark. At the neighboring Jablonów Synagogue, six of the ten major prayers painted on the walls were also associated with the Torah service (fig. 116).[67] This is a very high number of prayers related to the Torah service relative to the total number of prayers in the liturgy. This emphasis may be indicative of the paramount importance that the rituals of Torah service had acquired in Ashkenazi communities since the Middle Ages.[68]

Elite and Mystical Refinements to Prayer

The decision to use certain prayers from the common liturgy may also have been influenced, at least in part, by a highly educated segment of Polish Jewry, including Rabbis, scholars, or elite Kabbalists. The ways in which these respected individuals, usually from larger towns and cities, sought to influence liturgical practice are well documented, but the extent to which their efforts may have influenced the liturgy in smaller towns like Gwoździec is unknown.[69] It is possible that the painted prayers provide some insight into the extent of their influence.

Several inscriptions suggest Kabbalistic influences on liturgical practices and on the selection of the painted prayer texts. For example, "Ribono shel olam, malei misheloti," a mystical prayer, appears on the northern wall at Gwoździec and several times on the walls of the Jabłonów Synagogue. The prayer "Berirkh Shemei" was a passage from the mystical *Zohar*. Psalm 67, painted in Kabbalistic fashion within a seven-branched Menorah, appears at Gwoździec and Jabłonów and other wooden synagogues in the Podolian region (fig. 117). A Kabbalistic *kavanah* (a mystical prayer recited to aid intense focus or cleaving to God [*devekut*]) related to the Torah scroll appears inside the bimah. Several Kabbalistic additions, such as a reference to the angel Metatron, were also inserted into the introductory prayer, "Va'ani b'rov hasdecha."[70]

Despite the presence of these Kabbalistic influences in the prayers, it is not clear to what degree communities like Gwoździec actually incorporated them into their liturgy. While the prayers might reflect a popular liturgy heavily influenced by mysticism, they might reflect only the esoteric concerns of a scholarly elite or a small minority of the congregation.[71] In general, however, more Kabbalistic liturgical inscriptions appear at Gwoździec than one would have expected, given what little is known about the popular liturgy of the early eighteenth century.

The painted prayers in wooden synagogues such as Gwoździec may therefore provide a glimpse into the popular liturgy of small-town, pre-Hasidic Polish Jewry, although it must be stressed that much remains to be learned about their interpretation. They do represent, however, a rare form of direct evidence for a liturgy that is not entirely consistent with the early printed prayer books. Whether or to what extent the popular liturgy practiced in eastern Poland's small towns deviated from the urban, elite, and printed liturgies usually recorded has not been thoroughly studied. Such a study may shed light on whether later Hasidic liturgies were innovative or were, instead, further expressions of popular, small-

town liturgical practices that deviated from the traditions of the urban elite.

In the early eighteenth century, following the crises associated with the Sabbatian phenomenon and the advent of the Jewish Enlightenment, one might expect there to have been a weakening of mystical influence on Jewish popular culture and liturgy. Yet the selection and form of the liturgical excerpts found in wooden synagogue inscriptions suggest that mystical influence had a significant impact at the grassroots level in the Podolian region of the Polish Commonwealth. If this is correct, then the later Hasidic development of these mystical and Kabbalistic themes was less revolutionary and more typical of common worship than is now commonly believed.

Ashkenazi Sources

The search for artistic sources of the wall-paintings has frustrated researchers for over one hundred years. Today we are left with little tangible information about how the paintings may have developed. In order to approach the issue, I begin with a hypothesis about the depth of Ashkenazi cultural roots in the Jewish communities of Poland.

For a period of almost three hundred years, beginning around 1350, waves of Germanic Jews immigrated to Poland, creating a critical mass of Ashkenazi Jewry in the lands of the Polish state. Just as their medieval German language was transplanted and then transformed into Yiddish through contact with Eastern-European languages, I believe the art forms of Ashkenazi Jewry were similarly transplanted and transformed. Throughout this book, I have attempted to show the many ways that Polish Ashkenazi communities retained earlier patterns of art and architecture that they later applied to their synagogues. While almost all scholarship on Polish Jewry, including art history texts, acknowledges its broad Ashkenazi origins, the specific effects this Germanic culture had on Polish synagogue art and architecture have not been rigorously explored.[72]

The majority of Jews who immigrated to Poland came either from Franco-Germanic lands or from Ashkenazi settlements in surrounding regions. The Ashkenazi communities were located in a broad arc stretching across Europe from France, through Germany and Austria, and into Hungary and Romania. It is likely that the

FIG. 117. *Painted Menorah.* On the south wall of the Gwoździec Synagogue, the words to the 67th Psalm were inscribed in the branches of a painted menorah. Note the candle shelf below its base. (Courtesy of the Tel Aviv Museum of Art.)

FIG. 118. *Torah Shields.* These eighteenth-century torah shields are from the Galicia region of Poland. (Courtesy of the Museum of Ethnography and Crafts in Lviv, Ukraine.)

post-1300 Ashkenazi settlement of Poland overwhelmed earlier small communities from non-Ashkenazi regions. In any case, later demographic evidence establishes a broad Germanic derivation for the vast majority of Polish Jewry.[73] The strength of Ashkenazi culture for Polish Jewry is evident in the continuity of Ashkenazi language, social structure, education, religion, technology, folklore, and food practices. In fact, it is evident in all the critical components of Polish-Jewish culture.[74] While the exact numbers of immigrants and dates of immigration may be debated, it is clear that the majority of Jewish settlers brought Ashkenazi culture to Poland. Even though little material evidence is available, it is reasonable to assume that these immigrants also brought their artistic and architectural traditions. Such traditions would have had a direct impact on the art in Polish synagogues.

Both the artistic techniques and the symbolic content of the wall-paintings do indeed significantly reflect the influence of late-medieval Ashkenazi traditions maintained for hundreds of years in Poland. But since we know little about these original Ashkenazi sources, they are best approached through the study of their subse-

quent development in Poland. By the early eighteenth century, when the Gwoździec Synagogue was painted, several uniquely Jewish traditions had achieved a high level of artistic and technical sophistication in Poland and Eastern Europe, including metalwork and textiles for ritual and domestic objects, gravestone carving, manuscript and printed book art, and, of course, the synagogue wall-paintings (figs. 118, 119).[75] Although these art forms varied widely, their unity of motif and widespread diffusion throughout Eastern Europe indicate a long period of artistic development, involving generations of artists, craftsmen, and sponsors. Despite the little that we know about this development, it seems unlikely that such a refined, premodern, vernacular tradition could have developed in less than one or two centuries.[76] While there is precedent for rapid change in vernacular art forms—for example, Polish vernacular church paintings of the same era, which adopted Renaissance figural forms—there does not appear to have been a similar movement in Jewish art forms and synagogue paintings. The conservatism of Jewish liturgical art in the early modern period is perhaps explained both by

FIG. 119. *Gravestone Carving and Inscriptions.* Gravestones from the 1750s in Międzybóż, Ukraine, show standard inscriptions and decorative formats. Międzybóż was the home of the founder of Hasidism, the Baal Shem Tov. (Courtesy of Dr. D. Goberman.)

the restricted minority status of the Polish community and the conservative nature of the religious establishment, in which the weight of tradition was omnipresent.[77] All these factors suggest that the splendor and maturity of the early-eighteenth-century Gwoździec paintings necessitated a long period of development stretching back into medieval Ashkenazi culture.

This longevity of artistic tradition can readily be seen in the premodern or late-medieval Ashkenazi vocabulary of wall-painting motifs. It was a vocabulary that had been maintained for hundreds of years by Polish-Jewish artists who generally worked outside the major schools of Polish and Eastern-European art, environments in which Renaissance and Baroque influences and techniques had been selectively and unevenly assimilated. The isolation of Jewish liturgical artistic development

helps to explain many of the archaic features that appear in the seventeenth- and eighteenth-century synagogue paintings. For example, most of the columns and arches forming the decorative borders for the prayer inscriptions at the Gwoździec Synagogue preserve Romanesque/Byzantine architectural details long abandoned in European art and virtually unknown in Polish and Eastern-European vernacular art. On the north wall of the Gwoździec Synagogue, the columns and arches surrounding a painted prayer panel preserve the chevron motif in the arch and a basket-weave motif in the column capitals (fig. 120). Both architectural motifs were commonly employed in Romanesque and Medieval architecture and decorative arts between about 800 and 1500. Similarly, the painted architectural scenes atop the arched openings of several prayer panels were de-

FIG. 120. *Painted Prayer Panel, Detail, Gwoździec Synagogue.* A. This photograph shows the architectural column and capital motifs on the north wall. (Courtesy of the Tel Aviv Museum of Art.) B. A detail drawing highlighting the architectural elements.

picted in an elevation technique with crenellated walls, towers, and turrets (see figs. 89–92). This was a standard compositional technique in illuminated manuscripts throughout the Romanesque and Medieval periods (see figs. 123, 124).[78] While some of these motifs were also maintained through long periods of artistic development across many European cultures, the principal decorative and compositional patterns employed by Isaac and Israel as well as the other Jewish artists of the Gwoździec Synagogue had, by the seventeenth and eighteenth centuries, long been abandoned in most forms of European art.[79]

Gwoździec Synagogue's wall-paintings share many basic components with medieval Ashkenazi and German illuminated manuscript paintings, including similar compositions, colors, background motifs, and stylistic techniques. For example, the architectural arch or gate motif with flanking columns is a central component of the synagogue wall-paintings, and similar architectural arches or gates are one of the most consistent motifs found in German illuminated manuscripts as early as the Carolingian and Ottonian periods of the tenth and eleventh centuries. Two pages from German illuminated manuscripts are shown here to represent thousands of similar examples (figs. 121, 122).[80] In both examples, the arch and column arrangement as well as the details of construction follow conventions closely allied with the painted prayer surrounds of the Gwoździec Synagogue. These early German manuscript illuminations represent widely employed compositional motifs of great longevity, which I believe were gradually absorbed into the artistic milieu of medieval Ashkenazi Jewry.[81] Parallels

FIG. 121. *Carolingian Illuminated Manuscript Art.* St. Mark, *The Lorsch Gospels*, c. 815. (Copyright © George Braziller, Inc.)

FIG. 122. *Carolingian Illuminated Manuscript Art.* St. Matthew, *The Lorsch Gospels*, c. 800–815. (Copyright © George Braziller, Inc.)

may therefore be drawn to the few surviving examples of Jewish medieval illuminated manuscripts. Two pages from the famous *Worms Mahzor* are shown to represent examples of a much larger but now destroyed tradition of Jewish medieval art (figs. 123, 124). In both examples, the motif of the architectural surround and an abundance of animals are fundamental components to the illumination of the Hebrew text.

These examples drawn from medieval Jewish and Christian sources are not meant to imply a direct influence on the decorative surrounds or animal figures from the wall-paintings in the Polish wooden synagogues. In other words, I do not mean to suggest that the artists of the Gwoździec Synagogue actually copied from, or even knew about, the *Worms Mahzor* or any of the surviving Hebrew illuminated manuscripts (and certainly they did not consult Christian illuminated manuscripts). Therefore, one should not expect to find fully preserved examples of medieval Jewish manuscript art painted on the walls of the Gwoździec Synagogue or in any other eighteenth-century Polish synagogue. But the Gwoździec

painters did inherit a sophisticated Ashkenazi artistic tradition, which I believe is best exemplified in the surviving Hebrew illuminated manuscripts.[82] For a period of two hundred to four hundred years, Ashkenazi communities in Poland continued to develop their own traditions of synagogue art and architecture. Beginning in the fourteenth century, following large-scale immigration from German regions, Jewish communities in contact with Eastern-European cultures developed an indigenous Polish Ashkenazi culture. A few surviving fragments of illuminated book art, such as *Sefer Evronot* (fig. 125 and color plate 7), attest to the presence of what was a more widespread, but now largely destroyed, artistic tradition. When visiting the wall-paintings in the wooden synagogue at Mohilev in Belarus, El Lissitzky, a Russian painter, speculated that illustrations from early Hebrew books found in the synagogue might have influenced the wall-paintings. He observed: "Talmudic books and other old printed books with richly decorated title sheets, illustrations and tailpieces are standing on the bookshelves of old synagogues. In the olden days,

FIG. 123. *Medieval Hebrew Illuminated Manuscript Art*, Worms Mahzor, *Middle Rhine region, Germany, 1272*. JNUL ms Heb. 4°781/I, fol. 39v. Note the architectural surround with Romanesque and Medieval details. (Courtesy of the Jewish National and University Library in Jerusalem.)

FIG. 124. *Medieval Hebrew Illuminated Manuscript Art*, Worms Mahzor, *Middle Rhine region, Germany, 1272*. JNUL ms. Heb. 4°781/I, fol. 151r. Note the architectural surround supporting a medieval or celestial city. (Courtesy of the Jewish National and University Library in Jerusalem.)

those few pages played the role of today's illustrated magazines; they showed the recognized forms of art."[83] Like Lissitzky, I believe these sources, largely destroyed in the Holocaust, influenced the wall-paintings of wooden synagogues like Gwoździec.

By the late nineteenth century, Polish architectural historians recognized that the wooden synagogues, and particularly the synagogue wall-paintings, preserved some of the oldest surviving examples of Poland's most ancient art and architecture.[84] Mindful of the sweeping transformations previous traditions of Polish art and architecture brought about during the Baroque period, they struggled, as we still do today, to understand the pre-eighteenth-century sources for the art and architecture of the wooden synagogues. Here I have attempted to show that understanding the medieval Ashkenazi heritage of Polish Jews may illuminate some of these early sources.

FIG. 125. *Ashkenazi Book Art*, Sefer Evronot, *1664*. (Courtesy of the Hebrew Union College–Jewish Institute of Religion. Klau Library, Cincinnati. Ms. no. 906.)

Multicultural Sources

The importance of medieval Ashkenazi influences should not obscure other significant sources that contributed to the total aesthetic ensemble of the paintings, including Sephardic, Islamic, Italian/Baroque, Eastern-European vernacular, and international decorative arts sources. In the following sections, these influences are separated according to their Jewish and Gentile origins, although such a distinction is repeatedly blurred within the multinational milieu of the Jewish Diaspora experience.

Sephardic and Islamic Sources

By the beginning of the eighteenth century, European Jewish communities had been exposed to traditions of Islamic art and architecture through their contacts with Jewish communities from Islamic lands. After more than ten centuries, Jewish communities under Islamic rule had developed fundamental similarities between the form and decoration of synagogue and mosque. For example, in Islamic lands both mosques and synagogues had relatively plain exteriors and highly ornate interiors. The elaborate interior decoration of both kinds of religious buildings included walls that were entirely covered with intricate, geometric patterns and scribal art, for both religions prohibited figural art or scenographic rendering. Significantly, Sephardic Jews in Islamic lands followed such prohibitions much more closely than Ashkenazi communities in Christian lands.[85]

The influences of Islamic artistic traditions on Sephardic communities may account for some of the unique aesthetic qualities of the Gwoździec wall-paintings. For example, early observers consistently associated the wooden synagogue's dense paintings with Oriental textile motifs, especially noting similarities in the synagogue's floral and geometric borders and the ornate backgrounds of Oriental carpets. A specific Islamic motif in the wall-paintings is the arabesque, and four dominant arabesques are found in the upper peak of the cupola. Through continuous use in art forms of the synagogue, arabesque motifs integrated Sephardic and Islamic decorative sources (fig. 126, and see fig. 87). The absence of human figures and, for the most part, scenographic imagery is also an essential characteristic of both Jewish and Islamic religious art, one that distinctly separates these artistic traditions from equivalent

FIG. 126. *Arabesque Motif, Cupola, Gwoździec Synagogue.* This diagram shows one of the four large arabesques that flank the steeply sloping peak of the cupola.

FIG. 127. *Islamic/Ottoman Art in Poland.* This textile is part of an eighteenth-century tent from Brody, a large town north of Gwoździec. The repeating pendent/scallop motif at the bottom closely resembles the border motifs that circled the cupola of the Gwoździec Synagogue. (Courtesy of the Regional Museum of Tarnow, Poland.)

Christian and vernacular art forms of Eastern Europe.[86] Finally, as emphasized earlier, the shape of the entire interior cupola alludes to the Ottoman (Islamic) tent imported to Poland. Based on these many "oriental" parallels, one might even describe the overall quality of the Gwoździec Synagogue, and especially its wall-paintings, as significantly influenced by the art forms of Islamic and Sephardic cultures.

The influence of Islamic motifs was also reinforced by Polish contacts with Islamic lands. The Polish nobility had long cultivated an appreciation for oriental and Cossack themes as demonstrated by their appropriation of Ottoman tents into the Polish cultural heritage (fig. 127).[87] Seen as an overall pattern, Islamic and Sephardic sources appear to have been major factors in the development of the wall-paintings of the Gwoździec Synagogue.

European Decorative Arts and Vernacular Sources

Many types of European artistic influence are also evident in the wall-paintings of the Gwoździec Synagogue. They may be divided into Eastern-European vernacular sources and European elite sources and are most apparent in the decorative border and background motifs. While these motifs, in repetitive floral and geometric patterns, are not liturgically or symbolically significant, they are powerful aesthetic components of the wall-paintings, covering approximately 60 percent of the interior surface of the prayer hall, and helping to create the distinctive carpet-like density and "oriental" character of the space (fig. 128).[88] The decorative patterns reveal the influence of two contrasting sources: European commerce in decorative merchandise on the one hand, and a combination of older regional patterns of vernacular composition and decoration on the other.

In the seventeenth and eighteen centuries, an international commerce supplied European nobility with a wide range of decorative merchandise, including oriental textiles and carpets. These expensive goods came to Poland through extensive networks of trade between Europe and Asia, including exchange with Ottoman, Persian, and Indian centers of commerce. Through this trade, Polish magnates were able to import sophisticated forms of Asian and European decorative merchandise, which subsequently influenced Polish art and decorative works in all periods (fig. 129).[89]

From the fifteenth to the eighteenth century, a grow-

FIG. 128. *Floral Decorative Motifs, Wall-Paintings, Gwoździec Synagogue. (Top)* Floral motifs bordering prayer panels on the west wall. *(Bottom)* Three of the most commonly used floral motifs. (Courtesy of the Tel Aviv Museum of Art.)

FIG. 129. *Chevron Motifs, Polish Carpet.* This carpet was manufactured during the nineteenth century in the Tarnopol region north of Gwoździec. The drawing shows the stepped chevron motif in the photograph. (Courtesy of the National Museum in Cracow.)

ing commerce in European manufactured textiles, many inspired by imported oriental textiles, made a large volume of sophisticated fabrics available to the Polish upper classes.[90] Subsequently, the floral decorative patterns found in these contemporary fabrics may have supplied the Gwoździec painters with floral motifs used in the backgrounds of the wall-paintings (see fig. 128). Such transfer of decorative patterns from elite to folk interpretation may also have occurred simultaneously in Polish and Ukrainian vernacular culture, as for example, in some of the decorative floral patterns from the Church of St. George (1661), Drohobycz, Ukraine (fig. 130).[91] (Compare these patterns to traditional folk motifs as found, for example, at the Polish church of Debno [Fig. 131].)(Lacking documentation, these examples of elite to folk transfer can be no more than hypotheses.)

The probable application of contemporary patterns from European decorative art, however, did not transform the Gwoździec Synagogue's interior into a fash-

ionable Baroque palace. These newer motifs were integrated into an older compositional framework that dominated the overall aesthetic quality of the prayer hall.

Cosmopolitan Sources

Summarizing the varied influences that shaped the wall-paintings is a difficult task, for the paintings combine medieval-Germanic and early-modern Polish decorative motifs in a rich, variegated mixture that can rarely be attributed to a single artistic influence. Yet this hybrid mixture is what is most significant and uniquely Jewish about them.[92]

The artistic influences evident in the Gwoździec wall-paintings are probably best described not as stylistic trends or artistic sources in the traditional sense, but as the result of an artistic attitude formed within a cosmopolitan Jewish culture whose experience was multicultural. This artistic culture developed over many

FIG. 130. *Ukrainian Floral Motifs.* Seventeenth-century wall-paintings from the Church of Saint George in Drohobyc, Ukraine, combine folk and elite motifs. (From H. M. Zoltowskij, *Monumental Paintings in Ukraine, 17th–18th Century.* Reprinted courtesy of Naukova Dumka Publishers, Ukraine.)

FIG. 131. *Polish Folk Motifs, Wall-Paintings.* Seventeenth-century wall-paintings from a wooden church in Debno, Poland. (Photo: T. Chrzanowski, from *Gotyckie Kościoły Drewniane na Podhalu*, by Marin Kornecki.)

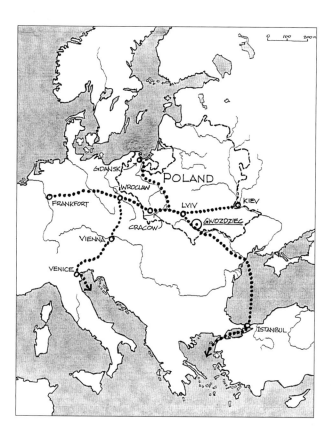

FIG. 132. *European Trade Routes, Sixteenth to Eighteenth Centuries.* The dotted lines show the major trade routes that facilitated the commercial development of Gwoździec and the small trading towns of southeastern Poland. (Based on P. R. Magocsi, *Historical Atlas of East Central Europe.*)

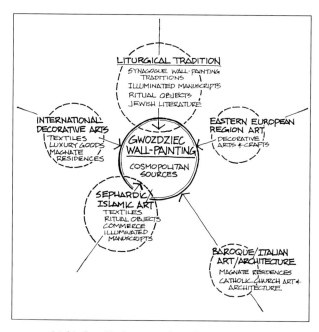

FIG. 133. *Multicultural Influences on the Wall-Paintings of Polish Wooden Synagogues.* Note the range and diversity of sources that influenced seventeenth- and eighteenth-century wall-paintings.

centuries as an extension of communications and travel among Jewish Diaspora communities throughout Europe, the Middle East, and North Africa. Widely dispersed Jewish communities maintained contact with one another through commercial and family networks, rabbinical communication, secular and religious educational exchanges, and scientific and medical discourse. These forms of communication were also facilitated by extensive traditions of written communication that included the circulation of manuscripts and published books.[93]

Extensive travel by Jews among the towns and cities of Eastern Europe has been noted by observers in all periods and was particularly evident in eastern Poland during the seventeenth and eighteenth centuries. Although probably only 5 to 20 percent of the adult male population of any small town traveled widely, this amounted to an unprecedented mobility when compared to the surrounding Eastern-European cultures, even within the region's upper classes (fig. 132).[94] These traditions of communication and travel contributed substantively to the creation of a worldly, educated, multilingual community with few equals in premodern Eastern Europe. The modern image of shtetl backwardness must give way to one of a Jewish popular culture penetrated deeply, at least at its upper levels, by cosmopolitan traditions.[95]

Here we find the necessary preconditions for the wide-ranging, multicultural art and architecture of the wooden synagogues (fig. 133). The small Jewish communities of eighteenth-century Poland cultivated an internal multiculturalism that is revealed in the variety of stylistic influences present in the interiors of the wooden synagogues.[96] As we have seen, in the particular case of the wall-paintings, these sources included Ashkenazi artistic traditions that had evolved in contact with Germanic and then with Eastern-European folk and elite cultures. Though we must still conclude that Jewish artistic development before 1800 remained largely isolated from the centers of Gentile artistic development, especially with regard to the liturgical aspects of the wall-paintings, the artistic totality of the wooden synagogues' paintings nevertheless represented a quiet distillation of many local and international Jewish and Gentile sources reflective of a unique, multicultural, Jewish cosmopolitanism.

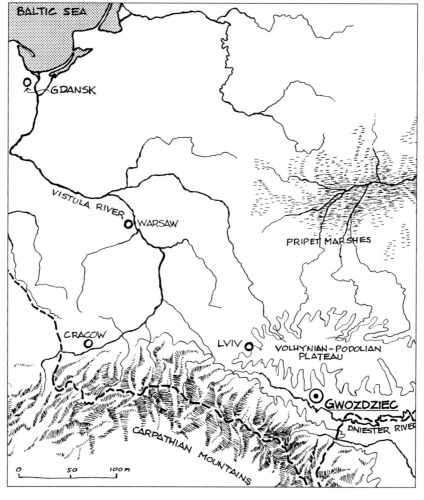

FIG. 134. *Geographic Regions of Central Eastern Europe near Gwoździec.* (Based on P. R. Magocsi, *Historical Atlas of East Central Europe.*)

HISTORICAL CONTEXT

This chapter examines the history of the Gwoź-dziec community with special regard for those ideas and events that influenced the building of the Gwoździec Synagogue. It is not a comprehensive history, but a selective search for those aspects of the past that contributed to the design and construction of the synagogue. Exploring the history of an eighteenth-century small town on the frontier of the Polish state is a challenging task, one made difficult by the scarcity of historical records. The documentation that does exist most often records the "great events" of history, but quite often these events had an uneven impact on tiny Gwoździec. For example, the Chmielnicki insurrection, so pivotal in Jewish and Polish histories of the region, seems to have had little effect on this Jewish community. Other events, such as the founding of the Bernardine Monastery and Church on land adjacent to the Gwoź-dziec Synagogue, did affect the Jewish community, but in ways slightly different from what we might expect given the history of the region. When national and local histories are seen together, the "little history" of the towns and rural regions is often assumed to reflect the "larger" history of the cities and the nation. But such is not always the case. Here we consider Gwoździec's "little history" and ask whether it was more or less successfully rendered by the "larger" historical record.[1]

There is much about Gwoździec and its Jewish community that may never be known, but more is known about other small towns and about the general history of the Podolian region. We shall, therefore, carefully apply what we know about these towns and their region to the particular case of Gwoździec.

History of Gwoździec

The region in which the Jews of Gwoździec settled was a vast upland plateau in what is now western Ukraine (fig. 134). The lands surrounding Gwoździec were a mixture of woodland and meadow with low hills laced by gentle ravines—a landscape more varied than Ukraine's great eastern steppes. Americans might imagine a rural region similar to eastern Iowa or southwest Wisconsin with more woodlands and far less agricultural and human presence. Conifer forests of pine, fir, and larch provided logs and shingles for the local buildings. Ukraine's fertile black soils have supported agrarian populations from ancient times, and it was Ukrainian peasant farmers working these lands who provided the Jewish traders and craftsmen of Gwoździec with their primary clientele.[2] Ancient trade routes crossed the region near Gwoździec, bypassing the Carpathian mountains to the southwest and connecting Western Europe with the Black Sea, the Ottoman Empire, and the "Orient" beyond.[3] It was the presence of trade along these routes that probably initiated Gwoździec's founding.

Gwoździec was situated in a region of prehistoric settlement, near the town of Halych, regional capital of the Kievian Rus during the twelfth and thirteen centuries. The history of Gwoździec begins, however, under Polish administration in the fourteenth century. Details of the early settlement of Polish towns such as Gwoździec are known to us through the records of their magnate owners and of the Catholic Church. The earliest historical documents record the awarding of the lands of Gwoździec to Chodko Łojowież in 1373 and Wasko Teptkowicz in 1375. In the sixteenth century, the town was owned by the Buczacki family and then the Potocki family, before being acquired by the Puzyna family, owners of the town during the building and remodeling of the Gwoździec Synagogue during the first quarter of the eighteenth century. In 1475, a Catholic church was first founded but was destroyed by the "Tartars" (Ottomans) in 1615 and 1623. By 1710, the destroyed church had been replaced with a new building. In 1715, the Puzyna family founded the Bernardine Monastery in Gwoździec and built a wooden church for the Bernardine Order. This wooden church was destroyed by fire in 1728. Immediately after the fire, the masonry church of the Bernardine Monastery was begun, again with support from the Puzyna family. It was this Bernardine Monastery church, under construction in 1731, that Gwoździec Synagogue worshipers saw from their synagogue courtyard.[4]

Jews are first mentioned in historical documents of Gwoździec in 1635, although small numbers may have arrived earlier. As outlined in chapter 3, there is conflicting information about when the wooden synagogue was built. Most researchers, interpreting obscure dates on the wall-paintings, have assumed that the synagogue was built between 1635 and 1650. By the beginning of the 1700s, the wooden synagogue certainly existed, and in 1712 there were at least 40 tax-paying Jewish families in Gwoździec. When the Gwoździec Synagogue ceiling remodeling was completed in 1731, I estimate there were approximately 30 to 50 Jewish households representing about 150 to 250 people. By 1765, Gwoździec had become a predominantly Jewish town with a Jewish population of 541, comprising 60 percent of Gwoździec's total population.[5]

Gwoździec was founded and developed under the sponsorship of a succession of Polish noble families. In the eastern Ukrainian provinces of Poland, Polish lords vied to control and enserf local Ukrainian farming populations, thereby establishing their own private trading towns and their private estates. Small-town development was initiated through the importation of a class of urban foreigners, typically Western-European artisans and merchants.[6] These urban settlers provided the critical commercial, craft, and entrepreneurial skills necessary to sustain a regional economy. It was to live in such a frontier environment that various ethnic and religious groups, including the Jews of Gwoździec, migrated to eastern Poland.

Jewish Settlement in Gwoździec, 1350–1650

The Jewish settlement in Gwoździec followed a pattern typical of European Jewish immigration to Polish lands. The major period of Jewish immigration to Poland, 1350 to 1650, was initiated by persecutions and expulsions throughout Europe and the subsequent opening of Polish lands to Jewish settlement. By 1731, when the Gwoździec Synagogue was remodeled, Poland's Jewish population is estimated to have been 500,000, constituting about 40 percent of the world's Jewish population. During the second half of the eighteenth century, Gwoździec's Podolian region (later called Galicia under Austro-Hungarian rule) was rapidly becoming one of the most densely populated Jewish regions in world.[7]

Ashkenazi Settlement

Although much about the premodern immigration of Jews to Poland is unknown, certain events have been extensively documented by Polish and Jewish historians. Significant high points such as royal invitations and privileges granted to Jewish immigrant groups are usually emphasized. For example, the first written grant of Jewish rights to be issued in Poland was given by Bolesław the Pious, duke of Kalisz, in 1264 and confirmed by King Kazimierz the Great in 1334, 1336, and 1367.[8] Such events were exceptional in Jewish history, standing out sharply against a background of intense Jewish persecution throughout Western and Central Europe during the late medieval period, including large-scale massacres and expulsions from most of the countries of Europe (fig. 135). Although the granting of privileges has correctly been interpreted as a landmark in the recognition of Jewish minority rights, historians also emphasize that such privileges were motivated by the economic and nationalistic objectives of the developing Polish monarchy. One of their key objectives was the settlement and administration of their expanding eastern territories, and the skills of the Jewish community in commerce and craft were highly valued components in

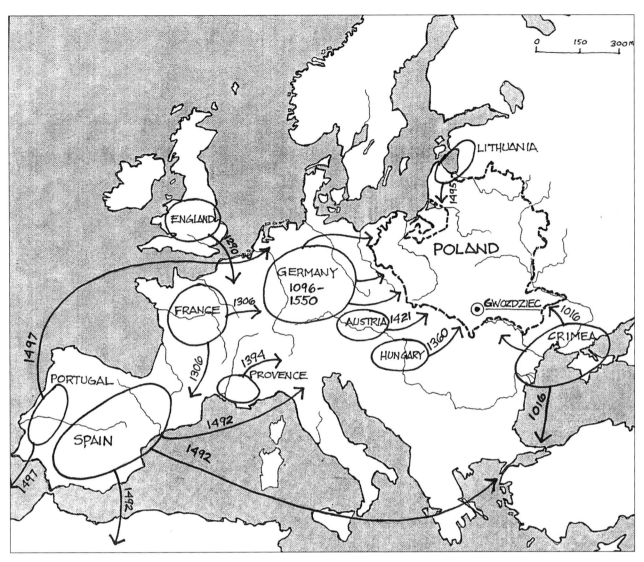

FIG. 135. *Patterns of Persecution of European Jews and Immigration to Poland, 1100–1497.* The dates show years of major persecutions or expulsions. (Based on E. Friesel, *Atlas of Modern Jewish History.*)

the establishment of these new towns (fig. 136). In order to attract such a skilled population, the Polish monarchy and later the independent Polish nobles granted Jewish communities privileges and, in many cases, directly supported local synagogue construction. In the town of Dobromił, one hundred miles northwest of Gwoździec, the town owner granted a typical charter of privileges to the Jewish community in 1612. Jacob Goldberg summarizes some of these privileges: "The Jews are permitted to pursue trade without restrictions, to produce and sell alcoholic beverages, to practice crafts without having to pay special dues to Christian guilds, to purchase property and build houses in all parts of the town without

restriction, to erect a synagogue without limits to size, and to lay out a cemetery." Goldberg also points out that the local nobility took pains to protect the local Jewish population, including "finding out and punishing persons guilty of damaging a synagogue or harming the Jews."[9] Such privileges and protections were not unique but typical of those granted to many Jewish communities within the eastern provinces of Polish settlement. Although there is no confirming documentation, it is not unreasonable to assume that such privileges and protections were granted to the Jews of Gwoździec as well. Jews entered Poland from many lands, but it was the expulsions of Ashkenazi communities from German lands

FIG. 136. *Eastern Expansion of the Polish State, 1250–1400.* The dates indicate territorial acquisition. (Based on W. Czaplinski, ed. *The Historical Atlas of Poland.*)

FIG. 137. *Persecution of Jewish Communities in German Regions and Immigration to Poland, 1350–1650.* The dashed lines show the regions and dates of the greatest persecutions. (Based on E. Friesel, *Atlas of Modern Jewish History.*)

that led to the largest waves of immigration to Poland. The earliest dates of the Polish charters granting rights to Jews roughly coincide with the first periods of German persecution. Although detailed demographic studies are not available, the major period of Ashkenazi immigration to Poland was precipitated by persecutions begun during the period of the Black Death (1348–49) and escalating throughout Europe between 1470 and 1570 (fig. 137).[10] These persecutions set the stage for the arrival of Jews in Poland.

The Small Trading Town

From about 1200 to about 1500, Jewish settlement was confined to the major towns in Poland's western regions nearest Germanic lands. After about 1500, following the path of Polish territorial expansion southward and eastward, Jews began settling in small trading towns and newly established regional centers such as Lviv and Kamieniec Podolski. After Poland's union with Lithuania in 1569, Jewish settlers, encouraged by the invitation of Polish kings and nobility, entered the newly acquired lands of Podolia and Volhynia (see fig. 136). Between about 1500 and 1600, the Jewish settlers began entering southern Podolia in the region of Gwoździec.

The eastward expansion of the Polish state into the frontier regions of what is now Ukraine and Belarus was a slow process, but it was not haphazard or disorganized. The growth of magnate-owned, private towns like Gwoździec frequently followed several standardized patterns of settlement shaped by a corpus of legal, spatial, and administrative traditions, the most influential of which was called Magdeburg law after the German town of the same name. These traditions of Germanic town settlement extended "westernization" (or "Germanization") into Eastern-European lands and provided a broad economic and social framework for the development of the small, private trading towns such as Gwoździec. To a significant degree, these westernized traditions sustained the long-term growth and prosperity of Poland's eastern provinces well into the eighteenth century. Although traditions such as Magdeburg law did not provide full liberties and citizenship to Jewish residents of small towns, it did help structure an open economic and social system in which Jews gained a considerable degree of independence to maximize both their traditions of autonomous self-government and their opportunities for craft and commerce.[11] Ashkenazi

Jewish settlers typically found the Germanic legal and cultural practices that guided Polish settlement compatible with their own cultural practices—a fact that has not been sufficiently emphasized. Such compatibility was probably a significant factor contributing to the long-term success of Jewish communities in the many Polish towns that were guided by the principles of Magdeberg law.[12]

Although we know very little about its history before the eighteenth century, in 1731, Gwoździec probably fit the typical profile of a small, economically expanding, multicultural trading town in eastern Poland. This type of settlement developed in Western Europe during the medieval period, and it continued to thrive in Eastern Europe well into the eighteenth century. One of the keys to the success of these towns was the settlement of westernized traders and artisans who organized themselves into separate community enclaves. During the years when the synagogue was being remodeled, Gwoździec was home to several distinct ethnic groups: Poles, native Ukrainians, Germans, and Jews (fig. 138). Typically these groups coexisted in a state of civic cooperation, economic competition, and social separation.[13]

Although archaic by eighteenth-century, Western-European standards, the economy of these small, multi-ethnic trading towns sustained an ancien-régime culture of manorial estates and enserfed agricultural peasantry into the late eighteenth century (fig. 139).[14] While the medieval precedents for these towns featured dense urban streets behind fortified walls, the Eastern-European versions were more spread out, less fortified, and more socially integrated. Although separate cultural enclaves were still maintained in the seventeenth and eighteenth centuries, it was not uncommon for groups to overlap spatially, as they did in Gwoździec and in most small towns of the eastern provinces. Such overlapping of boundaries is perhaps surprising to those familiar with the strict segregation of Jewish communities in the walled ghettos of medieval Europe, but there were no walled ghettos in Gwoździec. Only a few such ghettos were documented in Eastern Europe, most inhabited before 1500.[15]

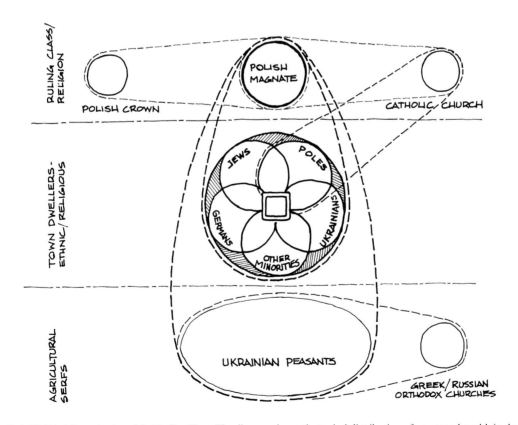

FIG. 138. *Social/Political Organization of the Trading Town.* The diagram shows the typical distribution of power and wealth in the small towns of eastern Poland during the early modern period.

FIG. 139. *Small Town Market, Hrubieszow, Lublin Province, Poland.* (Courtesy of YIVO Institute for Jewish Research.)

The Golden Age

Historians have cautiously characterized the late-medieval period of Jewish settlement in Poland (c. 1500–1650) as a "golden age" of Jewish culture. This characterization reflects the relative peace of this period between the previous persecutions in Germanic lands and the turmoil of later years. The accomplishments of Poland's Jewish community during this period include the expansion of economic and social privileges to many of Poland's Jewish communities, the establishment of centers for Jewish printing and book publication, the ascendancy of Polish Talmudic academies spurring a high level of popular education, and the general expansion of economic and artistic opportunities for a broad segment of

the Jewish population.[16] Perhaps their finest and most significant accomplishment of the period was the establishment and broadening of an elaborate network of local and regional Jewish self-government, the Kahal, including Jewish judicial systems under the overall direction of a national governing body called The Council of the Four Lands. Although subject to royal and local magnate control, the Kahal system had an unusual degree of autonomy at all levels of government within the Polish state. Overall, it served as a bulwark for protecting the welfare of Poland's expanding Jewish communities. In many respects, it was one of the most sophisticated systems of minority self-government existing in Europe before the modern period (fig. 140).[17]

Such a glowing appraisal of the Kahal structure is not

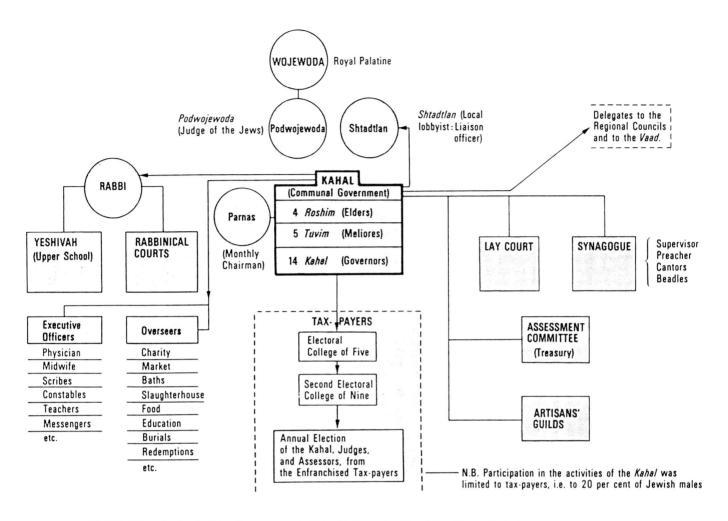

FIG. 140. *The Kahal Organization.* Jewish self-government in Poland before 1764. (Copyright © Norman Davies.)

often found in recent scholarship on Polish Jewry. It must be emphasized that the standard criticisms of the Kahal organization are most often directed toward its final period, when, after 1750, it had difficulty adjusting to the demands of the Jewish Enlightenment and the beginning of the modern era.[18] These well-chronicled failures should not, however, detract from its extraordinary success in nurturing and protecting the Jewish communities of Poland for hundreds of years prior to the modern era. When the Gwoździec Synagogue was built, the long-term stability of the Kahal system of local and regional self-government was at least partially responsible for securing the positive economic and social environment necessary to initiate such a synagogue construction project.

Jewish Development in Gwoździec, 1650–1750

In 1648, a disillusioned Ukrainian nobleman, Bogdan Chmielnicki, led a Cossack and Ukrainian peasant army against the Polish state. His forces nearly conquered the entire eastern half of Poland, including most of the Podolian region where Gwoździec was located (fig. 141). During five years of ensuing warfare with the Polish state, Chmielnicki's armies cut paths of destruction across the eastern provinces. Jewish chronicles recount the decimation of Jewish populations caught along this path, including instances where Polish authorities turned Jewish populations over to the rebels for slaughter.[19] The bloodshed and duplicity of local rulers irrevocably etched the Chmielnicki massacres in Jewish memory. They were the

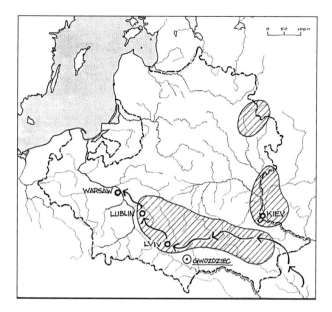

FIG. 141. *Chmielnicki Revolt and Jewish Massacres, 1648–1656.* The arrows follow the main path of Chmielnicki's armies. The shaded areas indicate the major regions of Jewish persecutions. (Based on D. Cohn-Sherbok, *Atlas of Jewish History*.)

worst persecutions to follow the Spanish expulsions, shattering an extended period of Jewish autonomy and community prosperity during the Golden Age of Polish Jewry.

From Polish historical perspective, the Chmielnicki insurrections marked the beginning of a series of foreign invasions called "The Deluge." The Deluge engulfed Poland between 1648 and 1673 and continued in another series of invasions between 1700 and 1721. Most historians agree that these invasions hastened the division of the Polish state at the end of the eighteenth century (fig. 142).[20] Consequently, it is not difficult to see why historians of Poland and Judaism have almost unanimously portrayed the post-Chmielnicki period as one of steady decline for Poland and its Jewish communities. Yet, this general decline did not occur uniformly in all areas of Poland, and it did not affect many of the small towns like Gwoździec in Poland's eastern provinces.

Disaster and Resurgence

Considering the destruction and displacement of Jewish communities in the eastern provinces during the Chmielnicki insurrections, it is surprising to learn that, in these same regions, an era of wooden synagogue construction began in the late seventeenth and early eighteenth centuries. Such seemingly irreconcilable historical developments, the destruction of Jewish populations during the Chmielnicki massacres and the resurgence of Jewish populations immediately after these terrors,

must be reconciled. While the extent of destruction suffered by Polish and Jewish communities continues to be debated, the subsequent reestablishment and expansion of Jewish communities in these same regions is not contested. Substantial evidence shows that Jewish communities stabilized, and their populations dramatically increased, under renewed Polish magnate sponsorship during the last quarter of the seventeenth century and the beginning of the eighteenth century.[21] In small towns like Gwoździec, Jewish community resurgence was accentuated by the construction and expansion of synagogues that began in the late seventeenth century.

Recent contextual studies of eighteenth-century Jewish communities in eastern Poland have amended the idea of a uniform post-Chmielnicki economic and social decline. Moshe Rosman and Gershon Hundert are in the forefront of scholars who have documented the presence of vigorous, expanding towns in the eighteenth-century Polish Commonwealth.[22] Their research confirms that Jewish communities flourished in the small private towns of the eastern provinces. While previous histories have focused on the older, larger cities of western Poland, which generally experienced stagnation or decline during the eighteenth century, the one hundred years following the Chmielnicki massacres might also be described as an era of small-town Jewish renaissance.[23] It was a renaissance, assisted by Polish magnates, that gained momentum in the early 1700s but had completely ended by 1800. In a detailed study of the town of Międzybóż in the Podolian region, 150 miles northeast

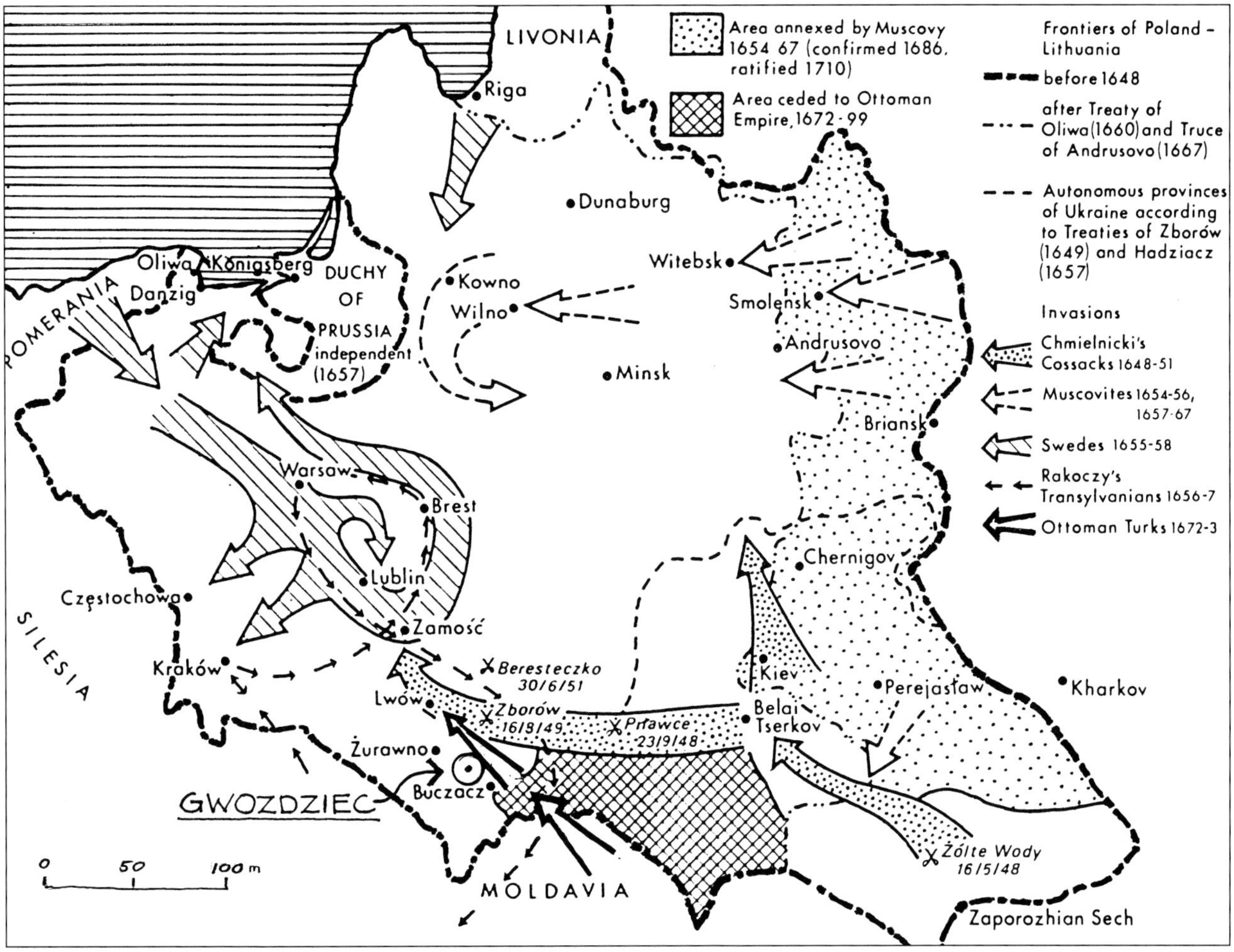

LIVONIA
Riga
Dunaburg
Area annexed by Muscovy 1654 67 (confirmed 1686, ratified 1710)
Area ceded to Ottoman Empire, 1672-99
Frontiers of Poland - Lithuania
before 1648
after Treaty of Oliwa (1660) and Truce of Andrusovo (1667)
Autonomous provinces of Ukraine according to Treaties of Zborów (1649) and Hadziacz (1657)
Invasions
Chmielnicki's Cossacks 1648-51
Muscovites 1654-56, 1657-67
Swedes 1655-58
Rakoczy's Transylvanians 1656-7
Ottoman Turks 1672-3
Oliwa
Königsberg
Danzig
POMERANIA
DUCHY OF PRUSSIA independent (1657)
Kowno
Wilno
Minsk
Witebsk
Smolensk
Andrusovo
Briansk
Warsaw
Brest
Lublin
Częstochowa
SILESIA
Zamość
Kraków
Beresteczko 30/6/51
Lwów
Zborów 16/8/49
Piławce 23/9/48
Żurawno
Buczacz
GWOZDZIEC
MOLDAVIA
Chernigov
Kiev
Belai Tserkov
Perejasław
Kharkov
Żółte Wody 16/5/48
Zaporozhian Sech
0 50 100 m

FIG. 142. *The "Deluge," Invasions of Poland, 1648–1710.* (Based on Norman Davies, *God's Playground*.)

of Gwoździec, Moshe Rosman affirms that "The successful recolonization of the Podolia region in the first half of the eighteenth century is a testimony to their [the Polish magnates'] political power and administrative talents." He stresses, "While the country [Poland] as a whole was in an economic downturn, Podolia was developing and growing. Population growth was up, new towns were established and old ones were revitalized. External trade was stable, and urban commerce was on the rise. Podolia was probably one of the more attractive places to live in Poland especially after the Great Northern War ended. . . . Jews responded to the new opportunities in Podolia by moving there as part of the recolonization movement, reaching by 1764, a population of almost forty thousand. . . ." Rosman concludes, "To see Podolia and its Jewish community as suffering the effects of debilitating crises fails to take into account steady growth and development during the first half of the eighteenth century."[24] This optimistic assessment for the prospects of the Podolian region sets the appropriate stage for the expansion of the Gwoździec Jewish community and the remodeling of its synagogue.

Historians have debated which factors led to the expansion of Jewish populations in Poland's eastern provinces. Most agree that, between 1600 and 1800, a fundamental change occurred in the multiethnic character of these small towns—specifically, the Jewish population grew dramatically relative to other ethnic communities. This expansion occurred despite continuing economic and social restrictions imposed on the Jewish community by local government and Catholic authorities. Some historians have suggested that this unprecedented expansion was in part a result of dietary laws and ritual bathing practices that led to fewer illnesses and increased

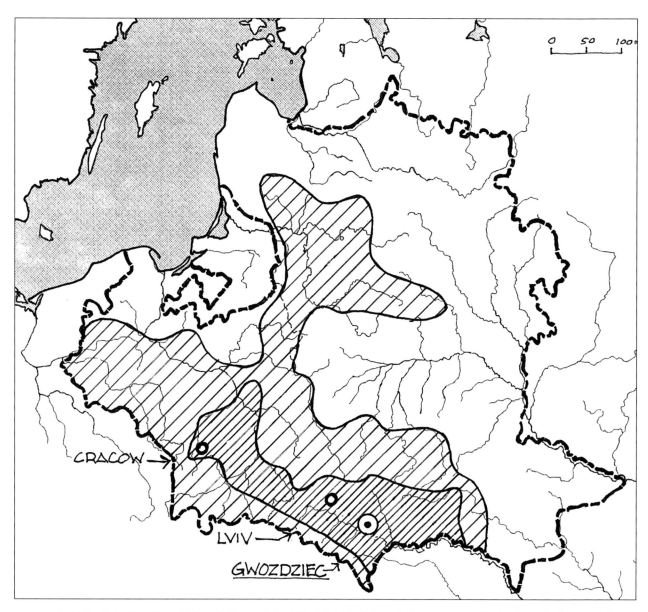

FIG. 143. *Jewish Population Densities in Eighteenth-Century Poland.* The lightly shaded area indicates regions with significant Jewish populations. The darker area, including the Gwoździec region, indicates the densest regions of Jewish population. (Based on Norman Davies, *God's Playground*.)

family size. The Jewish community's economic prosperity must also have benefited from the long-term success of the Kahal and broad magnate support for Jewish enterprises.[25] But whatever the exact causes, between 1600 and 1800 Jewish communities, historically only one of many ethnic and religious minorities in the trading towns of Eastern Europe, became in many towns the largest segment of the population.

Both the significant increase in the size of Jewish communities and the economic growth of Podolian towns like Gwoździec help to explain the construction of the wooden synagogues (fig. 143). Overall prosperity gradually translated itself into a community self-assurance, which found its expression architecturally in the building of synagogues. In no other land of the Jewish Diaspora before the middle of the eighteenth century did Jewish communities attain so much autonomy and such a high percentage of the total population as in the small towns of eastern Poland. This seems to have constituted a critical mass of Jewish culture, making possible the

construction of synagogues with some claim to originality and uniqueness. Such creative differentiation from
the dominant architectural models of their host countries was not achieved in other Diaspora communities
until the beginning of the modern period.[26]

Magnate Support

A critical factor in the expansion of Jewish settlements
like Gwoździec was the support provided by the ruling
nobility. With the weakening of international trade and
the depressed economic growth that followed the disas-
ters of the late eighteenth century, magnates increasingly
relied on Jewish entrepreneurial skills to sustain their
sagging economies.[27] Although most magnates were
Catholic and had the power to impose harsh church
restrictions on local Jewish communities, they generally
did not do so. Over long periods of reliance on their
Jewish subjects, these magnates had come to depend not
only on the skills of Jewish entrepreneurs and artisans
but also on Jewish tax revenues. Over time, many administrative positions on the magnates' estates were
held by Jews, including such important roles in the
small-town economy as innkeeping, selling alcoholic
beverages, marketing, milling, forestry, tax collection,
and general estate management. Consequently, a characteristic of manorial estates frequently noted by foreign
visitors was the presence and unparalleled importance of
the magnates' Jewish employees.[28] Yet, even this high
level of involvement with the magnates' affairs did not
guarantee continued magnate support for the Jewish
community, especially in times of crisis or social disorder
(fig. 144).[29]

The maintenance of a good relationship with the
local ruler was, therefore, critically important to the
Jewish community. Magnate approval was necessary for
most public activities, and this was especially true for the
construction of synagogues. As the most conspicuous
and potentially controversial symbol of a town's Jewish
presence, the building of a synagogue required both
magnate approval and the permission of Catholic
Church authorities, usually granted by local bishops. Because approval was required and because the structure
would be built by Gentile labor, a synagogue could not
be surreptitiously constructed by the Jewish community.
These communities lived in a climate of intense scrutiny,
and the ruling magnate's active or tacit support for the
construction project was absolutely essential.

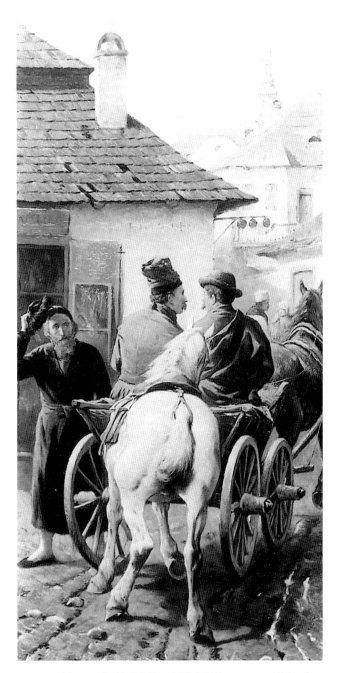

FIG. 144. *Magnate-Jewish Relations.* A Hasidic Jew removes his hat for
a Polish magnate in a painting by Zygmunt Ajdukiewicz, *Going to
Town*, 1885. Oil on canvas, 30 x 15 cm. (Courtesy of the National Museum
in Warsaw.)

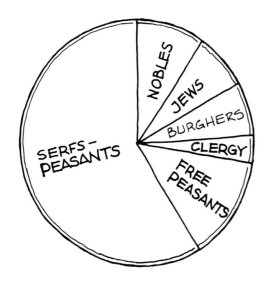

FIG. 145. *Polish "Estates."* Note the structure of social and political class within early modern Polish society. (Based on Norman Davies, *God's Playground*.)

FIG. 146. *Bernardine Church and Monastery, Gwoździec, Poland.* This drawing, found on an eighteenth-century map of the Podolian region drawn by the Bernardine Diocese, is an idealized version of the buildings. (Courtesy of the Bernardine Monastery Library, Lviv.)

Toward the end of the eighteenth and through the nineteenth century, when the failures of this antiquated manorial system increased and tensions between magnates and serfs escalated, Jewish communities found themselves inextricably enmeshed within a deteriorating social and economic order.[30] But during the seventeenth and eighteenth centuries, the magnates' private towns provided a unique window of opportunity that nurtured the growth of small-town Jewish culture throughout the eastern provinces of the Polish Commonwealth.

The Estates

The small-town Jewish communities of eastern Poland were a world defined by several constituencies or "estates": the magnates, the clergy (Catholic Church), the burghers (townspeople), and the peasants or serfs (fig. 145).[31] The most powerful of these estates was the magnates, followed by the Catholic Church, whose long opposition to Judaism took many covert and overt forms, from the creation of a climate of mistrust and suspicion toward the Jewish community, through anti-Semitic sermons and preaching, to direct encouragement of persecution and violence against the Jewish community. Particularly devastating was the Catholic Church's sanction or participation in the charges of blood libel (ritual murder accusation) and host desecration (destruction of the Catholic wafer symbolizing the body of Jesus), which periodically initiated destructive attacks against Jewish communities.[32] In relation to the physical environment, church authorities also frequently supported measures to prevent Jews from settling in the small towns, which in turn added to the estrangement of the Jews from their local communities.

There is no record, however, of the Catholic Church persecuting the Gwoździec Jewish community, nor is there evidence of anti-Jewish violence enacted by the local population. Because the Bernardine Monastery was located next door to the synagogue, we might expect greater intolerance of the Jewish population, but this does not seem to have been the case. Perhaps the possibility for conflict was offset by the power of the Puzyna/Kalinowski families, who were patrons of both church and synagogue.[33] In any case, this major regional center of Catholic Counter-Reformation activity existed in close proximity to the synagogue but did not curtail the steady expansion of Gwoździec's Jewish community through the seventeenth and eighteenth centuries.

FIG. 147. *Housing in a Farming Village, Borispol, Kiev Region, Ukraine.* (Courtesy of the Société de Géographie, Paris.)

The Gwoździec Synagogue ceiling was remodeled and most of the interior wall-paintings were completed during the same period that Bernardine Monastery was founded (1715) and its masonry church constructed (1728–1734) (fig. 146). Even with such a powerful and potentially antagonistic neighbor, the Jewish remodeling project went forward. In fact, despite its official status within the Polish state, the Catholic Church in Gwoździec and in similar Podolian towns often found its own power restricted because Catholics were often a minority. Towns like Gwoździec were typically surrounded by a population of Orthodox Greek (Uniate) and Russian Orthodox serfs. The majority of a small town's population, including its Jews, Protestants, and Orthodox Christians, did not belong to the Polish Catholic Chuch. Thus, in the Ukrainian heartland, the Catholic Church often found itself in an increasingly isolated position. Although it was the state church, it was confronted by non-Catholic majorities and an alienated and increasingly hostile Ukrainian rural population. Consequently, the Catholic Church in Gwoździec, although always a formidable threat to its Jewish neighbors, was neither as monolithic nor as overwhelming as it might initially appear.[34] The greatest restraint to the Catholic Church in eastern Poland, however, was not the competition of other religions, but the unpredictability of local magnates, whose near absolute power in the rural provinces could not be counted on to restrict or control local Jewish populations. Consequently, in many small towns like Gwoździec, the Catholic Church did not hold supreme power over the local Jewish population.[35]

The multiethnic town of Gwoździec was surrounded by a homogeneous agricultural population of Ukrainian peasantry (fig. 147). Throughout eastern Poland, these farmers were clustered in small agricultural villages or hamlets near market towns. The villages were organized

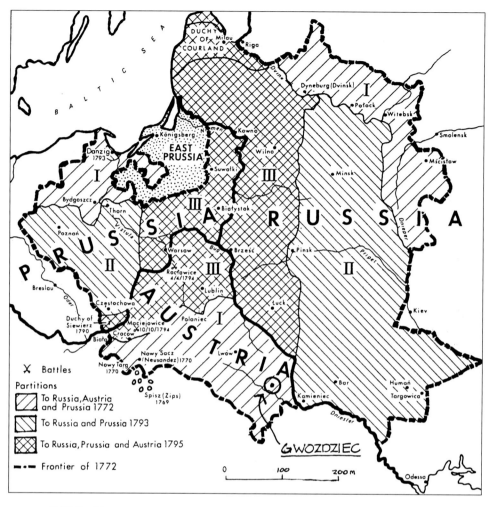

FIG. 148. *Polish Partitions, 1772–1795.* (Based on Norman Davies, *God's Playground.*)

into small districts of the Greek Orthodox or Russian Orthodox faiths. In a typical village, farmsteads lined a single road with a small wooden church at one end. These serfs lived under the control of the ruling magnate and their agricultural production was a central component of manorial wealth and power. Commercial activities, such as agricultural fairs, were held in the town's central square, where agricultural products from the countryside were exchanged for local crafts, services, and imported goods. This late-medieval model of small-town commercial exchange was the underpinning of the entire social, economic, and political system.[36]

Over time, Jews became the middlemen between magnate and serf, facilitating the critical components of commerce, craft production, and administration in their small towns. Lacking other opportunities for employ-

ment because of restrictions placed on the Jewish community, Jews became inextricably involved in the rising aspirations of an increasingly discontented population of Ukrainian serfs. One growing source of conflict was the tavern alcohol trade, which Jews, employed by magnates, frequently controlled. In the nineteenth century, this control became for the Ukrainian farmers a touchstone for growing dissatisfaction with their economic and social status. Tragically, Jews bore the brunt of attacks on the manorial system, which they served but over which they had little control.[37]

On the larger European stage where nation-states were emerging, the eighteenth-century era of stability in Eastern Europe—the era that fostered the production of wooden synagogues like Gwoździec—occupies a very minor place. From a modern political and economic perspective, the era of the synagogues was doomed to obsolescence because it preserved an ancient social and economic order. This region and its peoples are generally regarded as products of an ancient feudal system that extended into the seventeenth and eighteenth centuries, only to be rapidly submerged by the modern, industrial world of the nineteenth-century nation-state (fig. 148).[38] Yet in order to understand the emergence of the wooden synagogues, many of the most familiar concepts of progressive, premodern history, such as mercantilism, industrialization, and enlightenment, must be put aside. Instead of labeling Gwoździec a provincial backwater because it failed to thrive according to the criteria of the modern nation-state, we should strive to understand the particular conditions of small-town economy and society that allowed Gwoździec its brief moment of genuine prosperity during the eighteenth century.

During the last three quarters of the eighteenth century, synagogues with wooden vaulted cupolas became the dominant model for the small towns of eastern Poland. As we have seen in chapter 3, the aesthetic high point in this building genre occurred in the late eighteenth century in the small towns of the economically expanding Grodno-Bialystok region.[39] During the nineteenth century, wooden synagogues continued to be built on the lands of partitioned Poland, many within the Russian "Pale of Settlement," but many characteristics of the older wooden synagogues, such as the elaborately crafted cupolas and the traditional wall-paintings, were abandoned, severely modified, or continued in a diminished form.[40]

Beginning in the nineteenth century, no new additions or changes were recorded to the Gwoździec Synagogue. Nor do we see any stylistic or textural evidence of changes to the wall-paintings in extensive interior photographs. The only evidence of post-1800 change in the entire synagogue is a twentieth-century photograph of a stove pipe protruding from the roof of the beit midrash (house of study) addition to the front of the synagogue. (Such heating devices were late nineteenth- or early twentieth-century additions, usually in smaller outer rooms, and were not recorded within wooden synagogue prayer halls).

Yet violent change did come to the Gwoździec Synagogue in the twentieth century. During back-and-forth military action between Russian and Austro-Hungarian forces during the First World War, the town of Gwoździec was largely destroyed by fire, including its wooden synagogue. In accounts of Jewish residents, it was the Russian army that was responsible for the burning.[41]

Following hostilities, however, the Jewish community rebuilt its wooden synagogue. The new structure stood on the same location as the original, even using the same square plan and perhaps even using the original synagogue's squared log foundation. Tragically, it was this rebuilt synagogue that was destroyed by the Nazis in 1941–42 along with the destruction of the majority of the Jewish community.

Today there is little evidence of the Jewish presence in Gwoździec (Hvizdets in Western Ukraine) except for a late nineteenth-century yeshiva or school building, a few houses of the Jewish community, and the remnants of a Jewish graveyard.

FIG. 149. *Section, Looking South, Gwoździec Synagogue.* This drawing emphasizes the spatial volume of the interior as well as the complex wooden structure concealed within the roof. (Courtesy of the Tel Aviv Museum of Art.)

DESIGN OF THE SYNAGOGUE

How was the Gwoździec Synagogue designed? Given the destruction of the synagogue and its community, it is not surprising that there is little reliable information about how the building was designed, who the designers were, or whether they were Jewish. Now, more than eighty years after its destruction, it appears extremely unlikely that any of these questions can be answered.[1] Yet there are ways of answering that do not rely on standard historical sources.

In chapter 3, we examined the design of the synagogue primarily from the perspective of the Eastern-European contribution to the building process.[2] We must now consider in greater detail the Jewish community's contribution to the design of their synagogue. Although most scholars have assumed that there was some Jewish involvement in the design of wooden synagogues like Gwoździec, the precise role and degree of Jewish community participation has never been adequately established.[3] Here we will seek to determine the extent of that involvement.

I intend to explain what role the Jewish community played in the design of the Gwoździec Synagogue by exploring a literary source influential among Jewish communities in eighteenth-century Poland. I approach that source in search of underlying inspirations and motivations that may have buttressed the many practical design decisions that shaped the Gwoździec Synagogue.[4] By seeking the deeper inspirations and motivations for the design of the synagogue, I hope to place architectural design issues such as style and aesthetics within their appropriate relationship to the religious and cultural context of Gwoździec's eighteenth-century Jewish community.

Sources of Synagogue Design

Historians who have written about the development of the synagogue in Judaism emphasize the role of tradition.[5] The traces of this tradition are evident in a fundamental unity of synagogue design spanning all eras and regions of the Jewish Diaspora, a unity of architecture that was reinforced by the conservative nature of the liturgy. What we do not know is how these traditions of synagogue design were maintained and communicated to professional architects or builders in local communities. Design traditions may have been communicated through written documents that have not survived, or, more likely, they may have been communicated by members of the Jewish community through oral traditions that have also been lost.[6] Design information concerning pre-nineteenth-century synagogues worldwide is notoriously difficult to find. In most cases, we are left with little information about the design and building process and almost no information about the role the local Jewish community played in synagogue design.

The search for ideas influential to synagogue design and construction in the many branches of Jewish literature would seem to hold great promise. Yet thorough study of Jewish literature prior to 1800 has yielded little significant data to explain the building of wooden synagogues or any other type of synagogue.[7] This lack of reference is not surprising to scholars of Judaism, who recognize that within Jewish law certain subjects, such as dietary law, are analyzed in great detail, while other subjects, like daily prayer and, presumably, synagogue design, are resolved by tradition and custom.[8]

Although written or oral sources that specifically address synagogue design have not been found, rabbis and scholars have combed Jewish literature for references that may be applied to the synagogue. Consequently, a group of verses and quotations from biblical and talmudic sources have frequently been used to interpret the synagogue, for example, "Out of the depths I cry to Thee Lord" (Psalm 130), and "he who goes down before the ark" (Ta'an. 2:2, the Talmud's description of a prayer leader). It is important to emphasize that, although these passages may have influenced synagogue design, they were neither originally nor specifically intended to guide synagogue construction. Only later were they applied to the synagogue.[9] The same is true for references to the Tabernacle and the Temple, the two most frequently cited sources in Jewish literature for passages related to the synagogue. The architectural descriptions of both structures have posed special problems for practical interpretation, because it is unclear to what degree, if at all, the synagogue was supposed to be modeled after either the Tabernacle or the Temple(s).[10]

The Influence of the *Zohar*

I believe that an influential source of design ideas for Eastern-European wooden synagogues like Gwoździec was the *Zohar*, the major work of medieval Spanish Kabbalah. Frequently studied as an esoteric text, the *Zohar* is also a storehouse of pragmatic architectural advice on the design and construction of the synagogue. Such advice is evident in the following passage, which outlines a wide-ranging program for the organization of the synagogue. I quote the passage at length to show not only the *Zohar*'s advice about architectural elements of the synagogue, but also its fluid, metaphoric style.

> The place which Thou hast made for Thy dwelling-place, Lord, for the sanctuary, Lord, which Thy hands prepared. This implies the necessity of building a sanctuary below, corresponding to the Sanctuary above,

wherein the Holy One is daily served and worshipped [with prayer]. A synagogue should be a handsome structure, beautifully decorated, for it is an earthly copy of a heavenly prototype. The Temple below had its counterpart in the Temple above, and everything there, holy vessels and holy ministers, corresponded to something above. The same was true of the Tabernacle which Moses erected in the desert. And a synagogue must have the same object: it must be a true house of prayer. A sanctuary must have windows, as Daniel had in his upper chamber where he prayed (Daniel 6:11), corresponding to the "windows" in heaven, as it is written: "My beloved . . . he looketh forth at the windows, showing himself through the lattice" (Song of Songs 2:9). We might think that it is more proper to pray in the open air in order to allow the spirit a free ascent. This, however, is not so! There must be a house to correspond to the "House" above. Besides, prayer and the spirit must issue forth from a narrow, limited space, in a straight line towards Jerusalem, without deviating right or left. This is symbolized by the sound of the Shofar, which is thrust forth in a straight line from a narrow opening and breaks through the firmaments in order to stir up the Spirit above. It is true, we are told, that "Isaac did meditate in the field" (Genesis 24:63); but there are special reasons for this; and besides, the field where he prayed was not an ordinary field.[11]

This passage, surprisingly rich in detail about the synagogue, is just one in a series of references to the design and layout of the synagogue in the *Zohar*. In chapter 3, we saw how many of these basic criteria were applied to the Gwoździec Synagogue, for example the influence of the Temple's "holy vessels" and the orientation of the prayer hall toward Jerusalem. Other criteria for synagogue design, such as the use of lattice, the necessity for upper windows, the imagery of a synagogue above and below, and the issue of outdoor prayer, are discussed in what follows. These Zoharic directives form a substantial body of architectural advice on synagogues, which, when added to a more widely recognized body of spatial and visual imagery drawn from the *Zohar*, provided a myriad of architectural ideas for the synagogues' designers.

In the following sections, I demonstrate how the *Zohar* may have shaped, either directly or indirectly, many architectural features and interior decorations of eighteenth-century Polish synagogues, especially those found in wooden synagogues like Gwoździec. The *Zohar*'s specifications, like those quoted above, were frequently written in a direct, didactic fashion, leaving no doubt that they were intended to influence synagogue organization, construction, and worship. In a one-to-one comparison of text and building, the Zoharic specifications exactly match many aspects of the Gwoździec Synagogue, including specifications for the square plan organization, twelve windows in the prayer hall, six steps leading to the ark, and the special lattice window. The *Zohar* also provides general support for the beautification of the synagogue, the four pillar or clustered-column plan, and the use of the Tabernacle as a model for the synagogue.[12]

These detailed instructions for the design of the synagogue found in a source so influential to the premodern, Eastern-European Jewish community strongly suggest that the *Zohar*, or literature influenced by the *Zohar*, was a critical source of Jewish inspiration and design ideas. If this hypothesis is correct, it provides a partial answer to the question of how Jewish sources affected the design of the Gwoździec Synagogue.

However, we must be cautious about this hypothesis because the *Zohar* was and continues to be an extremely controversial book. Jewish sources contain considerable criticism of the *Zohar*, and the long history of Zoharic misinterpretation, both naive and willful, in Christian sources is enough to discredit even the most diligent attempts to use the *Zohar* as a meaningful source for academic inquiry.[13] Despite these problems, there are many compelling reasons to believe that Zoharic ideas and imagery influenced the art and architecture of Polish synagogues constructed during the seventeenth and eighteenth centuries.

The *Zohar* or *Book of Splendor* was for centuries known as the *Holy Zohar*, and it was widely believed to be the work of the second-century sage Rabbi Simeon ben Yohai (Rashbi). Modern scholars, however, have identified the *Zohar* as the central work of medieval Spanish Kabbalah. It was written between 1280 and 1300, by either Rabbi Moses de Leon or by a group of Kabbalists associated with him.[14] By 1600, the *Zohar* had become one of the most authoritative and venerated books in the history of Judaism. Extensive scholarship has been concentrated on the *Zohar*'s complex theosophy, especially on the elaborate interrelationships among the Sefirot (God's attributes or manifestations).[15] But the *Zohar* is not only a book of soaring theosophical exegesis; it is also a book of practical advice on the ethical conduct of daily life. Much of the book is written in an engaging narrative style with a vitality that has, over the centuries, inspired both expert and novice readers throughout the Jewish world.[16] While it is true that the majority of its stories contain complex metaphoric allusions to a rich variety of sources, considerable portions of these stories are also presented in a straightforward, practical manner and contain many pragmatic references to the synagogue.[17]

There are several possible reasons why the pragmatic Zoharic advice about the synagogue has been overlooked. Chief among them is the scholarly neglect and general condemnation of the *Zohar* during the era of rationalist historiography in the late eighteenth and nineteenth centuries.[18] Despite its subsequent reevaluation in the twentieth century, inspired by the works of Gershom Scholem,[19] the *Zohar* has most often been analyzed as a historical and philosophical text. Rarely has this influential book been analyzed from the perspective of its premodern Polish readers in order to assess the impact it might have had on their everyday religious life—an impact that is therefore almost completely unknown.[20]

The *Zohar* has not been completely ignored by scholars of art and architecture, although it is more often cited than read critically.[21] The possibility that the *Zohar* influenced synagogue design is mentioned in two influential sources. Both Ismar Elbogen, in his influential *Jewish Liturgy*, and Raphael Posner, in an entry titled "Synagogues" in the *Encyclopedia Judaica*, cite a passage from the *Zohar* on the necessity for twelve windows in the synagogue.[22] Yet in both sources, the citation is an isolated reference. Furthermore, as this chapter makes clear, the *Zohar* is not cited, where it could have been cited, in many other sections of these two comprehensive surveys of synagogue development.

In the passages quoted here, it will be clear that the author(s) of the *Zohar* sought to influence the architecture and the setting of worship in the synagogue. Yet it remains to be proven whether a late-thirteenth-century Spanish text could have influenced the construction of synagogues in distant Poland four hundred years later. There is no doubt that the *Zohar* was one of the most inspiring and influential works in Judaism. Gershom Scholem points out that it "succeeded in establishing itself for three centuries, from about 1500 to 1800, as a source of doctrine and revelation equal in authority to the Bible and the Talmud, and of the same canonical rank—this is a prerogative that can be claimed by no other work of Jewish literature."[23] Following Scholem, Isaiah Tishby claimed that, in post-sixteenth-century Europe, "the popular consciousness was full of stories from the *Zohar*. . . . In this way the *Zohar* was able to achieve the highest possible status. It attained a place in the national consciousness as a canonical text . . . [so that] the *Zohar* was placed in an even higher position than the Talmud."[24] In a recent article, Boaz Huss further argues that by the sixteenth century, for many influential Kabbalists, the *Zohar* had achieved the status of a sacred text whose authority was confirmed in revelation and reflected in the infinite structure of the divine world.[25] If such reverence was shared by members of the Polish communities involved in the design of the synagogues, then it is likely that the *Zohar*'s references to synagogues and its extensive spatial imagery would have influenced the design and construction of the Gwoździec Synagogue.

Of all the texts available to early-modern Polish Jewry that might have inspired the visual imagination, the *Zohar* probably had no equal in Jewish literature.[26] The tremendous breadth of the *Zohar*'s sources is one reason for its influence. As Isaiah Tishby has observed, it draws on "Targumim, aggadah and halakhah, liturgical poetry, philosophy, biblical commentary, lexicons, codes, and both hekhalot and Kabbalistic literature," to produce "a closely packed treasury of Jewish values in their totality."[27] But the volume and range of sources on which it drew were not the only appeal the *Zohar* held for the artistic and architectural imagination. As Tishby emphasizes, the "use of symbolic imagery instead of rational terminology in the expression of ideas . . . is a characteristic feature of practically every section of the *Zohar*."[28] Most scholars acknowledge the critical role of symbolic imagery in the *Zohar*. Moshe Idel, for instance, has described the *Zohar* as "a symbolic opus" and the "climax of Kabbalistic symbol creation."[29] The depth and vitality of Zoharic imagery has primarily been studied by modern scholars searching for its literary and philosophical associations. Yet, as Elliot Wolfson has convincingly demonstrated, the *Zohar* was also a vast storehouse of potent visual imagery and a major source for the Kabbalists' visual imagination.[30] The following research extends this line of inquiry by applying the *Zohar*'s vast array of visual imagery to the art and architecture of the synagogue.

In order to demonstrate that the *Zohar* influenced Polish synagogues, the following sections compare the art and architectural references found in the *Zohar* to the art and architecture found in Polish synagogues as they were actually built and decorated in the seventeenth and eighteenth centuries. Yet, although it is my purpose to show that the *Zohar* was highly influential, the overall effect of this text on the Polish synagogue should not be overestimated, especially in comparison to the importance of preexisting Jewish liturgical and Eastern European architectural traditions (as outlined in chapters 3 and 4). The *Zohar*'s influence should, therefore, be seen as an important contributing factor, both as a resource for reinforcing particular patterns of synagogue design and especially as a source of new or experimental ideas, such as those that influenced the remodeling of the Gwoździec cupola. Furthermore, the *Zohar* should primarily be seen as a generalized inspirational source for the Polish communities that still required considerable regional and local interpretation before its prescriptions and influences could be applied to the design of a synagogue like Gwoździec. Unfortunately, because of the destruction of these communities, the precise nature of this interpretation, between general inspirational source and particular local response, remains largely unknown. What remains is a highly suggestive Zoharic text and the documented evidence of the Polish synagogues—this chapter emphasizes their many points of unity.

Before delineating the *Zohar*'s likely influence on the synagogue, it is necessary to address two complex issues of Zoharic interpretation: the imagery of the *Zohar* and the diffusion of the *Zohar* into Poland.

Imagery of the Zohar

Controversies surrounding the authenticity of the *Zohar* have accompanied it from its inception, and the issue of its origins has been intensely debated.[31] For most Zoharic scholars, questions of authorship, textual sources, and the development of these sources within subsequent literature are immensely important. For this research concerning art and architecture, however, the most important aspect of a Zoharic passage is the strength of its imagery and its possible influence on the design of a synagogue. In this unusual respect, neither a passage's author nor its relationship to previous sources in Jewish literature are crucial to its applied artistic meaning. What matters, rather, are the internal cohesiveness of the

Zoharic imagery and its power to sway the hearts, the minds, and the imaginations of early-modern Polish readers in such a way as to have influenced the design of their synagogues.

My emphasis on the interpretation of the *Zohar*'s imagery is certainly not unique. Part of the *Zohar*'s immense attraction has always been the fluid power and vitality of its symbolic imagery—a vitality often achieved through recasting previous textual sources to produce fresh, revitalized expressions. As Elliot Ginsburg has emphasized about the Kabbalists of the *Zohar*, "their radical rereading of the earlier Jewish tradition has been called a model of 'mythopoeic revision,' a revision rooted in a world-view that stressed the interrelation of all worlds and levels of being."[32] While opponents of the *Zohar* have criticized these "revisions," because of the creative license they took with traditional sources, most analysts have agreed that, over time, the Zoharic recasting of traditional themes conferred new importance upon many sources and especially upon obscure or marginal sources.[33]

It is a central theory of the present study that the invigorated visual imagery of the *Zohar* inspired the art and the architecture of the seventeenth- and eighteenth-century Polish synagogues. Therefore, the issues of textual sources and authorship of the *Zohar*, while critically important for most studies, are overshadowed by the possibility that the Zoharic imagery itself had a practical, everyday potency for its seventeenth- and eighteenth-century Polish readership and therefore may have influenced the chain of architectural decision-making that linked designers, scholars, rabbis, and sponsors of the Polish synagogues. Unfortunately, since little is known about the everyday, practical influence of Zoharic imagery on the communities that built these synagogues, this research must be guided by the general assumption that the *Zohar* was a sacred, authoritative text for early-modern Polish Jewry.[34]

Diffusion of the Zohar

Over a three-hundred-year period directly following the expulsion of Jews from Spain in 1492, the *Zohar* became widely influential in much of the Jewish world, especially in the communities of Poland.[35] There is little agreement, however, about how and in what form the *Zohar* came to Poland. Controversies surrounding its content have made assessments of its diffusion more difficult. The *Zohar* was first printed in 1558–60, but it had been widely circulated while still in manuscript form. In addition to the distribution of the book itself, the popular spread of the *Zohar* to Poland may have been aided by unrecorded oral traditions, including the teachings of elite scholars and Kabbalists.[36]

But the most likely vehicles for spreading Zoharic ideas in Poland were the secondary sources inspired by the *Zohar*. Isaiah Tishby argues that the *Zohar* spread in Poland through the wide distribution of ethical writings, "which became a kind of popular branch of Kabbalistic thinking."[37] For example, the influential works of Menahem of Recanati and popular ethical (musar) and custom (Hanhagot) books like Isaiah Horowitz's *Shenei Luhot ha-Berit* (Two Tablets of the Covenant, 1598), and Zwi Hirsch Kaidanover's *Kav ha-Yashar* (The Honest Measure, 1705), all strongly influenced by the *Zohar*, were widely distributed and particularly influential in Poland during the eighteenth century.[38] Indeed, all branches of Jewish scholarship and communication both inside and outside Poland were influenced by the *Zohar*, including responsa (Rabbinical consultation on Jewish law),[39] preaching,[40] and some halachic (Jewish legal) literature.[41] To cite just one prominent halachic example, Joseph Caro, in the first volume of his book *Beit Yosef* (House of Joseph, 1555) and later in his influential *Shulhan Arukh* (Arranged Table, 1564–65), employs the instruction from the *Zohar* regarding the placement of twelve windows in the synagogue.[42] However, the task of tracing the popular spread of the Zoharic ideas through any one of these sources is hampered by the lack of detailed contextual studies.[43] Although the *Zohar*'s broader influence on Polish Jewry is well founded, we may never know how Zoharic ideas came to small towns like Gwoździec. They may have arrived in manuscript or print, through written or oral traditions, in elite or popular culture, from local Polish or distant Safed (Palestine) sources, or through a combination of any of these. Lacking in-depth contextual studies of eighteenth-century Jewish communities, we can only speculate on the paths of Zoharic diffusion and how these ideas influenced the wooden synagogues.[44]

By the middle of the seventeenth century, the *Zohar* had achieved the status of a sacred, canonical text and was used throughout the small towns of Poland.[45] Yet even its canonical status does not mean that the book was popularly read, nor does it guarantee that the *Zohar* was consulted for artistic and architectural inspiration by those who built the synagogues. We have only scattered records that show how the *Zohar* was popularly received, and, because of controversies surrounding the *Zohar*, these must be read cautiously. For example, Gershom Scholem quotes R. Moses Isserles, who wrote in 1570 to protest "emphatically against the enthusiasm of the 'ignorant crowd' for Kabbalistic lore: . . . And especially now that Kabbalistic books such as the *Zohar*, Recanati, and [Gikatila's] *Sha'arey 'Orah* [Gates of Light, 1561] are available in print every reader can indulge in their study believing that he has penetrated their meaning. . ."[46] While Isserles may have exaggerated the *Zohar*'s popular diffusion, it is still a remarkable observation about the *Zohar*'s popularity from one of Poland's leading rabbis and interpreters of Jewish law. Isserles made this observation just ten years after the *Zohar* was first printed in Italy in 1558–60. If the *Zohar* continued to enjoy such a degree of popularity in the small towns of eastern Poland, as I believe it did, then the design and painting of the Gwoździec Synagogue is likely to have been influenced by such a text.

The Synagogue Above and Below

In order to analyze the *Zohar*'s recommendations for the synagogue, it is important to understand how the term "synagogue" is used in the *Zohar* and how its author(s) typically formulated architectural advice. Three interrelated principles or beliefs define the *Zohar*'s synagogue. The first and most important stresses the belief that the earthly and heavenly realms exist in parallel dimensions, with the actions in one affecting the other. The *Zohar* states, "when the Holy One, blessed be He, created the world, He created it on the pattern of the world above, so that this world might be in the likeness of the world above. And all the facts of the world above were established by Him in the world below, so that one world might be connected and linked with the other" (II: 220b–221a).[47] This leitmotif linking "above and below" is used throughout the *Zohar*. It is a central tenet of Zoharic interpretation and a central theme of the *Zohar*'s synagogue.[48]

The second principle emphasizes that major buildings and places described in the *Zohar* have both earthly and heavenly equivalents. The Tabernacle and the Temple are the most frequently cited examples of buildings with both earthly and heavenly equivalents, and both

structures are models for the synagogue (II: 59b).[49] Other important spatial environments in the *Zohar*, besides the Tabernacle and the Temple, follow the same "above and below" correspondence—for example, Elijah's chair and the Bridal Canopy of Shekhinah (II: 169a).

This spatial imagery of above and below implies transference of divine perfection and approval from heavenly places to the places in which the Israelites dwell on earth, like the Tabernacle, the Temple(s), and the synagogue. The idea that divine inspiration or precedent guided the making of earthly buildings does not, of course, originate with the *Zohar*. The biblical instructions for constructing the Tabernacle and the Temple are well known,[50] and the idea of equivalence between the upper and lower worlds had many sources in earlier Jewish literature that greatly influenced the *Zohar*.[51] But, in typical Zoharic fashion, older themes were recast into more dynamic visualizations, so that the earthly Tabernacle, Temple, and synagogue were given new vitality and sanctity alongside their glorified heavenly equivalents. Through repeated mention in the *Zohar*, these three architectural structures and their heavenly equivalents become fused together in a richly overlapping spatial imagery.

The third principle broadens the idea of a lower synagogue (on earth) copying the upper synagogue (in heaven) by expanding the pool of upper synagogue prototypes to include other heavenly structures. Among these structures, the most frequently cited model for earthly synagogues is the heavenly Tabernacle. Many references are also made to the heavenly Temple, and further comparisons are made between synagogues and the Seven Halls or Palaces of the firmament and the Garden of Eden. For example, a previously cited passage illustrates the fluid spatial imagery typical of the *Zohar* where Temple, Tabernacle, and synagogue are united in overlapping images: "The Temple below had its counterpart in the Temple above, and everything there, holy vessels and holy ministers, corresponded to something above. The same was true of the Tabernacle which Moses erected in the desert. And a synagogue must have the same object: it must be a true house of prayer" (II: 59b). Here the *Zohar* links the Tabernacle and the synagogue relating them to the sanctity of the earthly and heavenly Temple.

The *Zohar* stresses the interrelatedness of heavenly and earthly places through fluid imagery where the real and the ideal are interwoven in a vibrant spatial tapestry uniting upper and lower structures. The constant in this complex dialogue between the real and the ideal is the idea that synagogues on earth should be modeled on celestial places above. So basic is this assumption that congregations like that of Gwoździec, influenced by the ideas of the *Zohar*, might have felt that their earthly synagogue was directly related to a heavenly synagogue.

Plan Organization

Earlier in this chapter, we examined a passage from the *Zohar* that outlined some of the basic features of the synagogue plan. This passage touched on the importance of using a confined building for prayer (instead of an outdoor space), the necessity for beauty in the synagogue, the importance of an eastern orientation toward Jerusalem (II: 59b–60a), and the need for high windows to facilitate prayer. By advocating a "confined, limited space" for prayer in the synagogue, the author(s) of the *Zohar* may have been commenting on the real or imagined practice of outdoor prayer.[52] Outdoor prayer was recommended in the Midrash and Genesis 24:63: "Isaac went out to meditate in the field at the evening time." Outdoor prayer is also implied in the *Zohar*'s own designation of Kabbalists as "workers (or reapers) of the field" (mechasdei chakla) (II: 240b).[53]

In several other passages, the *Zohar* addresses important issues related to the organization of a synagogue floor plan. These passages may have directly influenced the planning of seventeenth- and eighteenth-century Polish synagogues.

Square Plan

As we saw in chapter 3, the square plan of the Gwoździec Synagogue was only slightly different from the almost square plans typically used in neighboring synagogues.[54] Most scholars agree that square plans for Polish synagogues first emerged during the sixteenth to eighteenth centuries and became the most common type of floor plan for both masonry and wooden synagogues (see figs. 71, 76, 77).[55] As we have seen, arguments that connect the Polish square plan with the influence of Renaissance rationalism in general and with Italian Renaissance architecture in particular are quite convincing.[56] Yet, the *Zohar* may also have reinforced the acceptance of the square plan in Polish synagogues.

The geometrical ideas of the Renaissance may seem unrelated to the *Zohar*,[57] but there are similarities between Zoharic and Renaissance conceptions of space. For example, both schools of thought emphasize the ideal of geometric spatial perfection. For Renaissance architects, spatial perfection was often symbolized by the geometry of the circle and the square. The *Zohar* also describes many divinely inspired square and circular celestial spaces, and, in fact, the square is one spatial image repeatedly mentioned throughout the entire work. The *Zohar* uses the square as an organizing framework or image for various heavenly environments; for example, the spatial order of angels (hayyoth) (I: 211a), especially associated with the angels in Ezekiel's vision (I: 71b), and the Camp in the Wilderness. The *Zohar* also uses the square as a specific image for the twelve tribes (III: 154a) and the celestial throne (I: 211a), as well as for the spatial organization of celestial phenomena such as colors (II: 209b), the Divine Name (I: 159a), and heavenly beasts and celestial lights (II: 210b).

The *Zohar* uses the square as a basic geometric form and as a conceptual ideal. For example, the twelve tribes are camped in a square, and, as described in chapter 3, the Holy of Holies in the Tabernacle conforms to a square plan. In passages related to Ezekiel's vision, the angels (hayyoth) "turn their faces to the four cardinal points, and all revolve in a circle. The firmament is imprinted at the four corners of a square, with four figures: lion, eagle, ox and man. . . ." (I: 71b).[58] In most Zoharic references, the square functions as a symbol of divine perfection. Through repeated use, the author(s) of the *Zohar* assumes that the square symbolizes God's perfection, and thus employs the square as a leitmotif of divinely sanctioned, celestial space and, therefore, as a model for earthly architecture. The sanctity of the square plan and the cubic space in Judaism is not unique to the *Zohar*, but through repeated usage, the *Zohar* reinforced the sanctity of the square as a shape signifying perfection.[59]

Although the *Zohar* never explicitly instructs its readers to build synagogues with square plans or to use cubic volumes, repeated reference to the square places of celestial perfection must have created a climate favorable to the acceptance of a square plan among those influenced by the *Zohar*. The square that eventually became the model for most Polish synagogues, the plan usually attributed to Renaissance influence, may in fact have been inspired by the *Zohar*.

Unique West Wall

Most of the spatial imagery related to the square in the *Zohar* includes explicit mention of equal-sidedness. Yet equality of measure does not necessarily require that each side of a square be treated identically. The author(s) of the *Zohar* offered a variation on the equal-sided square plan in which one wall was different from the others. In a passage describing Moses raising the Tent of the Tabernacle, the *Zohar* says that he "first set up three sides of the Tabernacle, whereby the evil power was partly subjugated, and then [Moses] completed the fourth side, so that the evil power was completely subjugated" (II: 240a).[60] This strategy of varying treatments for three of the four sides may have influenced the wall treatment of Polish synagogues.

If the passage quoted above had been a single isolated reference, it might not have caught the attention of those seeking the *Zohar*'s guidance for synagogue design. But the 3-to-1 spatial relationship is often mentioned in the *Zohar*. The *Zohar* repeats the same spatial imagery contrasting three sides of a space with the fourth side, for example, in a description of the Temple courtyard (I: 130a), and in a passage about angels (hayyoth) praising God. Here the 3-to-1 relationship is described in more detail: "They [hayyoth] turn to the south and say 'Holy,' they turn to the north and say 'Holy,' they turn to the east and say 'Holy,' they turn to the west and say 'blessed'" (Isaiah 6:3; I: 71b). Here celestial praise is given a distinct spatial framework where the praise changes as the angels turn to the western side. If such a directive were applied to a synagogue (perhaps related to the western wall of the destroyed Second Temple), then the western wall would be different from the other three walls. Furthermore, this 3-to-1 relationship described in the *Zohar* is identical to the Bible's specification for the Tabernacle's tent walls. In Exodus 26:15–25, the structure and color of the Tabernacle's western wall was differentiated from that of the three other exterior walls. In the Gwoździec Synagogue, and in every other known wooden synagogue within its region, a 3-to-1 wall relationship was strictly followed (fig. 150).[61] In each of these synagogues, the north, east, and south walls of the prayer hall have identical pairs of high windows, while the western wall has only the entrance door and the lattice window.[62]

The functional reason used to explain the 3-to-1 wall relationship points out that various support rooms were built along the western facade of the synagogue. The placement of these rooms would have covered any windows on this wall, so that the prayer hall's western wall was different from the others. We cannot know for sure whether the western wall in Polish synagogues is different because of functional reasons or because of Zoharic influence. Perhaps both factors were mutually reinforcing. In any case, the vast majority of documented syna-

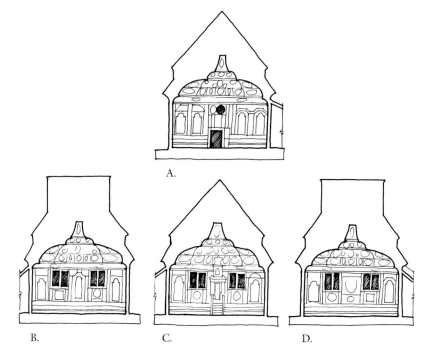

FIG. 150. *Unique West Wall, Gwoździec Synagogue.* A comparison of A. the west wall to B. the north wall, C. the east wall, and D. the south wall.

A.

B.

C.

D.

gogues constructed during the seventeenth, eighteenth, and nineteenth centuries were built on a square or nearly square plan, and these synagogues had three similar walls and a fourth, western wall that was noticeably different.[63]

Windows

Twelve Windows

Twelve large windows illuminated the main prayer hall of the Gwoździec Synagogue. This arrangement was typical for many types of seventeenth-, eighteenth-, and nineteenth-century Polish synagogues, both wooden and masonry (fig. 151). This standard window arrangement for Polish synagogues even continued into the twentieth century.[64] The twelve windows were arranged in six pairs. Two pairs, or four windows, were placed along the upper portion of the prayer hall's three exterior walls. While the *Zohar*'s recommendations for the square floor plan can be interpreted in several ways, its instruction about the number of windows in the synagogue is far more specific. The *Zohar* instructs:

> These [heavenly] windows exist in order to [submit prayer] before the Lord. This is why that if a synagogue does not have windows it is not a place for proper praying. There is a synagogue below parallel to a synagogue above. The upper synagogue has windows, as we have stated; so the lower one does also. This upper great synagogue has twelve upper windows, so also should the lower synagogue [on earth] exist in parallel to it. Because the worlds are parallel, God puts his dignity into both of them [above and below]. (II: 251a)

This passage provides precise directions for the placement of twelve windows in the synagogue. It is also an excellent example of the *Zohar*'s fluid method of linking heaven and earthly spaces together to reinforce their sacred interconnectedness. Here the recommendation for twelve upper windows in the synagogue is broadened into a discussion of the synagogue and prayer. Twelve windows are recommended not only because they imitate those of the heavenly synagogue, but also because windows in a synagogue allow prayers to ascend to God. Both of these points are repeatedly emphasized in the *Zohar*.[65] For example, another passage in the *Zohar* reads, "a synagogue must have windows as Daniel

had in his upper chamber where he prayed (Daniel 6:11), corresponding to the 'windows' in heaven" (II: 59b).[66] Here the high windows in the synagogue, which can direct the mind and prayer toward heaven, are linked to Daniel's prayer chamber, and both in turn are linked to a celestial synagogue that serves as a model for the synagogue on earth. The required windows in the earthly synagogue also reflect the *Zohar*'s elaborate analyses of prayer ascending to God. The *Zohar* develops themes of ascent to God in many elaborate images, for example, the architecture of the seven heavenly palaces that facilitate the ascent of prayer.[67]

A variation on the twelve window theme can be found in the *Zohar*'s reference to six windows in the heavenly Tabernacle: "Six of the windows [in the heavenly Tabernacle] are greater than all the others . . ." (II: 172a). While this might seem to contradict the recommendation for twelve windows, windows in premodern Polish synagogues were generally paired, producing six large window openings in synagogues but twelve separate windows (fig. 151).[68] At Gwoździec and at many neighboring synagogues, paired windows were constructed with segmented arch tops, giving a standard paired tablet profile.[69] Faced with variations in a sacred text, the standard six-opening, twelve-window synagogue plan is perhaps a sensitive resolution accomplished by Zoharic interpreters. In either case, it must be emphasized that the Gwoździec Synagogue and many Polish synagogues exactly followed the recommendation for twelve windows and six openings.[70]

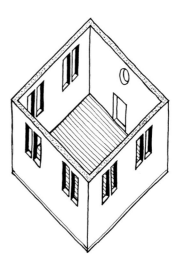

F I G. 151. *Window Locations, Gwoździec Synagogue.* Aerial diagram.

The twelve-window synagogue plan occurs in synagogues throughout the world. While it is possible that the *Zohar*'s directive for twelve windows in the synagogue may have articulated an earlier unarticulated, oral tradition, it is nevertheless true that the *Zohar* gave this tradition powerful, near-canonical support for Polish Jews. For example, even as late as 1928, a Rabbinical responsa, probably from Zlozitz in the Lviv region, answered a question about the required number of windows in a house of prayer: "As is written in the holy *Zohar*, a house suitable for prayer requires twelve windows and this is how it is here [in Zlozitz?] in the great synagogue that was begun in 1725 and completed in 1732."[71] It is my belief that many other passages from the *Zohar* provided this kind of specific guidance for the design of the synagogue.

Fifty Window Panes

Several photographs of the Gwoździec interior show what are probably two of the synagogue's original windows, both composed of very small panes of glass. These windows were located on the north wall and appear to have been abandoned after they were covered by the roof of the women's section. The other major windows of the prayer hall appear to be replacement windows with larger panes. Although we cannot determine the exact number of panes in the original windows, it is possible that they, too, followed a Zoharic directive concerning the number of windows in the heavenly synagogue. Two neighboring wooden synagogues with their original windows are suggestive in this regard.

At the Kamionka Strumiłowa Synagogue and the Jarychów Synagogue, both in the Lviv region, each of the 12 windows in the prayer hall had 49 and 50 individual glass panes respectively. This number of panes follows the *Zohar*'s directive: "These 100 windows [in Heaven] . . . are divided into fifties, and as we have said, in each one is a star" (II: 172a). The builders of the Kamionka Strumiłowa and the Jarychów Synagogues appear to have been influenced by this passage. At Kamionka Strumiłowa, each window had 49 panes set in rows with a star or "ray" pattern at the top of each rounded window frame. Altogether there were 588 panes of glass in 12 windows (fig. 152).[72] At Jarychów there were 50 panes in each window, a total of 600 panes, but they were not arranged in a star pattern. These examples suggest a very close, but not exact, reading of the Zoharic passage.[73] In

FIG. 152. *Window, Kamionka Strumiłowa Synagogue, Kamionka Strumiłowa, Ukraine.* This diagram shows one of the twelve windows in the prayer hall. Each window had forty-nine panes of glass and a star or ray pattern in the upper panes.

a survey of photographs from eighteenth-century Polish synagogues, 50-pane window units appear in both wooden and masonry synagogues.[74]

Precise correspondence between detailed prescriptions, such as found in the *Zohar* and in actual synagogue construction, is probably unprecedented in Jewish literature. It should be emphasized again that many biblical and talmudic references (such as Daniel 6:11) were not originally or specifically intended to guide synagogue construction, but were only later interpreted as practical advice applicable to synagogue design. But specifications drawn from the *Zohar*, such as the advice for synagogue windows, were indeed prescriptive for synagogue construction, and it is this specificity which leads me to believe that the *Zohar* was consulted by the builders of the Polish synagogues.

Pillars

Chapter 3 described the two major synagogue plans that used pillars or column supports surrounding the central bimah. The nine-vault plan, with four equally spaced pillars, produced equal-sized bays around a free-standing bimah (see figs. 74, 76). The clustered-column plan set four columns in a tight group around a central bimah (see figs. 74, 77).[75] Although the *Zohar* does not specify any type or placement of the bimah, the chapters describing the Seven Halls or Palaces of the Firmament are dominated by the recurring image of a hollow central pillar that closely resembles the clustered-column plan.[76] The *Zohar* states: "In the middle of this [first] hall a pillar has been fixed that goes up to the middle of the next hall, and it is hollow" (I: 42a) The *Zohar* proceeds to describe the manner in which spirits and prayer travel up and down the hollow pillar in communication with God. In the *Zohar*'s elaborate description of the architecture of the heavenly palaces, the central column is both a structural support and, more importantly, a hollow conduit for both the ascent and descent of angels, souls, divine blessings, and prayers.

The image of a central support and conduit built into the celestial palaces is further developed in passages that unite the Divine Throne with Ezekiel's vision of the four hayyoth (lion, ox, eagle, and man) (III: 240b). In these passages, the creatures act as four caryatid-like columns supporting the throne (I: 18b).[77] These two basic images, the conduit/pillar and the throne, are frequently united in the *Zohar* so that the central pillar with hollow or clustered columns is conceptually united with the supports for the Divine Throne—the four symbolic legs or columns. When this imagery is applied to the synagogue, the central bimah with surrounding columns can symbolize either a hollow, heavenly pillar or the legs of the Divine Throne. In the *Zohar*, these central pillar images are so vividly and repeatedly united, that it would not be surprising if the imagery of the hollow column were employed in the central space of the synagogue by those familiar with the *Zohar*.

The exact relationship between Zoharic references to columns and the development of central-column plans in Polish synagogues is unknown. There is, however, a close relationship between the widespread diffusion of the *Zohar* in Poland, following its first printing in 1558–60, and the subsequent alteration of synagogue plans to build or to add columns surrounding the central bimah (c. 1600–1700). The clustered-column plan is closest in spirit to the *Zohar*'s heavenly pillar imagery (see fig. 77). While recognizing the simultaneous influence of Renaissance architectural ideas on the development of symmetrically ordered, central-pillar plans, we must also consider the influence of the *Zohar*, a source far more familiar to the Jewish communities that built these synagogues.

Although it was the most common plan used in seventeenth- and eighteenth-century masonry synagogues, central-column plans were used in only a few Polish wooden synagogues in the late eighteenth century.[78] The central column plan is still significant for this study, however, because the central wooden vaults of synagogues like Gwoździec manifest the same spirit of ascent as that which may have inspired the clustered-column plan. Therefore, the Zoharic emphasis on the central pillar or conduit may have provided indirect support for Gwoździec's centralized vaulted cupola.

Summary

A close relationship exists between the *Zohar*, written in the late thirteenth century, and the Gwoździec Synagogue, built and decorated in the late seventeenth and early eighteenth centuries. The *Zohar*'s many directives and references to synagogue architecture are closely aligned with actual construction and decorative practices used in the Gwoździec Synagogue and other Polish synagogues of the eighteenth century.

The *Zohar* was a canonical, sacred text in early-modern Poland. Just as it was inspirational to the development of Ashkenazi liturgy and popular culture in the Polish community, so I believe the *Zohar* would have inspired the art and architecture of the synagogue. The *Zohar*'s influence may have been specific, as with the directives recommending twelve windows in the synagogue, or it may have been more general, such as lending strong support to the beautification of the synagogue.

The *Zohar*'s most direct influence on the design of the Gwoździec Synagogue was probably its elevation of the Tabernacle, and to a lesser extent the Temple, as models for synagogue construction. In fluid spatial imagery, the *Zohar* constantly interweaves the Tabernacle, Temple, and synagogue so that selected characteristics of the divinely inspired buildings become embedded in the advice and specifications for earthly synagogues.

As I have attempted to prove in the previous chapters, the *Zohar*'s practical advice about synagogues was assimilated into the popular mainstream of one stratum of Polish Judaism earlier, and with far greater impact, than has generally been acknowledged. Future research may well reveal the precise nature and extent of this Zoharic influence, but such research will not find that its impact was minor or temporary. To have affected the design of so many synagogues required the sustained recognition of the *Zohar* by many Jewish communities over a long period of time. Thus the *Zohar* must have found broad-based acceptance among all segments of the Jewish community in eighteenth-century Poland, from rabbis and leading citizens to the common people.

FIG. 153. *Section, Looking West, Gwoździec Synagogue*. This drawing emphasizes the density of the wall-paintings and the contrast between the exterior form and the tent-like interior cupola.

THE MEANING OF THE
REMODELED CUPOLA

Each chapter of this book has contributed something new to our understanding of the cupola at the Gwoździec Synagogue. Together, they tell us a great deal about how the cupola was built, how it was painted, and how it related to other synagogues of its region (figs. 153, 154). Yet, while we know much about what happened, we know far less about why it happened. In this final chapter, I will attempt to determine why the Jewish community of Gwoździec initiated their synagogue remodeling project and specifically why they raised an elaborate tent-like cupola over their existing prayer hall.

This book has been guided by a basic premise of material-culture study—that architecture investigation can reveal essential ideas about a people and their culture.[1] While there are many reasons to suppose that Jewish architecture in general and Diaspora synagogues in particular are less receptive to this form of analysis, I have nevertheless pursued this line of reasoning while moving from the material analysis of the Gwoździec Synagogue toward greater degrees of cultural and religious interpretation.

In order to summarize how synagogue architecture might be used to reveal patterns of culture and religion, let us briefly examine the synagogue development of late-nineteenth- and early-twentieth-century American Jews. American synagogues around the turn of the nineteenth century clearly demonstrate the gradual abandonment of an "old world," Eastern-European synagogue plan, with a central bimah and a separate women's

gallery. This old world model was gradually displaced by the American Reform synagogue arrangement, one that combines the bimah and ark at the front of the congregation and eliminates the separate women's section. Some might argue that these architectural changes, in and of themselves, mean very little. In some synagogues, these changes were made by simply moving a railing, rearranging the seating, and eliminating a wall. But, in fact, these changes in synagogue architecture reflect one of the most decisive turning points in the history of American Judaism. They mark the gradual abandonment of a long tradition of Ashkenazi Orthodoxy and the ascendancy of the American Reform movement, a change symbolized by the relocation of the bimah and the elimination of the separate women's section.[2] While we must always keep in mind that architectural developments may or may not reflect essential patterns of religion and culture, I believe that the remodeling of the Gwoździec ceiling, like the remodeling of the American synagogue, was expressive of fundamental themes in the religious life and culture of its Polish community.

In this chapter, three intertwining narratives are intended to reveal the underlying inspiration and motivating ideas behind the ceiling remodeling project. The first focuses on a special lattice window above the entrance door and its symbolic meaning as a "Gate of Heaven." The second focuses on the ceiling's painted animal figures or "creatures of heaven" and analyzes their meaning and purpose in the synagogue. The third links the Tent of the Tabernacle with changing ideas about the imagery of the Sabbath. Taken together, these three narratives explore the ideas that shaped the cupola of the Gwoździec Synagogue. If I am successful, they will show why the Jewish community of Gwoździec built a "Tent of Heaven" within the prayer hall of their synagogue.

The Lattice Window and the Gate of Heaven

In chapter 6, we learned that the *Zohar* prescribed twelve major windows for the prayer hall of the synagogue. To this standard twelve-window arrangement, we must now add a thirteenth window (a window that has been described in previous chapters but not yet analyzed).[3] In most synagogues of the Gwoździec region, a small window was placed high above the doorway on the western wall[4] (fig. 153). At Gwoździec and at several other synagogues, a painting of this window was also placed immediately below the actual window (fig. 155, 156, and see

fig. 97). In most cases, the circular window was a blind opening designed to provide neither exterior lighting nor interior communication. At Gwoździec, for example, this window opened into a dark attic space above the main entry and so had no obvious practical function. If they served no function, why were such windows found in so many of the wooden synagogues of the Gwoździec region?

The *Zohar* points to the function of this special window in several frequently cited stories about a fleeing deer or gazelle (see the deer section of chapter 4).[5] These stories are based, in part, on a passage from the Song of Songs, where the Lord yearns for the sight of the exiled Israelites. In the *Zohar* we find this passage: "He goes up on roofs to gain a sight of them [Israelites] through the chinks of the wall, as it says, 'He looketh in at the windows, he glanceth through the lattice,' in synagogues and houses of learning" (III: 114b).[6] Here the author(s) of the *Zohar* makes explicit the purpose of a single lattice

FIG. 154. *Section, Looking East, Gwoździec Synagogue.*

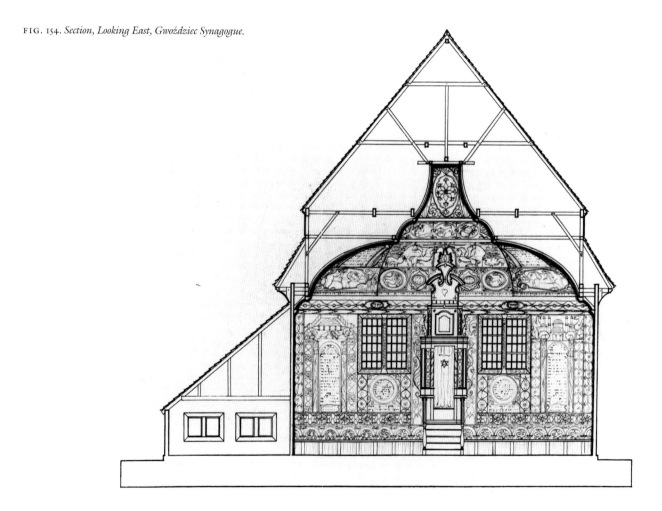

window placed high on a wall—it is an opening through which God can look in on the congregation in the synagogue. In eighteenth-century synagogues of the Gwoździec region, these windows were located on the upper portion of the western wall, and they were either covered with lattice, vertical slats, or painted to look as if they were covered with lattice. Thus the secretive upper lattice windows in the synagogues of the Gwoździec region closely follow the *Zohar*'s suggestion. The word *lattice* (charakim) also means "angel" in the *Zohar* (II: 250b), and the double meaning of this term is particularly appropriate. God may thus be imagined as watching a congregation either through lattice or through a lattice of angels.[7]

At Gwoździec, the window painted directly below the actual lattice window was also filled with lattice (fig. 156). It showed opened casement window sashes containing a diagonal lattice pattern of late-medieval diamond-shaped window panes (see fig. 97). This pairing of real and painted lattice windows was not an arbitrary decision made by the Gwoździec painters; it was, as we have seen, a standard arrangement found in other wooden synagogues of the region (fig. 155). Inside the opening of the painted window was written a passage beginning with the lines, "All the gates were locked except the gates of tears. Therefore every man should force his heart and shall pray with tears . . ."[8] This passage is based on the Babylonian Talmud (Berachot 32b and Baba Metsi'a 59a) and reoccurs, with variations, in several places in the *Zohar*.[9] In these passages, the *Zohar* emphasizes a Divine window or "Gate of Heaven" through which prayers ascend to God and answers to prayer descend from God.

These "Gate of Heaven" windows in the Polish wooden synagogues are also associated with Jacob's ladder as described in Genesis 28:17–18: "How frightening is this place! This is no other than the house of God, and this is the gate of heaven."[10] This well-known verse is interpreted in the *Zohar* as an image of gates both above and below. The *Zohar* states: "For indeed this is the Gate of Heaven . . . the gate assuredly through which pass the blessings downward, so that it is attached both on high and below: on high, as being the gate of heaven, and below, as being none other than the house of God [the synagogue]" (I: 150b). Thus the real and painted lattice windows of the Gwoździec Synagogue may also be labeled "Gate(s) of Heaven," for both gates reinforce the symbolism of making an opening or gate for prayer

FIG. 155. *Painted Lattice Window, West Wall, Jabłonów Synagogue.* Note the lattice shutters on either side of the arched window. This painted window, just like the painted window at the Gwoździec Synagogue, contains the Hebrew inscription: "All the gates were locked except the gates of tears." (Courtesy of the Tel Aviv Museum of Art.)

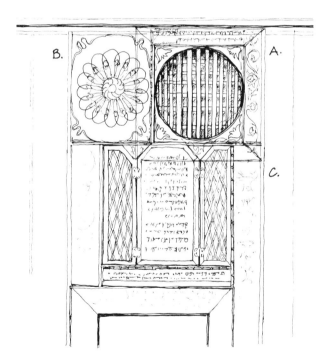

FIG. 156. *Lattice Window and Painted Windows, Gwoździec Synagogue.* A. Circular window covered by lattice; B. Painted circular window with rays next to the lattice window; C. Painted arched window with open lattice shutters on either side.

to ascend to God and for God's angelic messengers to return to the congregation at prayer.[11] In chapter 6, we saw how the imagery of a heavenly conduit influenced the clustered-column plans used in masonry synagogues. In the vaulted wooden synagogues, the conduit to God was provided by the "Gate of Heaven" window on the western wall. Thus, at Gwoździec and at other eighteenth-century wooden synagogues, the lattice window opening facilitated communication with God and conveyed the idea of God's symbolic presence in the synagogue.

The *Zohar* reinforces the idea that the lattice window is a "Gate of Heaven" by frequently depicting God/Shekhinah looking in on the Jewish people at prayer. The quote that opens this section, "He glanceth through the lattice," confirms God's concealed presence as He observes the worshipers in the synagogue.[12] The association of a lattice window on the western wall of the synagogue (or the entire western wall and its doorway) with the Shekhinah is certainly not a minor or hypothetical linkage. The prayer "Lekhah Dodi" painted on the western wall near the doorway of the neighboring Chodorów Synagogue (see fig. 115) clearly demonstrates the connection between the liturgy of seventeenth- and eighteenth-century Ashkenazi Jewry and the entrance of the Shekhinah through the doorway of the prayer hall. The lattice window above the entrance may have provided an additional focal point for the congregation, as they turned toward the western wall to welcome Shekhinah, the Sabbath bride, at the completion of the prayer "Lekhah Dodi."[13] It is likely that this lattice window became a standard component of wooden synagogues in the Gwoździec region at the same time that the "Lekhah Dodi" prayer, along with the rituals of Kabbalat Shabbat, were introduced into the popular liturgy of Ashkenazi Jewry between the sixteenth and eighteenth centuries.

In sum, because of the many references to the lattice window as a heavenly portal in Jewish literature, especially in the *Zohar*, I believe that the lattice window in the Gwoździec Synagogue indeed symbolized a "Gate of Heaven" for its congregation. It was a gateway with two primary functions: it was a conduit for the passage of prayer to God and a place within the synagogue through which God/Shekhinah, concealed behind the lattice, could observe the congregation. The image of Shekhinah observing the congregation from behind a lattice is a powerful, dynamic image of God's symbolic

presence in the synagogue. The lattice serves as an architectural device to simultaneously conceal and reveal God's presence to the congregation in order to articulate His symbolic presence.[14] Thus the lattice window facilitated an understanding of the Divine as neither a theoretical abstraction nor a remote messianic ideal, but as an immediate, accessible image of God's close proximity to the congregation. Whether this conceptualization of God's immediate presence was central or peripheral to the conduct of worship for early-eighteenth-century congregations requires further contextual study, but the adoption of the Gate of Heaven as a standard motif in other synagogues of the Gwoździec region suggests that the concept of a present but concealed God may well have been a component of their daily worship.

The Ceiling Paintings and the Creatures of Heaven

In 1731, the newly painted ceiling of the Gwoździec prayer hall glistened with an abundance of plant and animal life. The figures in these paintings were neither the simplistic creation of shtetl artists nor naive copies of Eastern-European folk art. They represented, instead, a distinctive iconography related to liturgy that was developed within the Jewish communities of Poland, probably beginning in the earliest periods of Ashkenazi settlement. Although portions of the wall-paintings were purely decorative, as we have seen in chapter 4, the animal figures were primarily used to communicate liturgical themes and ethical stories.

Although several animals in the wall-paintings have already been analyzed, we do not know the collective meaning of these creatures and the extent to which their meaning was understood by the Gwoździec community. These are difficult questions to answer in any circumstances, but they are made immeasurably more difficult by the destruction of the wall-paintings and of most of their historic sources. Even general comparative evaluation is difficult because so little remains of any synagogue art produced from late antiquity until the late 1600s, when these elaborate art forms were first recorded in the synagogues of the Gwoździec region. Because these wall-paintings are so isolated from other sources of synagogue art, it is not surprising that scholars have been unable to answer even basic questions about the paintings and their animal figures.[15]

To approach these questions, I turn again to the *Zohar*. In this case, the *Zohar*'s vivid imagery and likely artistic influence is less important than its role in creating and sustaining a climate favorable to the acceptance of synagogue art. Without repeating the many issues regarding the extent of Zoharic influence in the small towns of Poland, already outlined in chapter 6, this section examines passages from the *Zohar* that demonstrate general support for the visual arts and specific support for the use of animal figures as an accompaniment to worship in the synagogue.[16] Given the many direct connections between the *Zohar*'s text and the architecture of the Gwoździec Synagogue already cited, it seems reasonable to ask whether the paintings in the wooden synagogues might also have been inspired and sanctioned by this influential text.

The *Zohar* is well known for its wealth of vivid and distinctive visual imagery, which makes it an obvious source of inspiration for the painters of the synagogue. Less well known is the *Zohar*'s positive attitude toward visual imagery and painting. The *Zohar* clearly states: "Therefore the graving and painting of all forms is permitted, except the human form."[17] This positive support for the visual arts is followed by warnings about the dangers of visual images, so it is clear that the author(s) of the *Zohar* was well aware of the traditional prohibitions against and general concern about the visual arts in Jewish worship and Jewish life.[18] On balance, however, the *Zohar* communicates an extremely positive and supportive attitude toward the process of visualization and the creation of visual arts within Judaism. Through its widespread and long-term influence, I believe that the Zoharic sanction for visualization and the visual arts had a considerable effect upon the development of synagogue art in the Polish Ashkenazi communities.[19]

Yet, even this general sanction for visual arts in the synagogue may not appear to justify the unusual collection of exotic animal figures found on the ceiling and walls of the Gwoździec Synagogue (figs. 157, 158, 159). The camels, elephants, turkeys, squirrels, as well as fantastic creatures like griffins, unicorns, and serpents, are difficult to reconcile within a Jewish religious context. Although most of these creatures, including the fantastic ones, appear in Jewish literature and legend, their density on the Gwoździec ceiling still requires further explanation.[20] The *Zohar*'s influence provides such explanation. Close analysis of the *Zohar* yields interpretations of the collective meaning of these animal figures, including the many fantastic creatures.

For the Gwoździec congregation in 1731, the profusion of painted creatures on the ceiling of the prayer hall may have reminded them of the awe one should feel in the presence of God's creations. Therefore, the depiction of these creatures would have represented a way of honoring God, the creator of an unfathomable world of natural wonder. This wonder encompassed a profusion of living creatures, both familiar and unfamiliar. In the world view of premodern Ashkenazi Jewry, the study of unusual or miraculous phenomena was traditionally seen as a way of understanding and honoring God's true nature. In an article about Eleazar of Worms, whose writings may have influenced the art forms of later Polish Jewry, Joseph Dan stresses this fundamental concept about the miraculous: "the goodness of God is apparent in the created world by the unusual and the miraculous and not by the usual, ordinary and natural." Dan continues, "God's true nature, according to this [medieval Hasidic] system, is revealed by those phenomena which contradict natural law."[21] Although it is an ancient topic in Jewish literature, the theme of wonderment felt for the natural world, and especially its curiosities, was given renewed emphasis under the powerful influence of the *Zohar*.

The *Zohar* stresses the important role visualization plays in honoring God. By meditating on his varied, exotic creations, including both heavenly and earthly creatures, a person honors God's majesty. While reading the following passage from the *Zohar*, visualize the ceiling of the Gwoździec Synagogue and its profusion of earthly and heavenly creatures. Think of these many figures as honoring God in their unfathomable diversity (see figs. 157, 158, and 159) (emphasis added):

"In the beginning God created the heaven and the earth," means that the lower world was created after the pattern of the upper. Now, the Tabernacle below was likewise made after the pattern of the supernal Tabernacle in all its details. For the Tabernacle in all its works embraced all the works and achievements of the upper world and the lower, whereby the Shekhinah was made to abide in the world, both in the higher spheres and the lower. Similarly, the Lower Paradise is made after the pattern of the Upper Paradise, and the latter contains all the varieties of forms and images to be found in the former. Hence the work of the tabernacle, and that of

FIG. 157. *Animal Figures, East Ceiling above the Ark, Gwoździec Synagogue.* Note the lion and squirrel in medallions (center), the rooster and griffin beside the Tablets of Law (upper center), and the dove with an olive branch (top center). Note also the wooden, two-headed eagle wearing a crown that sits atop the ark just above a pair of hands symbolizing the sign of the Priestly Blessing. (Courtesy of the Tel Aviv Museum of Art.)

heaven and earth, come under one and the same mystery. *It is written: "Lift up your eyes on high, and see: who hath created these? He that bringeth out their hosts by number. . . . Not one faileth" (Isaiah 40:26). Are we to imagine from this that by lifting his eyes upwards a man can know and see what he is not permitted to know and see? No. The true meaning of the passage is that whoever desires to reflect on and to obtain a knowledge of works of the Holy One, blessed be He, let him lift his eyes upwards and gaze on the myriads of the hosts and legions of existence there, each different from the other, each mightier than the other.* Then will he, while gazing, ask, "Who created these?" Indeed, as has already been expounded elsewhere, "Who created these?" amounts to saying that the whole of creation springs from a region that remains an everlasting "Who?," in that it remains undisclosed. [The *Zohar* answers:] *"He that bringeth out their host by number,"* for inasmuch as that region is undisclosed it brings forth everything by means of the sound that issues from the trumpet, the sound that constitutes the "number" of all the celestial hosts and the sum of the whole of creation; and from thence also proceeds the mystery of sublime faith through all the supernal "sides," and then extending in grade after grade downwards, and widening out into numerous hosts after their kinds, all of whom are numbered, and "He calleth them all by name." [The verse continues:] "By the greatness of His might" —an allusion to the "right side," "for that He is strong in power"—alluding to the "left side," "no one faileth," this in allusion to the forces emanating from the two sides." [The *Zohar* continues:] According to an alternative interpretation, the verse, *"Lift up your eyes on high, and see: who hath created these?" contains an allusion to the erection and completion of the Tabernacle. For whoever then looked at the Tabernacle saw in it an epitome of the upper world and the lower; for all the works of the universe were contained in the equipment of the Tabernacle. Thus whoever gazed with attention at the clasps of the Tabernacle saw in their gleam the radiance of the stars inasmuch as they were disposed in the same way as the stars in heaven.* (II: 231b–232a)[22]

The last section of this quotation describes the Tabernacle's curtains as a kind of interior sky full of heavenly creatures that confirm God's majesty. This allusion to the Tabernacle assumes even greater significance when the interior curtains of the Tabernacle are understood to be decorated with "Keruvim [angels] of artistic work" (Exodus 26:1). When the imagery of heavenly angels is added to the imagery of clasps and stars in the tent

fabric of the Tabernacle, this final section of the passage reinforces the idea that God's wondrous angelic creations are revealed to those who "lift up their eyes" within the heavenly Tabernacle. Throughout this book, I have described the cupola of the Gwoździec Synagogue as shaped by the Tent of the Tabernacle and reflective of a heavenly environment. It was toward this end that I believe the Gwoździec community remodeled their prayer hall, to create a more heaven-like space for worship.

The entire passage vividly and repeatedly demonstrates the *Zohar*'s sanction for visualization pursued with open, curious eyes. Here the act of questioning through seeing becomes a vehicle for honoring God's majesty in the visual contemplation of his varied creations. It is a process of worshiping God that Elliot Wolfson has described as uniting scriptural interpretation with the visual imagination.[23] Furthermore, this exhortation to "Lift up your eyes" is neither an isolated nor a unique example. Various themes related to the act of seeing and marveling at God's wondrous creations permeate the *Zohar*. In fact, the emblematic homily, "Lift up your eyes," is cited ten times in the *Zohar*, and each time it is used to draw the reader's attention to a significant passage.[24]

The importance of architectural beauty is also mentioned several times in the *Zohar*, especially when the Tabernacle, the Temple, and the synagogue are linked. One example can be found in the passage cited at the beginning of chapter 6: "A synagogue should be a handsome structure, beautifully decorated" (II: 59b). If a congregation (or the authorities responsible for building a synagogue) were familiar with such Zoharic ideas, it does not seem strange that they would commission beautiful art works for the synagogue, works that served to honor God through allusions to his unfathomable wonder.

Within the literary and liturgical traditions of the sixteenth, seventeenth, and eighteenth centuries, the *Zohar*'s sanction for visualization, especially for visual art within the synagogue, is extremely rare. A later book that was strongly influenced by the *Zohar*, the popular *Kav Ha Yasher* (The Honest Measure, 1705), by Zwi Hirsch Kaidanover, shows far greater concern for and frequent prohibition against the act of seeing in general and the dangers of seeing evil in particular.[25] The *Zohar* does contain the standard rabbinical restrictions and prohibitions against inappropriate visualization and

FIG. 158. *Animal Figures, North Ceiling, Gwoździec Synagogue.* Note the lion battling a unicorn, the turkey, the raven-like bird, and the composite, leopard-like animal with a human face. (Courtesy of the Tel Aviv Museum of Art.)

FIG. 159. *Ceiling, Gwoździec Synagogue.* This drawing shows the paintings that were completed in 1729. Note how the ark extends into the ceiling at the top center of the drawing.

seeing. For example, it repeats the standard prohibition against looking at a rainbow associated with the avoidance of looking at God's presence (III: 84a). Such Zoharic prohibitions against looking at visual phenomena, however, are vastly outnumbered by passages that encourage one to see and to exercise one's visual imagination, as long as such visualization is conducted, of course, within the context of Jewish law and tradition.

It would be difficult to imagine the long-term development and sponsorship of an elaborate liturgical art such as that found at the Gwoździec Synagogue without the kind of influential sanction provided by the *Zohar*.

The *Zohar* encourages the visual aspects of worship in several other ways. For example, it suggests methods of visualization that could be used in ecstatic or mystical worship. In an analysis of the visionary experience in worship, Elliot Wolfson observes, "the *Zohar* repeatedly employs metaphors derived from the phenomenon of sight. God is said to hide secret matters within the Torah and clothe them in a garment, the removal of which allows them to be seen by the sage. Hence, the mystic is called the 'wise one full of eyes,' and 'master of the eyes.'"[26] Throughout its text, the *Zohar* maintains a surprisingly persistent emphasis on the visual over the auditory aspects of worship. Wolfson concludes: "The goal of the [*Zohar's*] Kabbalistic exposition, however, is not hearing the word of God as related in the text, but rather seeing the hidden mysteries. . . . In sum, then, mystical gnosis [esoteric knowledge] for the *Zohar* is primarily visual and not auditory."[27] Both quotations emphasize the significance of sight and seeing as a primary vehicle for the act of worshiping God.

To those who have studied Jewish scripture, liturgy, and law, the Zoharic emphasis on seeing and visual inquiry must sound unusual. It is certainly not typical of Jewish experience today. After all, "the people of the book" are not generally known for pursuing visual inquiry as a vehicle of liturgy and prayer, as the *Zohar* so strongly and consistently recommends. But if this study is correct in its conclusions about the premodern, pro-Zoharic, pre-Hasidic emphasis on visualization in the conduct of prayer and liturgy, then something in the conduct of worship must have radically changed between then and now.

I believe that the tent-like cupola and the elaborate wall-paintings of the Gwoździec Synagogue reflect an earlier, more visually oriented, premodern or "medieval" approach to worship. Although the term "medieval" may seem temporally inappropriate, it does convey a premodern, pre-Enlightenment world view in which the act of seeing and visual exploration within religious devotion was a fundamental component of worship. Therefore, when the worshipers in the community of Gwoździec lifted up their eyes, they would have been exercising a standard visual component of worship that included the recognition of the exotic animals on the synagogue's ceiling as a sign and confirmation of God's unfathomable wonder.[28]

With the advent of both Hasidism and Haskalah (Jewish Enlightenment) during the second half of the eighteenth century, the visually oriented aspect of worship, so powerfully expressed in the art and architecture of the Gwoździec Synagogue, was to change rapidly and irrevocably.[29] As I have stressed throughout this book, the ideas that sustained the remodeling and painting of the Gwoździec Synagogue were generated by a pre-Hasidic, popular Judaism characterized by a nonmystical, popular, pietistic approach that flourished during the seventeenth and eighteenth centuries in the small towns of eastern Poland.[30]

Current scholarship has reexamined previous assumptions about this region and era and raised questions about the popular transition to Hasidism in Eastern Europe. This transition was typically depicted as a struggle between establishment mitnagdim (opponents) and rebel Hasidim (pious). Such depictions were frequently based on the well-chronicled accounts of the Gaon of Vilna's attacks on the early Hasidic sects. Within the small towns of eastern Poland, transition to Hasidism appears to have occurred without major clashes between opposing sides, yet the transformation in the conduct and meaning of popular worship were most likely profound.[31] One result of the transformation is clear: there was a stunning, absolute break in the art of the small-town wooden synagogues that accompanied the rise of Hasidism. The elaborate wall-paintings, so central to the seventeenth- and eighteenth-century synagogues of the Gwoździec region, were greatly diminished or discontinued in later synagogues. This fundamental change in the spatial environment of the synagogue, which occurred during the second half of the eighteenth century, directly parallels the rise of the Hasidic and Haskalah (Jewish Enlightenment) movements in the small towns of eastern Poland.[32] As was explained in chapter 4, the abrupt termination of the wall-paintings at the Kamionka Strumiłowa Synagogue during the middle of the eighteenth century may have signaled a dramatic turning point in this popular liturgical art form, which, in any case, was not substantively continued in synagogues after 1800.[33] The abandonment of the highly developed traditions of synagogue wall-painting can be attributed to many external factors stemming from the external sociopolitical and economic transformations of the modern period. But internal factors related to changes in popular worship introduced by Hasidim may also have been influential. Here I stress one such internal factor: the performance of Hasidic prayer.

In several recent publications, Moshe Idel has described the transition in Hasidic worship from visually oriented pre-Hasidic prayer to vocally oriented Hasidic prayer. He writes: "Hasidic mysticism of prayer is primarily interested in the vocal aspect of prayer, i.e., the pronounced letters rather than the contemplation of its written letters."[34] Here Idel emphasizes the inwardly directed, contemplative nature of Hasidic prayer, frequently conducted with closed eyes and an intense internal focus. Compare this Hasidic practice of prayer with the method of contemplation described in the passage quoted from the *Zohar*, where the worshiper is invited to contemplate, with eyes wide open, the wonder of God's many creations. It is extremely difficult even to imagine a Hasidic congregation lifting up their eyes in prayer and studying the sky or the ceiling of their synagogue as directed in the *Zohar*.[35] And yet, within the small Ashkenazi towns of eastern Poland during the seventeenth and early eighteenth centuries, before the rise of Hasidism, the practice of lifting the head and eyes upward in prayer was widely practiced.[36]

For later nineteenth- and twentieth-century Ashkenazi congregations in Poland, perhaps influenced by Hasidic notions of prayer and less mindful of stories from the *Zohar*, the paintings on Gwoździec's ceiling may have appeared to be images only distantly related to Jewish legends. But in 1731, when the Gwoździec community finished remodeling its synagogue, the ceiling's ensemble of art and architecture would have been far more meaningful for most worshipers. Some of this meaning may have come from a tradition of worship where visual experience and visual associations played a more prominent role. Within this earlier, more visual context, the elaborate ceiling paintings with their profuse animal imagery would have been a meaningful accompaniment to worship.

Looking again at the figures on the Gwoździec ceiling, we can better appreciate their presence as a surviving record of a pre-Hasidic approach to worship, an approach that placed considerable value on the visual aspects of worship (see figs. 157, 158, 159). (The extent to which contemporary viewers have generally lost this sense of wonderment for the creatures of the natural world should not blind us to the potency such images may have had for the Gwoździec community.) Although the animal figures are just one part of these complex paintings, the many fantastic and heavenly creatures honored God by drawing attention to the unfathomable variety and incomprehensibility of his wonders. Through their powerful artistic creations, the artists illuminated the splendor of God's creation and brought the heavenly world closer to the worshipers of Gwoździec. Thus, when the congregation lifted up their eyes, they combined visually oriented prayer with an awe for God's unfathomable being.[37]

The Tent of the Tabernacle and the Tent of Heaven

This book has illustrated the many ways that tent imagery, especially related to the Tent of the Tabernacle, influenced the creation of Gwoździec's wooden cupola.[38] In mutually reinforcing ways, the designers, builders, and artists who created the synagogue's cupola alluded to the shape, materials, details, and symbolism of the Bible's Tabernacle tent. It is now time to ask: why was tent imagery used during the eighteenth century, and what did this imagery mean to the Gwoździec community?

I believe that the designers of the Gwoździec cupola intended to erect a heavenly tent above the prayer hall— a "tent of heaven" that was inspired by the Tent of the Tabernacle. Although the Tabernacle has been interpreted in all periods of Jewish literature, it was the *Zohar*'s recasting of Tabernacle imagery that probably had the most direct impact on the cupola of the Gwoździec Synagogue.[39] Although the *Zohar* does not specify that a tent-like cupola should be constructed over the prayer hall of the synagogue, it does provide an extensive repertoire of imagery referring to sacred tents, canopies for prayer, and holy meetings within tents. Frequently in the *Zohar*, the Bible's specifications for the Tent of the Tabernacle are used to describe other tent-like environments intended for worship and prayer.[40] The similarity of Tabernacle imagery in neighboring wooden synagogues, coupled with the *Zohar*'s canonical status and widespread influence, makes the *Zohar*'s Tabernacle a likely influence on Gwoździec's tent-like ceiling. It must be stressed, however, that there were many other potential sources for Tabernacle imagery in Jewish literary and oral sources, so that one source, no matter how influential, should not be overemphasized.[41] We should, therefore, imagine a religious context where references to the Tabernacle were reinforced in multiple texts. Whatever the exact sources that inspired the tent references, we have already seen that the designers of the Gwoździec Synagogue's interior made repeated reference to tents and specifically to the Tent of the Tabernacle. We shall now explore why they did so.

From the sixteenth through the eighteenth century,

the imagery of the Tent of the Tabernacle and the Temple received renewed emphasis within the liturgy of Ashkenazi Jewry. Joseph Gutmann has stressed that such an emphasis on the Tabernacle and Temple was part of a wider liturgical reform movement that strengthened the link between the synagogue and the ancient rituals of the Tabernacle and Temple. Gutmann notes that one consequence of this linkage was that "the synagogue itself constituted a surrogate, temporary substitute for the Temple."[42] Gutmann lists the rituals and physical characteristics of the Temple and Tabernacle that were newly emphasized within Polish synagogues between the fourteenth and eighteenth centuries. These Temple/Tabernacle characteristics include: inscribing the Ten Commandments (Decalogue) on the inside doors of the ark, utilizing a curtain (parochet) and valance (kapporet) to cover the ark, suspending an eternal light (ner tamid) in front of it, and placing a Menorah (seven-branched candelabrum) on its south side. Although Gutmann makes a compelling case for the messianic symbolism of these renewed features, I believe that the theme of Tabernacle/Temple restoration also had important implications for both Sabbath worship and the performance of liturgy.[43]

In the three centuries prior to the construction of the Gwoździec Synagogue, the image of the Tabernacle's tent became more closely associated with rituals of Sabbath worship. In one particularly influential Sabbath image, the Tabernacle's canopy shelters the bride, Shekhinah (the female aspect of God), in a sacred marriage to God. Although the association of this Divine marriage with Sabbath worship reflected the contribution of Kabbalists over a long period, the *Zohar*'s many prominent references to the Tabernacle as a Divine bridal canopy revitalized this sacred marriage imagery for Ashkenazi Jewry. In a repeated Zoharic formula, the Tabernacle was envisioned as a wedding canopy sheltering the bride Shekhinah and this image was then used to symbolize the performance of Sabbath worship.[44]

This broad mythopoeic revision of the Sabbath evolved over a long period but was finally popularized in Polish communities by the disciples of the Safed, Palestine, Kabbalist Isaac Luria after about 1600. One result was that the entire Sabbath was reenvisioned and overlaid with the unifying image of a Divine marriage ceremony. Frequently, this use of Divine marriage imagery for the Sabbath accompanied the widely adopted liturgical practices for the Friday evening service preparation,

Kabbalat Shabbat.[45] The historical development of Divine marriage imagery for Ashkenazi Jewry has been analyzed by various scholars including Gershom Scholem and Moshe Idel, and is extensively analyzed by Elliot K. Ginsburg in *The Sabbath in the Classical Kabbalah*.[46] Ginsburg emphasizes that the central image of a sacred marriage ceremony was further reinforced by associative imagery, such as: the return of Shekhinah from the captivity of the demonic forces,[47] preparations of Shekhinah for the sacred marriage to God, and the sacred union of God with his bride. What is significant for this research is the fact that these intertwining images of God's sacred marriage were frequently envisioned as occurring under a sacred tent. Also important is the fact that these images were applied to all functions and rituals of the Sabbath, including: domestic customs, especially associated with Sabbath meals; rituals of preparation for and termination of the Sabbath; customs for marital union; and imagery for the entire liturgy of the Sabbath.[48] In a related development, the now almost universal use of the four-posted wedding canopy, or chuppah, was also developed and standardized in Ashkenazi communities during the same period when the imagery of the sacred marriage ceremony came to be associated with the Sabbath.[49]

The simultaneous development of the chuppah (the canopy for Jewish marriage) and Gwoździec Synagogue's cupola (the Tabernacle's canopy for God's sacred marriage) provides the underlying rationale for the remodeling of the Gwoździec ceiling. The critical link connecting the Tabernacle's tent with the design of the cupola at Gwoździec is the imagery of the Divine marriage. Reinforcing this association for the Gwoździec community, the entire Sabbath liturgy, and particularly the Friday evening service, was overlaid with the imagery of God's marriage and union with his bride, Shekhinah.[50] This sacred marriage was depicted as occurring in a tent-like setting, and it is this Tabernacle tent for the Divine marriage that I believe inspired those who remodeled the Gwoździec ceiling into the shape of a tent. Perhaps the most widely accepted liturgical custom associated with this sacred marriage ceremony was the prayer "Lekhah Dodi" (Come my beloved friend let us welcome the [Sabbath] bride).[51] I believe that the same motivations that inspired the sacred marriage allusions in "Lekhah Dodi" also inspired the Tabernacle/marriage-tent imagery of the Gwoździec ceiling remodeling.

The popular dissemination of sacred marriage imagery that shaped the conduct of worship in the small towns of eastern Poland must await more detailed contextual studies. Enough is known, however, to strongly suggest that the tent-like shape of the synagogue's interior, embedded with tent and Tabernacle imagery, was intended to reinforce the imagery of a sacred marriage ceremony as it was emphasized in the liturgy of Kabbalat Shabbat and as it was so consistently emphasized in the *Zohar*. Thus the Tent of the Tabernacle serving as a synagogue's marriage chuppah might have risen, as the "Lekah Dodi" recommends, to welcome the Sabbath bride, Shekhinah (fig. 160).

The Meaning of the Gwoździec Synagogue

In this final chapter, we have inquired into the ideas that shaped the remodeled cupola of the Gwoździec Synagogue. Previous observers have generally agreed that the synagogue's completed cupola intensified the visual and spatial qualities of the prayer hall and created an experientially powerful setting for worship. For those with a skeptical or unfavorable impression of the Polish/Eastern-European shtetl experience, the spatial intensity of the prayer hall might only confirm the difficult or even desperate circumstances of Jewish communities in the small towns of Poland. Seen from this perspective, the unique shape and elaborate decoration of the prayer hall might only reflect long-term community despair and pessimism—the effects of Eastern-European impoverishment, persecutions, and pogroms. But from the evidence presented in this book, the Gwoździec Synagogue remodeling project demonstrates the presence of a positively motivated and unified religious community, no matter how fragile or illusionary its values and beliefs might appear in retrospect. When the Gwoździec Synagogue was remodeled in 1731, there was little about the architecture or the community to indicate pessimism for the long-term prospects of the Gwoździec community, even though the Jews of Gwoździec could not have been misinformed or naive about their vulnerable minority status, living as they did under the absolute rule of a Polish Catholic magnate and in the literal shadow of a powerful Bernardine Monastery Church. This book strives to illustrate the many ways that the initial synagogue construction and the later ceiling remodeling project reflected the rising aspirations of Gwoździec's demo-graphically expanding, economically viable, reasonably secure, and largely unified Jewish community in 1731.

At the beginning of this book, we observed the Gwoździec community as they prayed beneath the glistening cupola of their newly remodeled synagogue. We found that the dramatic cupola and its elaborate paintings were not unusual but were typical accompaniments to worship in the small towns of seventeenth- and eighteenth-century eastern Poland. Although the liturgical implications remain unproven, I have attempted to show the many ways that the art and architecture of the Gwoździec Synagogue represented the popular mainstream culture of small-town, Ashkenazi communities in eighteenth-century Poland.

In the last two chapters, I have shown that significant portions of the artistic and architectural traditions that shaped the wooden synagogues were drawn from sources within the larger Jewish community, especially from liturgical and literary sources. Without underestimating the central role that non-Jewish, Eastern-European regional sources played in the architecture and the paintings, I have identified the significant role that Jewish ideas had in shaping the individuality and distinctiveness of wooden synagogues like Gwoździec. When the critical contribution of these Jewish sources is fully recognized, wooden synagogues like Gwoździec can finally be appreciated as powerful, original expressions of their Polish-Jewish communities, and perhaps as some of the most original expressions of Jewish art and architecture ever created.

The purpose of this book has been to give new life to a destroyed synagogue and its community from one small town of Polish Jewry. Whatever the success of this effort, it can only begin to depict the patterns of life and worship of a formerly vibrant community that is now barely discernible amid the few remaining scraps of historical documentation. A well-known Hasidic legend about the founder of the Hasidic movement, the Baal Shem Tov, quoted by Gershom Scholem, best illustrates the difficulty of such efforts to recover the spirit of this past.[52]

When the Baal Shem had a difficult task before him, he would go to a certain place in the woods, light a fire and meditate in prayer and what he had set out to perform was done. When a generation later the "Maggid" of Mescritz was faced with the same task he would go to the same place in the woods and say: We can no longer light the fire, but we can speak the prayers—and what he

FIG. 160. *Worship in the Synagogue.* A rabbi stands at the railing of the bimah in the Jabłonów Synagogue, his back to the door, in this painting by Isidor Kaufmann, *Rabbi at the wooden synagogue of Jabłonów,* 1897–1898, oil on wood, 28 x 26 cm. (Courtesy of the Sussi Collection.)

wanted done became reality. Again a generation later Rabbi Moshe Leib of Sassov had to perform this task. And he too went into the woods and said: We can no longer light a fire, nor do we know the secret meditations belonging to the prayer, but we do know the place in the woods to which it all belongs—and that must be sufficient; and sufficient it was. But when another generation had passed and Rabbi Israel of Rishin was called upon to perform the task, he sat down on his golden chair in his castle and said: We cannot light the fire, we cannot speak the prayers, we do not know the place, but we can tell the story of how it was done.

I borrow the ending of this Hasidic story to complete the story of the Gwoździec Synagogue. We too are greatly distanced from the spark of religious inspiration that sustained its creation; we too do not know the prayers that were once spoken. When we go to the place where the synagogue once stood, nothing can be found, and when we ask about the synagogue and its community nothing is remembered. But we can still tell the story of how the Gwoździec Synagogue was built. And if we have told this story with integrity and conviction, we too might discern a faint glow. Perhaps it is the same glow of inspiration that created the synagogue and its resplendent painted ceiling . . . if we can only . . . "Lift up our eyes."

Sergey R. Kravtsov

AFTERWORD

Lift Up Your Eyes on High, and See!

Almost twenty years have elapsed since the publication of *Resplendent Synagogue*. It is not a very long time for architectural history, particularly for synagogue architecture, where numerous concepts dating to the mid-twentieth century survive well into the twenty-first. Architectural history is written at a noticeably slower pace than many other branches of the humanities, perhaps due to the paucity of connoisseurs and an even narrower number of researchers. For this reason, a new edition of Thomas Hubka's monograph is an important event for those interested in this almost esoteric field.

Several reviews have been published since its appearance in 2003, and some new ideas have emerged in the meantime.[1] The arguments of *Resplendent Synagogue* are being continuously reconsidered, mostly by researchers vis-à-vis their own work, often in lively discussions with colleagues, and—explicitly and implicitly —in their new publications.

For those reading the monograph for the first time, the challenges the author had to overcome should be explained anew. These included a scarcity of historical records concerning the Jewish community of Gwoździec (today Hvizdets), complicacy of its religious, cultural, social, and demographic milieu in the eighteenth century, the complexity of the wooden synagogue as it was reconstructed and decorated by 1731, and its novelty versus regional/vernacular traditions. The author overcame these difficulties painstakingly and courageously, avoiding the lines of the least resistance. He greatly benefited from the investigation of heterogeneous sources and built components, which is a principal virtue of an architectural historian.

The core of the book is a material-cultural and social-cultural analysis of a wooden synagogue. Social and cultural historians have, however, focused on Hubka's discovery that the *Zohar* (and its surrounding ethical literature) did contain many direct prescrip-

tions for building and decorating a synagogue. Esoteric and perplexing, the Book of Splendor or the *Zohar* is a foundational work of Jewish mystical thought known as kabbalah, which first appeared in thirteenth-century Spain. Though the origins of the *Zohar* were remote in time and space from Eastern Europe, the book became influential in that region from the late sixteenth century, when several printed editions became available and when Lurianic kabbalah penetrated the Polish Ashkenazi realm and reinvigorated its worldview and liturgy. In Eastern European Jewish communities, devastated by peasants' uprisings, wars, and epidemics, the *Zohar* found grateful readers seeking spiritual respite.

Thomas Hubka reads the *Zohar* mostly as a didactic text for straightforward instructions about the shape and function of a synagogue—factors not emphasized by readers interested in the symbolic and esoteric readings of this sacred text—and as visual material for the architect's spatial interpretation, though the book's visual sequence aims to conceptualize its mystical content. Semantically, the *Zohar* establishes vertical links between the heavenly Temple, the Tabernacle, the Throne of Glory, Seven Palaces, and the "upper" synagogue above with the earthly synagogues below. According to Hubka, the designers of the Hvizdets synagogue were mindful of these links and used them as a blueprint to shape their actual place of prayer.

Hubka's approach to the *Zohar* as a didactic-prescriptive source also contrasts with some art historians, who distance themselves from the complex esoteric weight of the *Zohar*'s elaborate mystical symbolism. Instead, they tend to explain the synagogue's built and decorative forms through standard/traditional liturgical texts and ceremonial sequences, looking for proof of suggested meanings in the texts inscribed immediately on the built members or in spatial reference to them.

However, no such inscriptions have been noticed so far in Eastern European synagogues.

Despite this methodological difference, Hubka's study fits well within a relatively new trend in Jewish studies, where connections between kabbalah and halacha, homily, liturgy, conduct, and other expressions of religious life—including ritual art—are exposed. Within this emerging trend, many historians of art and architecture cautiously accept many of Hubka's insights.

This trend is obvious regarding the twelve windows of the "upper" synagogue supposedly repeated in the "lower," earthly synagogue.[2] The proof is in the statistics of analyzed edifices across Eastern Europe and, as more synagogues are surveyed, Hubka's findings and interpretation are affirmed. On the other hand, the call for twelve windows was repeated, with due reference to the *Zohar*, in the halachic code Shulḥan Arukh (1564–65). This secondary instance reinforces the position of those art historians who privilege halakhic references to kabbalistic ones.

There is less consensus regarding the attribution of the fifty window panes to the *Zohar*.[3] Though a provable numeric indicator, it seems to be a new signification that the historian imbued into the artifact. This interpretation is akin to a similar trope regarding the Great Portuguese Synagogue of Amsterdam, whose seventy-two windows allegedly remind the believers of the numerical value of the Lord's name written in full.[4] Random numbers are subject to myriad interpretation, particularly with the preoccupation in Jewish mysticism with gematria (an alphanumeric code assigning a numerical value to a name, word, or phrase according to its letters).

Hubka's interpretation of the synagogue's composite —concave and convex—interior cupola as a tent or a Tabernacle has met with more serious opposition from art historians. Their criticism derives from the medieval iconography, Jewish and non-Jewish, where the biblical Tabernacle appears as a rectangular box with plane faces and roof. Hubka's theory is drawn from the well-documented influence of Ottoman tents in Polish society and Jewish tent trade with the Ottoman East. The "architect" of the Hvizdets synagogue could model his cupola, particularly its upper convex tier, either on these images or on actual Ottoman tents in Polish possession, as suggested by Hubka.

The critiques of *Resplendent Synagogue* notwithstanding, the monograph has had a wide and significant impact on recent research and has earned a place in the history of synagogue architecture.

Maria Piechotka (1920–2020), a seminal researcher in synagogue architecture, named Thomas Hubka as a successor of her and her husband Kazimierz's life enterprise.[5] The Piechotkas' and Hubka's studies are among the challenges to drive the study on, to reconstruct this building.

Bracha Yaniv is one of the foremost scholars of Jewish ritual art and has commented on *Resplendent Synagogue*. She has examined the biblical, midrashic, and kabbalistic sources referring to the six stairs of the celestial Throne of Glory: according to the *Zohar* and *Tikunei hazohar*, six steps, similar to the six sefirot of Malchut, should ascend to the Torah ark and bimah in an earthly synagogue.[6] With this finding, Yaniv placed the Zoharic vision within a train of multilayered Jewish thought rather than interpreting it as having a unique formative role in Jewish art. That scholar's survey of archival photographs and drawings clearly supported the six-step kabbalistic element of Torah arks, in keeping with Hubka's discovery in Hvizdets.[7] Conversely, the number of steps leading to the bimah is habitually smaller, according to Yaniv.

Tamar Shadmi has undertaken a thorough study of inscriptions in the seventeenth- and eighteenth-century Eastern European synagogues.[8] She outlined the penetration of Lurianic kabbalah into Ashkenazi liturgy through the prayer books and wall inscriptions, which gave new meanings to the synagogue space. Her study laid the foundation allowing for the interpretation of figurative paintings covering the synagogues' interior surfaces, while Hubka's book recognizes many of Shadmi's sources. A new joint comprehensive study on inscriptions and paintings in Eastern European synagogues by Yaniv and Shadmi is forthcoming.

Another scholar of that school, Zvi Orgad, researched the technique, iconography, composition, paleography, and other aspects of murals in the same synagogues.[9] Primarily focused on itinerant eighteenth-century Jewish artist Eliezer Zusman from the Ruthenian town Brody, Orgad traced the formative sources of this art and the paths of its dissemination from Eastern Europe to Germany. Orgad's work helps us to understand many technical and substantive aspects of the work completed by another itinerant artist, Itzhak ben

Yehuda Ha-Cohen from Yarychiv, in Hvizdets. Hubka also reviews Zusman's synagogue painting and the implications of his exported work in German synagogues.

My own study also attempted to refine Hubka's theory and place the Hvizdets synagogue within the architectural history of the Polish-Lithuanian Commonwealth. The substantial conclusion of *Resplendent Synagogue* is that in 1729 the Jewish community had undertaken an effort to heighten their prayer hall by constructing a multitiered, central wooden dome, ultimately penetrating its attic space and compromising the stability of its roof construction. Hubka convincingly explains this reconstruction as the desire to emphasize the vertical dimension of the hall and the meaningful connection between the celestial and earthly realms.

Various scholars have written about the origins and development of similar central domes in Eastern European wooden synagogues. Hubka discerns the further development of centralized domes four decades later and hundreds of miles north, in the four-pillar wooden synagogues of the Hrodna-Białystok group. He is correct when connecting this pattern in wooden synagogues to their masonry predecessors. However, he might have looked at a group of Ruthenian and Podolian masonry synagogues whose pillars bore a cupola boldly protruding into the attic space but still invisible from outside, as it was in Hvizdets. These were the Old and the New synagogues in Brody (both built during the second quarter of the eighteenth century), the great synagogues in Zbarazh (Zbaraż, the 1740s), Sharhorod (Szarogród, the 1740s), Raşcov (Raszków, 1749), and Soroca (1775).[10] In the synagogues of Zbarazh and Raşcov, decorated in stucco and stone carving, the southern and northern walls bore representations of the menorah and the shew-bread table, which reinforced the reference of these synagogues to the Tabernacle and Temple, as in the case of the wooden synagogue of Hvizdets. In my opinion, these masonry synagogues drew inspiration from the same elevation idea as their wooden precursor in Hvizdets, and they could be a nexus between the early and late eighteenth-century, southern and northern wooden synagogues.

Whereas the cupola of Hvizdets resembled a portable tent or Tabernacle, a later series of wooden synagogues in the Podolian towns of Smotrych (Smotricz, 1746), Mykhalpil (Michałpol, 1763–73), Yaryshiv (Jaryszów, 1780), and Min'kivtsi (Mińkowce, ca. 1780),[11] and in the Volhynian Norynsk (Noryńsk, late eighteenth or early nineteenth century), had convex cove domes. Their cupolas penetrated the roof space from the outset and transposed contemporary masonry forms, also those of the stone synagogues, into wooden vernacular construction. Hence, the Hvizdets synagogue secured a pioneering and unique position in the entire trend.[12]

Hubka's book and his educational efforts promoted the construction of wooden synagogue replicas, placed either in enclosed museum spaces or in the open-air "skansens." The Hvizdets replica in the POLIN museum in Warsaw was followed by the large-scale models of the wooden synagogues of Belarussian Vowpa (Wołpa, reconstructed in Polish Biłgoraj in 2015) and Polaniec (replicated for the Folk Architecture Museum in Sanok in 2014–21). These replicas, as tangible illustrations of once-vibrant religious and material culture, have yet another added benefit: they served the study of traditional arts and crafts shared by diverse ethnic and religious groups of the Old Commonwealth.

Moreover, in a broader European context, the building of these replicas brings to mind a largely forgotten technical revolution. Indeed, the Age of Discovery depended on capacious and fast ships, on the carvel-smooth hulls attached to a frame, possible only with standard boards produced on sawmills, which were reinvented in early modern Europe. These technical advances speedily spread across richly forested Eastern Europe. They facilitated not only massive timber exports to Holland and England, but in addition they made countless vernacular purposes affordable, such as for baroque domes, smoothly joined and covered with shingles or tin, and interior coves, "sham" vaults, and cupolas, one among them in Hvizdets.[13]

The reader has before her a book rich in images and thought. It is a book by an architect and architectural historian who comprehends the built environment both visually and culturally. He conveys his understanding of space and history through drawings, archival photographs, and narration, and invites you, as in Isaiah, to "Lift up your eyes on high, and see!"

October 2021

Sergey R. Kravtsov is a Research Fellow
at the Center for Jewish Art at the
Hebrew University of Jerusalem.

APPENDIX

Hebrew Prayers and Inscriptions on the Walls of Gwoździec Synagogue

The following Hebrew prayers and inscriptions were painted on the walls and ceiling of the Gwoździec Synagogue. The ten major text panels with painted architectural surrounds, described in the book as the "painted prayer panels," are listed by number, beginning on the southwest corner of the western wall and running clockwise around the prayer hall. The texts on the upper ceiling are listed in ascending order, moving toward the center of the cupola. The names of the zodiac signs, appearing at the top of the cupola, are listed last. The translation was edited by Avriel Bar-Levav using several English references, including *The Complete Artscroll Siddur*, by Rabbi Nosson Scherman (New York, 1992); abbreviated *A.S.* In many cases, the Gwoździec prayers differed from currently accepted versions.

WEST WALL

Painted Prayer Panel I (far left, west wall)

Prayers and benediction recited by priests before and after blessing the congregation:

"May it please You, O Lord our God and God of our fathers, that His blessing which You have commanded us to pronounce upon Your people Israel may be a perfect blessing, forever free from any stumbling or iniquity." (*A.S.* pp. 694–95)

"Blessed are You, O Lord our God, King of the universe, Who has sanctified us with the holiness of Aaron and commanded us to bless Your people Israel with love." (*A.S.* pp. 694–95)

"Sovereign of the universe, we have performed what You decreed for us; do You, too, fulfill what You have Promised us. Look down from Your [holy] abode, from heaven, and bless Your people Israel and the soil You have given us, as You have sworn to our fathers, a land flowing with milk and honey." (*A.S.* pp. 700–1)

Dedication:

"This is the donation of the noble brothers . . . [illegible, Katz brothers?]."

Painted Prayer Panel 2 (middle left, west wall)

Prelude to Thirteen Attributes:

"Almighty King, sitting on the throne of mercy, You act graciously, pardoning the sins of Your people and making them pass away one by one. You grant abundant pardon to sinners, forgiveness to transgressors, dealing generously with all mortals and not treating them according to their wickedness. O God, Who instructed us to recite the thirteen divine attributes, remember in our favor the covenant of the thirteen attributes, as You revealed them to the humble [Moses] of old, as it is written in Your Torah: 'The Lord came down in a cloud; He stood with him there, and proclaimed the name Lord. The Lord passed before him and proclaimed: "[The Lord!] the Lord! A God compassionate and gracious, slow to anger, abounding in kindness and faithfulness, extending kindness to the thousandth generation, forgiving iniquity, transgression and sin, and remitting our sins" [Exodus 34:5–7]. Pardon our iniquity and our sin, and take us for Your own' [ibid., v. 9]. Our Father, forgive us, for we have sinned; Our King, pardon us, for we have transgressed. For You, O Lord, are truly kind, forgiving and merciful to all who call upon You." (*A.S.* pp. 822–23)

Dedication:

"This was donated by the noble Rabbi Judah Leib son of Rabbi Israel of blessed memory, in the year [Date unclear: 1691 or 1721] 'The scepter shall not depart from Judah' (Genesis 49:10)."

Inscription above Painted Prayer Panels I and 2
(middle left, west wall)

"Black on white, to commemorate the Destruction"

The following six inscriptions are located above or near the doorway to the prayer hall at the center of the western wall.

Inscription above the Circular Lattice Window
(center, west wall)

[Only partly legible] "A person is vexed by the loss of his money but not [by the loss of his days; his money does not help, his days do not return]." (A variation of this verse is found in *Der Sucht Spiegel* [The Mirror of Ethics], Auerbach, 1716.)

Inscription above the Doorway, within a Painted Window (center, west wall)

[Only partially legible] "All the gates have been [sealed] except for the gates of tears. Therefore every man shall pray in tears . . . King David . . . because God heard his voice. . . ."

On the basis of the words that are legible, the inscription is probably the same as that located in the same position at the neighboring Jabłonów Synagogue: "All the gates were locked except the gates of tears. Therefore every man should force his heart and shall pray with tears. And if he can not pray with tears in any case, he will be able to make a [low] sound in his heart. About this said King David that God heard his voice of weeping" [Psalms 6:9]. (Based upon Babylonian Talmud, Berachot 32b, but modified)

Inscription above the Door (center, west wall)

Dedication:

"Joseph son of Yehuda Leib. May the Lord of our fathers increase your numbers a thousand fold." (Deuteronomy 1:11)

Inscription on the Door Lintel (center, west wall)

"At [that] time (1718), I will bring you again together [. . . I turn back your captivity before your eyes, saith the Lord]." (Adapted from Zephaniah 3:20)

Inscription on the Left Door Jamb (center, west wall)

"I will turn their mourning to joy, I will comfort them and cheer them in their grief." (Jeremiah 31:13)

Inscription on the Right Door Jamb (center, west wall)

"Righteousness shall go before Him; and shall set us in the way of His steps." (Psalms 85:13)

The next inscription either continues the passage above or is a new passage:

"Anyone who gives charity . . . health . . ."

Below the inscription is a charity box.

Painted Prayer Panel 3 (middle right, west wall)

Prayer said after the morning and evening services:

"May the Lord our God be with us, as He was with our fathers. May He never abandon or forsake us. May He incline our hearts to Him, that we may walk in all His ways and keep the commandments, the laws, and the rules, which He enjoined upon our fathers. And may these words of mine, which I have offered in supplication before the Lord, be close to the Lord our God day and night, that He may provide for His servant and for His people Israel, according to each day's needs—to

the end that the peoples of the earth may know that the Lord alone is God. . . ." (I Kings 8:57–60)

"O Lord, lead me along Your righteous path because of my watchful foes; make Your way straight before me [Psalms 5:9]. But I walk without blame; redeem me, have mercy on me, for I am alone and afflicted. My feet are on level ground. In assemblies I will bless the Lord [Psalms 26:11–12 and 25:16]. The Lord is my guardian, the Lord is my protection at my right hand. My help comes from the Lord, maker of heaven and earth. The Lord will guard my going and coming [for life and peace] now and forever [paraphrase of verses from Psalm 121, in first person]."

Note that the artist may have (inadvertently?) conflated two verses, Psalms 26:11 and 25:16, probably owing to the similarity of the last words of the former and the first of the latter.

Dedication:

"Donated by the noble Asher son of [illegible] Mordecai of blessed memory, for his son, the child Aaron, may he grow up to the Torah, to the nuptial canopy and to good deeds. In this year of (1723) 'Asher's bread shall be rich.'" (Genesis 49:20)

Painted Prayer Panel 4 (far right, west wall)

Prayer said by individuals to themselves, but only after a bad dream, in order to better a bad dream. (From B. T. Ber. 55b with the addition: "May it please you O Lord . . ." [second line]):

"Sovereign of the universe, I am Yours and my dreams are Yours. I have dreamt a dream and know not what it is. May it please You, O Lord my God and God of my fathers, that all my dreams concerning myself and concerning all Israel should be beneficial, whether those I have dreamt concerning myself, or those I have dreamt concerning others, or those that others have dreamt concerning me. If they are good, reinforce and strengthen them, and may they be fulfilled for me and for them like the dreams of Joseph the Righteous. If they require healing, heal them as You healed Hezekiah King of Judah from his sickness, Miriam the prophetess from her leprosy and Naaman from his leprosy. [Sweeten them] as the waters of Marah were sweetened by Moses and the waters of Jericho by Elisha. Just as You turned the curse of the wicked Balaam into a blessing, so may you turn all my dreams into happiness for myself and for all Israel. Protect me, be gracious to me and favor me. Amen."

Prayer recited by congregation during and after Priestly Blessing:

"Supreme and mighty are You on high; You are peace and Your name is peace. May it please You to grant life and blessing and enduring peace to us and to all Your people Israel" (A.S. pp. 700–701)

Dedication:

"This is the donation of the noble Rabbi Solomon Kalman [. . .] (1728) [date unclear] for his grandson, the child S[. . .]m[. . .] [may he be] reared to Torah, the nuptial canopy and good deeds."

NORTH WALL

Painted Prayer Panel 5 (far left, north wall)

Prayer for the New Year and the Day of Atonement. (Recited when the scroll is taken out, after saying thirteen attributes):

"Master of the world, fulfill the requests of my heart for good, satisfy my desire, and grant my wish, and forgive all my sins and all the sins of the members of my household—a pardon of kindness, a pardon of mercy, and cleanse me of my wrong-doing, my sins and my transgressions, remember me favorably before You and be mindful of me for deliverance and mercy. Remember me for a long life, for a good and peaceful life, good livelihood and sustenance, food to eat and clothes to wear, wealth, honor and longevity [being occupied] in Your Torah and in Your mitzvoth, and intelligence and understanding to perceive and comprehend the depths of Your mysteries. Grant a complete healing to all our pains, and bless all the work of our hands. Enact for us favorable decrees, salvations and conso-lations; nullify all severe and harsh decrees against us; and dis-pose the heart of the government, its advisers and ministers favorably toward us. Amen, and so let it be Your will. May the words of my mouth and the meditation of my heart be accept-able before You, Lord, my strength and Redeemer. Make my prayer to You, Lord, be at a propitious time; God, in Your abounding kindness, answer me with Your true deliverance." (*A.S.* pp. 434–35; Birnbaum, *High Holydays Prayer Book for Yom Kippur*, pp. 401–2)

Dedication:

"[Illegible] in the year . . ., may he strengthen them. . . ."

Inscription above Painted Prayer Panel 5
(far left, north wall)

The following are within a painting of a leopard, eagle, gazelle, and lion (partially illegible):

"[Be bold as a leopard]
and light as an eagle
[and swift as a gazelle and strong as a lion]
to do the will of your Father in heaven"
     (*Sayings of the Fathers* 5:20)

Inscription below the Window
(right middle, north wall)

"And the angels shall sing, the cherubs glorify, the seraphim exalt in song, and the angels bless the Lord; and the face of every angel and cherub; also the seraphim opposite each other."

An identical passage occurs on the painted ceiling of the Horb Synagogue, from Horb, Germany, relocated in the Israel Mu-seum, Jerusalem.

Dedication (?):

Illegible.

Painted Prayer Panel 6 (far right, north wall)

Prayer recited by congregation after the Torah scroll has been re-moved from the Ark and placed on the table preparatory to reading:

"Magnified and hallowed, praised and glorified, exalted and extolled above all be the name of the supreme King of Kings, the Holy One, blessed be He, in the worlds which He has created—this world and the world to come—in accordance with His will and the will of all those who revere Him, and the will of all the House of Israel. He is the eternal stronghold, the Lord of all creatures, the God of all souls, Who dwells in the expanses on high, Who inhabits the ancient high heavens; Whose holiness is above the celestial beings and above the throne of glory. Now, Your name, O Lord our God, shall be sanctified among us in the sight of all the living. Let us sing a new song before Him, as it is written: Sing to God, chant hymns to His name, extol Him Who rides the clouds, the Lord is His name, exult in His presence. May we see Him eye to eye when He returns to His abode, as it is written: For eye to eye they shall behold the Lord's return to Zion. And it is said: The presence of the Lord shall appear, and all flesh, as one, shall behold—for the Lord Himself has spoken." (*A.S.* pp. 438–9)

Dedication:

[Partially legible] "donation of the noble men [?] the noble . . . Rabbi Meir . . . Abraham, may God protect and nourish him, with his sons . . ."

"This was donated by the noble Rabbi Isaac son of Rabbi Simon Segal for his son . . . S[imon?], in the year (1728) 'for it is through Isaac that offspring shall be continued for you.'" (Genesis 21:12)

EAST WALL

Painted Prayer Panel 7 (far left, east wall)

Prayer recited upon entering the synagogue:

"And I, through Your abundant loving kindness, enter Your house, by the grace of Abraham, who was called the man of loving kindness; I bow down at Your holy temple, by the grace of Isaac, who was bound on the altar in a holy place; in awe of You, by the grace of Jacob, who said, 'How awesome in this place!' O Sovereign of all worlds, by the grace of these three Patriarchs may I enter the synagogue to offer my prayer before You, and by their grace may my prayer, the prayer of a humble person, be considered worthy of mercy and good will before Your glorious throne, and rise and be placed as a crown upon Your head by Metatron the Prince of the Countenance. Amen Selah."

Inscription under the Window (left middle, east wall)

Dedication (?):

Illegible.

Inscription under the Window (right middle, east wall)

Artist's dedication (?):

"In the year (1730 or 1731) the handiwork in which I glory . . . he who engages in the holy work."

Painted Prayer Panel 8 (far right, east wall)

Modim of the Rabbis:

"We thank You, Who are the Lord our God and God of our fathers, God of all mankind, our Creator and Creator of the universe. Blessings and thanks are due to Your great and holy name, because You have kept us and sustained us. So may You ever grant us life and sustain us and gather our exiles to Your holy courts, to observe Your laws, to do Your will and worship You with a perfect heart. For this we thank You. Blessed be God, to Whom all thanks are due." (*A.S.* pp. 112–13)

Dedication:

"This was donated by the noble and exalted leader, Rabbi Jacob son of Rabbi Abraham . . ."

SOUTH WALL

Painted Prayer Panel 9 (far left, south wall)

This prayer cannot be translated from existing photographs.

Inscription within the Branches of the Painted Menorah (center, south wall)

"God be gracious to us, and bless us; and cause His face to shine upon us; (Selah) that Thy way may be known upon the earth, Thy salvation among all nations. Let the peoples praise Thee, O God: let all the peoples give thanks to Thee. O let the nations be glad and sing for joy: for Thou shalt judge the peoples with equity, and govern the nations upon the earth. (Selah) Let the peoples praise Thee, O God; let all the peoples give Thee thanks. The earth has yielded her increase; and God, our own God, shall bless us. God shall bless us; and let all the ends of the earth fear Him." (Psalms 67)

Dedication:

Illegible.

Painted Prayer Panel 10 (far right, south wall)

This prayer cannot be translated from existing photographs.

Inscriptions on the Inside of the Bimah

"I am now preparing to stand and make the benediction over the Torah scroll, for the unification of the Holy Only, blessed be He, [and His Holy Presence?] through the Hidden One, in the name of all Israel."

"It is forbidden to talk during the reading of the Torah."

"May it please You, O Lord our God, that Your mercy should . . . and that You should treat Your sons with the attribute of mercy and deal leniently with them."

CUPOLA CEILING

Inscriptions on the Lowest Cove of the Ceiling

There are eight medallions containing acronyms, with two acronyms on each of the four walls. These are painted on the coves that run continuously around the prayer hall at the top of four walls. Only three of the eight acronyms can be translated:

"May [the King] answer us when we call." (Psalms 20:9)

"The tents of the righteous resound with joyous shouts of deliverance."

"Shun evil and do good." (Psalms 34:15)

Inscriptions in a Continuous Frieze at the Top of the Lowest Cove:

[East wall] "Said R. Simeon b. Lakish: Any person who answers Amen with all his might—the gates of paradise are opened for him [Bab. Talmud, Shabbat 119b]. Said R. Joshua b. Gaddi: Any [northeast wall] person who answers Amen in this world is deemed worthy of answering Amen in the world [north wall] to come, as Scripture says, Blessed be the Lord forever, Amen and Amen—Amen in this world and Amen in the world to come. [northwest wall] Said R. Joshua b. Levi: Any person who answers "Amen, may his great name [be blessed]" with all his might—[west wall] the sentence decreed against him will be annulled [Bab. Talmud, Shabbat 119b]. Said R. Isaac: Anyone who is accustomed to come to the synagogue and fails to come one day, the Holy One, blessed be He, [southwest wall] asks after him, as Scripture says [Isaiah 50:10], Who among you reveres the Lord and heeds the voice of His servant [Bab. Talmud 6b]. [south wall] Said R. Joshua b. Levi, come and see, how great are the humble before the Lord, for when the Temple was standing, a person who brought a burnt offering was rewarded accordingly, a person who brought a meal offering . . . [illegible] [Bab. Talmud, Sotah 5b]. [southeast wall] [One who says] Amen is greater than one who makes a benediction." (Bab. Talmud, Berachot 53b, modified).

Inscriptions on the Lower Tier Panels of the Eight-Sided Ceiling

Artist's "signature" (far left, west arch panel)

"By the worker, engaged in the holy labor, quote [?] the artist Israel, son of the venerable Rabbi Mordecai from the holy community of Jaryczów, district of the holy community of Lviv."

Artist's "signature" (far right, west arch panel)

"See, all this was made by my hand [Isaiah 66:2], for the glory of the place and the glory of the community, quote [?] the artist Isaac son of Rabbi Judah Leib haCohen from the holy community of Jaryczów. (1729) This is my handiwork, in which I glory." (Isaiah 60:21)

Ostrich (west arch panel)

This painting is labeled "ostrich."

Inscription in a Medallion above a Leviathan
(northwest arch panel)

Verses recited after the Aleinu prayer:

"You will not fear sudden terror or the disaster that comes upon the wicked [Proverb 3:25]. Hatch a plot . . . agree on action—it shall not succeed, for with us is God! [Isaiah 8:10]. Till you grow old, I will still be the same; when you turn gray, it is I who will carry; I was the Maker and I will be the Bearer; and I will carry and rescue you [Isaiah 46:4]. This is always said after Aleinu." (*A.S.* pp. 350–53)

The last sentence could either be a directive to the congregation, or a copy (inadvertent?) by the artist from a prayer book.

Inscription in a Medallion above a Painted Elephant (northeast arch panel)

Prayer recited before returning the Torah scroll to the Ark [Numbers 10:36]

And when it halted, he would say: Return, O Lord, to the tens of thousands of the families of Israel! Advance, O Lord, to Your resting place, You and Your mighty Ark! Your priests are clothed in triumph; Your loyal ones sing for joy. For the sake of Your servant David do not reject Your anointed one. For I give you good instruction, do not forsake My teaching." (*A.S.* pp. 148–49)

Inscription painted on Crown of Torah above Ark (east arch panel)

"Crown of the Torah."

Inscription in a Medallion above a Painted Elephant (southeast arch panel)

Prayer recited before the Torah scroll is removed from the Ark, prior to reading of the Torah:

"When the Ark was to set out, Moses would say: Advance, O Lord! May Your enemies be scattered and may Your foes flee before You! For instruction shall come forth from Zion, the word of the Lord from Jerusalem.

   "And then one says [the prayer] 'Blessed be the name of the Lord. . . .'" (*A.S.* pp. 138–39)

The last sentence, partially from the *Zohar*, could either be a directive to the congregation or instructions copied (inadvertently?) by the artist from a prayer book.

Inscription above a Painting of an Ox (Behemoth) (southwest arch panel)

A portion of a prayer for sustenance

"Cast your burden on the Lord and He will sustain you [Psalms 55:23]. Mark the blameless, note the upright, for there is a future for the man of integrity [Psalms 37:37]. Trust in the Lord and do good, abide in the land and remain loyal [Psalms 37:3]. Behold the God Who gives me triumph! I am confident, unafraid; for the Lord is my strength and might, and He has been my deliverance." (Isaiah 12:2)

Inscriptions at the Junction of the Lower and Upper Tiers of the Ceiling (continuous band on four walls)

[East wall] "Said R. Levi, wherever there is a house of [. . .] [Said Resh Lakish: Whosoever has a synagogue in his home town but does not enter it] [north wall] to pray is called an evil neighbor [Bab. Talmud, Berachot 8a]. Said R. Yohanan: when the Holy One, blessed be He, enters [west wall] a synagogue and does not find there ten men, He immediately becomes angry [Bab. Talmud, Berachot 6b]. We have learned that Abba Benjamin [south wall] says: A man's prayer is heard nowhere but in the synagogue, as Scripture says, 'to hear the cry . . . [illegible]." (Bab. Talmud, Berachot 6a, I Kings 8:28)

Zodiac Figure Inscriptions, Upper Tier of the Ceiling

Each zodiac figure is given the month of the Jewish year with which it is associated.

(East)	Sign of Tammuz—Cancer
	Sign of Av—Leo
	Sign of Elul—Virgo
(North)	Sign of Tishri—Libra
	Sign of Heshvan—Scorpio
	Sign of Kislev—Sagittarius
(West)	Sign of Tevet—Capricorn
	Sign of Shevat—Aquarius
	Sign of Adar—Pisces
(South)	Sign of Nisan—Aries
	Sign of Iyyar—Taurus
	Sign of Sivan—Gemini

1. Synagogue and Community

1. Because the opening of this book is a narrative intended to set the stage for later arguments, the sources used in chapter 1 are not cited. The ideas and sources for this chapter are referenced in notes found in the following chapters. A large portion of the material in chapter 1 is based on archival sources in Lviv, Ukraine; a site investigation by the author in Gwoździec (Gvozdets), Ukraine; and documentation of wooden synagogues found in Polish sources, particularly in the works of Maria and Kazimierz Piechotka.

2. Conceptions and Misconceptions

1. The theories of material cultural studies that underlie this book are analyzed in Henry Glassie, *Passing the Time in Ballymenone*, pp. 721–32; Dell Upton, "The Power of Things," pp. 262–79; and Dell Upton, "Outside the Academy," pp. 199–213. I have been particularly influenced by the works of Henry Glassie, especially *Folk Housing in Middle Virginia* and *Passing the Time in Ballymenone*.

2. Many themes in this chapter parallel Barbara Kirshenblatt-Gimblett's "Introduction" to *Life Is with People*, by Mark Zborowski and Elizabeth Herzog, pp. ix–xlviii. She writes an authoritative summary of Jewish-American attitudes toward pre-Holocaust, Eastern-European Jewish life and especially toward the interpretation of the shtetl.

3. The difficulty of analyzing pre-Holocaust Jewish history from a post-Holocaust historical perspective is sensitively presented by Steven J. Zipperstein in *Imagining Russian Jewry: Memory, History, Identity*, pp. 88–105. On the postmodern critique of historiography, see Hayden V. White, *Tropics of Discourse: Essays in Cultural Criticism*, and Michel Foucalt, *Archaeology of Knowledge*.

4. On the subsequent influences of *Fiddler on the Roof*, see Seth Wolitz, "The Americanization of Tevye or Boarding the Jewish Mayflower," pp. 525–36; Steven J. Zipperstein, *Imagining Russian Jewry*, pp. 31–39; Richard Altman, *The Making of a Musical*, and David G. Roskies, *The Jewish Search for a Usable Past*, pp. 9–16.

5. There has been uncritical acceptance of endemic Jewish impoverishment in the small shtetl towns of Eastern Europe. Even very good historical studies may assume a uniform decline in the quality of small-town life for Polish and Russian Jews after about 1650, as, for example, Robert M. Seltzer, *Jewish People, Jewish Thought*, pp. 480–496. These assumptions are frequently based on extremely biased earlier studies, for example, S. M. Dubnow, *History of the Jews in Russia and Poland*, vol. 1, pp. 139–187. During the last fifty years, photographic publications depicting the poverty of Eastern-European Jewish communities have also reinforced popular and scholarly perceptions of perpetual poverty in these regions; see Lucjan Dobroszycki and Barbara Kirshenblatt-Gimblett, *Image Before My Eyes*, pp. 39–101. For Polish views of the shtetl, see Eugenia Prokopowna, "The Image of the Shtetl in Polish Literature," pp. 129–142.

6. On Jewish memory of Eastern Europe and the issue of geographic placelessness, especially following the Holocaust, see Barbara Kirshenblatt-Gimblett, "Introduction" to *Life Is with People*, pp. xiv–xix, xxxiii–xxxiv, and Steven J. Zipperstein, *Imagining Russian Jewry*, pp. 16–39. Further complicating the issue of Jewish geographic memory are Gentile perceptions of Jewish mobility, as illustrated in cultural and antisemitic stereotypes like the "Wandering Jew"; for example, see Galit Hasan-Rokem and Alan Dundes, eds., *The Wandering Jew: Essays in the Interpretation of a Christian Legend*.

7. Romantic imagery of the shtetl was popularized in the influential *Life Is with People* as analyzed in Barbara Kirshenblatt-Gimblett's "Introduction" to the book, pp. ix–xlviii. Romantic and nostalgic themes of the Eastern-European shtetl are also analyzed in David G. Roskies, *The Jewish Search for a Usable Past*, pp. 2–16, 41–66, and Richard Altman, *The Making of a Musical*.

8. On the shtetl myths of cultural unity and homogeneous isolation, see Kirshenblatt-Gimblett, "Introduction" to *Life Is with People*, pp. xx–xxii; Steven J. Zipperstein, *Imagining Russian Jewry*, pp. 42–62; and David G. Roskies, *The Jewish Search for a Usable Past*, pp. 46–57. On legends from the shtetl as ethnographic sources, see Jack Kugelmass and Jonathan Boyarin, *From a Ruined Garden*, pp. 1–19; Lucy S. Dawidowicz, *The Golden Tradition*, pp. 5–90; and Diane K. Roskies and David G. Roskies,

The Shtetl Book. Numerous photographic surveys reinforce a mixture of romantic and impoverishment imagery, for example, Zvi Gitelman, *A Century of Ambivalence*; Marion Wiesel, ed., *To Give Them Light*; Lucjan Dobroszycki and Barbara Kirshenblatt-Gimblett, *Images Before My Eyes*; and Roman Vishniac, *Polish Jews*. Other sources emphasize a stark imagery of Jewish impoverishment and destruction following the Holocaust, for example, Earl Vinecour, *Polish Jews*; Shlomit Shakked, *Poland: Aperture to a World Laid Waste*; Małgorzata Niezabitowska, *Remnants: The Last Jews in Poland*; and Yaffa Eliach, *There Once Was a World*. Abraham Joshua Heschel gives a bittersweet summary of this lost world in "The Eastern European Era in Jewish History," pp. 1–21. An extensive collection of art and photographs of Jewish life survives in Polish collections, for example: Halina Nelken, *Images of a Lost World*.

9. On the issues of Jewish community separation from and integration with surrounding Eastern-European cultures, see M. J. Rosman, "A Minority Views the Majority," pp. 39–47; Jacob Katz, *Exclusiveness and Tolerance*, pp. 132–68; Aleksander Hertz, *The Jews in Polish Culture*. A summary of Polish perceptions of Jewish community "separateness" is given in Harold B. Segel, ed., *Stranger in Our Midst*.

10. A negative impression of Eastern-European shtetl Jewry, the "Ostjuden," was conveyed by nineteenth-century rationalist historians and writers such as Heinrich Graetz, *History of the Jews*, vol. 5, pp. 51–55, 199–231, 375–94; S. M. Dubnow, *History of the Jews in Russia and Poland*, vol. 1, pp. 198–241, and vol. 2, pp. 11–139; Karl Emil Franzos, *The Jews of Barnow*, continued by twentieth-century historians Solomon Grayzel, *A History of the Jews*, pp. 505–20, and Howard Morley Sachar, *The Course of Modern Jewish History*, pp. 25–35. Disdain for the Ostjuden should also be seen in the wider context of Western-European skepticism and criticism of Eastern Europe, for example, Larry Wolf, *Inventing Eastern Europe*, pp. 1–143; and Daniel Chirot, ed., *The Origins of Backwardness in Eastern Europe*. Eastern-European Jews were also negatively portrayed as "Orientals," as for example, in Paul Mendes-Flohr, "*Fin-de-Siecle* Orientalism, the *Ostjuden* and the Aesthetics of Jewish Self-Affirmation."

11. A central component of Haskalah criticism of Eastern-European Orthodoxy was the implicit or explicit link with ignorance and poverty, especially the association of Jewish mysticism with cultural backwardness; see Heinrich Graetz, *History of the Jews*, vol. 5, pp. 51–85, 199–231, 374–94; and S. M. Dubnow, *History of the Jews in Russia and Poland*, pp. 199–241. Recent studies have challenged these interpretations, for example, M. J. Rosman, *Lords' Jews*, p. 211, concludes that early Hasidism began in flourishing times, not amidst extreme poverty and persecution. Summarizing the findings of several scholars, Gerson Cohen, *Messianic Postures of Ashkenazim and Sephardim (Prior to Sabbethai Zevi)*, states, "For, if there is any

one conclusion that the data force upon us, it is that, contrary to the popular impression, there is no discernible connection between persecution and messianic movements." Cohen observes that Jewish messianic movements were not "the religion of the oppressed." After listing the major persecutions and expulsions, he concludes that these tragedies "did not generate a single messianic movement," and paradoxically, the major messianic movements "were undertaken in areas and periods of relative stability." See note 6, chapter 4.

12. Joseph Gutmann has explored the relationship between Jewish art and the Second Commandment in many publications, including "The Second Commandment and the Image in Judaism," pp. 1–14. Other studies include Lionel Kochan, *Beyond the Graven Image*, pp. 3–52; Ernest Namenyi, *The Essence of Jewish Art*, pp. 1–24; Vivian B. Mann, *Jewish Texts on the Visual Arts*, pp. 1–18. Kalman P. Bland summarizes the premodern myths of Jewish anti-iconism in *The Artless Jew*.

13. On the conflicting sources of approval, disapproval, restriction, and caution about synagogue art in Jewish literature, see Carol Krinsky, *Synagogues of Europe*, pp. 56–60; Dan Urman and Paul V. M. Flesher, "Ancient Synagogues," pp. xxxiii–xxxvi; Rachel Hachlili, "Synagogues in the Land of Israel," pp. 96–129.

14. On the changing styles and periods in the art and decoration of synagogues, see Carol Krinsky, *Synagogues of Europe*, pp. 73–96, and Samuel D. Gruber, *Synagogues*.

15. The division between medieval and modern periods can be found in many histories of Judaism before 1980, for example, H. H. Ben-Sasson, ed., *A History of the Jewish People*, and Solomon Grayzel, *A History of the Jews*.

16. On the lack of attention to the practical performance of Jewish religion and daily life, see Zeev Gries, *Conduct Literature*; Chava Weissler, *Voices of the Matriarchs*, pp. 54–59, 89–93, including a review of relevant sources, note 2, p. 192; and Barbara Kirshenblatt-Gimblett, "Introduction" to *Life Is with People*, pp. xiv–xix. For an attempt to formulate a definition of popular Jewish culture, see Dov Noy, "Is There a Jewish Folk Religion?" pp. 273–285. Stephen D. Benin explores the meaning of Jewish popular culture in "A Hen Crowing like a Cock," pp. 261–81. Benin reviews the difficulties of applying the term "popular culture" to Judaism's text-centered, scholarly religious, and communal governance system. He also includes comparisons to medieval Christian culture, where he finds a greater socioeconomic disparity between laity and clergy and between aristocracy and peasantry. He correctly argues that a traditional "two-tiered" medieval Christian approach, contrasting elite and popular religion, should not be applied to Jewish communities, where he finds social organizations that recognize "a broad, complex, and seemingly continuous spectrum of religious sensibility, knowledge, level of practice, and commitment . . ." (p. 269).

17. The origins of the Hasidic movement during the middle

of the eighteenth century have received intensive study, and new research has extended the development period and widened the scope of the initial movement beyond the circle of the Ba'al Shem Tov, as in Joseph Weiss, *Studies in Eastern European Jewish Mysticism* pp. 27–42; Louis Jacobs, *Hasidic Prayer*, pp. 8–9, and Rachel Elior, *The Paradoxical Ascent to God*, pp. 8–9. There is little information, however, about the spread of Hasidism to the general population of the Jewish people and the resulting influence on popular culture. For example, when, where, and to what degree did a certain percentage of Jewish society adopt Hasidic ideas? From the sources available, it appears that the acceptance of Hasidism by large numbers of Jews occurred some time after initial organized opposition to Hasidism began in about 1772; see Gershom Scholem, *Major Trends in Jewish Mysticism*, pp. 323, 328, 337. Because interior-vaulted wooden synagogues became popular in the communities of eastern Poland in the first half of the eighteenth century, before popular acceptance of Hasidism, the term "pre-Hasidic" is applied to these Jewish communities.

18. The strengths and weaknesses of Polish historiography are reviewed in Piotr S. Wandycz, "Historiography of the Countries of Eastern Europe," pp. 1011–25. Poland's minority populations or "territorial minorities" have generally been under-represented in Polish sources.

19. The political history surrounding the Polish partitions dominates seventeenth- and eighteenth-century Polish historiography, as analyzed in Piotr S. Wandycz, "Historiography," pp. 1011–18. For the Ukrainian interpretation of this era, see Stephen Velychenko, *National History as Cultural Process*, pp. 3–15, 47–78, 141–64, 214–29.

20. In their otherwise detailed analysis of the eighteenth century, Polish historians have not generally emphasized the anomaly of magnate prosperity during the declines of the partition era. See Aleksander Gieysztor, *History of Poland*, pp. 272–319. Norman Davies gives more attention to this issue in *God's Playground, A History of Poland*, pp. 363–72, 525–30, and Norman Davies, *Heart of Europe*, pp. 316–54. Magnate prosperity is analyzed from Jewish community perspective by M. J. Rosman, *Lords' Jews*, pp. 23–35.

21. The collective works of M. J. Rosman and Gershon Hundert and the journal *Polin* exemplify some of the finest efforts to combine both Polish and Jewish historical perspectives and sources. For ethnographic studies about Polish Jews before the First World War, see Olga Goldberg-Mulkiewicz, *Ethnographic Topics Relating to Jews in Polish Studies*, pp. 9–25.

22. One of the most challenging themes in Polish/Jewish historical scholarship has been the definition of Jewish minority culture separation and/or integration with Polish majority culture, as attempted, for example, in Aleksander Hertz, *The Jews in Polish Culture*, and Jacob Katz, *Exclusiveness and Tolerance*. Current studies generally recognize a greater degree of social and economic integration than in previous studies; see Gershon David Hundert, *Polish Private Town*, and M. J. Rosman, *Lords' Jews*.

23. On the complexities of pre- and post-Holocaust Polish/Jewish identity, see Michael C. Steinlauf, "Whose Poland? Returning to Aleksander Hertz," pp. 131–42; and Michael C. Steinlauf, *Bondage to the Dead*, pp. 1–22. On the religious dimensions of Polish/Jewish reconciliation, see Byron L. Sherwin, *Sparks Amidst the Ashes*. David Roskies reviews the problems of multiple interpretive frameworks, explaining how "a free market of pasthoods" hampers Jewish historical study, in *Jewish Search for a Usable Past*, pp. 14–16. Similar issues are explored from a Polish perspective: Joseph L. Lichten, "Polish Americans and American Jews," pp. 52–62; and Krzysztof Śliwiński, "Towards a Polish-Jewish Dialogue," pp. xvii–xxvii.

24. On the inappropriateness of conceiving current historical study outside an awareness of the Holocaust, see Steven J. Zipperstein, *Imagining Russian Jewry*, pp. 88–105. While I acknowledge that current discourse unavoidably structures the understandings of the past, as argued from different perspectives by David Lowenthal, *The Past Is a Foreign Country*, Hayden V. White, *Content of the Form: Narrative Discourse and Historical Representation*, and Peter Novick, *That Noble Dream*, pp. 415–629; research for this book is grounded on the necessity to maximize the insights of historical context to inform theorization about the past, as outlined in Henry Glassie, *Passing the Time in Ballymenone*, pp. 648–55; and Michael Baxandall, *Patterns of Intention*, pp. 12–40, 105–37.

25. Because the following summary of reasons for building the wooden synagogues is presented as a group of introductory hypotheses, this section does not contain scholarly notes. All sources supporting these hypotheses are cited in the notes to the following chapters.

3. Architecture

1. On the discourses between majority and minority cultures applicable to the eighteenth-century Jewish community of Gwoździec, see Homi Bhabha, *The Location of Culture*.

2. An extensive literature traces the transition from Temple to synagogue and the development of the early synagogue. See Dan Urman and Paul V. M. Flesher, eds., *Ancient Synagogues: Historical Analysis and Archaeological Discovery*, vols. 1 and 2, including a summary of related literature, "Ancient Synagogues—A Reader's Guide," pp. xvii–xxxvii; and Steven Fine, ed., *Sacred Realm*. On the spiritual consequence of the change from Temple to synagogue, see Arthur Green, "Sabbath as Temple," pp. 290–92.

3. On the importance of the central axis or axis mundi as the central principle for organizing religious space, see Mircea Eliade, *The Sacred and the Profane*, pp. 33–44.

Eliade's ideas are placed within a Jewish perspective by Arthur Green, "The Zaddiq as Axis Mundi in Later Judaism," pp. 327–48.

4. On the development of the ark, see Carol Krinsky, *Synagogues of Europe*, pp. 24–26; Lee I. Levine, *The Ancient Synagogue*, pp. 319–323; and Joseph Gutmann, *Sacred Images*, pp. 22–29.

5. In some early synagogues, the main doorway faced east. By the fourth century the location of the ark and its niche at the center of the eastern wall became standardized. See Joan R. Branham, "Sacred Space under Erasure in Ancient Synagogues and Early Churches," *The Art Bulletin*, pp. 383–85; and David Amit, "Architectural Plans of Synagogues in the Southern Judean Hills and the 'Halakah,'" pp. 129–56.

6. For more on the eastern, Jerusalem-facing orientation of the synagogue's central axis, see Franz Landsberger, "The Sacred Direction in Synagogue and Church," pp. 239–64; and Amit, "Architectural Plans of Synagogues," pp. 136–56.

7. The reading table is located at or very near the center of more than half the wooden synagogues showing bimahs in their plan. See Maria and Kazimierz Piechotka, *Bramy Nieba: Bóżnice drewniane*. I wish to thank David Kaufmann for identifying this characteristic of Polish synagogues. Two slightly different locations for the bimah are shown in drawings of the Gwoździec Synagogue in Maria and Kazimierz Piechotka, *Wooden Synagogues*, figs. 41 and 43, unnumbered pages; and Maria and Kazimierz Piechotka, *Bramy Nieba, Bóżnice drewniane*, figs. 311, 314, pp. 208, 210. Consequently the reading table, located on the portion of the bimah's platform closest to the ark, would be centered in one sectional drawing and almost centered in the other.

8. On the relationships between arks and altars, see Maria and Kazimierz Piechotka, *Bramy Nieba: Bóżnice murowane*, pp. 81–89; Maria and Kazimierz Piechotka, *Bramy Nieba: Bóżnice drewniane*, pp. 94–105, and Richard I. Cohen, *Jewish Icons: Art and Society in Modern Europe*, p. 78.

9. On the relationship of the ark to the bimah, see Maria and Kazimierz Piechotka, *Bramy Nieba: Bóżnice drewniane*, pp. 25–34, 81–95, and Carol Krinsky, *Synagogues of Europe*, pp. 21–27. See also Arthur Green, "Sabbath as Temple," pp. 290–92, and Robert Goldenberg, "The Broken Axis," pp. 869–82. Steven Fine has written about the transference of holiness and sanctity from the Temple to the synagogue in *The Holy Place*. The complex relationship between the Tabernacle and the Temple(s) as central symbols in Judaism is analyzed in Jon D. Levenson, "The Jerusalem Temple in Devotional and Visionary Experience," pp. 32–61, and Joan R. Branham, "Vicarious Sacrality," pp. 319–345.

10. On the comparison of spatial axis and entry systems in synagogues and churches, see Franz Landsberger, "The Sacred Direction in Synagogue and Church," pp. 239–64; and Jonathan Z. Smith, *To Take Place*, pp. 45–95. On the overall relationship of the performance of liturgy to the spatial environment of the synagogue, see Arthur Green, "Sabbath as Temple," pp. 287–305.

11. The "almost square" plans of the wooden synagogues are documented in Maria and Kazimierz Piechotka's *Wooden Synagogues* (unnumbered pages accompanying town names, between pp. 51 and 195) and their *Bramy Nieba: Bóżnice drewniane*, pp. 173–382. These were not failed attempts by their builders to realize a square plan, as is often assumed by historians and architects. This common error is reinforced by current Cartesian and Euclidean spatial terminology, which fails to provide neutral, nonpejorative terms for these "asymmetrical," "irregular" plans. The wooden synagogue builders possessed sufficient technical skills to produce perfectly square measurements, and they did so when they desired. The consistency of the "almost square" plans in ratios of 9:10 and 10:11 suggests that design determinants, as yet unknown, repeatedly shaped most synagogue plans toward a consistent, nonequal-sided, "almost square" arrangement. Interestingly, the 10:11 ratio of length to width is the same recorded in fifteen synagogues in Galilee dating from the third to the fourth centuries c.e., see Michael Avi-Yonah, "Synagogue," pp. 595–96. See note 85, chapter 3.

12. The square plan has been used in sacred and monumental buildings of most world cultures from prehistoric eras to the present; see Spiro Kostof, *A History of Architecture*, pp. 20–95. The square plan and the cubic volume in Jewish architecture occur in the specifications for the Temple and are assumed, but not specified in the Tabernacle; see "Tabernacle," *Anchor Bible Dictionary*, pp. 295–96. Both Temple and Tabernacle specifications are repeated and combined in a variety of later sources, from the Temple visions of Ezekiel (Ezekiel 40–48) to many variations in the *Zohar*. The Enlightenment focus on the Jewish Temple as an architectural model also influenced later synagogue designs. See Lola Kantor Kazovsky, "Piranesi and Villalpando: The Concept of the Temple in European Architectural Theory," pp. 226–44. See notes 37 and 85, chapter 3.

13. On the Italian Baroque influences on Polish architecture and planning, see Adam Miłobędzki, *Architektura polska XVII wieku*. For the influence of foreign, neoclassical architecture treatises on Polish architecture, see Adam Małkiewicz, *Teoria Architektury w Nowożytnym Piśmiennictwie Polskim*, and Zygmunt Mieszkowski, *Podstawowe Problemy Architektury w Polskich Traktatach od połowy XVI do początku XIX w.* The absence of formal geometrical designs, such as the square plan, in the design traditions of Eastern-European vernacular architecture is cited in Adam Miłobędzki, "Architecture in Wood," pp. 185–86. The Piechotkas find some basis for the presence of non-vernacular, formal, geometric design composition in the elevations for some wooden synagogues. See Maria and

Kazimierz Piechotka, *Bramy Nieba: Bóżnice drewniane*, pp. 75–77.

14. Zofia Puzyna's support for the construction of the synagogue is cited in a letter by Karol Maszkowski, dated September 4, 1899, in records for the town of Gwoździec found in the Bernardine Archives, Lviv, Ukraine, Maszkowski letters file, Archiwum Polskiej Akademii Nauk, Krakow.

15. Vernacular architecture designers typically incorporate new ideas from elite or avant-garde sources through selective borrowing. For example, the designers of the Gwoździec Synagogue integrated some of the most up-to-date Baroque features of surface plasticity into the curving cupola, yet they also maintained most traditional characteristics of their regional wooden buildings. The issues of borrowing and creativity within vernacular tradition are addressed by Henry Glassie, *Folk Housing in Middle Virginia*, pp. 66–113, and Thomas C. Hubka, "Just Folks Designing," pp. 426–32.

16. On the use of the Ottoman/Turkish tents, see Maria and Kazimierz Piechotka's *Bramy Nieba: Bóżnice drewniane*, pp. 120–33, and "Polichromie polskich bóżnic drewnianych," pp. 74–76. On the history of European perception of the Islamic world, see Edward W. Said, *Orientalism*, and Timothy Mitchell, *Colonizing Egypt*.

17. On the European depiction of Jerusalem as a European city, see numerous articles in Bianca Kuhnel, ed., *The Real and Ideal Jerusalem in Jewish, Christian, and Islamic Art*, especially, Jonathan J. G. Alexander, "'Jerusalem the Golden': Image and Myth in the Middle Ages in Western Europe," pp. 255–64; Martina Pippal, "Relations of Time and Space: The Temple of Jerusalem as the *Domus Ecclesiae* in the Carolingian Period," pp. 67–78; and Bianca Kuhnel, "The Use and Abuse of Jerusalem," pp. xix–xxxviii. The wooden synagogue painter Eliezer Sussmann, from Brody, Ukraine, depicted Jerusalem as a European city in several German synagogue paintings; see Iris Fishof, "Depictions of Jerusalem by Eliezer Sussman of Brody," pp. 67–82. See note 10, chapter 4.

18. On Sarmatian culture within the Polish aristocracy, see Michael J. Mikoś, *Polish Baroque and Enlightenment Literature* pp. 44–46, and Norman Davies, *God's Playground: A History of Poland*, vol. 1, pp. 201–55.

19. On Sobieski's siege of Vienna and the captured Turkish tents, see Norman Davies, *God's Playground*, pp. 473–89. On the later influences of these tents, see Piechotka, *Bramy Nieba: Bóżnice drewniane*, pp. 120–33. On the significance of the Ottoman tent, see Cenap Curuk and Ersin Cicekciler, *Ornekleriyle Turk Cadirlari*, pp. 1–41.

20. On tent manufacture and trading associated with Jewish merchants in the Lviv region, see Maria and Kazimierz Piechotka's "Polychrome Paintings," pp. 74–76, and *Bramy Nieba: Bóżnice drewniane*, pp. 122–28.

21. Compared to many types of Eastern-European churches and to much of the world's religious architecture, the premodern prayer hall, the principal space of Jewish worship, is noteworthy for the absence of major centralized domes, transept crossings, and centralized vaulted cupolas. This conspicuous spatial difference is perhaps a reflection of the nonsacred precinct of synagogues where, as far as is known, dramatic cupolas or domes were not constructed before the modern era. This is why the introduction of the centralized wooden cupola in Polish wooden synagogues at the beginning of the eighteenth century was such an innovation. To clarify the distinctiveness of the central vaulting in wooden synagogues like Gwoździec, it should be noted that masonry vaulting had been employed in synagogues since the Medieval period, and this practice was continued in Poland. See Maria and Kazimierz Piechotka, *Bramy Nieba: Bóżnice murowane*, pp. 25–81. A distinction should be made, however, between the groin or barrel vaults, common to masonry synagogues, and the distinctive central cupolas of the later wooden synagogues like Gwoździec. See note 103, chapter 3.

22. Little information is available on the spatial performance of daily worship in the pre-Hasidic, Polish Ashkenazi community. There is no ethnographic study approaching, for example, the completeness of Samuel C. Heilman's study of a modern Orthodox congregation in *Synagogue Life*.

23. The painted arches behind the built-in seats at Gwoździec Synagogue are faded and only partially visible. In the neighboring Jabłonów Synagogue, which closely follows the same layout as Gwoździec, there were fifty-three arches painted above the built-in benches lining the prayer hall; see Jabłonów Synagogue drawings by Ludwik Wierzbicki, 1891, *Sprawozdania Komisji do Badań Historii Sztuki w Polsce*.

24. Built-in benches lining the perimeter of the synagogue are a tradition dating to the earliest recorded synagogues; see Lee I. Levine, *The Ancient Synagogue*, pp. 313–16, 446–47. There is a remote possibility that the benches could have been added later, but the artistic style of the arches painted above the benches, containing dated donor inscriptions, suggests that the benches were installed before 1720.

25. The primacy of synagogue seats along the eastern wall nearest the ark is cited in many sources, including Levine, *Ancient Synagogue*, pp. 408, 447. The assigning and purchasing of seats in Polish synagogues is also cited in many sources, for example, Nisson E. Shulman, *Authority and Community*, pp. 20–21, and Daniel Tollet, "The Private Life of Polish Jews in the Vasa Period," pp. 58–59.

26. On the scarcity of individually owned prayer books before 1750, see Stefan C. Reif, *Hebrew Prayer*, pp. 215–38; Elchanan Reiner, "The Ashkenazi Elite at the Beginning of the Modern Era," pp. 90–98; and Stefan C. Reif, *Shabbethai Sofer and his Prayer-book*, pp. 39–52. See note 59, chapter 4.

27. On synagogue lecterns and individual prayer book stands, see Zussia Efron, "Carved Wooden Lecterns and Torah Pointers," pp. 115–119.

28. The evaluation of photographs for evidence of spatial usage poses many difficulties. The most serious problem for this study is that the photographs of the Gwoździec Synagogue were taken more than a century and a half after it was built and remodeled. Yet if my analysis is correct, the prayer hall, and perhaps its pattern of community worship, may have remained relatively unchanged. In other words, as we look at early-twentieth-century photographs of the prayer hall, there is the possibility that we may be observing the room much as it was used and decorated in 1731, the year of its final remodeling. Another interpretive problem is the analysis of the nonregular furniture arrangement in the prayer halls of Polish wooden synagogues. The furniture arrangement seen in early-twentieth-century photographs could be interpreted as either a sign of continuous community usage or of carelessness and disorder, depending upon the opinion of the viewer. Deciding whether such photographs of prayer halls demonstrate community piety or decline marks a significant fault line in Christian-Jewish discourse. The long-term Christian and later European Enlightenment evaluation of Jewish worship as unsystematic and disordered followed a standard, dominant-culture, antisemitic critique, as outlined in Janusz Tazbir, "Images of the Jew in the Polish Commonwealth," pp. 18–29, and Aleksander Hertz, *The Jews in Polish Culture*, pp. 59–85. For late medieval, Christian depictions and misrepresentations of Jewish worship, see Heinz Schreckenberg, *The Jews in Christian Art*, and Richard I. Cohen, *Jewish Icons*, pp. 16–25. Christian interpreters generally failed to understand that the highly organized patterns of Jewish liturgy allowed for variation in individual spatial movement and expression. This was especially true in comparison to the more uniform and regimented practices of congregational assembly in Christian worship during most periods. Current patterns of Orthodox spatial worship are sensitively analyzed in Samuel C. Heilman, *Synagogue Life*.

29. For the range of functions the support rooms served, see Maria and Kazimierz Piechotka, *Wooden Synagogues*, pp. 35–36 and, listed by synagogue, pp. 196–215.

30. Little precise information about Gwoździec's Jewish community facilities and buildings exists before the nineteenth century. The depiction of Gwoździec's environment is supplemented by descriptions of similarly scaled communities, including the author's survey of neighboring towns such as Chodorów, Poland, and detailed information from two larger towns, Opatów, Poland, in Gershon David Hundert, *The Jews in a Polish Private Town*, pp. 85–93; and Międzybóż, Ukraine, in M. J. Rosman, *Lords' Jews*, pp. 41–73. The diagrams and maps showing Gwoździec in 1731 were extrapolated from several nineteenth- and early-twentieth-century maps in the Central State Historical Archives of Ukraine, Lviv; Mendel Zilbur, ed., *The Gwoździec Memory Book*, and site investigation in Gwoździec, Ukraine. Town maps from other Jewish community "memory books," often drawn from memory, also provided useful comparative information about the geography of the small Jewish towns; see for example, the map of the shtetl Tishevits, in Diane K. Roskies and David G. Roskies, *The Shtetl Book*, p. 2.

31. On the issue of women's role in the synagogue, see Emily Taitz, "Women's Voices, Women's Prayers," pp. 59–72. Chava Weissler has skillfully demonstrated that various traditions of women's worship existed alongside the standard male service, in *Voices of the Matriarchs*, and "Prayers in Yiddish and the Religious World of Ashkenazi Women."

32. The emergence of women's galleries in Polish synagogues is analyzed by Maria and Kazimierz Piechotka, *Bramy Nieba, Bóżnice murowane*, pp. 96–100, and Carol Krinsky, *Synagogues of Europe*, pp. 28–32. A commonly recorded practice was the addition of a second-floor women's gallery above the entrance to an existing wooden synagogue; for example, the synagogues at Zabłudów, Przedbórz, and Grodno, in Maria and Kazimierz Piechotka, *Wooden Synagogues*, unnumbered pages by town name, between pp. 51 and 195.

33. Before the nineteenth century, wooden synagogues are not known to have contained any heating devices—fireplaces, masonry stoves, or chimneys. In a few masonry synagogues, masonry stoves heated rooms attached to the main prayer hall. For example, two chimneys in attached structures can be seen in a photograph of the Pińsk Synagogue; see Maria and Kazimierz Piechotka, *Bramy Nieba, Bóżnice murowane*, fig. 241, p. 196. However, most of these chimneys and stoves were not original, but nineteenth-century additions. In the case of wooden synagogues, the highly flammable structure generally prohibited the use of any heating devices. A twentieth-century photograph shows a metal stove pipe extending from the roof of Gwoździec's masonry addition (see fig. 20); both the stove and the annex building were later additions. Interior photographs of the Gwoździec prayer hall also reveal what are probably portable coal or charcoal heating stands, indicating a modern, late-nineteenth- or twentieth-century method of temporary, portable heating (see fig. 114). Typically, however, even throughout the modern period, the prayer halls of most wooden synagogues were unheated. Perhaps only a smaller beit midrash (house of study) would have been heated.

34. See Isidor Kaufmann's *Beth Hamidrash*, a painting and watercolor study, in *Bilder des Wiener Malers*, G. Tobias Natter, ed., pp. 266–71. Kaufmann frequently used human models from his Vienna studio to complete his shtetl paintings. Nevertheless, he was deeply impressed by the Gwoździec and Jabłonów synagogues, and he spent considerable time in both prayer halls, as his extremely accurate paintings of both synagogue interiors reveal (pp. 308–13). Kaufmann's romantic depiction of Jewish culture is analyzed in Richard I. Cohen, *Jewish Icons*, pp. 171–75.

35. The limited documentation for Gwoździec does not reveal whether there were alternative synagogues or houses of study. I speculate that, when the Gwoździec Synagogue remodeling was completed in 1731, there were no other synagogues or "competing minyan" until later in the eighteenth century. In 1741, the larger town of Międzybóż, 200 miles northeast of Gwoździec, had several competing, pre-Hasidic synagogues associated with workers guilds; see Moshe Rosman, *Founder of Hasidism*, pp. 90–94. In smaller communities such as Gwoździec, with no urban guild organizations, multiple synagogues probably began with the arrival of Hasidism, usually after the late 1700s. It is interesting to note that, by 1930, there were four Hasidic houses of prayer in Gwoździec; see Mendel Zilbur, *The Gwoździec Memory Book*, p. 46.

36. Based on limited sources, I hypothesize a basic social and religious unity within the pre-Hasidic, small-town community of Gwoździec. I am aware, however, that such a romantic image of Jewish community homogeneity, including an exclusive focus on its single synagogue, has been largely discredited in recent studies, for example, Barbara Kirshenblatt-Gimblett, "Introduction," *Life Is with People*, pp. ix–xix. Much of this scholarship, however, is based on later, post-partition sources. For the pre-Hasidic, pre-Jewish Enlightenment community of Gwoździec, finishing what was almost certainly its only synagogue in 1729, the image of a largely unified community seems largely accurate.

37. See note 68, chapter 3.

38. On the overlapping boundaries between ethnic/religious neighborhoods in Polish small towns, see Moshe Rosman, *Founder of Hasidism*, p. 160. Rosman writes that, in 1730, in the town of Międzybóż (containing a similar percentage of Jewish residents as Gwoździec) "more than a third of the Jewish householders (75 out of 204) had at least one Christian neighbor." On the unified pattern of spatial and social order in the small Jewish town, see Maria and Kazimierz Piechotka, "Jewish Districts in the Spatial Structure of Polish Towns," pp. 24–39; and Harold Brodsky, "A Map of the Shtetl Vinograd," pp. 349–55.

39. On the ancient practice of locating a synagogue near water, see Isaac Levy, *The Synagogue*, p. 31; and Flavius Josephus, *The Works of Flavius Josephus*, vol. 14, p. 258.

40. On the spatial pattern of Polish towns, see Maria and Kazimierz Piechotka, "Jewish Districts," pp. 24–39. On common commercial and residential architecture often inhabited by Jews in the small towns of the eastern provinces, see Alla Sokolowa, "Architecture in the Small Towns of Western Podolia," pp. 53–82; and Alla Sokolowa, "Architectural Space of the Shtetl-Street-House," pp. 35–85.

41. On restrictions placed on Jewish residents in Polish towns and cities, see Gershon David Hundert, "Jewish Urban Residence in the Polish Commonwealth in the Early Modern Period," pp. 26–31.

42. See *Słownik Geograficzny Królestwa Polskiego*, p. 924, and *Pinkas Hakehillot: Encyclopaedia of Jewish Communities*, p. 135.

43. Between 1889 and 1939, Gwoździec was visited by most of the major prewar investigators of wooden synagogues, but little ethnographic or local historical information was recorded; see Maria and Kazimierz Piechotka, "Polichromie polskich bóżnic," pp. 75–76, and *Bramy Nieba, Bóżnice drewniane*, pp. 208–12. Several legends about the synagogue and community were recorded in Mendel Zilbur, *The Gwoździec Memory Book*, pp. 42–44. For example, a legend is told of the Baal Shem Tov's visit to the Gwoździec Synagogue and his meeting with Rabbi Schor. Although many legends of the Besht (Baal Shem Tov) have little basis in fact, it is interesting to note that in the 1730s the then unheralded Besht passed through the Gwoździec region on his way from Kutów and Tluste to his future home in Międzybóż; see Evyatar Friesel, *Atlas of Modern Jewish History*, pp. 50–51. It is not inconceivable that a wandering, charismatic preacher would have met with the up-and-coming, soon-to-be well-known Rabbi Schor of Gwoździec. Their meeting was said to have taken place within the synagogue. If such a meeting did take place, it may have occurred under the same ceiling that is the focus of this book.

44. On misconceptions about the role of the architect in vernacular building, see Henry Glassie, *Folk Housing*, pp. 19–40, and Thomas C. Hubka, "Just Folks Designing," pp. 429–32.

45. On the role of tradition in vernacular building design, see Henry Glassie, *Folk Housing*, pp. 114–75, and Thomas C. Hubka, "Just Folks Designing," pp. 426–30.

46. On the builders, materials, and construction techniques used to build the wooden synagogues, see Maria and Kazimierz Piechotka's, *Wooden Synagogues*, pp. 35–47, and their *Bramy Nieba: Bóżnice drewniane*, pp. 43–72.

47. On the possible contribution of Jewish architects and builders, see Maria and Kazimierz Piechotka's *Wooden Synagogues*, pp. 36–44, and their "Polish Synagogues in the Nineteenth Century," pp. 179–98.

48. Since no documented accounts of synagogue building have been located, the construction records of similarly scaled wooden churches and monumental buildings of Poland provide a general comparison. See Czeslaw Krassowski and Adam Miłobędzki, "Studia nad zabudową miasteczka Ciężkowice," pp. 33–36; Henryk Samsonowicz, "Uwagi o budownictwie w Polsce u schyłku wieków średnich," pp. 117–19; Jerzy Paszenda, *Kościół Jezuitów w Shucku*, pp. 221–35; and Tadeusz Mankowski, *Fabrica Ecclesiae*, pp. 5–54. Each of these studies details eighteenth-century construction practices including estimates of costs, which were always considerable and usually required substantial royal, church, and magnate patronage. No study based on building construction documentation drawn from eighteenth-century, Eastern-European sources has stated or implied that wooden construction,

on the scale needed to build the wooden synagogues, was ever inexpensive.

49. Although no existing records document Jewish construction associations, regional Jewish craftsmen and regional builders still might have existed. The names of Jewish craftsmen and architects appear in nineteenth-century records, yet in earlier periods, it is very difficult to locate Jews associated with the building trades. The absence of records listing Jewish artisans in the building trades is noted in Moses Kremer, "Jewish Artisans and Guilds in Former Poland, 16th–18th Centuries," pp. 34–65; Therese and Mendel Metzger, *Jewish Life in the Middle Ages*, p. 163, and Mark Wischnitzer, *A History of Jewish Crafts and Guilds*, pp. 206–75. It must be stressed, however, that within the premodern, small Jewish towns of eastern Poland, part-time Jewish craftsmen with woodworking and construction skills probably existed, although their presence may have gone unrecorded. Various restrictions placed on employment in the building trades may also have limited Jewish access to the building professions before the nineteenth century; see Gershon Hundert, "Jewish Urban Residences in the Polish Commonwealth in the Early Modern Period," pp. 27–30.

50. In several articles, Adam Miłobędzki has emphasized the overall impact and importance of Germanic building traditions and techniques on premodern Polish architectural development; see "Medieval Architectural Tradition in the Cultural Landscape of 16th–18th Centuries, Central Europe," pp. 42–48; "Architecture in Wood," pp. 183–98; and "The Survival of Gothic in Vernacular and 'Neo-Vernacular' Architecture," pp. 149–54.

51. For premodern, Polish wooden construction details, see Witold Krassowski, "Ze Studiów nad Detalami Zabytkowych Konstrukcji Ciesielskich," pp. 3–25.

52. On the craftsmanship of wooden decoration, see Franciszek Kopkowicz, *Ciesielstwo Polskie*, pp. 1–93, 342–75, and Titus Hewryk, *Masterpieces in Wood*, pp. 13–36.

53. For artistic and cultural connections between Ashkenazi and Sephardic communities, see Esther Juhasz, "Synagogues," pp. 36–59. On cultural contacts between early-modern Ashkenazi and Sephardi communities, see Sophia Menache, "Communication in the Jewish Diaspora," pp. 15–56.

54. I make this general, untested hypothesis comparing the spatial volume of religious structures based on a review of Jewish, Polish, and Ukrainian architecture literature and on site visitation to hundreds of Polish and Ukrainian churches and surviving masonry synagogues. In the specific case of Gwoździec, the volume of the synagogue's prayer hall was three to four times larger than the volume of the naves of the two Greek Orthodox village churches on the outskirts of the town. While the nave of the Bernardine Monastery Church was over five times larger than the prayer hall of the synagogue, it was an atypical regional church. Typically, Catholic churches and Russian and Greek Orthodox churches from the small

towns of the Gwoździec region were smaller than the wooden synagogues; see Ryszard Brykowski, *Drewniana Architektura Cerkiewna*.

55. Restrictions on the height of synagogues were often imposed on Jewish communities in Poland and throughout the Diaspora; see Isaac Levy, *The Synagogue*, p. 30. In many cases, restrictions were imposed but not always enforced; see Maria and Kazimierz Piechotka, *Wooden Synagogues*, p. 17.

56. On the prevalent use of log construction for most pre-nineteenth-century buildings in the small towns of Poland, see Zygmunt Gloger, *Budownictwo drzewne i wyroby z drzewa w dawnej Polsce*.

57. On log construction techniques in Poland, see Witold Kassowski, "Ze studiów nad detalami zabytkowych konstrukcji ciesielskich," pp. 5–13. Although the American log cabin built with rounded logs has considerable mythic value, most historic American log buildings, like the Gwoździec Synagogue, were constructed of square hewn logs.

58. Wooden synagogue files, Department of Prints and Drawings, Tel Aviv Museum of Art. Before the modern era, the date carved into the door frame of a Polish vernacular building almost always commemorated the original date of construction completion. The 1718 date carved on the prominent lintel of the Gwoździec Synagogue has long been noted, but it has not been evaluated as a possible date of construction, probably because it conflicted with the widely accepted dates of construction, 1640 and 1652, initially proposed by Alois Breier, Max Eisler, and Max Grunwald, *Holzsynagogen in Polen*. These two seventeenth-century dates were never confirmed in photographs or in the reports of other investigators who visited the synagogue, but have been accepted in all later studies of wooden synagogues. The earliest date, 1640, was based on an admittedly faded inscription (recorded during Breier's fieldwork conducted before 1913 and published in 1934 after the destruction of the synagogue in 1916). Neither the 1640 date nor the 1652 date was ever recorded in the many detailed photographs of the interior taken by Alois Breier and still available for inspection in the Tel Aviv Museum of Art collection. Furthermore, neither date was ever confirmed by the many other investigators who studied the Gwoździec Synagogue, all of whom searched for evidence of an original construction date. Although current scholarship has accepted these mid-seventeenth-century dates, I believe that several later dates should also be considered as possible dates of original construction (see notes 68 and 69, chapter 3). It is to the credit of Maria and Kazimierz Piechotka that they so patiently and objectively recorded the many controversies surrounding the early dates for the Gwoździec Synagogue and consistently provided a fair evaluation of the relevant data in their many publications. See, for example, "Polichromie polskich bóżnic drewnianych," note 69, chapter 3.

59. Vertical timbers attached to horizontal log walls were often used to stiffen aging or failing walls, but it is also possible that these members were components of the original construction system; see the entry for Olkienniki Synagogue, in Maria and Kazimierz Piechotka, *Wooden Synagogues*, unnumbered pages by town name. In twentieth-century photographs, the vertical posts are sometimes shown with iron rods and bolts holding the vertical stiffeners to the walls. This method of joining would indicate a later, nineteenth-century repair. It is not known, however, if bolts were used to hold the stiffeners at the Gwoździec Synagogue.

60. On the high cost of logs, see Franciszek Kopkowicz, *Ciesielstwo Polskie*, pp. 5–25, and Czesław Krassowski, "Ze studiów nad detalami zabytkowych konstrukcji ciesielskich," pp. 3–7.

61. Magnate donation of logs for the synagogue is recorded in Mariella Beukers and Renee Waale, *Tracing An-sky*, pp. 76–77. Stories of Polish magnate support for synagogue construction were collected by Shlomo An-sky (Shlomo Zanvil Rapoport) and later published by Abraham Rechtman, *Jewish Ethnography and Folklore*, pp. 45, 60. Magnate support for synagogue construction was frequently cited in post-Holocaust, Jewish community memory (Yiskor) books, for example, Shlomo Farber, *Olkienniki in Flames*, p. 84. These memory books were often the work of many contributors and, despite their uneven scholarship, they are an important source of information for the small towns. The fact that positive memories of Polish magnates were still recorded, despite the Holocaust, attests to the strength and probable accuracy of these accounts.

62. For examples of such roof structures on typical manor houses, see Maciej Rydel, *Jam Dwór Polski*. For the variety of roof structures used in traditional Polish wooden architecture, see Jerzy Raczynski, "Przyczynki do Historji Ciesielskich Konstrukcyj Dachowych w Polsce," pp. 95–124.

63. The sophistication of the roof truss systems in Polish synagogues has received extensive documentation; see Maria and Kazimierz Piechotka's *Wooden Synagogues*, pp. 38–43, and their *Bramy Nieba: Bóżnice drewniane*, pp. 43–72. Adam Miłobędzki suggests that the trusses and cupolas of the wooden synagogues may have been designed by architects employed by local magnates because these advanced structural techniques were not usually employed by local builders; "Architecture in Wood," pp. 195–98. See notes 48 and 49, chapter 3.

64. Modern structural theory has consistently emphasized the link between structural systems and architectural expression so that both are seen as unified and highly integrated. Yet structural systems may or may not reflect architectural expression, and in the Baroque and postmodern periods, structural expression became secondary to the expression of form. On the plastic expression of the Baroque period, see Christian Norberg-Schulz, *Late Baroque and Rococo Architecture*, pp. 9–92, and Giulio Carlo Argan, *The Baroque Age*, pp. 64–66, 100–3. A related problem is the tendency of modern scholarship to assume that excellence in structural form requires minimal expression. In the Gothic and postmodern eras, structural clarity and its rational expression followed a different, more elaborately expressive structural logic, as emphasized by John Ruskin, *The Seven Lamps of Architecture*, pp. 25–56, and currently practiced by architects such as Renzo Piano and Frank Gehry. Nor should it be assumed that the minimalism in structural expression had a universal inevitability or modernist Zeitgeist; see Reyner Banham, *Concrete Atlantis*, pp. 1–21. Banham observed that minimalism in structural expression was, and still is, a stylistic and ideological decision, as confirmed in the nonminimalist works of late-nineteenth-century engineering, such as Gustave Eiffel's landmark tower.

65. There is no complete statistical tabulation of Eastern-European synagogues. Maria and Kazimierz Piechotka have compiled the most complete list of major wooden synagogues in their many works; see especially *Wooden Synagogues*, pp. 196–210, 221 (unnumbered flyleaf), and *Bramy Nieba: Bóżnice drewniane*, pp. 412–14. Masonry synagogues are listed in the Piechotkas' *Bramy Nieba: Bóżnice murowane*, pp. 113–229, 324–25, and in Eleonora Bergman and Jan Jagielski, "The Function of Synagogues in the PPR," pp. 42–43. Other surveys of Polish synagogues include G. K. Loukomski, *Jewish Art*, pp. 63–65, David Davidovitch, *The Synagogues in Poland and Their Destruction*, p. 97 flyleaf; and Z. Yargina, *Wooden Synagogues*, pp. 72–73, unnumbered pages by town name. However, the complete tabulation of all previous synagogues on the Polish lands of Eastern Europe would require an immense effort, involving case study research in towns with Jewish populations of fifty or more people, as listed in Shaul Stampfer, "The 1764 Census of Polish Jewry," pp. 60–147, and *Słownik Geograficzny*. Present surveys do not reflect a complete historical documentation of all recorded synagogues, but rather a selective editing, based largely on incomplete photographic and architectural survey information. When a complete historical survey is taken of all the synagogues ever built in a single medium-sized town, as for example, that by Eleonora Bergman, "Góra Kalwaria," pp. 13–15, 22–23, the quantity and complexity of synagogue development through time becomes evident. Bergman's current research on the synagogues of Warsaw analyzes an exceedingly complex architectural history where over three hundred synagogues and houses of prayer existed in 1900 (documentation shown to author). In previous efforts to document Eastern-European synagogues, there can be little doubt that the most "architecturally significant" examples of wooden synagogues that existed into the late nineteenth century were recorded, and this documentation accurately represents the finest available examples. These documented structures were typically the most architec-

turally exotic synagogues, ones that captured the imaginations of early historians, but many more ordinary structures were left unrecorded. A different interpretation of synagogue architecture and its relationship to the Jewish communities will emerge, however, if the complete record of Polish synagogue development, including all masonry and wooden synagogues, houses of prayer, and other supporting religious structures, is compiled. Such a complete demographic history has yet to be written, but it would communicate, as few current sources do, the active presence and deep-rootedness of Jewish communities in Poland.

66. Maria and Kazimierz Piechotka, *Wooden Synagogues*, pp. 7–8, and *Bramy Nieba*, pp. 6–8; and Carol Krinsky, *Synagogues of Europe*, pp. 96–97.

67. All known wooden cupola construction within wooden synagogues originates in the eighteenth century; and no cupolas can be dated before 1700; see Maria and Kazimierz Piechotka, *Wooden Synagogues*, pp. 35–47. Care must be taken to distinguish between the dates of building and cupola construction, which, as in the case of Gwoździec, were different. See notes 69 and 70, chapter 3.

68. Data for the synagogue and town of Gwoździec were primarily compiled from documents, maps, and inventory files at the Central State Historical Archives of Ukraine, Lviv. Other sources include: a census of Gwoździec's Jewish community in 1712; Files of the Potocki Family of Radzyń, p. 23, no. 242, Old Documents Archives, Warsaw; Letters of Karol Maszkowski, files: WI-108, Archiwum Polskiej Akademii Nauk (Polish Academy of Science Library), Cracow; Mendel Zilbur, *The Gwoździec Memory Book*; and Andrzej Betlej, "The Church of the Immaculate Conception and the Bernardine Monastery in Gwoździec," pp. 19–38, plus figures on unnumbered pages. For the definitive bibliography of sources for the Polish wooden synagogues, see Maria and Kazimierz Piechotka, *Bramy Nieba: Bóżnice drewniane*, pp. 383–411.

69. Maria and Kazimierz Piechotka review the major sources for dating the Gwoździec Synagogue, in "Polychrome Paintings," p. 74, n. 38, *Wooden Synagogues*, p. 198, and *Bramy Nieba: Bóżnice drewniane*, pp. 124–32, 208–12. They acknowledge the problems and discrepancies with seventeenth-century dates for the Gwoździec wall-paintings; see notes 1 and 14, chapter 4. Synagogues that can be dated with accuracy were almost all produced during the eighteenth and nineteenth centuries. Several other wooden synagogues are assumed to have been built in the seventeenth century, but these structures lack documentation of any kind. My research confirms that many wooden synagogues were indeed built before 1700, but it is doubtful whether many of these structures survived, in their original form, into the late nineteenth century to be documented by modern historians. Several factors make the seventeenth-century dating problematic: (1) the general lack of written documentation for the seventeenth century, (2) the practice of remodeling and/or replacing existing synagogues on the same site, especially after destruction by fire, (3) the possibility that a recorded date may refer to a previous or remodeled synagogue on the same site, or to a founding event in the Jewish community, (4) the common tendency of antiquarian historians of all eras to exaggerate the age of wooden structures, often for nationalistic purposes, and (5) the extreme difficulty of reading Hebrew numerical calculation (the placement of small marks above Hebrew letters representing numerical equivalents) on the faded painted surfaces of the wooden synagogues. No interior cupola can accurately be dated before about 1700, as suggested by Maria and Kazimierz Piechotka, *Wooden Synagogues*, p. 39, and "Polichromie polskich bóżnic drewnianych," p. 74. The late nineteenth and early twentieth century was an era of national romantic movements where the age of vernacular buildings became associated with issues of national origin and ethnic identity. There is the strong possibility that early-twentieth-century researchers and historians, motivated by these antiquarian and nationalistic objectives, may have exaggerated the age of the wooden synagogues. All these factors combine to suggest that the 1640 and 1652 dates commonly given for the construction of the Gwoździec Synagogue should be cautiously evaluated. See note 58, chapter 3.

70. On the ceiling remodeling, see Maria and Kazimierz Piechotka, *Wooden Synagogues*, p. 198, and *Bramy Nieba: Bóżnice drewniane*, pp. 208–212. These assessments are primarily based on the site investigations of Alois Breier, *Holzsynagogen*, pp. 12–14.

71. Ceilings with stylistically advanced, Baroque-inspired, double curves first appeared in Poland during the middle of the seventeenth century, primarily in the largest cities accompanying the most advanced commissions of the period; see Adam Miłobędzki, *Architektura polska*, p. 336. The use of barrel vaults in Polish monumental structures probably reached its peak during the same mid-seventeenth-century period, although barrel vaults were continuously used in Polish church architecture beginning in the fourteenth and fifteenth centuries. See Hanna Kozaczewska-Gołasz, "Drewniane kolebki w budownictwie średniowiecznym," pp. 91–121, and "Drewniane kolebki w średniowiecznych kościołach ziemi chełmińskiej i ich wpływ na architekturę," pp. 361–70.

72. Diary of Martin Greenewegs, File no. 406-386/90, Biblioteka Gdańska, Gdańsk, Poland. The diary is analyzed in Iaroslav Isaievych, "Naidavnishyi Istorychnyi Opys Lvova," pp. 109–13. I would like to thank Iaroslav Isaievych for bringing this document to my attention.

73. Maria and Kazimierz Piechotka, *Wooden Synagogues*, pp. 198–99, and *Bramy Nieba: Bóżnice drewniane* pp. 214–17.

74. Maria and Kazimierz Piechotka, "Polichromie," pp. 74–75, and *Bramy Nieba: Bóżnice drewniane*, pp. 113–20.

75. Maria and Kazimierz Piechotka, *Wooden Synagogues*, p. 196, and *Bramy Nieba: Bóżnice drewniane*, pp. 182–85.

76. Maria and Kazimierz Piechotka, "Polichromie," pp. 74–76, and *Bramy Nieba: Bóżnice drewniane*, pp. 120–32.

77. Maria and Kazimierz Piechotka, *Wooden Synagogues*, p. 209, and *Bramy Nieba: Bóżnice drewniane*, pp. 363–70.

78. On the termination of the wall-painting tradition, see Maria and Kazimierz Piechotka, "Polichromie polskich bóżnic drewnianych," pp. 79–87, and *Bramy Nieba: Bóżnice drewniane*, pp. 148–56.

79. Barbara Kirshenblatt-Gimblett, "Introduction" to *Life Is with People*, p. xvi, summarizes the diverse factors promoting social and cultural change in the small-town, Eastern-European Jewish community including "modernization, Enlightenment, Westernization, urbanization, secularization, industrialization, assimilation, nationalism, and political mobilization," factors that also contributed to the decline of premodern wooden synagogues at the beginning of the nineteenth century. For various articles exploring these topics, see Deborah Dash Moore, ed., *East European Jews in Two Worlds*; Frances Malino and David Sorkin, eds., *From East and West*; and Chimen Abramsky, Maciej Jachimczyk, and Antony Polonsky, eds., *The Jews of Poland*.

80. Isaac Ze'ev Kahana, *Studies in Responsa Literature*, pp. 349–395. In his chapter, "Synagogue Art in Halachic Literature," Kahana lists 115 whole and partial responsa correspondences concerning the art and decoration of the synagogue. Increasingly after the late eighteenth century and into the nineteenth century, Ashkenazi responsa from communities outside of Poland, especially from Germany and Central Europe, recommended the removal of wall-paintings and imagery (except for God's name) from synagogues.

81. The Hasidic response to the art and architecture of synagogues has not been adequately documented or analyzed. From the limited information available, it appears that early Hasidic communities maintained the art and architecture they inherited. In most cases, these communities did not significantly add to, but only modestly extended, the art and architectural inheritance of their synagogues; see Eleonora Bergman, "Góra Kalwaria," pp. 3–23. Eastern-European and Russian Jewish folk and decorative art produced during the Hasidic period can be seen in Alexander Kantsedikas, "Semyon An-sky and the Jewish Artistic Heritage," pp. 17–128. Richard Cohen analyzes various European Jewish art forms that paralleled the rise of Hasidism, in *Jewish Icons: Art and Society in Modern Europe*. The establishment of special houses or palaces for the Zaddic ("righteous man," or Hasidic leader) is a special topic requiring further research; see Eleonora Bergman, "Góra Kalwaria," pp. 14–15.

82. Maria and Kazimierz Piechotka, "Polichromie polskich bóżnic drewnianych," pp. 79–81.

83. On the ubiquitous use of wooden architecture in the small towns of the Podolia region, see Alla Sokolowa, "Architectural Space of the Shtetl-Street-House," pp. 35–85; and Zygmunt Gloger, *Budownictwo drzewne*. On the replacement of wood by masonry in seventeenth- and eighteenth-century buildings, see Adam Miłobędzki, *Architektura polska*, pp. 485–86. In the neighboring town of Chodorów, which had a wooden synagogue similar to Gwoździec, detailed property maps from 1846 show that, out of a total of approximately 350 houses and commercial buildings, only nine structures were masonry. Seven of the masonry buildings were owned by either the Catholic Church or the local magnate, and two masonry structures may have belonged to Jewish residents; File no. 186/4/38, pp. 494–510, Central State Historical Archives of Ukraine, Lviv. In my study of ten towns with wooden synagogues in the Lviv region, all had similar ratios of wood to masonry buildings. Similar conclusions are drawn in Maria and Kazimierz Piechotka, *Wooden Synagogues*, p. 35. For Jews in the small private towns of the eastern provinces, masonry buildings might even have been associated with the architecture of the Catholic Church or the ruling nobility and thus may have represented an unsuitable model for local synagogue construction.

84. The development of Polish masonry synagogues is analyzed by Maria and Kazimierz Piechotka in *Bramy Nieba: Bóżnice murowane* and in *Wooden Synagogues*, pp. 23–34; Rachel Wischnitzer, *European Synagogues*, pp. 107–24; Carol Krinsky, *Synagogues of Europe*, pp. 200–25; and Sergei R. Kravtsov, "Synagogues of Eastern Galicja," pp. 37–49. On the development of the nine-vault plan, see Maria and Kazimierz Piechotka, *Wooden Synagogues*, pp. 29–34; Carol Krinsky, *European Synagogue*, pp. 200–25; and Sergei R. Kravtsov, "On the Genesis of the Nine-Bay Synagogue," pp. 23–40.

85. There is considerable debate about the development of the square synagogue plan, including Polish, Spanish, Italian, and Dutch sources from both Jewish and non-Jewish building traditions. The diversity of possible sources suggests a fluidity of design experimentation and development in the sixteenth through eighteenth centuries, probably aided by literary sources, in Jewish communities throughout Europe. See Carol Krinsky, *Synagogues of Europe*, pp. 46–52; Rachel Wischnitzer, "Mutual Influences Between Eastern and Western Europe in the Synagogue Architecture From the 12th to the 18th Century," pp. 25–68; and Aharon Kashtan, "Synagogue Architecture of the Medieval and Pre-Emancipation Periods," pp. 103–17.

86. Carol Krinsky, *Synagogues of Europe*, pp. 212–14; Maria and Kazimierz Piechotka, *Bramy Nieba: Bóżnice murowane*, pp. 151–56.

87. Carol Krinsky, *Synagogues of Europe*, pp. 215–17; Maria and Kazimierz Piechotka, *Bramy Nieba: Bóżnice murowane*, pp. 216–19. The development of Lviv's Suburban Synagogue plan is usually associated with Renaissance influences; see Sergei R. Kravtsov, "On the Genesis of the Nine-Bay Synagogue," pp. 23–40. The existence of a similar nine-bay, Sephardic synagogue dating from the

fifteenth century in Tomar, Portugal, may suggest mutual sources; see Jerrilynn D. Dodds, "Mudejar Tradition and the Synagogues of Medieval Spain," pp. 129–30. Aharon Kastan cites these sources, but claims that the Tomar Synagogue is an isolated example, perhaps influenced by synagogues in Jewish communities along the African coast; see "Architectural Confrontations in the Old City of Jerusalem," pp. 262–64.

88. Carol Krinsky, *Synagogues of Europe*, pp. 208–9, and Maria and Kazimierz Piechotka, *Bramy Nieba: Bóżnice murowane*, pp. 72–73.

89. Most historians have divided Polish synagogues into wooden and masonry groups with various subcategories. See Rachel Wischnitzer, *The Architecture of the European Synagogue*, pp. 125–47. While the Piechotkas make this distinction, they also emphasize the similarities between wooden and masonry types in *Wooden Synagogues*, p. 35. Adam Miłobędzki has proposed that the interior-vaulted wooden synagogue represented an innovative departure from earlier forms of medieval wood construction in "Architecture in Wood," pp. 195–98. The seemingly obvious grouping of buildings according to construction material is, however, only one of several ways to classify architecture. In many building traditions, changes in building materials do not reflect substantive changes to other basic features of a building, such as the plan arrangement. See Thomas C. Hubka, *Big House, Little House, Back House, Barn*, pp. 138–44.

90. Several sources provide evidence that wooden synagogues predated masonry synagogues: in Lviv, 1624–1632, and in Gniezno, 1582, Maria and Kazimierz Piechotka, *Wooden Synagogues*, p. 49; and in Cracow, 1553–1557, Roman Spira, *Rabbis and Jewish Scholars in Poland in the 16th, 17th, and 18th Centuries*. Spira quotes Moses Isserles describing the evolution of Cracow's Kazimierz Synagogue: "The first one [synagogue] of timber perished in a great fire in 1523 [and was] rebuilt in masonry in 1537" (p. 23).

91. The underlying differences between the larger and smaller towns that may have generated fundamental differences in their synagogues are paralleled by the differences between larger, royal towns in western Poland and smaller, private towns in eastern Poland. See Moshe Rosman, *Founder of Hasidism*, pp. 42–62.

92. Only after about 1775, when both wooden and masonry synagogue types were firmly established, did masonry synagogues directly influence the wooden synagogues. For example, after 1775, wooden synagogue builders in the Grodno-Białystok region freely combined the wooden vaulted cupola and the clustered column plan of the masonry synagogue to produce a dramatic new type of wooden synagogue, such as the Wołpa Synagogue; see Maria and Kazimierz Piechotka, *Wooden Synagogues*, pp. 38–47, and *Bramy Nieba: Bóżnice drewniane*, pp. 43–72.

93. On the power and widespread influence of the local magnates see Norman Davies, *God's Playground*, pp. 245–255. On the likelihood of magnate architectural influence, see

Adam Miłobędzki, "Medieval Architectural Tradition in the Cultural Landscape of 16th–18th Centuries, Central Europe," pp. 40–48, and *Zarys dziejów architektury w Polsce*, pp. 192–205; and Marta Leśniakowska, *Polski Dwór: Wzorce Architektoniczne, Mit, Symbol*.

94. For the influence of the manor house on synagogue architecture, see Maria and Kazimierz Piechotka, *Wooden Synagogues*, pp. 18–22, and *Bramy Nieba: Bóżnice drewniane*, pp. 29–37. Other parallels between the manor houses and wooden synagogues can be discerned in a survey of Polish manor houses in V. A. Chanturya, *A History of Belarusian Architecture*, pp. 242–64.

95. Various building types in Eastern Europe share elements of the typical wooden synagogue's construction vocabulary; for example, the common tavern or inn, as documented in Bohdan Baranowski, *Polska Karczma*, pp. 1–30 and figs. 1–51, plus unnumbered pages; and Maciej Rydel, *Jam Dwór Polski*. For the full range of small-town architecture potentially influential to synagogue architecture, see Zygmunt Gloger, *Budownictwo Drzewne i Wyroby z Drzewa w Dawnej Polsce*; and for the range of buildings in one town, see Czesław Krassowski and Adam Miłobędzki, "Studies of the Buildings in the Town of Ciężkowice," pp. 31–60, figures, unnumbered pages.

96. On the Jewish exposure to Baroque styles, see Mendel Metzger, "Style in Jewish Art of the 17th and 18th Centuries in Relation to the Baroque and the Rococo," pp. 181–93. For magnate influence, see Jan Samek, *Polskie rzemiosło artystyczne*, pp. 194–428, and Norman Davies, *God's Playground*, pp. 213, 219.

97. On the extent and influences of Baroque theater decoration, see Barbara Król-Kaczorowska, *Teatr Dawnej Polski*, pp. 25–87.

98. The finest work on the wooden churches of Gwoździec's Podolian region is Ryszard Brykowski, *Drewniana Architektura Cerkiewna*. See also Titus Hewryk, *Masterpieces*, pp. 54–62, and David Buxton, *The Wooden Churches of Eastern Europe*, pp. 162–88. The region's wooden churches combine an ancient, vernacular, Slavic log building tradition with spatial and decorative concepts borrowed from Byzantine, Russian Orthodox, and Baroque church architecture to produce soaring interior cupolas. Many of these churches were built during the same eighteenth-century period as the interior vaulted synagogues. Related Polish Catholic wooden churches are analyzed in Adolf Szyszko-Bohusz, "Kościoły w Tomaszowie i Mnichowie," pp. 311–326; Marian Kornecki, "Małopolskie Kościoły Drewniane Doby Baroku," part 1, vol. 7 (1978), pp. 205–18, part 2, vol. 8 (1979), pp. 117–134, and part 3, vol. 14 (1980), pp. 123–33.

99. Some investigators have overemphasized the similarities between wooden churches and wooden synagogues; for example, Stefan Szyller, *Czy mamy polską architekturę?* pp. 45–51. But scholars who are familiar with these structures, Maria and Kazimierz Piechotka, *Wooden Synagogues*, pp. 37–46, present a much more balanced interpretation,

emphasizing both the similarities and the differences between wooden synagogues and churches. For comparison of wooden churches and synagogues, see Adam Miłobędzki, "Sakralne Budownictwo Drewniane," pp. 336–38. On the differences in synagogue and church plans, see pp. 337–38. Several detailed studies by Marian Kornecki demonstrate the similarities and differences between similarly scaled, eighteenth-century wooden churches and synagogues, for example, "Małopolskie kościoły drewniane." Several Eastern-European wooden churches have been repeatedly compared to the wooden synagogues. One of these is the Church of the Annunciation, 1727, Tomaszów Lubelski, Poland (fig. 83). Although there are many points of comparison, the essential differences between these two traditions might just as easily be emphasized. To compare the Tomaszów Lubelski Church to wooden synagogue construction, see Ryszard Brykowski, "Początki drewnianej fary w Tomaszowie Lubelskim," pp. 345–52.

100. Regarding arks and altars, compare Catholic altars in Adam Miłobędzki, *Architektura polską*, pp. 276–82, 334–38, and Greek and Russian Orthodox iconostases (altar screens in Orthodox churches) in Hewryk, *Masterpieces*, pp. 30–34, to Jewish arks in Maria and Kazimierz Piechotka, *Bramy Nieba*, pp. 94–105. For an account of the design and building of an ark in a wooden synagogue, see Shlomo Farber, ed., *Olkienniki in Flames: A Memorial Book*, pp. 83–85.

101. On the Jesuits' influence on Poland's art and architecture, see I. Jaffe and R. Wittkower, *Baroque Art*, pp. 73–80. For an overview of Jesuit/Catholic influence in Poland, see Norman Davies, *God's Playground*, pp. 166–72.

102. For the finest analysis of Baroque architecture as a powerful symbol of the Catholic Church in Poland, see Adam Miłobędzki, *Architektura polska*, pp. 478–79l. Also see note 103, chapter 3. Architectural historians are often correctly criticized by cultural historians for inflating the overall importance of architectural styles, especially as generators of ideas and movements in culture. In the case of the Polish Baroque style, however, claims to its overall importance have greater justification. More than an aesthetic style, the Baroque architecture of the Catholic Church evolved into a powerful cultural vehicle for a trans-European movement intended to reverse the gains of the Protestant Reformation. In Eastern Europe and especially in Poland, Baroque church, civic, and residential architecture also became a national symbol of the Polish Enlightenment, uniting religious and secular culture within a common trans-European aristocratic culture.

103. On the development of Baroque vaulting for Catholic churches and monumental secular buildings, see Adam Miłobędzki, *Architektura polska*, pp. 45–80, Stanisław Mossakowski, *Tylman z Gameren*, and Thomas DaCosta Kaufmann, *Court, Cloister, and City*, pp. 51–73, 282–92. On the development of vaulting and cupolas in Ukrainian wooden churches built during the same period and in

the same regions as wooden synagogues, see Titus D. Hewryk, *Masterpieces in Wood*, pp. 22–36, and G. N. Logvin, *Monuments of Art in the Soviet Union, Ukraine, and Moldavia*, pp. 9–13, plus figures throughout the text. While providing a clear referential source for the wooden synagogues, these heavy wooden vaults are also quite small and dark, being derived from an ancient log construction tradition. The large, soaring volume of the wooden synagogue vaults created an entirely different, more expansive spatial experience.

104. On the influence of Eastern-European masonry vaulting precedents on the wooden synagogues, see Maria and Kazimierz Piechotka's *Wooden Synagogues*, pp. 38–47, and *Bramy Nieba*, pp. 59–72.

105. A massive campaign of Jesuit church building brought Italian and other foreign architects and advanced ideas of the European Baroque to Poland during the seventeenth and eighteenth centuries. This importation generated a sophisticated period of Baroque church building, for example, in the work of the architect Tylman van Gameren; in Stanisław Mossakowski, *Tylman z Gameren*, pp. 36–52, and as summarized by Adam Miłobędzki in *Architektura polska*, pp. 475–93.

4. Wall-Paintings

1. The wall-paintings in Polish wooden synagogues are recorded and analyzed in Maria and Kazimierz Piechotka's many works, including; "Polichromie Polskich bóżnic drawnianych," pp. 65–87, *Bramy Nieba: Bóżnice drewniane*, pp. 112–57, and *Bramy Nieba: Bóżnice murowane*, pp. 310–15.

2. If read as a continuous band of illuminated text, the wall-paintings resemble the linked pages of a decorated Esther Scroll (the text of the Book of Esther is traditionally written on a long parchment scroll divided into sequential columns, often surrounded by decorative frames). I do not believe, however, that Esther Scrolls served as models for the wall-paintings, although they may have been part of a larger tradition of liturgical art that inspired the wall-painters.

3. For background information on the painters, see Maria and Kazimierz Piechotka, "Polichromie Polskich bóżnic drawnianych," pp. 69–70, and *Bramy Nieba: Bóżnice drewniane*, pp. 113–36; and David Davidovitch, *Wall-Paintings of Synagogues in Poland*, pp. 53–68.

4. The wealth of visual imagery in the Gwoździec wall-paintings is related to liturgical stories and legends for which the contemporary viewer may have little precedent. In order to appreciate this dense narrative complexity, a contemporary viewer should recognize the limits of current visually oriented discourse to address religious art forms. The modern emphasis on abstract, visual/aesthetic criteria to interpret visual art tends to minimize or confuse the depth of traditional, narrative-based,

liturgical art such as the synagogue wall-paintings. Such a liturgically based art necessitates a historical and contextual reading requiring that the paintings be interpreted from the point of view of the artists and audiences of the early eighteenth century. This approach does not deny purely aesthetic, noncontextual or universal criteria, it only cautions that such criteria should be interpreted within a cultural or religious perspective; see John Berger, *Ways of Seeing*, and Henry Glassie, *The Spirit of Folk Art*.

5. Maria and Kazimierz Piechotka have assembled the most complete list of early researchers and their publications in *Bramy Nieba: Bóżnice drewniane*, pp. 383–411.

6. Gershom Scholem, *Sabbatai Sevi*, pp. 2–5, 20–21, helped to dispel the association of Jewish messianic movements with eras of persecution or impoverishment, like the Jewish expulsions from Spain. Recently, Moshe Idel has further suggested that, instead of hopelessness, we might envision "the kindling of hope as a prelude to messianic awareness"; *Messianic Mystics*, pp. 8, 103. Idel identifies a "non-apocalyptic messianism" (p. 105) characterized by "a collective of Jews, namely a situation where perfection has already been attained by a collective and cumulative effort" (p. 223). I emphasize Idel's reevaluation of the sources of messianic movements to disassociate the wall-paintings from the charge that messianic despair generated their development. This book emphasizes themes of positivism, even theurgic optimism, underlying and sustaining the worship, and by extension, the art forms of early-eighteenth-century Polish Jews; see Moshe Idel, *Kabbalah: New Perspectives*, pp. 256–71.

7. Alois Breier, Max Eisler, and Max Grunwald, *Holzsynagogen in Polen*, based on Alois Breier, "Die holzernen Synagoen in Galizien und Russisch-Polen aus dem 16, 17 und 18 Jahrhundert."

8. The artists' signatures can be seen in enlarged photographs of Gwoździec Synagogue, in the wooden synagogue files, Department of Prints and Drawings, Tel Aviv Museum of Art. According to the conventions of the early modern period, the title "rabbi" can apply to any adult Jewish male. Therefore, the painters were not sons of rabbis, as has occasionally been surmised. However, it would not be unreasonable to assume that the painters may have had an uncommonly high level of learning. Beyond their artistic and technical skills as painters, they may have possessed more than average knowledge of Hebrew, manuscript calligraphy, and liturgical history. It is also likely that these painters had high standing in their regional communities.

9. On the likelihood that Jewish artistic guilds were involved in the production of the wall-paintings, see Maria and Kazimierz Piechotka, "Polichromie polskich bóżnic drewnianych," pp. 70–76. During the seventeenth and eighteen centuries, the town of Brody, near Lviv, maintained organizations or schools of Polish and Ukrainian painters; see Volodymyr Alekandrovich, "Painters' Cir-

cles in Brody," pp. 113–18. On the skills and techniques of medieval artists, perhaps similar to those of the Gwoździec artists, see Virginia Wylie Egbert, *The Medieval Artist at Work*, pp. 19–37. See also note 49, chapter 3.

10. On the synagogue wall-paintings of Eliezer Sussman, see Iris Fishof, "Depictions of Jerusalem by Eliezer Sussmann of Brody," pp. 67–82; David Davidovitch, *Wandmalereien in alten Synagogen*, pp. 7–56; and Max Untermayer-Raymer, "German Synagogue Art," pp. 64–68.

11. My compositional analysis of the western wall is based on the premise that the prayer hall door is offset to the south (or to the left, as seen from the prayer hall floor) with respect to the center line of the wall and the room. In a plan of the Gwoździec Synagogue (Maria and Kazimierz Piechotka, *Wooden Synagogues*, fig. 41, unnumbered pages by town name), the door is shown offset to the left (as seen from the prayer hall). I have confirmed this offset arrangement by measuring various repeating decorative motifs on the walls and ceiling. In the Piechotkas' later book (*Bramy Nieba: Bóżnice drewniane*, fig. 311, p. 208, and repeated in a sectional drawing in fig. 82, p. 62), the Gwoździec Synagogue floor plan shows the doorway drawn in the center of the west wall with the small window above the door offset to the right (as seen from the prayer hall). I believe this later depiction is an understandable minor error, perhaps drawn by a draftsperson who assumed that the doorway was centered in the room. The photograph of the west wall (fig. 97) clearly shows the nonalignment in the center line of the lattice window with respect to the center line of the door below; the question is whether the door or the window is centered in the room. I believe that a study of all the photographs of the west wall will confirm that the lattice window is centered and the door is off-centered to the left with respect to the center line of the room, as drawn in the earliest Piechotka plan. I belabor this very minor point only to bring consistency to my discussion of the painters' compositional strategy for Gwoździec's western wall. In hundreds of other synagogue drawings, the Piechotkas have maintained a very high standard of technical accuracy.

12. The necessity for this four quadrant configuration of Holy Vessels is reiterated in many variations in the *Zohar*. See note 62, chapter 6.

13. For a comparison of interior photographs from the wooden synagogues of Gwoździec, Chodorów, Jabłonów, and Kamionka Strumiłowa in the Lviv region, see wooden synagogue files, Department of Prints and Drawings, Tel Aviv Museum of Art.

14. On the color of the wall-paintings in the Gwoździec Synagogue, see Maria and Kazimierz Piechotka, *Bramy Nieba: Bóżnice drewniane*, pp. 124–36, *Bramy Nieba: Bóżnice murowane*, pp. 310–15, and "Polichromie," pp. 3–5; Davidovitch, *Wall-Paintings*, pp. 29–68; and descriptions of color in the Letters of Karol Maszkowski, files WI-108, Archives of the Polish Academy of Science, Cracow,

Poland. The surviving records of colors used in the Gwoździec Synagogue include three primary sources: a painting by Isidor Kaufmann titled *Portal of the Rabbis* (c. 1897–98), Magyar Nemzeti Galeria, Budapest, inventory no. 1692 (incorrectly labeled as a painting of the Jabłonów Synagogue in *Bilder des Wiener Malers: Isidor Kaufmann, 1853–1921*, G. Tobias Natter, ed., pp. 284–85, fig. 87, and color plate 1); a colored elevation drawing of a portion of the ceiling, copied from an original by Alois Breier (current status unknown), in David Davidovitch, *Wall-Paintings*, color plate between pages 40 and 41 (fig. 88, and color plate 3); and a colored elevation drawing of a portion of the northern wall by Alois Breier, in a photograph, wooden synagogue files, Department of Prints and Drawings, Tel Aviv Museum of Art (color plate 4). From these color samples and accompanying written analyses, the range of colors in the Gwoździec wall-paintings appears similar to those colors employed in early-eighteenth-century Eastern-European secular and ecclesiastical buildings — only the large prayer tablets with their brilliant white background and black letters were unique to the synagogues. For the use of colors in Greek Orthodox churches of the same era, see H. M. Zoltowskij, *Monumental Paintings in Ukraine*. For the use of color on Jewish gravestones see Andrzej Trzcinski, "Polichromia Nagrobków na Cmentarzach Żydowskich w Polsce Południowo-Wschodniej" (Paintings [Polychrome] on the Tombstones in Jewish Cemeteries in Southeastern Poland), pp. 63–64.

15. Correspondence of Karol Maszkowski, September 4, 1899, p. 5. files WI-108, Archives of the Polish Academy of Science, Cracow, Poland.

16. Colors in the wall-paintings of Polish wooden synagogues have frequently been interpreted in relation to the colorful painted model of the Chodorów Synagogue ceiling, at the Nahum Goldmann Museum of the Jewish Diaspora in Tel Aviv; for example, see the jacket of Ida Huberman's *Living Symbols*. While this model is a very skillful reproduction, it contains compositional errors and minor distortions. Small areas of the model's ceiling appear to have been freely interpreted when photographic evidence was lacking. More significantly, the color selection is based on sources that cannot be located or verified. This assessment of the Chodorów model is based on a review of all known photographic sources and on an interview with David Davidovitch in 1990.

17. Moshe Idel describes the significance of color in Kabbalistic prayer, and particularly in the *Zohar*, in "Kabbalistic Prayer and Colors," pp. 17–28. Idel discusses the color symbolism in mystical techniques of the Kabbalah, *Kabbalah: New Perspectives*, pp. 103–11. In several works, Elliot Wolfson also identifies the significance of color in prayer and worship, as in *Through a Speculum That Shines*, pp. 380–83.

18. The use of color in the wall-paintings of the Gwoździec Synagogue follows premodern techniques probably closest to medieval techniques. John Ruskin's analysis of color in medieval architecture is still the finest available; see a summary of Ruskin's extensive color theories in John Unrau, *Looking at Architecture with Ruskin*, pp. 40–52. According to some art historical interpretations, a dominant aesthetic strategy of the wall-paintings is the composition strategy labeled *horror vacui* (fear of emptiness), a label often used to describe medieval decorative arts. This widely accepted interpretation has the unfortunate consequence of attributing the dense pattern of many forms of medieval and premodern art to a kind of weakness or insecurity on the part of the artist, causing him to mechanically fill or clutter a composition. But to describe the skillful artists of the Gwoździec Synagogue as fearful of emptiness would be equivalent to interpreting modern artists as fearful of complexity or narrative. The dense compositional style of premodern artists, such as the Gwoździec painters, is sensitively analyzed by E. H. Gombrich, *The Sense of Order*, pp. 63–94, and Henry Glassie, *Art and Life in Bangladesh*, pp. 169–79. Instead of *horror vacui*, Gombrich suggests that the term *amor infiniti* (love of the infinite) be applied to art forms with dense compositions (p. 80).

19. See note 13, chapter 7.

20. On the motif of the architectural gate, see Shalom Sabar, *Mazal Tov*, pp. 19–25. Annette Weber also documents the sixteenth- and seventeenth-century Italian development of the gate/column/curtain motif, particularly in book art, and emphasizes the emergence of the twisted column within this motif as a messianic symbol; see "Ark and Curtain," pp. 94–99. The architectural gate motif in the European ark curtain (parochet) is described by Bracha Yaniv, "The Origins of the 'Two-Column Motif' in European Paroket," pp. 26–43.

21. The *Zohar* does not specify that ten tapestries be hung in the synagogue, as they were hung in the Tabernacle, so the association of the ten tapestries in the Tabernacle to the ten painted tablets of the Gwoździec Synagogue is speculative. The *Zohar*'s passage does, however, continue with an extended analysis of the Tabernacle linking in rapid succession ten worshipers (minyon), ten supports of the King (throne), the absence of Shekhinah (not included in ten), and the ten curtains of the Tabernacle (II: 164b). These references to the number ten are cited in a rapid, rhythmic fashion, typical of the *Zohar*, as if to bind together the multiple, reinforcing references. It is this repetition of metaphoric reference that may have contributed to the decision to paint ten prayer tablets in the Gwoździec Synagogue. See note 29, chapter 6.

22. The decorative, scalloped border appears in many cultures, East and West, folk and elite; see E. H. Gombrich, *The Sense of Order*, pp. 67–83. For a discussion of Turkish tent influences on Polish decorative art, see Maria and Kazimierz Piechotka, *Bramy Nieba: Bóżnice drewniane*, pp. 124–37. For an analysis of Jewish decorative motifs in

the art of papercuts from a later period, see Joseph and Yehudit Shadur, *Traditional Jewish Papercuts*.

23. For a discussion of the visual strategy in rope motifs, see E. H. Gombrich, *Sense of Order*, pp. 75–83.

24. The possibility of this edging motif representing fabric stitching was kindly suggested by Judith Kenny.

25. On Polish carpet manufacture in the Lviv region, see Beata Biedrońska-Słotowa, *Orient w Sztuce Polskiej*, pp. 7–40, and Maria and Kazimierz Piechotka, "Polichromie polskich bóżnic drewnianych," p. 80.

26. It has often been uncritically assumed that animal motifs in the synagogue wall-paintings drew upon and paralleled animal depictions in Eastern-European folk art, yet this assumption has not been thoroughly investigated. The primarily decorative use of animals in Polish and Ukrainian folk art (see Józef Grabowski, *Sztuka Ludowa: formy i regiony w Polsce*) and the primary liturgical/ethical usage of animal figures in the synagogue wall-paintings are, despite some similarities in artistic application, fundamentally different.

27. For the earliest attempts to catalog the animal motifs of the wall-paintings, see Max Grundwald, "Anhang zur Iconographie der Malerei in unseren Holzsynagogen" (Appendix on Iconography of Paintings in Our Synagogues), pp. 13–21; David Davidovitch, *Wall Paintings*, pp. 20–26; and Maria and Kazimierz Piechotka, "Polichromie polskich bóżnic drewnianych," pp. 68–69. Efforts to analyze animal symbolism are summarized in Piechotka, "Polichromie polskich bóżnice drewnianych," p. 87. Many sources dealing with the wall-paintings offer a generalized interpretation of animal motifs within a broad context of Jewish art; see, for example, Abram Kahof, *Jewish Symbolic Art*, pp. 67–75. Unfortunately, an understanding of the abundance of animal and plant imagery in Jewish literature is complicated because many animals have multiple meanings and because some species have different meanings in different periods and regions. This complexity is catalogued in Louis Ginzberg, *The Legends of the Jews*; Hayim Nahman Bialik and Yehoshua Hana Ravnitzky, eds., *The Book of Legends*; and Angelo S. Rappoport, *The Folklore of the Jews*.

28. See Marc Michael Epstein, *Dreams of Subversion in Medieval Jewish Art*, and "The Elephant and the Law," pp. 465–478. The problems of understanding the popular meaning of animal figures for a premodern constituency are explored in Michael Camille's discussion of decorative motifs used in Christian medieval illuminated manuscripts; see *Mirror in Parchment*, pp. 239–257.

29. On the desire of Polish Jewry to recall and honor their former Ashkenazi homeland, see Israel M. Ta-Shma, "On the History of the Jews in Twelfth- and Thirteenth-Century Poland," pp. 307–20; Ephraim Kanarfogel, "*Peering Through the Lattices*," pp. 112–13, 125, 251–58; and Marvin Herzog, *The Yiddish Language in Northern Poland*, pp. 235–46.

30. Jewish symbolic communication may also have appropriated some Christian symbols, as analyzed in several works by Marc Michael Epstein, including "'If lions could carve stones . . .' Medieval Jewry and the Allegorization of the Animal Kingdom," pp. 33–76, 372–83. For example, Epstein reviews the elaborate symbolism of the hare hunt scenes in Jewish and Christian medieval literature. He concludes that, although the hare hunt was generally understood to convey the pursuit of Israel by the nations of the world, in the hands of Jewish artists, the symbolism was turned "topsy-turvy" to become a sign of hope, not distress, when presented to Jewish audiences (pp. 111–14).

31. Characteristics of medieval folk painting similar to Gwoździec's are analyzed by A. J. Gurevich, *Categories of Medieval Culture*, pp. 35–89.

32. On fantastic creatures, see Marc Michael Epstein, "'If lions could carve stones,'" pp. 243–90, 307–32; and David B. Ruderman, "Unicorns, Great Beasts and the Marvelous Variety of Things in Nature in the Thought of Abraham B. Hananiah Yagel," pp. 343–64. Jewish medieval and Kabbalistic literature describes many fantastic animals. For example, imagery associated with the transmigration of souls (gilgul) involving many types of animal/human combinations, is outlined by Gershom Scholem, in the chapter "Gilgul: The Transmigration of Souls," in *On the Mystical Shape of the Godhead*, pp. 197–250.

33. The influence of Eleazar of Worms on Polish Jewry is emphasized in Israel M. Ta-Shma, "On the History of the Jews in Twelfth- and Thirteenth-Century Poland," pp. 307–20.

34. The fertility of Eleazar's imagery and its subsequent influence in Jewish literature are analyzed by Elliot R. Wolfson in his chapter "The Image of Jacob Engraved Upon the Throne: Further Reflection on the Esoteric Doctrine of the German Pietists," in *Along the Path*, pp. 1–62. In other works, Wolfson explores themes of visual imagination and imagery in Eleazar's works; see "The Mystical Significance of Torah Study in German Pietism," pp. 43–77; and "The Face of Jacob in the Moon: Mystical Transformation of an Aggadic Myth," pp. 240–45. On the use of allegory in medieval Jewish literature, see Frank Talmage, "Apples of Gold: The Inner Meaning of Sacred Texts in Medieval Judaism," pp. 312–55.

35. On the nut imagery in works by Eleazar and his school, see Joseph Dan's "Hokhmath Ha-'Egoz, its origin and development," pp. 73–82, and Joseph Dan, "The Book of the Divine Name by Rabbi Eleazar of Worms," pp. 27–60.

36. Alexander Altmann, "Eleazar of Worms' Symbol of the Merkabah," p. 163.

37. The significance of animal imagery for the Gwoździec congregation should be understood within a context of worship where animal symbolism played a significant role; see Joyce E. Salisbury, *The Beast Within: Animals in the Middle Ages*, pp. 103–82. Animal imagery was an important vehicle for symbolic expression in the Bible,

Talmud, and Midrash (see *The Book of Legends*, ed. Hayim Nahman Bialik and Yehoshua Hana Ravnitzky), and was continued in the medieval era. See Marc Michael Epstein, "'If lions could carve stones.'"

38. See Marc Michael Epstein, "'If lions could carve stones,'" pp. 115–19. The hind or deer is described in several biblical stories as "pious among the animals"; see Louis Ginzburg, *The Legends of the Jews*, p. 59.

39. In addition to painting the deer with a turned head, the artist also shows the deer raising its hind leg. This depiction could represent a common artistic convention, now lost, or it may relate to other stories about deer. For example, in another passage concerning deer, a serpent assists at a birth by biting the deer (II: 219b). The Zoharic deer initiates this process by putting its own head between its legs (II: 52b). Perhaps the raised leg of the Gwoździec deer alludes to the beginning of this process, as outlined in Isaiah Tishby, *The Wisdom of the Zohar*, p. 359, and Gershom Scholem, *Sabbatai Sevi*, p. 807. This interpretation is only a suggestion, but it is offered as one example of the multiple possible interpretations for the synagogue's imagery. Also see Joseph and Yehudit Shadur, *Traditional Jewish Papercuts*, where the decorative aspects of animal imagery are frequently emphasized. Although nonreligious papercuts from the nineteenth century differ from the liturgical wall-paintings of eighteenth-century synagogues, they share a similar vocabulary of animals and decorative motifs. While the possible decorative, practical, or nonsymbolic use of the major animal figures in the wooden synagogues should be acknowledged, this book demonstrates that the widespread tradition of animal symbolism was closely associated with, and symbolic of, liturgical themes for the premodern Jewish community.

40. Tishby argues that the theme of the Shekhinah in exile became "the cornerstone of [an] immense mythical structure" in Lurianic Kabbalah. Isaiah Tishby, *The Wisdom of the Zohar*, p. 385. In the *Zohar*, the image of the Shekhinah associated with the turning deer is also linked to the lattice window on the synagogue's western wall. In several stories, the lattice window motif is combined with the image of the deer and the Shekhinah in exile, both hiding or waiting behind a wall. See note 12, chapter 7.

41. The painter's intention is clarified by the inscription "ostrich," but there are other possible meanings of this inscription and the bird image. For example: did the artist write "ostrich" and mean another bird, such as the peacock? There is also the possibility of covert symbolism where the eagle-like ostrich may have communicated other meanings to its Jewish audience. For a discussion of the range of possible meanings in similar painting and manuscript art, see Marc Michael Epstein, *Dreams of Subversion*, pp. 1–15.

42. Jewish literature contains many stories, like the story of the ostrich's vision, about the power of the eye to do good or evil. Many of these stories are related to the "evil

eye," as analyzed in Rivka Ulmer, *The Evil Eye in the Bible and in Rabbinic Literature*. Elliot Wolfson also describes various esoteric meanings of the ostrich-egg-vision motif in *Through a Speculum That Shines*, pp. 317–25.

43. *Kav Ha Yashar* was based on the composition *Yesod Yosef* written by Kaidanover's teacher Rabbi Yosef. *Yesod Yosef* remained in manuscript form for a long time and was printed only after *Kav Ha Yashar*. Rabbi Yosef writes: "Looking is a significant thing, and the ostrich's case proves that, for through his looking at eggs which are laid in front of it, it makes a hole in the eggshells, and chicks come out." See *Yesod Yosef*, R. Yosef of Dubnow, ch. 2, p. 1d. Another source that mentions this story is Hayyim Vital, *'Es Hayyim* (Tree of Life), sec. 8: "We have seen some power in the looking of the eye as we see in the natural sense of the eye, as in the case of the ostrich's. The chick is born through its mother's sustained gaze, without her sitting on the eggs to incubate them, as the rest of the birds do, and that shows that the gaze of the eyes holds real power."

44. Predator imagery in Jewish art and literature has been used to symbolize the persecution of Jewish community; see listings in Elijah Judah Schocet, *Animal Life in Jewish Tradition*. Predatory animals, however, have communicated many other meanings; see for example, Rachel Wischnitzer, "The Messianic Fox," pp. 70–80. Marc Michael Epstein further suggests a reversal of the standard notion of a predator attacking the Jewish community in medieval sources; see *Dreams of Subversion*, pp. 16–38.

45. The loss of man's divinity and his subsequent acquisition of animal characteristics is an ancient theme (Psalms 49:13, Shabbat 151b, and Numbers 14:9). The theme is described in the medieval Ashkenazi book *Sefer Hasidim*, as analyzed in Moshe Idel, "Gazing at the Head in Ashkenazi Hasidism," pp. 281–82.

46. Predatory animals are found in the surviving wall-paintings of eighteenth-century Polish synagogues but, from the limited amount of comparable examples, it cannot be determined whether they were more or less plentiful in synagogues from other lands or eras; see four predators in the Chodorów Synagogue wall-paintings, wooden synagogue files, Department of Prints and Drawings, Tel Aviv Museum of Art.

47. Photographs of predators from the model of the Chodorów Synagogue ceiling at the Nahum Goldmann Museum of the Jewish Diaspora, Tel Aviv, are often used in place of original photographs; see Maria and Kazimierz Piechotka, *Bramy Nieba, Bóżnice drewniane*, p. 113. The model is painted in brilliant colors, but all current surviving photographs of the prayer hall are in black and white, and the color sources for the model cannot be located. While the Chodorów Synagogue model is a very good technical reproduction, its colors should be cautiously evaluated. See note 16, chapter 4.

48. The portrayal of evil powers or beings is prohibited by Jewish law, and this prohibition relates to the existence of

evil powers or beings outside or independent of God; see Gershom Scholem, *Shape of the Godhead*, pp. 56–87. Rachel Elior explores this issue in the period preceding the construction of the Gwoździec Synagogue in "The Doctrine of Transmigration in Galya Raza," pp. 243–69. The *Zohar*'s vivid and influential portrayal of evil, evil creatures, and the struggle between good and evil is summarized by Isaiah Tishby in *The Wisdom of the Zohar*, vol. 2, pp. 447–512.

49. While rarely seen in synagogues outside Poland, in Polish wooden synagogue wall-paintings, predators were commonly depicted. Representations of animals attacking other animals have a long history in European medieval manuscripts, and it is this tradition that is likely to have influenced the Polish synagogues. Unfortunately, almost nothing is known about the wall-paintings in northern European medieval synagogues. One item, frequently cited, is a responsa from Cologne, Germany, from about 1260, that acknowledges the painting of lions and snakes on the synagogue windows but rules against their presence; see Isaac Ze'ev Kahana, *Studies in Responsa*, p. 371.

50. In the *Zohar*, these predators may represent God's avenging Hayyoth (angels), which are often described as "shield bearing" Hayyoth from the "Fourth Palace of the Firmament" whose responsibility is to "complete their work of judgment and punishment throughout the four corners of the world" (I: 41b–42b).

51. See Wilma George, "Sources and Background to Discoveries of New Animals in the Sixteenth and Seventeenth Centuries," pp. 79–104; and Lorraine Daston and Katharine Park, *Wonders and the Order of Nature*, pp. 13–66.

52. See *Perek Shirah*, "Introduction" by Malachi Beit-Arie, The Jewish National and University Library, Jerusalem, Heb. 8° 4295, unnumbered pages. First mentioned in the tenth century, *Perek Shirah* is an anonymous tract containing hymnic sayings praising God, as if spoken by the animals or the features of the physical world. See Malachi Beit-Arie, *Perek Shirah*, and Louis Ginzburg, *The Legends of the Jews*, pp. 60–62.

53. The theme of honoring God through the contemplation of the diversity in the natural world is reminiscent of Bahya Paquada's second chapter, "On the Explanation of the Aspects of Meditation upon the Creation and God's Abundant Grace Shown in It," in *The Book of Directions to Duties of the Heart*, pp. 150–75. See note 20, chapter 7.

54. The Appendix provides a translation of all the prayers and inscriptions from the Gwoździec Synagogue. Translations from Hebrew are by Avriel Bar-Levav from photographs of the Gwoździec Synagogue, wooden synagogue files, Department of Prints and Drawings, Tel Aviv Museum of Art. I wish to thank Avriel Bar-Levav for his generous assistance.

55. For a review of inscriptions from the earliest synagogues, see Louis H. Feldman, "Diaspora Synagogues," pp. 48–66; and Leonard Victor Rutgers, "Diaspora Synagogues," pp. 67–95. These sources confirm that inscriptions served

as dedications, donor acknowledgments, and proverbs, but rarely as vehicles for prayer quotation as they were developed in northern Europe.

56. See Dr. Ad. Jellinek, *Märtyrere und Memorbuch*, pp. 35–36. (I wish to thank Boaz Huss for this reference.) The prayers and inscriptions seen in surviving photographs of synagogues throughout the former Polish-Lithuanian Commonwealth have not been systematically catalogued or analyzed. Research for this book focused on a group of nine partially documented wooden synagogues from the Podolian region of western Ukraine. Only two synagogues, Gwoździec and Jabłonów, have nearly complete documentation for the entire interior, including all their painted inscriptions. This documentation permits a rare comparison of the complete prayer texts of these neighboring synagogues. More than half of the liturgical inscriptions in the Jabłonów Synagogue, as well as six other proverbs and ethical inscriptions, are identical to those in the Gwoździec Synagogue. Fragmentary photographic documentation from other wooden synagogues of the region reveals a similar pattern of prayers and inscription duplication, suggesting some regional consensus. A preliminary review of the surviving photographs of all Polish wooden and masonry synagogues also reveals duplications of inscriptions, but exploration of this topic remains incomplete. Numerous inscription duplications and parallels also exist between the wall-paintings in the Gwoździec region and the German synagogue paintings of Eliezer Sussman. See note 10, chapter 4. Recent archival discoveries in Ukraine have brought attention to synagogues in the eastern Podolian towns of Michalpol, Smotrich, Minkovtsy, and Jarochow (located between Lviv and Kiev, northeast of Gwoździec), which share similar wall-painting characteristics with synagogues of the Gwoździec region. Photographic records of the wooden synagogues from Michalpol, Smotrich, Minkovtsy, and Jarochow can be found in the S. Taranushchenko Collection, Central Scientific Library of the Academy of Sciences of Ukraine, Kiev; and the D. Shcherbakivsky Collection, Ukrainian Institute for Archaeology, Kiev. These Ukrainian sources were kindly brought to my attention by Siergiej Kratsov.

57. On the diffusion and the availability of printed prayer books in seventeenth- and eighteenth-century Poland, see Stefan C. Reif, *Judaism and Hebrew Prayer*, pp. 176–87; and Zeev Gries, *The Book in Early Hasidism* and *Conduct Literature*. On the unsuccessful efforts to standardize prayer books in seventeenth-century Poland, see Stefan C. Reif, *Shabbethai Sofer and his Prayer-book*, pp. 3–62.

58. On the Hasidic adoption of the Sephardic or Lurianic rite, see Mordecai L. Wilensky, "Hasidic-Mitnaggedic Polemics in the Jewish Communities of Eastern Europe," pp. 248–53, and Louis Jacobs, *Hasidic Prayer*, pp. 36–45.

59. On the performance of an oral and text-based liturgy see, Stefan C. Reif, *Judaism and Hebrew Prayer*, pp. 178–82, 221–55; and Zeev Gries, *Conduct Literature* and *The Book*

in Early Hasidim. On the issue of prayer book availability, Ruth Langer writes, "Indeed before the widespread availability of printed prayer books, the average Jew did not own a siddur [prayer book]; normal practice was to memorize the standard prayers and to rely on the sheliah tzibbur's [hazzan, leader of the congregation] repetition for the more infrequent holiday prayer." *To Worship God Properly*, p. 243. On the complex interrelationship between manuscript and printed text, see Elchanan Reiner, "The Ashkenazi Elite at the Beginning of the Modern Era," pp. 85–98.

60. Chava Weissler, *Voices of the Matriarchs*, pp. 52–59, helps to define these common worshipers by quoting Moses ben Henoch Yerushalmi Altshuler's (c. 1546–1633) popular ethical book *Brantshpigl* (Burning mirror), which was written in Yiddish "for women and for men who are like women." In this definition, a major distinction among common and elite worshipers is made between those who can understand only Yiddish and those who can also understand Hebrew. Although most males had some familiarity with Hebrew, only a well-educated Jew would have had the ability to speak and read Hebrew fluently in the small towns of the seventeenth and eighteenth centuries. It must be stressed, however, that beyond these general observations, little is known about the ability of most Jews from small towns like Gwoździec to understand the Hebrew liturgy. See Nisson E. Shulman, *Authority and Community*, pp. 82–90; Chava Weissler, *Voices of the Matriarchs*, pp. 6–9, 38–50; and Daniel Stone, "Knowledge of Foreign Languages among Eighteenth-Century Polish Jews," pp. 200–20.

61. The assessment of scribal errors engages larger problems of intent and meaning among patrons, users, and artists. Marc Michael Epstein addresses these issues in *Dreams of Subversion*, pp. 1–15.

62. See Louis H. Feldman, "Diaspora Synagogues," pp. 48–66; Carol Krinsky, *Synagogues of Europe*, pp. 21–59; and Isaac Levy, *The Synagogue*, pp. 28–73.

63. This donor dedication is shown in a photograph of the western wall below prayers that accompanied the Priestly Blessing. Wooden synagogue files, Department of Prints and Drawings, Tel Aviv Museum of Art.

64. Although some parallels exist, a symbolic reading of Hebrew prayer in the synagogue would not be the same as a Christian liturgical reading of the art in medieval churches, as analyzed in Michael Camille, *Gothic Art*, pp. 41–69. For various modes of approaching and seeing God through the esoteric reading of Hebrew texts and prayer, see Frank Talmage, "Apples of Gold," pp. 321–45; Elliot R. Wolfson, *Through a Speculum That Shines*, pp. 33–44, 326–45, 383–92; and Joseph Dan, "Prayer as Text and Prayer as Mystical Experience," pp. 33–45.

65. Moshe Idel has examined the increasing emphasis on the sanctity of Hebrew letters, words, and divine names in prayer during the period immediately preceding the remodeling of the Gwoździec Synagogue; see "Perceptions

of Kabbalah in the Second Half of the 18th century," pp. 75–104. Elliot Wolfson has written extensively on the sanctity and rituals of Torah reading, for example in "The Mystical Significance of Torah Study in German Pietism," pp. 43–77. The scribal art of micrography (masorah figurata), the creation of textual figures from Hebrew script developed by Jewish scribes, is a unique art form that honors the Hebrew script, see Leila Avrin, "Micrography as Art," pp. 43–80 plus unnumbered figures; and Joseph Gutmann, "Masorah Figurata," pp. 49–62 plus unnumbered figures. On the sanctity of Hebrew letters and words of the prayer book in the Hasidei Ashkenaz of medieval Germany, see Arnold S. Rosenberg, *Jewish Liturgy as a Spiritual System*, p. 51.

66. See Jerrilynn D. Dodds, "Mudejar Tradition and the Synagogues of Medieval Spain," pp. 113–31; Ittai Tamari, "The Inscriptions Adorning the Synagogue Hall," pp. 135–46 (pagination in reverse order).

67. The Jabłonów Synagogue prayers are copied in elevation drawings in Ludwik Wierzbicki, *Proceedings of the Commission*. The synagogues at Gwoździec and Jabłonów contain the only completely documented interiors showing painted prayers on each of the four walls.

68. On the development of the rituals of the Torah Service, see Ruth Langer, "From Study of Scripture to a Reenactment of Sinai," pp. 43–67; and Stefan C. Reif, *Judaism and Hebrew Prayer*, pp. 215–218. In an e-mail, H-Judaica listserv, Jan. 31, 2000, Ruth Langer emphasized that the ritual of lifting the Torah scroll, although mentioned in scattered earlier sources, became "common among both Ashkenazi and Sephardi Jews only in the 16th century." She speculated that the practice of pointing to the Torah scroll originated in "popular custom and it may be concurrent with some eighteenth-century customs to accompany each movement connected to the Torah ritual with an appropriate biblical verse, essentially calling on deeper personal involvement and attention with what the received ritual dictated."

69. The attempts of scholars and rabbis from larger towns to influence the common liturgy is well documented by Stefan C. Reif, *Shabbethai Sofer and his Prayer Book*, pp. 53–62, and *Judaism and Hebrew Prayer*, pp. 151–255; Ismar Elbogan, *Jewish Liturgy: A Comprehensive History*, pp. 271–95; and Elchanan Reiner, "The Ashkenazi Elite," pp. 85–98. But the extent to which these efforts actually influenced the practical liturgy from small towns like Gwoździec is unknown.

70. On the influence of Kabbalism on early-modern Ashkenazi liturgy, see Moshe Hallamish, "The Influence of the Kabbalah on Jewish Liturgy," pp. 121–31; Abraham I. Schechter, "Cabbalistic Interpolations in the Prayer Book," pp. 39–60; and Stefan C. Reif, *Judaism and Hebrew Prayer*, pp. 226–55.

71. Stephen D. Benin explores the degree to which elite Kabbalistic themes could influence popular liturgy, including the complex interaction between local custom (minhag)

and Jewish law (halakhah), on religious life, in "A Hen Crowing like a Cock," pp. 261–281.

72. On the problem of analyzing German influence on Jewish and Polish cultural development, see Jan M. Piskorski, "The Historiography of the So-Called 'East Colonization' and the Current State of Research," pp. 654–67. On the basic Ashkenazi roots of Polish Jewry, see Israel M. Ta-Shma, "On the History of the Jews in Twelfth- and Thirteenth-Century Poland," pp. 287–320.

73. There have been many attempts to trace non-Ashkenazi Jewish settlement in Poland. Scholars have suggested that such settlers could have arrived through immigration from the tenth-century Kazar Kingdom, Sephardic and Karaite settlement, gradual settlement by traders along eastern trade routes, and immigration of the "lost tribes"; see Omeljan Pritsak, "The Pre-Ashkenazic Jews of Eastern Europe," pp. 6–10. Kazar Kingdom immigration theories, although unsubstantiated in demographic research and Polish historical sources, have remained popular. See for example, Arthur Koestler, *The Thirteenth Tribe: The Khazar Empire and Its Heritage*, pp. 159–80; and Norman Golb and Omeljan Pritsak, *Khazarian Hebrew Documents of the Tenth Century*, pp. xiii–xvi. Although there were non-Ashkenazi settlements in Poland, most were small communities that cannot begin to explain larger patterns of migration and cultural development that produced an overwhelmingly Ashkenazi culture in Poland. For an overview of Ashkenazi immigration, see Bernard D. Weinryb, *The Jews of Poland*, pp. 19–35.

74. On the Germanic/Ashkenazic derivation of the major forms of Polish-Jewish culture, see Israel M. Ta-Shma, "On the History of the Jews in Twelfth- and Thirteenth-Century Poland," pp. 307–20, and Ephraim Kanarfogel, "*Peering Through the Lattices*," pp. 112–13, 125, 251–58. Both studies establish the long-term Germanic religious roots of Polish Jewry. Alice Faber and Robert King, "Yiddish and the Settlement of Ashkenazi Jews," pp. 73–108, attempt an objective appraisal of Jewish immigration to Poland based solely on Yiddish linguistic evidence. Although it is a good summary of data, similar studies demonstrate the weakness of single criteria investigations to fully account for historical development.

75. On the advanced level of Polish-Jewish artistic development in a range of art forms, see Sarah Harel Hoshen, ed., *Treasures of Jewish Galicja*; and Maksymiljan Goldstein, Karol Dresdner, and Majer Balabon, *Kultura i sztuka ludu żydowskiego na ziemiach Polskich*.

76. On the need for an extended period of development for folk art and architecture, see Henry Glassie, *The Spirit of Folk Art*, pp. 198–228, and Aron Gurevich, *Medieval Popular Culture*, pp. 54–60.

77. The liturgy of Jewish worship, although not unchanging, has proven resistant to rapid change; see Stefan C. Reif, *Judaism and Hebrew Prayer*, pp. 22–52, and A. Z. Idelsohn, *Jewish Liturgy and Its Development*, pp. 3–70. This study has shown the many ways that the art and the liturgy of the synagogue were closely related. The conservative nature of liturgical development is assumed to have influenced the development of synagogue wall-paintings, although this point lacks documentation.

78. The depiction of the medieval city in Jewish art is detailed in Therese and Mendel Metzger, *Jewish Life in the Middle Ages*, pp. 44–57. On the architectural representation of Jerusalem in forms of medieval art, see Jonathan J. G. Alexander, "*Jerusalem the Golden*: Image and Myth in the Middle Ages in Western Europe," pp. 255–64. The particular motif of a European medieval city, often symbolizing Jerusalem, atop an arched structure is, however, a common image in Hebrew illuminated manuscripts. Several types of medieval German manuscripts and early-modern Eastern-European manuscripts and printed books have similar architectural surrounds. See Bianca Kuhnel, "The Use and Abuse of Jerusalem," pp. xix–xxviii; Therese and Mendel Metzger, *Jewish Life in the Middle Ages*, pp. 39–86; and Bezalel Narkiss, *Hebrew Illuminated Manuscripts*, pp. 88–120. On the occurrence of Temple motifs in Romanesque art, see Walter Cahn, "Solomonic Elements in Romanesque Art," pp. 45–72.

79. On the artistic isolation of many dominant art forms and motifs in the wooden synagogue paintings from the major artistic currents of eighteenth-century sources, see Adam Miłobędzki, "Medieval Architectural Tradition," pp. 39–43. On the wall-paintings' similarities to and differences from surrounding folk traditions, see Barbara Wolff-Łozińska, *Malowidła stropów polskich I połowy XVI w*, pp. 7–25, and Adam Miłobędzki, "Survival of Gothic," pp. 149–51.

80. See Henry Mayr-Harting, *Ottonian Book Illumination*, Part 1, pp. 25–55; also see Adolph Goldschmidt, *German Illumination*, vol. 1, pp. 1–30.

81. Christian artistic traditions borrowed and reinterpreted by Jews are analyzed by Marc Michael Epstein, *Dreams of Subversion*, pp. 1–15, 96–119; Joseph Gutmann, *Hebrew Manuscript Painting*, pp. 12–13; Franz Landsberger, "The Illumination of Hebrew Manuscripts in the Middle Ages and Renaissance," pp. 146–48; and Gabrielle Sed-Rajna, "Filigree Ornaments in Fourteenth-Century Hebrew Manuscripts of the Upper Rhine," pp. 45–54. Byzantine illuminated manuscripts may also have influenced Eastern-European communities. See Alexander Saminsky, "A Reference to Jerusalem in a Georgian Gospel Book," pp. 354–69; Alexei Lidov, "Heavenly Jerusalem," pp. 341–53; Otto Demus, *Byzantine Art and the West*; Kurt Wietzmann et al., *The Place of Book Illumination in Byzantine Art*.

82. On the continuation of these medieval art forms in Poland, see Iris Fishof, "The Origin of the *Siddur* of the Rabbi of Ruzhin," pp. 73–82. Medieval manuscript motifs appear to continue in *Sefer Evronot*, 1664, and similar motifs are further developed in elaborate fashion in a 1780 version of Joseph Vital, *Sefer Ets Hayim*. A range of Eastern-European Jewish art forms collected by Semyon

An-sky that contain earlier Ashkenazi motifs are organized by Alexander Kantsedikas, "Semyon An-sky and the Jewish Artistic Heritage," pp. 17–122. Other material from An-sky's collection is presented in Beukers and Waale, *Tracing An-sky*. A tombstone dated 1203 from Breslau (Wrocław), western Poland, was decorated and lettered in a style characteristic of the regions near Worms and Mainz (Germany), cited in M. Brann, "Ein Breslauer Grabdenkmal aus dem Jahre 1203," pp. 11–16.

83. El Lissitzky, "The Synagogue of Mohilev," p. 12.

84. Stefan Szyller, *Czy mamy polską Architekturę?* pp. 45–51, 116–20.

85. Similarities between synagogues and mosques are emphasized in Jerrilynn D. Dodds, "Mudejar Tradition and the Synagogues of Medieval Spain," pp. 113–31.

86. On Sephardi and Islamic cultural and artistic influences, see Esther Benbassa and Aron Rodrigue, *Sephardi Jewry*, pp. 36–64; Aron Rodrigue, "The Sephardim in the Ottoman Empire," pp. 162–88; Leo Ary Mayer, "Jewish Art in the Moslem World," pp. 353–76; Basilio Pavon Maldonado, "The Mudejar Elements of the El Transito Synagogue," pp. 151–135 (English pages in reverse order); and Esther Juhasz, "Textiles for the Home and Synagogue," pp. 64–119. For an overview of the Sephardi/Islamic relationship, see S. D. Goitein, *Jews and Arabs*, pp. 125–211; and Jacob Elbaum, "The Influence of Spanish-Jewish Culture on the Jews of Ashkenaz and Poland in the Fifteenth–Seventeenth Centuries," pp. 179–97.

87. On the Ottoman/Islamic artistic influence in Gwoździec and Poland, see Dariusz Kołodziejczyk, *Podole pod panowaniem tureckim, 1672–1699*, pp. 45–133; Zdzisław Żygulski, Jr., *Sztuka Islamu w Zbiorach Polskich*, pp. 5–43, unnumbered illustrations; and Beata Biedrońska-Słotowa, *Orient w Sztuce Polskiej*. Turkish carpets and their motifs are also analyzed by Beata Biedrońska-Słotowa, *Kobierce tureckie*. See note 16, chapter 3.

88. On themes of decorative backgrounds and borders, see E. H. Gombrich, *Sense of Order*, pp. 149–70.

89. On Polish trade routes to Asia and the artistic influence of Islam and the Ottomans that such trade routes made possible, see Tadeusz Mankowski, *Orient w Polskiej Kulturze Artystycznej*, pp. 50–64, 89–111, and Zdzisław Żygulski, Jr., *Sztuka Islamu w Zbiorach Polskich*, pp. 5–35, plus figures, unnumbered pages.

90. On Jewish participation in the European textile trade, see Bracha Yaniv, "Ceremonial Textiles for the Synagogue," pp. 101–13. On the European textile trade to Poland and magnate involvement in such trade, see Tadeusz Mankowski, *Orient w Sztuce Polskiej*, pp. 150–89. The dominance of the European textile trade is evident in the 10,000-piece fabric collection in the Czechoslovak State Jewish Museum in Prague. See Hana Volavkova, *The Synagogue Treasures of Bohemia and Moravia*, pp. xiv–xv and figures. This collection demonstrates the frequent use of eastern/Ottoman motifs in Polish textiles; see Zdzisław Żygulski, *Sztuka Islamu*.

91. A similar tradition of Ukrainian wooden church painting, one that combines vernacular and high style influences, is preserved at the Church of St. George, Drohobycz, Ukraine; see H. M. Zoltowskij, *Monumental Paintings in Ukraine*. Similarities in the interior paintings of Polish Catholic churches, Ukrainian Orthodox churches, and the wooden synagogues are noted by Piechotka, "Polichromie polskich bóżnic drewnianych," pp. 65, 73. Parallels can also be drawn between Ukrainian and Russian Orthodox decorative art traditions and the wooden synagogues; see G. K. Loukomski, *L'Art Decoratif Russe*, plates 7–17, 44–52, 110–33, 172–91. When the ceiling motifs of wooden synagogues and churches are compared, pre-1700 Polish wooden churches generally follow older folk traditions with geometrical patterns integrated into floral backgrounds; see Barbara Wolff-Łozińska, *Malowidła stropów polskich I połowy XVI w*, pp. 7–26, and unpaginated figures 27–185.

92. The word "cosmopolitan" is used here to describe the multicultural, hybrid art of the Polish synagogue. Unfortunately, the term has also been used antisemitically to criticize Jewish urbanity. This is certainly not the intent of the term "cosmopolitan" as used in this research, where it is intended to communicate a worldly, multicultural sophistication of the Polish Jewish community. On the appropriateness of the term "multiculturalism" to describe European Jewish experience, see Oded Heilbronner, "Introduction: European Jews as a Factor in Multicultural Society," pp. 63–68; and, in a later period, Shulamit Volkov, "Minorities and the Nation-State," pp. 69–88. It should also be noted that the term "international culture," when applied to the Jewish community, has also been used in antisemitic literature to mean or imply an "international Jewish conspiracy." For related issues, see Janusz Tazbir, "Conspiracy Theories and the Reception of The Protocols of the Elders of Zion in Poland," pp. 171–82, and Richard I. Cohen, *Jewish Icons*, pp. 221–60.

93. On the sophistication of Jewish patterns of communication, education, and travel, see Jonathan Israel, *European Jewry in the Age of Mercantilism, 1550–1750*, pp. 170–83, 207–16; Sophia Menache, "Communication in the Jewish Diaspora," pp. 15–57; Daniel Stone, "Knowledge of Foreign Languages among Eighteenth-Century Polish Jews," pp. 200–20; and Gershon Hundert, *The Jews in a Polish Private Town*, pp. 50–68.

94. On the widespread tradition of premodern Jewish travel, see Sophia Menache, "Communication in the Jewish Diaspora," pp. 34–39. The frequency of merchant travel is detailed in a diary from the Podolian region written just before the Gwoździec Synagogue was remodeled; M. Vishnitzer trans., *The Memoirs of Ber of Bolechow*, pp. 1–49. On the issue of Gentile perceptions of Jewish travel, especially as crystallized in legends of the "wandering Jew," see Galit Hasan-Rokem and Alan Dundes, *The Wandering Jew*, and George K. Anderson, *The Legend of*

the Wandering Jew. The complexities of Jewish walking, wandering, and the "itinerant motif" are developed in such varied sources as Richard I. Cohen, *Jewish Icons*, pp. 221–55; Elliot R. Wolfson, in the chapter, "Walking as a Sacred Duty," in *Along the Path*, pp. 89–109.

95. The remarkable sophistication and cohesiveness of European Jewish culture in the seventeenth and eighteenth centuries is outlined by Jonathan Israel, *European Jewry in the Age of Mercantilism*, pp. 123–236. Many of the central themes of Israel's thesis are applied to seventeenth- and eighteenth-century eastern Poland.

96. Jewish artistic development follows current multicultural and hybridization models, as outlined in Homi Bhabha, *The Location of Culture*.

5. Historical Context

1. This relationship between great and little history, analyzed by Henry Glassie, *Folk Housing*, pp. 8–25, has more commonly been interpreted as a struggle between elite and popular cultural history, as developed in E. P. Thompson, *The Making of the English Working Class*, and Clifford Geertz, *Interpretation of Culture*, pp. 193–254.

2. On the geography of the Gwoździec region, see Orest Subtelney, *Ukraine: A History*, pp. 3–15, and Paul Robert Magocsi, *Historical Atlas of East Central Europe*, pp. 2–10.

3. On trade routes and connections between Asia and Europe, see M. J. Rosman, *The Lords' Jews*, pp. 75–105; Gershon David Hundert, *The Jews in a Polish Private Town*, pp. 50–63; Orest Subtelney, *Ukraine: A History*, pp. 81–91, 178–181; and Paul Robert Magocsi, *Historical Atlas of East Central Europe*, pp. 34–45. On Jewish participation in the Polish-Ottoman trade routes, especially those in Lviv, see H. H. Ben-Sasson, *A History of the Jewish People*, pp. 580–82.

4. See note 68, chapter 3.

5. On the sources for Jewish demographic information on Gwoździec, see *Słownik Geograficzny*, p. 924, Document: "Register of damages suffered from the Crown Army by the town of Gwoździec in the land of Halicz, 1712," Potocki family files of Radzyń, p. 23, no. 242, Main Archives for Historic Records, AGAD, Warsaw; *Pinkas Hakehillot*, pp. 135–37 (this source lists two different population figures, 541 and 126, for 1765, p. 135); and Mendel Zilbur, *The Gwoździec Memory Book*, p. 41. This information on early Jewish settlement must be interpreted cautiously. Early records may include itinerant Jewish presence, such as the visits of Jewish traders. Later sources may have undercounted minority populations, especially in towns where restrictions were placed on Jewish settlement and land ownership. Such inaccuracies are standard problems in Jewish community demography of pre-1764 Poland; see Stampfer, "The 1764 Census," pp. 44–59. In Chodorów, Ukraine, a similar-sized town with a well-documented wooden synagogue 50 miles northwest of Gwoździec, the Jewish population in the 1660s was 128. By 1720, a few years after the Chodorów Synagogue was remodeled and the ceiling painted, the population was 702 (file no. 146/85/2368, Central State Historical Archives of Ukraine, Lviv). Another method for determining Jewish population is the study of religious activity; see for example Israel M. Ta-Shma, "On the History of the Jews in Twelfth- and Thirteenth-Century Poland," pp. 287–320. General population assessments for Gwoździec may be gleaned from Mendel Zilbur, *The Gwoździec Memory Book*, pp. 38–42, 78. On the complexities of settlement demographics in similar Polish towns, see Gershon David Hundert, *Polish Private Town*, pp. 1–8, and M. J. Rosman, *The Lords' Jews*, pp. 39–48. Jewish population statistics are summarized in earlier studies such as S. M. Dubnow, *History of the Jews*, pp. 13–58, and Bernard D. Weinryb, *The Jews of Poland*, pp. 17–32.

6. On the frontier development of eastern provinces in the Polish state, see M. J. Rosman, *The Lords' Jews*, pp. 36–54, and Moshe Rosman, *Founder of Hasidim*, pp. 42–62. When seen from the perspective of a postindustrial/ nation-state history, eastern Poland was an underdeveloped agricultural region that was left behind by the major movements of the modern era; Robert Brenner, "Economic Backwardness in Eastern Europe in Light of Developments in the West," pp. 15–52, and Jerome Blum, *The End of the Old Order in Rural Europe*, pp. 241–331.

7. The 1764 census of Polish Jewry has been the basis for many scholarly assessments of Jewish population trends in Eastern Europe; see Shaul Stampfer, "The 1764 Census of Polish Jewry," pp. 41–147. On Podolian regional population estimates see M. J. Rosman, *The Lords' Jews*, pp. 38–48, and Moshe Rosman, *Founder of Hasidism*, pp. 60–69.

8. See Jacob Goldberg, *Jewish Privileges in the Polish Commonwealth*, pp. 6–7; for a summary of privileges, see pp. 1–52. See also A. Cygielman, "The Basic Privileges of the Jews of Great Poland as Reflected in Polish Historiography," pp. 117–49. On the social and economic traditions of religious tolerance underlying these privileges in Poland, see Janusz Tazbir, *A State Without Stakes*, pp. 198–210.

9. Jacob Goldberg, *Jewish Privileges in the Polish Commonwealth*, p. 83. Goldberg's work is particularly important for this study because he provides a detailed list of Jewish privileges in many Polish towns, and he demonstrates the ways magnate support attracted Jews, particularly to the small eastern towns (pp. 1–46). Although many of the town privileges recorded by Goldberg date from the second half of the eighteenth century, most of these documents were initiated by Jewish communities seeking to reconfirm previously existing privileges during the turmoil of the Polish partitions and especially following the dissolution of the Kahal organization in 1764.

10. For a summary of the European expulsions of Jews that initiated the major waves of Ashkenazi immigration to

Poland, see Zenon Guldon and Waldemar Kowalski, "Between Tolerance and Abomination," pp. 161–75. For a general review of immigration, see Leonard B. Glick, *Abraham's Heirs*, pp. 234–73; and Bernard D. Weinryb, *The Jews of Poland*, pp. 19–35.

11. On the influence and importance of Magdeburg Law for Eastern Europe and Jewish settlement, see Jan M. Piskorski, "The Historiography of the So-Called 'East Colonization' and Current State of Research," pp. 654–67; and Jacob Goldberg, "The Privileges Granted to Jewish Communities of the Polish Commonwealth," pp. 43–45.

12. On the issue of Germanization and the difficulties of articulating these concepts in Jewish and Eastern-European historiography, see Jan M. Piskorski, "The Historiography of the So-Called 'East Colonization' and the Current State of Research," pp. 654–67.

13. On the development of Eastern-European multicultural trading towns, see M. J. Rosman, *The Lords' Jews*, pp. 36–74, and Gershon David Hundert, *The Jews in a Polish Private Town*, pp. 36–68. For an overview of this phenomenon, see Thomas DaCosta Kaufmann, *Court, Cloister, and City*, pp. 13–27.

14. While the rural economy of seventeenth- and eighteenth-century eastern Poland expanded, it had serious, long-term problems. See Jacek Kochanowicz, "The Polish Economy and the Evolution of Dependency," pp. 92–130.

15. Several walled, ghetto-like enclaves were recorded during the medieval period in the largest Polish towns, for example, in Kazimierz, Cracow's suburban Jewish district. Punitive walled ghettos, however, were not found in Poland's eastern provinces during the settlement period for Gwoździec. On the complexities of settlement patterns and the continuing restrictions placed on the Jewish community during the early modern era, see Gershon David Hundert's "The Role of the Jews in Commerce in Early Modern Poland-Lithuania," pp. 245–75, and "Jewish Urban Residence in the Polish Commonwealth in the Early Modern Era," pp. 25–34. Jacob Katz's balanced assessment of the external segregation and internal separation of the Polish Jewish community, *Exclusiveness and Tolerance*, pp. 131–68, is one of the finest works to address this difficult topic.

16. See Nisson E. Shulman, *Authority and Community*, pp. 3–92; Shmuel A. Arthur Cygielman, *Jewish Autonomy in Poland and Lithuania*, pp. 13–44; and Shmul Ettinger, "The Council of the Four Lands," pp. 93–109.

17. On the Kahal's sophisticated system of governance, see Gershon David Hundert, *The Jews in a Polish Private Town*, pp. 85–115; Jacob Goldberg, "The Jewish Sejm," pp. 147–65; Mordekhai Nadav, "Regional Aspects of the Autonomy of Polish Jews," pp. 166–73; and Gershon David Hundert, "The *Kehilla* and the Municipality in Private Towns at the End of the Early Modern Period," pp. 174–85. David Baile stresses the unique political aspects and advantages of the "corporate" Kahal system of self-government, especially in relation to other forms of government before the modern era, in *Power and Powerlessness in Jewish History*, pp. 58–83.

18. On the failures of the Kahal system of Jewish self-government in the early modern period, see S. M. Dubnow, *History of the Jews in Russia and Poland*, pp. 189–98; Raphael Mahler, *A History of Modern Jewry*, pp. 291–98; H. H. Ben-Sasson, *A History of the Jewish People*, pp. 711, 766–67. Eli Lederhendler, *From Autonomy to Auto-Emancipation*, pp. 102–70. For objective appraisals of the Kahal system and the reasons for its later failures, see Benzion Dinur, "The Origins of Hasidism and Its Social and Messianic Foundations," pp. 95–98; Gershon David Hundert, "The *Kehilla* and the Municipality in Private Towns at the End of the Early Modern Period," pp. 174–85.

19. The problems of analyzing Jewish losses in the Chmielnicki massacres are analyzed by Edward Fram, "Creating a Tale of Martyrdom in Tulczyn, 1648," pp. 89–112; and Daniel Beauvois, "Polish-Jewish Relations in the Territories Annexed by the Russian Empire in the First Half of the Nineteenth Century," pp. 78–90. The destruction of Jewish populations during the Chmielnicki revolt in eastern Poland suggests that Jewish culture in these regions was irrevocably damaged. For example, see S. M. Dubnow, *History of the Jews in Russia and Poland*, pp. 139–53; and Robert M. Seltzer, *Jewish People, Jewish Thought*, pp. 480–96. The resurgence of Jewish populations in these same regions within 50 to 100 years of the massacres is, however, noted by most demographic and economic historians, for example, Andrzej Link-Lenczowski, "The Jewish Population in the Light of the Resolutions of the Dietines in the Sixteenth to the Eighteenth Centuries," pp. 36–44. For a Ukrainian perspective, see Orest Subtelny, *Ukraine: A History*, pp. 123–38; and Frank E. Sysyn, "The Jewish Factor in the Chmielnicki Uprising," pp. 43–54.

20. See Norman Davies, *God's Playground*, pp. 463–510.

21. Eighteenth-century population and economic expansion in the eastern Polish provinces is cited in Norman Davies, *God's Playground*, pp. 433–69; Orest Subtelny, *Ukraine: A History*, pp. 155–57, 178–98; M. J. Rosman, *Lords' Jews*, pp. 185–212; Shmuel Ettinger, "Jewish Participation in the Settlement of Ukraine in the Sixteenth and Seventeenth Centuries," pp. 23–30; and Jacob Litman, *The Economic Role of Jews in Medieval Poland*, pp. 154–223. For previously accepted theories of post-1648 social and economic deterioration in Eastern-European Jewry, see S. M. Dubnow, *History of Jews of Russia and Poland*, pp. 138–87; and Hinrich Graetz, *History of the Jews*, pp. 51–56, 375–94. Although these and later studies, such as Moses A. Shulvass, *From East to West*, pp. 19–78, have assumed large-scale Jewish emigration from Poland following the Chmielnicki massacres, this emigration has not been confirmed in detailed studies; see, for example, Moshe Rosman, *Founder of Hasidism*, pp. 49–82.

22. On the expansion of private towns, see Gershon David Hundert, *The Jews in a Polish Private Town*, pp. 36–68,

134–55; M. J. Rosman, *Lords' Jews*, pp. 37–105, and "The Polish Magnates and the Jews." Both authors also provide ample documentation of the prohibitions and restrictions placed on the Jewish minority population, but, in balance, they present documentation of pre-1764 communities that were expanding, self-governing, and, by eighteenth-century, Eastern-European socioeconomic standards, relatively stable and prosperous. For a negative assessment of the same eighteenth-century era, see Jacek Kochanowicz, "The Polish Economy and the Evolution of Dependency," pp. 92–130. For a balanced assessment of the era, see Ignacy Schiper, *Dzieje handlu żydowskiego na ziemiach polskich*, pp. 1–24. For a positive assessment of the era, see Jonathan Israel, *European Jewry in the Age of Mercantilism*, pp. 145–83, esp. p. 182. The Podolian region was also a spawning ground for major movements of Jewish and Ukrainian religious and social reform; see Evyatar Friesel, *Atlas of Modern Jewish History*, pp. 50–51. This was the same region that Gershom Scholem described as a hotbed of Kabbalistic activity: "There is no doubt that in the first half of the seventeenth century, Poland, and more particularly its southern parts Galicja, Podolia, and Volhynia, was the scene of a considerable kabbalistic revival" (*Sabbatai Sevi; The Mystical Messiah, 1626–1676*, p. 79).

23. On the economic prosperity of small private towns of eastern Poland during the eighteenth century, see Gershon David Hundert, "The Role of the Jews in Commerce in Early Modern Poland-Lithuania," pp. 245–75, esp. 246–49; and "The Implications of Jewish Economic Activities for Christian-Jewish Relations in the Polish Commonwealth," pp. 55–63. In nine similarly sized towns in Gwoździec's regions surveyed for this research, relative economic prosperity supported synagogue construction or remodeling.

24. See Moshe Rosman, *Founder of Hasidism*, p. 61. Gershon Hundert reviews the positive perception of Poland by Polish Jewry in "Poland: Paradisus Judaeorum," pp. 335–48.

25. On the possible factors contributing to Jewish population and economic expansion, see Gershon David Hundert, "Jewish Children and Childhood in Early Modern East Central Europe," pp. 81–94.

26. The creativity and originality of the Polish wooden synagogue is made evident in comparison to synagogues in other Diaspora communities. In surveys of synagogues throughout the world, the surrounding architectural context is seldom analyzed to determine the degree to which Diaspora synagogues departed from or conformed to the architecture of their regions; see Gruber, *Synagogues*, and H. A. Meek, *The Synagogue*. In most of the Diaspora, pre-1800 synagogues closely followed the architectural precedents of their surrounding cultures. This pattern is consistent for synagogues in both elite urban communities, such as seventeenth-century Amsterdam, and rural vernacular communities, such as medieval Moroccan villages. Several factors allowed Polish communities to begin to stand outside the standard architectural conventions of their host culture. The most important was that their population grew to a significant proportion in many Polish towns. This produced a unique critical mass of Jewish popular culture in the towns of eastern Poland, including a dominant physical and spatial presence unique to Jewish communities since the late Roman era. In most Diaspora settlements worldwide with less size or longevity of Jewish presence, synagogue architecture followed regional precedents much more closely. In Muslim countries where Jews resided for even longer periods than in Poland, Jewish communities never developed a large-scale, autonomous, popular culture with a dominant spatial and cultural presence like the ones that developed so consistently in Poland. Consequently, a specific Jewish-Islamic architecture never emerged.

27. Magnate support for the Jewish populations of their privately owned towns is well documented; see Gershon David Hundert, *The Jews in a Polish Private Town*, pp. 75–85; Maria and Kazimierz Piechotka, *Wooden Synagogues*, pp. 13–22; Gershon David Hundert, "The Role of the Jews in Commerce in Early Modern Poland-Lithuania," pp. 257–64, and M. J. Rosman, *The Lords' Jews*, pp. 136–37, 145–46.

28. See Norman Davies, *God's Playground*, p. 213.

29. The pre-partition historic diversity and changes in Polish society's perception of the Jews are analyzed in Janusz Tazbir, "Images of the Jew in the Polish Commonwealth," pp. 18–30; Jewish attitudes toward Poles in the same period are analyzed by M. J. Rosman, "A Minority Views the Majority," pp. 31–52; and Israel Bartal, "The *Porets* and the *Arendar*: The Depiction of Poles in Jewish Literature," pp. 357–69.

30. On the declining economic and social status of post-partition Polish Jews and the deterioration of magnate kingdoms that accompanied the rise of Polish and Ukrainian nationalism, see Daniel Beauvois, "Polish-Jewish Relations in the Territories Annexed by the Russian Empire in the First Half of the Nineteenth Century," pp. 78–90; and Robert M. Seltzer, *Jewish People, Jewish Thought*, pp. 482–96. On the lingering survival and consequences of ancient regime serfdom in Eastern Europe, see Jerome Blum, *The End of the Old Order in Rural Europe*, pp. 197–215, 357–76; and Peter Gunst, "Agrarian Systems of Central and Eastern Europe," pp. 53–91. Historians have interpreted in various ways the failure of this ancient regime and the Polish culture it sustained; see Norman Davies, *God's Playground*, pp. 492–546; Hillel Levine, *Economic Origins of AntiSemitism*, pp. 20–74, 145–60; and Daniel Chirot, "Causes and Consequences of Backwardness," pp. 1–14.

31. See Norman Davies, *God's Playground*, pp. 201–7; and Gershon David Hundert, *The Jews in a Polish Private Town*, pp. 36–45.

32. On Catholic antagonism and persecution of Polish Jews, see Zenon Guldon and Jacek Wijaczka, "The Accusation of Ritual Murder in Poland," pp. 99–140; Jacob Goldberg, "The Changes in the Attitude of Polish Society Toward the Jews in the 18th Century," pp. 35–48; Hillel Levine, *Economic Origins of AntiSemitism*, pp. 183–90, and summarized by H. H. Ben-Sasson, "The Middle Ages," pp. 403–20, 733–40.

33. Gwoździec's history shows no record of acts of violence or pogroms against the Jewish population. The Gwoździec Synagogue, along with a majority of the town's wooden buildings, was burned in military action between Austro-Hungarian and Russian forces during the First World War. There are conflicting accounts of the burning of the synagogue during fighting in which Russian forces occupied the town on three separate occasions between 1914 to 1916. In Jewish accounts, the Russians deliberately set fire to the synagogue during their final occupation. Several stories in the town's memory book describe the difficulty the Russian arsonists had in starting the fire; Mendel Zilbur, *The Gwoździec Memory Book*, pp. 36, 133.

34. On the limits of Catholic Church authority in Ukraine, see Orest Subtelny, *Ukraine: A History*, pp. 193–98, and Moshe Rosman, *Founder of Hasidism*, pp. 42–62.

35. On the local magnate's influence and control of the Catholic Church, especially in the eastern provinces, see Norman Davies, *God's Playground*, pp. 201–40.

36. On the ownership of serfs by magnates and on the serfs' farming practices, see Jerome Blum, *The End of the Old Order in Rural Europe*, pp. 116–96; and Norman Davies, *God's Playground*, pp. 201–14, 240–46. For a negative appraisal of this social and economic system, see the articles in Daniel Chirot, ed., *The Origins of Backwardness in Eastern Europe*.

37. On nineteenth-century impoverishment and the concurrent rising violence against Jewish communities, primarily on lands under Russian administration, see Shmuel Ettinger, "The Modern Period," pp. 733–40, 813–33, 881–90; and Hillel Levine, *Economic Origins of Anti-Semitism*, pp. 160–239. On the deterioration of conditions for Jewish communities during the period of the partitions during the second half of the eighteenth century, see Jacob Goldberg, "The Changes in the Attitude of Polish Society Toward the Jews in the 18th Century," pp. 35–48.

38. On Eastern-European backwardness and the rise of the nation-state, see Robert Brenner, "Economic Backwardness," pp. 15–52, and Norman Davies, *God's Playground*, pp. 492–546.

39. On the wooden synagogues in Grodno-Białystok region, see Maria and Kazimierz Piechotka, *Wooden Synagogues*, pp. 39–46.

40. On the complex factors contributing to the abandonment of wooden synagogue traditions, see Jacob Katz, *Out of the Ghetto*, pp. 1–41, and "Introduction" and "Jewry and Judaism in the Nineteenth Century" in *Emancipation and Assimilation*, pp. ix–xii and 1–20.

41. See note 33 above.

6. Design of the Synagogue

1. See Maria and Kazimierz Piechotka, *Wooden Synagogues*, pp. 7–8.

2. See notes 48, 50, and 52, chapter 3.

3. My emphasis on the Jewish contributions to the synagogue design is not meant to de-emphasize the considerable Eastern-European contribution. It is important, however, to carefully differentiate the role of Jewish ideas in the design of the synagogue from Eastern-European ideas because the influence of these Jewish ideas has been so uncritically assumed and so insufficiently documented in current scholarship. Besides the names of the Jewish artists who painted the ceiling, little is known about the design of the Gwoździec Synagogue or any other pre-1800 Polish wooden synagogue. See Maria and Kazimierz Piechotka, *Wooden Synagogues*, pp. 35–47, and *Bramy Nieba: Bóżnice drewniane*, pp. 29–37.

4. On the limitations of "common-sense," functional, and popular explanations for vernacular design, see Henry Glassie, *Folk Housing*, pp. 13–24. Such explanations for architectural development are not without merit; for example, communities did, and still do, copy synagogue designs from adjacent towns. But the question of motivation becomes more difficult to resolve when one realizes that, in the eighteenth century, there were several different types of synagogues in surrounding towns. This problem of multiple precedents is especially evident with regard to the masonry synagogues in larger towns, which could have served as models for the wooden synagogue builders. Suddenly, the common-sense, practical question becomes far more complicated: Why did the Gwoździec community develop its unique vaulted wooden ceiling instead of copying other styles of synagogue design? Why especially did they not borrow the example of the masonry synagogues built in older, larger surrounding towns like Tarnopol and Lviv? As we have seen, the Jewish community of Gwoździec did not choose to copy these synagogues.

5. On the role of tradition in synagogue design across time, see Lee I. Levine, *The Ancient Synagogue*, pp. 291–356, and Carol Krinsky, *Synagogues of Europe*, pp. 5–34.

6. On the role of oral decision-making in the design of vernacular architecture, see Henry Glassie, *Folk Housing*, pp. 13–65, and Walter J. Ong, *Orality and Literacy*, pp. 5–30.

7. The scarcity of synagogue documentation in Jewish literature before the modern period is frequently noted. Joseph M. Baumgarten observes, "One of the remarkable aspects of Rabbinical teaching concerning prayer is the paucity of laws dealing with the architecture appropriate to the house of worship" ("Art in the Synagogue, Some Talmudic Views," p. 79). Raphael Posner writes, "Ha-

lakhah governs only very specific components of synagogue design and makes no stipulation for the building's general external appearance" ("Synagogues," p. 591). A significant exception, Joseph Caro, *Shulhan Arukh*, OH 90:4, 150:1–5, contains synagogue analysis, although most advice refers to conduct directives for worship and not to architectural design recommendations. In some cases, Caro's advice was influenced by recommendations from the *Zohar*.

8. The complex interplay between local custom (minhag) and Jewish law (halakhah) and their ability to influence religious life are discussed by Stephen D. Benin, "A Hen Crowing like a Cock: 'Popular Religion' and Jewish Law," pp. 261–81; see also Jacob Katz, *The "Shabbes Goy."*

9. While we are reasonably sure that both verses were not originally intended as specifications for synagogue construction, it is entirely possible that, through repeated reference over time, these verses may have provided guidance to those involved with synagogue design. This is especially true in relation to the themes of ascent and descent, which have multiple associations throughout Jewish literature; see Moshe Idel, *Kabbalah, New Perspectives*, pp. 166–70, 191–97; Elliot R. Wolfson, "Yeridah la-Merkavah," pp. 13–44; Annelies Kuyt, *The "Descent" to the Chariot*; and Martha Himmelfarb, *Ascent to Heaven in Jewish and Christian Apocalypses*, pp. 29–46.

10. Some of the complex issues relating the synagogue to the Tabernacle and Temple are summarized by Arthur Green, "Sabbath as Temple," pp. 287–305. The difficulty of analyzing synagogue/Temple relationships is explored in Victor Aptowitzer, "The Celestial Temple as Viewed in the Aggadah," pp. 2–27.

11. *Zohar*, II: 59b–60a. Except where cited, all references are taken from what Gershom Scholem, *Kabbalah*, p. 220, has described as the "main body" of the *Zohar*. This main body, first printed in 1558 in three volumes, is now the standard Mantua edition. Subsequent quotations from the *Zohar* will be indicated by volume and page number in the text. Except where noted, English quotations from the *Zohar* are based on Harry Sperling and Maurice Simon, *The Zohar*, and Isaiah Tishby, *The Wisdom of the Zohar*. All English translations, however, have been evaluated through comparison to the Aramaic original. The controversies about authorship and the sources for the *Zohar* are reviewed by Isaiah Tishby in *The Wisdom of the Zohar*, pp. 55–96.

12. The *Zohar*'s direct references to the synagogue include: plan, II: 59b; twelve windows, II: 251a; lattice window, III: 114b; four pillars, I: 18b; wall-paintings, II: 59b; synagogue beautification, II: 59b; and the Tabernacle, II: 231b, 232a. Each of these topics is examined in chapters 6 and 7.

13. On the scholarly criticism of the *Zohar*, see Isaiah Tishby, *The Wisdom of the Zohar*, pp. 30–55.

14. On the author of the *Zohar*, see Isaiah Tishby, *The Wisdom of the Zohar*, vol. 1, pp. 53, 55; and Joseph Dan,

"Introduction," pp. viii–ix. Gershom Scholem describes Moshe de Leon as the author of the major portions of the *Zohar*. This conclusion was challenged by Yehuda Liebes, *Studies in the Zohar*, pp. 85–138. Liebes attributes the authorship of the *Zohar* to the joint composition of an entire group of Kabbalists in the circle of Moshe de Leon.

15. Yehuda Liebes, "New Trends in the Research of Kabbalah," pp. 159–61. Scholem's general historical-philological approach to Jewish mystical studies has structured the modern exploration of the *Zohar*. Scholem stresses the issue of historical development, focusing on authorship, sources, criticism, and especially the complex theosophical ideas related to the Sefiroth and Kabbalistic symbolism. These approaches are summarized by Isaiah Tishby, *The Wisdom of the Zohar*, pp. 52–54, and Idel, *Hasidism*, pp. 2–9.

16. In an attempt to explain the popularity of the *Zohar*, Tishby stresses that "the *Zohar* is a book that deals with real life. The life of the Jew with its spiritual turbulence is reflected here just as it is, with its lights and shades, and there is hardly a single corner of existence not touched upon somehow within its pages" (*The Wisdom of the Zohar*, p. 8). Moshe Idel also emphasizes its wide-ranging appeal: "the *Zohar* was written in a special literary style . . . intended from the outset for a double audience: the ordinary Jew interested in a more exciting understanding of the text, and those few seeking its esoteric sense" (*New Perspectives*, p. 209). Gershom Scholem was certainly aware of the popular content of the *Zohar* and its success in dealing with issues of real life; see, for example, *Major Trends in Jewish Mysticism*, pp. 174–76. But he chose not to develop these ideas. Although Yehuda Liebes analyzes, in "*Zohar* and Eros," some of the *Zohar*'s most complex metaphoric passages, he nevertheless observes that "according to its own consciousness, the *Zohar* does not speak in riddles and is not difficult to understand" (p. 181). For an analysis of the practical, Halachic elements in the *Zohar*, see Israel M. Ta-Shma, *The Halachic Residue in the Zohar*. Liebes outlines the *Zohar*'s remarkable versatility: "The supreme sanctity of the *Zohar* does not contradict at all its greatness as a charming literary masterpiece, among the greatest in the world's literature" ("*Zohar* and Eros," p. 181). Arthur Green summarizes the logic of the *Zohar*'s popular appeal through time, in "The Zohar: Jewish Mysticism in Medieval Spain," pp. 97–134.

17. For example, in an important passage analyzed at the beginning of this chapter (II: 59a–60a), the author(s) of the *Zohar* reviews the major requirements of a synagogue in a clear, step-by-step manner that provides succinct references and precedents. Similar pragmatic advice is found throughout the *Zohar*. Yet even generally objective observers, such as Gershom Scholem, repeatedly emphasize the *Zohar*'s unsystematic nature. For example, he finds the *Zohar*'s "deliberately unsystematic" structure to be a product of the author's homiletical style, so that

the author(s) of the *Zohar* frequently loses himself in "mystical allegorizations." But Scholem also acknowledges the *Zohar*'s moments of "magnificent clarity of expression," which are worth the many inconsistencies in the text. See *Major Trends in Jewish Mysticism*, p. 158.

18. Isaiah Tishby, *The Wisdom of the Zohar*, pp. 38–50, reviews the modern, Enlightenment historiography, which was often extremely critical of the *Zohar*, although there were exceptions, such as the work of Aaron Jellinek.

19. Gershom Scholem, *Major Trends in Jewish Mysticism*, pp. 1–39. The history of the *Zohar*'s modern reassessment is analyzed by Isaiah Tishby, *The Wisdom of the Zohar*, pp. 51–55.

20. For example, Zeev Gries has evaluated the types of popular literature and their effect on European Jewry in several works, "The Copying and Printing of Kabbalistic Books," *Conduct Literature*, and "From Myth to Ethos." See also Sylvie-Anne Goldberg, *Crossing the Jabbok*. The effects of popular conduct literature on average Jews are also examined by Eugene Newman, *Life and Teaching of Isaiah Horowitz*, pp. 73–199. Generally, the study of the relationship between religious ideas and their expression in practical life, including material culture, has only developed in Western historiography in the last fifty years. It developed in the study of Judaism even later. Thus, the role of the synagogue as a center of religious life and experience, in which abstract ideas find concrete expression in art and architecture, has received little scholarly attention, especially in the pre-Hasidic period in Eastern Europe. For a summary of the issues related to material cultural study, see Barbara Kirshenblatt-Gimblett, "Introduction," *Fabric of Jewish Life*, pp. 37–40.

21. For example, see Ida Huberman, *Living Symbols*, pp. 38, 57, 84.

22. Both Raphael Posner, *Encyclopedia Judaica*, p. 591, and Ismar Elbogen, *Jewish Liturgy*, n. 42, p. 451, cite the *Zohar* as the source of the twelve window specification for the synagogue. Both authors also cite Joseph Caro, *Shulhan Arukh* (OH 90:4), as a later source for the twelve window reference. It is important to note that in *Beit Yosef* (OH 90:4), Joseph Caro also traces the specification for twelve windows to the *Zohar*.

23. Gershom Scholem, *Zohar: The Book of Splendor*, p. 7. Scholem elaborates on the influence of the *Zohar* in *Major Trends in Jewish Mysticism*, pp. 156–57; and *Kabbalah*, pp. 70–83. See also Isaiah Tishby, *The Wisdom of the Zohar*, pp. 25–26.

24. Isaiah Tishby, *The Wisdom of the Zohar*, p. 25. Jacob Katz analyzes the relationship between Halakhah (Jewish law) and Kabbalah (tradition), emphasizing the increasing stature of Kabbalah after the sixteenth century in "Halakhah and Kabbalah as Competing Disciplines of Study," pp. 34–63.

25. Boaz Huss, "Sefer ha-Zohar as a Canonical, Sacred and Holy Text," pp. 257–307.

26. Isaiah Tishby, *The Wisdom of the Zohar*, pp. 7–9. In many works, Elliot Wolfson has emphasized the *Zohar* and its related literature as major sources of Kabbalistic imagery; see "Iconic Visualization and the Imaginal Body of God," in *Modern Theology*, pp. 137–62, and "Letter Symbolism and Merkavah Imagery in the Zohar," pp. 195–236.

27. Isaiah Tishby, *The Wisdom of the Zohar*, pp. 7, 74.

28. Ibid., p. 7. Frank Talmage emphasizes the use of allegory as a significant vehicle for literary expression in Jewish medieval sources such as the *Zohar*; see "Apples of Gold," pp. 315–53. He concludes that the use of allegorical expression has helped to maintain textual vitality and to sustain it throughout Jewish history; see also Eliezer Segal, "The Exegetical Craft of the Zohar," pp. 31–50.

29. Moshe Idel, *Kabbalah, New Perspectives*, pp. 213, 215. Elliot K. Ginsburg, in "Zelem 'Elohim: The Image of the Divine and Person in Zoharic Kabbalah," emphasizes "that in the *Zohar* in particular, there is a remarkable fluidity to the imagery, a 'looseness' of association, even, at times, a kind of synesthesia, all of which attest to (and help create) an altered state of mind, a 'symbolic consciousness' conducive to mystical experience" (p. 71).

30. See Elliot Wolfson's many groundbreaking studies on the themes of visual imagery in Kabbalist sources such as the *Zohar*, "The Hermeneutics of Visionary Experience," pp. 311–45. Wolfson's theories of visualization are summarized in *Through a Speculum That Shines*.

31. Isaiah Tishby, *The Wisdom of the Zohar*, pp. 74–96. This exploration continues, for example, in the recent work of Yehuda Liebes who has reopened the issue of the *Zohar*'s authorship by challenging Scholem's long uncontested assertion that Moshe de Leon was the sole author.

32. Elliot K. Ginsburg, "Zelem 'Elohim: The Image of the Divine and Person in Zoharic Kabbalah", p. 61.

33. Jacob Katz emphasizes the power of the Zoharic "self-referential" system when he writes, "Once a detail of law is interpreted in Kabbalah [particularly the *Zohar*], it receives a metaphysical dignity irrespective of its place in the Halakhic hierarchy" ("Post Zoharic Relations Between Halakhah and Kabbalah," p. 286). In an extended textual analysis, Arthur Green analyzes a typical Zoharic transformation of a biblical narrative, "The Zohar: Jewish Mysticism in Medieval Spain," pp. 107–9. Gershom Scholem places particular stress on the author's [Moses de Leon] "sovereign contempt for the literal text, using it freely as a plastic material for his own constructive purposes and giving free rein to his imagination. . . . His favorite method is to take the motifs of the old Aggadah and weave them into his own fabric of thought" (*Major Trends in Jewish Mysticism*, p. 174).

34. See notes 20 and 25, chapter 6.

35. Gershom Scholem, *Sabbatai Sevi*, pp. 66–87; and Boaz Huss, *Sefer ha-Zohar*, pp. 268–300.

36. Printed copies of the *Zohar* were not widely available until the beginning of the eighteenth century; see Zeev Gries, "The Printing of Kabbalah Books," p. 210. Also see

Moshe N. Rosenfeld, "The Development of Hebrew Printing in the Sixteenth and Seventeenth Centuries," pp. 92–100. The nonliterary means for the transmission of the *Zohar* remain largely unexplored, yet they may have played an important role in its diffusion. Cultural ideas have always been transmitted through more than literary means, including forms of oral, visual/symbolic, and material culture communication. Nonliterary forms of communication existed prior to reading, handwriting, and printing. Among the researchers who emphasize these forms of communication are Walter J. Ong, *Orality and Literacy*; Gerardus van der Leeuw, *Sacred and Profane Beauty*; Henry Glassie, *Folk Housing in Middle Virginia*; E. H. Gombrich, *The Sense of Order*; and Johan Huizinga, *Homo Ludens*. In eighteenth-century eastern Poland, both literary and nonliterary sources may have been equally important to the spread of Zoharic ideas that influenced the design of the Gwoździec Synagogue.

37. Isaiah Tishby, *The Wisdom of the Zohar*, p. 25.

38. See Zeev Gries, *Conduct Literature*, and "The Copying and Printing of Kabbalistic Books"; and Jacob Elbaum, "Aspects of Hebrew Ethical Literature in Sixteenth-Century Poland," pp. 146–66. Following widespread acceptance of Zoharic ideas in conduct literature available throughout Eastern Europe, the *Zohar* was further popularized in "anthologies of commentaries" described by Boaz Huss, "The Anthological Interpretation," pp. 1–19.

39. An important source for responsa concerning the architecture and painting of the synagogue is Isaac Zeev Kahana's chapter, "The Synagogue Art in Halachic Literature," in his *Studies in Responsa Literature*, pp. 349–94. A review of the more than 100 synagogue-related responsa from Eastern and Central Europe collected by Kahana reveals that their primary purpose was to respond to existing synagogue architecture, usually to comment on some feature or practice in the synagogue. The responsa were generally not used as a generative source for new, innovative ideas about synagogue construction or decoration, but were primarily regulatory. Despite these limitations, responsa literature is a fertile source for many topics related to synagogues.

40. Zeev Gries explores the important role preaching played in the spread of popular religious ideas that affected daily life. He also stresses the difficulty in obtaining these sources; see "Between History and Literature," pp. 1–10.

41. See Jacob Katz, "Post-Zoharic Relations Between Halakah and Kabbalah," pp. 284–89, and *Halacha and Kabbalah*.

42. Joseph Caro, *Beit Yosef* (OH 90: 4), and *Shulhan Aruch* (OH 90: 4).

43. Scholem outlines the basic literary sources for pre-1800 Polish Kabbalah in *Sabbatai Sevi*, pp. 77–88; Zeev Gries has traced the spread of the printed editions of the *Zohar* in "Kabbalistic Books," p. 210; Moshe Idel analyzes the large amount of Hasidic commentaries on the *Zohar* in

Hasidism, p. 15; Isaiah Tishby finds it difficult to trace manuscript diffusion in Eastern Europe, see *The Wisdom of the Zohar*, pp. 99–101. None of these studies, however, permit a detailed contextual analysis of the evolving influence of Kabbalism in general, or the *Zohar* in particular, within a specific Eastern-European community or region.

44. On the multiple paths of Zoharic influence to Poland, see Isaiah Tishby, *The Wisdom of the Zohar*, pp. 22–30, and Gershom Scholem, *Sabbatai Sevi*, pp. 49–88.

45. On the acceptance of the *Zohar* as a sacred text, see Boaz Huss, "Sefer ha-Zohar," pp. 280–99. On the controversial issue of Isaac Luria's role in the popular acceptance of the *Zohar*, Scholem has emphasized Luria's influence in many works; see, for example, *Kabbalah*, pp. 74–80. While recognizing multiple Kabbalistic sources, Yehuda Liebes finds that Isaac Luria "stands out as the greatest interpreter of the *Zohar* of all time," in "Myth vs. Symbol in the Zohar and in Lurianic Kabbalah," p. 225. In a recent work, Moshe Idel has challenged the idea of widespread Lurianic influence before the mid-eighteenth century, "One from a Town, two from a Clan—The Diffusion of Lurianic Kabbalah and Sabbatianism," pp. 79–104.

46. Gershom Scholem, *Sabbatai Sevi*, p. 78. Scholem proceeds to outline the presence of an original but "folkloric" Polish Kabbalah where "Everything was grist for the mill, the classical tradition of Spanish Kabbalism as well as the teaching of the German Hasidim." This combination produced a unique, unsystematic Kabbalism that emphasized an elaborate demonology and gematrid (numerology) (p. 80).

47. The mutual relationship between earthly and heavenly worlds is analyzed in Isaiah Tishby, *The Wisdom of the Zohar*, pp. 423–29, 450–58, 909–11.

48. Gershom Scholem interprets "above and below" as "everything is in everything else," and "everything acts upon everything else" (*On the Kabbalah and Its Symbolism*, p. 123). He emphasizes that the above/below metaphor linked human action with cosmic import (pp. 124–28). Moshe Idel stresses the theurgic implications that occur when the linkage is made between earthly and heavenly action, *New Perspectives*, pp. 156–72. The ancient roots of the "above and below" theme are analyzed by Arthur Green, *Keter*, pp. 3–11.

49. On the complex relationships between Tabernacle and Temple in the *Zohar*, see Isaiah Tishby, *The Wisdom of the Zohar*, pp. 867–940.

50. Divine instruction and design for the First Temple: I Kings 6:8; II Chronicles 2:4; for the Second Temple: Isaiah 44:28; II Chronicles 36:22–23; and for the Tabernacle: Exodus 25:31, 35–40.

51. See Victor Aptowitzer, "The Celestial Temple as Viewed in the Aggada," pp. 1–30; and E. E. Urbach, "Heavenly Jerusalem and Earthly Jerusalem," pp. 156–71. The interrelationships between Tabernacle and Temple are reviewed in Craig R. Koester, *The Dwelling of God*, pp. 1–75.

52. On the practice of outdoor prayer by Spanish Kabbalists and its possible influence on the *Zohar*, see Efraim Gottlieb, "The Meaning of Prayer in Kabbalah," pp. 38–55. The *Zohar* addresses the issue of outdoor prayer as if it were an existing practice, or at least an alternative practice. But the *Zohar* does not sanction outdoor prayer: "We might think that it is more proper to pray in open air in order to allow the spirit a free ascent. This, however, is not so" (II: 59b). The Safedian Kabbalists, although strongly influenced by the *Zohar* would, however, go on to emphasize outdoor prayer and meditation; see R. J. Zwi Werblowsky, "The Safed Revival and Its Aftermath," pp. 15–16.

53. Concerning the phrase "workers or reapers of the field," see Yehuda Liebes, *Studies in the Zohar*, pp. 31 (n. 99), 160, 175–76.

54. See note 11, chapter 3.

55. See Carol Krinsky, *Synagogues of Europe*, pp. 46–47; Rachel Wischnitzer, *European Synagogue*, pp. 111–15; and Maria and Kazimierz Piechotka, *Wooden Synagogues*, pp. 23–27.

56. See note 13, chapter 3.

57. See note 12, chapter 3.

58. Although Ezekiel's vision of the four animal faces of the keruvim (angels) associated with God's throne (Ezekiel 10:10–22) is the primary reference, the *Zohar* develops multiple interpretations and settings for these four figures; for example, see Isaiah Tishby, *The Wisdom of the Zohar*, pp. 597–632.

59. See notes 49 and 50, chapter 6.

60. On the various forms of evil in the *Zohar*, see Isaiah Tishby, *The Wisdom of the Zohar*, pp. 447–70.

61. There are slight variations in the 3-to-1 wall treatments among the nine synagogues used as case studies. For example, at the Chodorów Synagogue, the twelve windows are not paired; at the Janów Trembowelski Synagogue, a major renovation may have altered the eastern wall; and at the Jarychów Synagogue, the plan measurements are unknown. Generally, however, the synagogues of this region had walls that were organized similarly; Maria and Kazimierz Piechotka, *Wooden Synagogues*, pp. 196, 198–99, 201, 205, 210, plus unpaginated figures.

62. The distinct differentiation of three of the walls from the fourth wall of the prayer hall may also reflect an effort to differentiate the synagogue from the Christian church. Renaissance architectural theorists had heightened the search for perfect, symmetrical geometries for church architecture. Although their "perfect" plans were seldom implemented—Michelangelo's symmetrical plan for St. Peter's Basilica, for instance, was altered to a more traditional elongated nave—the perfectionist architectural theories of the Renaissance, continuing into the Baroque period, had a wide-ranging influence on church architecture, as was the case in sixteenth- through eighteenth-century Poland. In their search for perfect models, church designers sought scriptural precedent, for example Revelations (John 21:10, 12, 16, 21), where a celestial Jerusalem has a square plan and twelve gates, with the gates arranged symmetrically—three gates on each of the four walls. An extensive early printed literature promoted similar rationalist, symmetrical schemes for churches and other monumental buildings. Imported to Poland, such schemes had set the dominant national style by 1700. Within this Renaissance and Baroque architectural context, Jewish communities may have sought similar types of rationalist plans for their synagogues. The wide circulation of Italian architectural literature in Poland is analyzed by Adam Miłobędzki, *Architektura polska*, pp. 5–45. For a detailed account of one of Poland's finest classical architects, see Stanislaw Mossakowski, *Tylman z Gameren*, pp. 10–65.

63. Functional requirements contributed to the differentiation of the western wall. For example, entrance and auxiliary rooms were most often placed on the western side of the synagogue nearest the entrance door to the prayer hall. This practice often restricted or prevented west-facing exterior windows from being put into the prayer hall, as was the case in all the documented wooden synagogues in Gwoździec region. See Maria and Kazimierz Piechotka, *Wooden Synagogues*, pp. 196–210, and unnumbered pages by town name.

64. Over 75 percent of the wooden synagogues recorded in Maria and Kazimierz Piechotka, *Wooden Synagogues*, follow this general window arrangement.

65. The ascent of prayer is analyzed in Isaiah Tishby, *The Wisdom of the Zohar*, pp. 951–74; Moseh Idel, *Kabbalah: New Perspectives*, pp. 191–99; and Gershom Scholem, *Kabbalah*, pp. 125–27. Idel and Scholem also emphasize the theurgic implications of the ascent of prayer.

66. See Moshe Hallamish, "Notes on the Thirteen Gates in Heaven," pp. 147–51.

67. Isaiah Tishby, *The Wisdom of the Zohar*, pp. 597–614.

68. At the neighboring Chodorów Synagogue, the four windows on each wall are separated, not paired, and at Janów Trembowelski in the same Lviv region, the east interior wall may have been altered during later construction. Maria and Kazimierz Piechotka, *Wooden Synagogues*, see unnumbered pages by town names.

69. It is tempting to associate these rounded windows with the paired Tablets of Law, a common symbol for Judaism in Jewish and Christian sources after the sixteenth century; see Ruth Mellinkoff, "The Round-Topped Tablet of the Law," pp. 28–43. But this window arrangement was also found in many types of Christian and secular, Eastern-European monumental buildings constructed during the same period. Whether these windows were ever actually intended to symbolize the Tablets of Law by their designers or users, or were simply seen that way by Gentile observers in their eighteenth-century context, is a complicated issue involving multiple perspectives that cannot be answered from the limited data available.

70. See Maria and Kazimierz Piechotka, *Wooden Synagogues*, unnumbered pages by town names.

71. Responsa, from R. Nathan N. Leiter, Zlozitz, Ukraine, 1928, in Isaac Ze'ev Kahana, *Studies in Responsa Literature*, p. 388.

72. The specification for 50 windows and the making of 49 windows closely parallels Rav and Shmuel's discussion (B.T., Rosh ha-Shana 21b and Nedarim 38a) "that 50 gates of understanding were created in the world, and all but one were given to Moses, for it is said (Psalms 8:6), 'For Thou hast made him [Moses] but a little lower than the angels'" (p. 394). In this interpretation, the making of 49 windows recognizes that the Divine portion of 50 should not be approached by humans. While 49 panes of glass in a window may seem prohibitively expensive, hand-size window panes were the standard before about 1750, so that large windows in important buildings, especially in rural regions, required many panes of glass. Many synagogue windows depicted in photographs in Maria and Kazimierz Piechotka, *Wooden Synagogues*, show post-1800 replacement windows that used larger panes of glass.

73. The *Zohar*'s abundant numerological interpretations and their possible mystical significance have not been emphasized in this book, because their fluidity and complexity makes it difficult to develop adequate proofs. Therefore, although 50 window panes were cited and 49 made, I have made no attempt to interpret the meaning of the relationship between the numbers 49 and 50 as presented in the *Zohar* (II: 183a, and I: 3b–4a). See note 72 above. Although number relationships permeate the *Zohar*, the numerology of the *Zohar* has not been systematically analyzed. As in the case of the synagogue's windows, the *Zohar*'s number relationships are extremely fluid, often changing, and therefore easily exaggerated and misinterpreted. Therefore, I have refrained from speculative numerology, while still emphasizing the importance of numbers in the *Zohar*. For numerology in association with the letters of the Divine Name, see Idel, *Kabbalah: New Perspectives*, pp. 97–103; and for numerology in various other forms, see Gershom Scholem, *Kabbalah*, pp. 119–22, 172–74. On the development of numerology possibly influential to the *Zohar*, see Daniel Abrams, "From Germany to Spain: Numerology as a Mystical Technique," pp. 85–101.

74. In one of the most extensive photographic surveys of Polish masonry synagogues, Loukomski, *Jewish Art*, pp. 67–144, almost 20 percent of the synagogue windows (from prayer halls where the window panes could be counted) had 48 to 52 panes per window. It must be emphasized that when these photographs were taken in the twentieth century, many windows may have been nineteenth-century replacements using fewer and larger panes of glass. Furthermore, many of these synagogues were built after 1775–1800 when the 50-pane window tradition may have been discontinued.

75. See Maria and Kazimierz Piechotka, *Bramy Nieba:*

Bóżnice murowane, pp. 54–81, and *Wooden Synagogues*, pp. 29–34; and Carol Krinsky, *Synagogues of Europe*, p. 51.

76. The role of the pillar in the *Zohar* is far more important than it is in earlier Hekhalot literature; see Peter Schafer, *Synopse zur Hekhalot-Literatur*, p. 55. The development of Hekhalot literature is examined by David J. Halperin, *The Faces of the Chariot*, pp. 359–405.

77. Isaiah Tishby, *The Wisdom of the Zohar*, pp. 587–614.

78. See note 92, chapter 3.

7. The Meaning of the Remodeled Cupola

1. See note 1, chapter 2.

2. On the architecture of the American synagogue and the development of the American Reform synagogue, see Leon A. Jick, "The Reform Synagogue," pp. 85–110; Jack Wertheimer, ed., *The American Synagogue*, and Leon A. Jick, *The Americanization of the Synagogue*.

3. Although the *Zohar* clearly specifies twelve windows for the synagogue, a complementary arrangement of thirteen windows is also mentioned. The *Zohar* states, "there are thirteen window frames of the firmament" (*Zohar*, Ruth 76c). If the small circular window on the western wall is added to the twelve standard windows of the prayer hall, the total number of windows is thirteen. In this reading, the isolated thirteenth window also parallels the *Zohar*'s standard imagery for the Shekhinah frequently standing alone or exiled, either outside the twelve tribes, outside the Sefirot, or outside the synagogue; see *Zohar*, III: 114b. Therefore, the single, differentiated lattice window associated with Shekhinah might be added to the twelve standard windows of the prayer hall to produce thirteen. This theme of the separation or exile of the Shekhinah is analyzed by Isaiah Tishby, in *The Wisdom of the Zohar*, pp. 371–76, and especially in the chapter "The Exile of the Shekhinah," pp. 382–85.

4. Lattice windows on the interior west walls can be seen in photographs and drawings of Polish wooden synagogues in Maria and Kazimierz Piechotka's *Wooden Synagogues* and *Bramy Nieba: Bóżnice drewniane*. Determining the frequency of "Gate of Heaven" type windows is complicated by the presence of similar screens and lattice openings in women's galleries found along the upper west wall. Therefore, all lattice screens are not Gate of Heaven windows; see Maria and Kazimierz Piechotka, *Wooden Synagogues*, pp. 35–36, 196–210. It should also be noted that from the seventeenth to the nineteenth centuries, small circular or semicircular lunette windows were commonly used for special lighting effects in Polish Baroque churches and monumental secular buildings—the period that they were used in wooden and masonry synagogues. For example, note the lunette-type window above the ark and the entrance in the Janów Sokolski Synagogue, figures 328–37 in Maria and Kazimierz Piechotka, *Bramy Nieba: Bóżnice drewniane*, pp. 219–23.

The fact that a similar kind of lunette window was found at Gwoździec and at synagogues throughout Poland might suggest that these windows were the influence of the larger dominant culture. As we have seen in other instances, the Jewish minority borrowed from the dominant surrounding culture, but the lattice window was given a specific, Jewish, Gate of Heaven meaning within the context of the synagogue.

5. The *Zohar* repeatedly combines the images of a deer/Shekhinah hiding behind walls and watching the Israelites; see Isaiah Tishby, *The Wisdom of the Zohar*, pp. 379–85. See notes 38 and 39, chapter 4.

6. Song of Songs (2:9–10). The extensive influence of the Song of Songs on the *Zohar* is emphasized by Arthur Green in "The Song of Songs in Early Jewish Mysticism," pp. 59–62.

7. On the depiction of stiff-legged angels, see Hayim Nahman Bialik and Yehoshua Hana Ravnitzky, *Book of Legends*, p. 181 (based on Ezekiel 1:7 and B. Yoma 19b and En Yaakov). The conception of God looking through lattice into the synagogue is also related to the image of the Cohanim looking through raised, lattice-like hands and fingers, as described in Nosson Schermann and Meir Zlotowitz, eds., *Bircas Kohanim: The Priestly Blessing*, pp. 31–32, 41–42. The "chinks" (kostei kotla) mentioned in the passage could also refer to lattice-like openings in masonry walls, presumably in masonry synagogues (with either wood or masonry lattice openings), which were either known or imagined by the Spanish author(s) of the *Zohar*. In Polish wooden synagogues, these "chinks" were reinterpreted in wooden lattice construction.

8. At Gwoździec Synagogue, this inscription was faded and only partially visible (see fig. 97). At the neighboring Jabłonów Synagogue, the full verse was inscribed within a similar painted lattice window set above the doorway in the same location as the painted window in the Gwoździec Synagogue (see fig. 155 and Appendix for full translation). The prescription for praying with tears has a long history in Jewish literature; see Moseh Idel, *Kabbalah: New Perspectives*, pp. 75–88; for the theurgic importance of praying with tears, see Idel, pp. 197–199. The occurrence of this inscription at Gwoździec and Jabłonów Synagogues may also relate to the Kabbalistic emphasis of this practice as repeatedly advised in the *Zohar*, for example, (I: 223a), and (II: 165a), and echoed in influential conduct literature of the early modern period, for example, Kaidanover, *Kav ha Yashar*, chapter 8.

9. Babylonian Talmud (Berachot 32b and Baba Metsi'a 59a) and reworked in several Zoharic variations (I: 32a, II: 12b, II: 165a–b)

10. On the "Gate of Heaven" motif in the Polish wooden synagogues, see Maria and Kazimierz Piechotka, "Polychrome Paintings," p. 68, and *Bramy Nieba: Bóżnice drewniane*, pp. 113–55. "Gate of Heaven" is apparently one of the ancient names for synagogues; see Isaiah Sonne, "Secondary Names for Synagogues," pp. 557–59. The idea of a heavenly portal is an ancient theme in Judaism (see Bernard Goldman, *The Sacred Portal*, pp. 69–100), as it is in most religions of the world (see Mircea Eliade, *The Sacred and the Profane*, pp. 26, 81).

11. See note 65, chapter 6.

12. There are several Zoharic variations on the story of the exiled Shekhinah concealed behind lattice; see *Zohar* III: 114b.

13. "Lekhah Dodi" was composed by Solomon Alkabez (1505–76) probably in Safed, Palestine. It was inspired by the Talmud (Shabbath 119a and Baba Kama 32 a–b) and was among the latest *piyyutim* (liturgical poetry) to be incorporated into the prayer book. According to Yehuda Ratshabi, "Lekhah Dodi" "achieved unparalleled popularity . . . and was accepted into the prayer book soon after it was written" (Sephardic version, Venice, 1584, and printed in *Seder ha Yom*, Venice, 1599); in "Lekhah Dodi of Rabbi Shlomo Alkabez and its Sources," pp. 162–69. Also see Reuven Kimelman, "A Prolegomena to Lekhah Dodi and Qabbalat Shabbat"; Abraham I. Schechter, *Lectures on Jewish Liturgy* pp. 57–60, and Reuven Kimelman, "'Awaken, Awaken, for Your Light has Come': From Garments of Skin to Garments of Light," pp. 141–44.

14. On the complex issues of concealing and revealing God's presence to the Jewish people, see Elliot R. Wolfson, *Through a Speculum That Shines*, pp. 85–98, 108–24, and "Iconic Visualization and the Imaginal Body of God," pp. 137–62.

15. Given the lack of data on the development of art forms in the synagogue, it is tempting to borrow interpretive models from medieval Christian art analyzing the creation of painting, sculpture, and stained glass. Although these arts were once interpreted simply as a "bible in stone" communicating religious doctrine to the masses, recent scholarship has developed more comprehensive interpretations, for example, Umberto Eco, *Art and Beauty in the Middle Ages*; Emile Male, *The Gothic Image* pp. 1–70; and Umberto Eco, *Interpretation and Overinterpretation*, pp. 60–66. Yet, the application of theory and insights gathered from the study of Christian art and worship to the study of Jewish art and worship poses major difficulties and can never be assumed. Consequently, these theories have been addressed very cautiously.

16. See notes 16 and 23, chapter 6.

17. *Zohar*, II: 86a, and II: 87a, and based on Rosh Ha-Shana 24a.

18. While clearly supporting themes of visualization, the authorship of the *Zohar* also recognized the powers and dangers of imagery and visualization (I: 239a, II: 87a, and III: 84a).

19. In many original works, Elliot R. Wolfson has explored the power of visualization in Jewish literature. He particularly focuses on the *Zohar* as a vehicle of revelation, concluding that "Gnosis for the *Zohar* is primarily visual and not auditory" ("The Hermeneutics of Visionary Experi-

ence," p. 324). Wolfson summarizes and extends much of his previous work on visual imagery and visual imagination throughout *Through a Speculum That Shines*.

20. On the overall significance of animal themes within Jewish literature, see Epstein, "'If Lions Could Carve Stones,'" pp. 41–52. On the theme of wonderment toward fantastic creatures, see David B. Ruderman, who emphasizes "the acquisition of Jewish and naturalistic knowledge," particularly including fantastic creatures, in "Unicorns, Great Beasts and the Marvelous Variety of Things in Nature in the Thought of Abraham B. Hananiah Yagel," p. 361. For a broader discussion of this theme, see Lorraine Daston and Katharine Park, *Wonders and the Order of Nature*, pp. 13–66.

21. Joseph Dan, "The Book of the Divine Name by Rabbi Eleazar of Worms," pp. 50–51.

22. This passage demonstrates a typical style for Zoharic expression, featuring a dense weave of overlapping metaphors presented in an intense narrative fashion. It is a style that has contributed to the attraction of adherents and the frustration of detractors for centuries. On the *Zohar*'s literary style and its background, see Yehuda Liebes, "How the *Zohar* Was Written," pp. 85–138, and Isaiah Tishby, *The Wisdom of the Zohar*, pp. 64–71.

23. Elliot R. Wolfson, "The Hermeneutics of Visionary Experience," pp. 312–13. Wolfson identifies the link between visual and scriptural interpretation as a theurgic/mystical method of worship, pp. 313, 324–25.

24. The verse, "Lift up your eyes . . ." (Isaiah 40:26) appears in *Zohar* I: 1b, 29b, 30a; II: 105a, 126b, 226a, 231b, 232a, 253b; and III: 233a. Another verse about lifting up the eyes, "Unto thee I lift up mine eyes . . ." (I: 208), begins a passage about the methods of drawing down blessings from God. In a story about lifting up one's eyes based on the *Zohar*, R. Yosef, son of R. Yehuda of Dubnow, writes: "therefore, people of deeds (Kabbalists) are accustomed to looking at the sky when there is a multitude of stars illuminating a bright light, to give praise and thanks to the Blessed Holy One," *Yesod Yosef*, chapter 2, p. 2a.

25. See Zwi Hirsch Kaidanover, *Kav ha-Yashar*, chapter 2 and passim.

26. See Elliot R. Wolfson, *Through a Speculum*, p. 385.

27. See Elliot R. Wolfson, "The Hermeneutics of Visionary Experience," p. 324.

28. On the medieval approach to worship and the issue of seeing and believing, see Aron Gurevich, *Categories of Medieval Culture*, pp. 26–79, and *Medieval Popular Culture*, pp. 1–77; G. G. Coulton, *Medieval Faith and Symbolism*, pp. 1–25, 242–320; and Umberto Eco, *Art and Beauty in the Middle Ages*, pp. 28–51.

29. See note 40, chapter 5.

30. There are no commonly accepted terms for the pre-Hasidic popular Judaism of eastern Poland. The term "popular pietism" is cautiously used in this book to describe a nonmessianic, non-Sabbatian, nonmystical Judaism that I believe characterized the common religious orientation in early-eighteenth-century eastern Podolian small towns like Gwoździec. On the difficulty of defining Jewish popular culture, see Stephen D. Benin, "A Hen Crowing like a Cock," pp. 261–70. Joseph Weiss summarizes the religious characteristics of an early Hasidic Judaism; see "Some Notes on the Social Background of Early Hasidism," pp. 3–26. Zwi Werblowsky provides a summary of post-Lurianic/pre-Hasidic Ashkenazi spirituality in "The Safed Revival and Its Aftermath," pp. 31–33. He describes the spirituality of this pre-Hasidic, non-Sabbatian popular culture as "another type of spirituality which is often neglected—perhaps because [it is] less spectacular, less exotic, and more rational than the Kabbalah. Very often this type of piety was propagated by men who, as we know, were themselves Kabbalists but who felt that this part of their teaching should be reserved to the chosen few only. It is spirituality usually called *mussar*" (p. 32)

31. In a detailed study of the Międzybóż, the later home of the Ba'al Shem Tov, Moshe Rosman emphasizes the nonradical social and political nature of early Hasidism; see *Founder of Hasidism*, pp. 63–94. In many Podolian towns similar to Gwoździec, the advent of Hasidism was not marked by clashes between supporters and opponents. On the popular transition to Hasidism, see Louis Jacobs, *Hasidic Prayer*, pp. 17–45, and Moshe Idel, *Kabbalah: New Perspectives*, pp. 256–71.

32. Gershom Scholem, in *Major Trends in Jewish Mysticism*, pp. 325–50, describes the successful efforts of the early Hasidim to recast or rechannel the destructive aspects of apocalyptic messianism, related to the Sabbatian movement, into a more worldly, personally meaningful orientation. I believe that the synagogue designers also attempted to recast and reformulate Jewish worship in terms more meaningful to an emergent Jewish popular culture and to infuse common worship with a greater sense of experiential meaning related to ritual. That Hasidism finally achieved this popular transformation through means other than altering the environment of worship should not distract from the interim success of the communities that constructed wooden synagogues to accomplish some of the same goals through changes in the environment for worship.

33. This does not mean that synagogue wall-painting completely ended at the beginning of the nineteenth century. Limited photographic evidence reveals that some synagogues continued the tradition of wall-painting; see Maria and Kazimierz Piechotka, *Bramy Nieba: Bóżnice drewniane*, pp. 158–66. However, the premodern style of the wall-paintings, as practiced by the Jarychów School of painters at the beginning of the eighteenth century, was probably not continued after 1800. This hypothesis is seemingly contradicted by the continued existence of many eighteenth- and nineteenth-century Jewish decorative art forms, as evidenced, for example, in East-European tombstones, ritual and domestic objects, and textiles, as well as in illustrated literature; see, for exam-

ple, Mariella Beukers and Renee Waale, *Tracing An-sky*, pp. 62–77. It is, perhaps, the special nature of synagogue art, tied so closely to liturgical function, that may explain the termination of the wall-painting traditions and the continuation of some of their themes and motifs in other types of artistic expression, such as textiles and domestic objects. Further complicating this aesthetic problem is the unknown Hasidic relationship to art forms in nineteenth-century synagogues. Adequate data are lacking concerning Hasidic sponsorship of synagogue building and re-modeling projects, with the exception of a few courts of tsaddiks; see, for example, Eleonora Bergman, "Góra Kalwaria," pp. 14–16, 20. A related, underexplored issue is the relationship of Hasidism to other forms of artistic expression, such as portraiture. Some of these issues were investigated by Richard Cohen in a lecture, " 'And Your Eyes Shall See Your Teachers,' " pp. 114–53.

34. Moshe Idel, "Perceptions of Kabbalah in the Second Half of the 18th Century," p. 75. In a related approach, Haviva Pedaya emphasizes the transference of the Divine in Hasidism from inhabiting a heavenly plane parallel to the earthly, to a supernal place with little reference to physical places or synagogues on earth, "The Divinity as Place and Time and Holy Place in Jewish Mysticism," pp. 97–101.

35. On the characteristics of Hasidic prayer, see Louis Jacobs, *Hasidic Prayer*, pp. 17–35; Rivka Schatz Uffenheimer, *Hasidism as Mysticism*, pp. 144–214; and Weiss, *Jewish Mysticism*, pp. 95–130.

36. I. G. Marcus emphasizes that medieval German Pietist prayers involved looking upward and concentrating on God. Postulating the continuation of these practices into the modern period, Marcus writes, "And as late as the eighteenth century, Rabbi Jacob Emden, a fierce anti-Kabbalist, reports as unnecessary the practice of looking up during prayers whenever the Name of God is mentioned," in "Prayer Gestures in German Hasidim," p. 52–53. It is important to emphasize that the specific quality of looking upward with open eyes and actually seeing is uncharacteristic of later Hasidic worship. This should be understood as distinct from exaggerated prayer expressionism in some Hasidic sects, such as lifting the hands and head heavenward but with closed eyes; see Jacobs, *Hasidic Prayer*, pp. 54, 57.

37. Various forms of the verse "Lift up your eyes . . ." (Isaiah. 40:26) introduce significant Zoharic passages where the power and importance of vision is emphasized. For example, "Unto thee I lift up mine eyes" (I: 208) begins a story about the methods of drawing down blessings from God and assisting God by means of prayer. Moshe Idel describes this Kabbalistic effort to fashion a mythology for the repair of the cosmos (God) with man's help as "Jewish theurgical anthropology," in *Kabbalah: New Perspectives*, pp. 173–99. He then describes a dilution of this theurgic effort in Hasidism including the elimination of Zoharic symbolism and linguistic experimentation in Hasidic practice, pp. 205–10, 267–71.

38. See notes 16, 19, and 20, chapter 3.

39. See notes 12 and 33, chapter 6.

40. The *Zohar*'s tent or canopy imagery was frequently incorporated into synagogue-like settings; for example, when two righteous men traveled together to the Garden of Eden, they sat down in a temple and "lifted up their eyes and saw a tent embroidered with all sorts of figures, in various colors and over it a curtain of flashing light too dazzling to behold" (III: 162b). This passage recalls the description of the Tabernacle (Exodus 26:1) where the curtains of the tent were covered with elaborately decorated angels.

41. See note 38, chapter 6.

42. Joseph Gutmann, "Return in Mercy to Zion," p. 238.

43. See Joseph Gutmann, "Return in Mercy to Zion," p. 240. The general outline of Gutmann's arguments are reinforced in this section. Although Gutmann emphasizes the messianic implications of the adoption of Temple restorative rituals, I would broaden this interpretation to include the impact of Temple rituals on the performance of normative, daily worship in the synagogue.

44. The early-modern development of the sacred marriage theme is analyzed by Gershom Scholem, *On the Kabbalah and Its Symbolism*, pp. 137–46, and Elliot K. Ginsburg, *The Sabbath in Classical Kabbalah*, pp. 101–20. The theme of God's female aspect associated with sacred marriage is analyzed by Gershom Scholem in his chapter "Shekhinah: The Feminine Element in Divinity," in *On the Mystical Shape of the Godhead*, pp. 140–96. Arthur Green provides an excellent analysis of the unity of the Sabbath-Temple/Tabernacle tent relationship in "Sabbath as Temple," pp. 287–305. In another article, Green links the "Song of Songs" with the themes of the sacred marriage of God, "The 'Song of Songs' in Early Jewish Mysticism," pp. 53–62. On the bride/Shekhinah as a symbol of Torah, see Elliot R. Wolfson's chapter "Female Imaging of the Torah: From Literary Metaphor to Religious Symbol," in *Circle and Square*, pp. 1–28. Wolfson also emphasizes the interrelationships between the Tabernacle and Shekhinah in "Forms of Visionary Ascent as Ecstatic Experience in the Zoharic Literature," pp. 212–14.

45. On the historical development of the liturgy of Kabbalat Shabbat, see Reuven Kimelman, "A Prolegomena to Lekhah Dodi and Qabbalat Shabbat."

46. Elliot K. Ginsburg, *The Sabbath in Classical Kabbalah*.

47. The weekly exile of the bride Shekhinah became a popular theme in women's prayer, where, for example, fervent prayer with tears was widely encouraged; see Chava Weissler, *Voices of the Matriarchs*, pp. 110–25.

48. On the customs and ritual practices of Shabbat influenced by Kabbalah, see Elliot K. Ginsburg, *The Sabbath in Classical Kabbalah*, pp. 186–277; Moshe Hallamish, "The Influence of the Kabbalah on Jewish Liturgy," pp. 121–31; Abraham I. Schechter, "Cabbalistic Interpolations in the Prayer Book," pp. 39–60; and Gershom Scholem, *On the Kabbalah and Its Symbolism*, pp. 118–57. Scholem summa-

rizes the widespread effect of new Kabbalistic practices on every phase of religious and daily life: "The main influence of Kabbalah on Jewish life must be sought in the three areas of prayer, custom and ethics. Here the Kabbalah had practically unlimited freedom to exert its influence, which expressed itself in the creation of a broad body of literature that was directed at every Jewish home. From the middle of the seventeenth century onward, Kabbalistic motifs entered the everyday prayer book and inspired special liturgies intended for a variety of specific occasions and rituals, many of which were in essence Kabbalistic creations" (p. 193).

49. On the development of the chuppah in the early modern period, see Joseph Gutmann, *The Jewish Life Cycle*, pp. 16–17. While some marriage rituals are very old, like the tradition of covering the head of the bride, the ritual using the four-posted wedding canopy emerged in Ashkenazi communities between the sixteenth and seventeenth centuries. See Solomon B. Freehof, "The Chuppah," pp. 186–93.

50. Isaiah Tishby presents a detailed analysis of the marriage and sacred coupling themes that were applied to specific prayers in the liturgy, particularly the Amidah and the Shema, in his essay "Prayer and Devotion in the Zohar," in Isaiah Tishby, *The Wisdom of the Zohar*, pp. 966–74. A general discussion of mythological themes in sacred marriage imagery is given by Raphael Patai in *The Hebrew Goddess*, pp. 255–94. For ancient sources of the sacred marriage theme, see Arthur Green, *Keter*, pp. 78–87. A detailed analysis of the sacred marriage theme is presented by Elliot R. Wolfson, "Coronation of the Sabbath Bride," pp. 301–44. Wolfson also addresses the general issue of God's iconic image in many publications; see for example, "Iconic Visualization and the Imaginal Body of God," pp. 137–62.

51. Reuven Kimelman analyzes the complex symbolism of "Lekhah Dodi" especially related to the Sabbath and to Jerusalem in "A Prolegomena to 'Lekhah Dodi' and Qabbalat Shabbat," pp. 393–454.

52. Gershom Scholem, *Major Trends in Jewish Mysticism*, pp. 349–50. Scholem summarizes the story told by the Hebrew novelist S. J. Agnon about the founder of the Hasidic movement. For other variations on this story, see Moshe Idel, *New Perspectives*, pp. 270–71, 391 n.92, attributed to R. Israel of Ruzhin, in *Knesset Israel*, fol. 12a; and Elie Wiesel, *Souls on Fire*, pp. 167–68.

Afterword

1. Milda B. Richardson, review of *Resplendent Synagogue: Architecture and Worship in an Eighteenth-Century Polish Community* by Thomas C. Hubka, *Perspectives in Vernacular Architecture* 12 (2005): 84–86; Moshe Rosman, "Resplendent Book," review of *Resplendent Synagogue: Architecture and Worship in an Eighteenth-Century Polish Community* by Thomas C. Hubka, *Ars Judaica* 6 (2006):

165–68; Adam Teller, review of *Resplendent Synagogue: Architecture and Worship in an Eighteenth-Century Polish Community* by Thomas C. Hubka, *AJS Review* 31/2 (2007): 409–12.

2. This dependence has been introduced into architectural history by Rachel Wischnitzer-Bernstein, *The Architecture of the European Synagogue* (Philadelphia: Jewish Publication Society, 1964), 120–21.

3. Thomas C. Hubka, *Resplendent Synagogue: Architecture and Worship in an Eighteenth-Century Polish Community* (Hanover, NH, and London: Brandeis University Press, published by the University Press of New England, 2003), 148.

4. Judith C. E. Belinfante, et al., *The Esnoga: A Monument to Portuguese-Jewish Culture* (Amsterdam: D'ARTS, 1991), 56.

5. This was said at the First Congress of Jewish Art in Poland, Kazimierz on the Vistula River, October 27, 2008.

6. *Zohar*, "Vayakhel" 205a; *Tikunei hazohar*, ed. Reuven Margaliot, no. 69; Bracha Yaniv, *The Carved Wooden Torah Arks of Eastern Europe* (Liverpool, UK: Liverpool University Press, 2017), 79–97.

7. Hubka, *Resplendent Synagogue*, 141.

8. Tamar Shadmi, "From Functional Solution to Decorative Concept," *Ars Judaica* 6 (2010): 69–80; Tamar Shadmi, "Wall Inscriptions in East European Synagogues: Their Sources, Meanings, and Role in Shaping the Concept of Space and Worship," PhD diss., 3 vols., Bar-Ilan University, 2011.

9. Zvi Orgad, "Transferring Visual Culture: The Case of Eliezer-Zusman," in *Warsaw and Jerusalem: Polish-Jewish History, Culture, Values, and Education Between Paradise and Inferno*, eds. Nitza Davidovitch and Eyal Lewin (Boca Raton, FL: Brown Walker Press, 2019), 47–57; Zvi Orgad, *Eliezer-Zusman at Work: The Early Modern Synagogue Artisan and His World* (Boston: Brill, forthcoming).

10. Sergey R. Kravtsov, "Na ratunek Wielkiej Synagodze w Brodach," *Art and Criticism* 10/85 (2019): 24–31; the English online version: www.academia.edu/40490165/ Great_Synagogue_in_Brody_History_and_Present, accessed October 1, 2021. My paper, "Domed Synagogues in Ruthenia, Podolia and Volhynia: Space, Decoration, Meaning," was presented at the GEOP Workshop, Building Culture and Community: Jewish Architecture and Urbanism in Poland, held at the POLIN Museum in Warsaw on May 29, 2019.

11. The dates are quoted from dated paintings of these synagogues.

12. Sergey R. Kravtsov, "Synagogue Architecture of Volhynia," in Sergey R. Kravtsov and Vladimir Levin, *Synagogues in Ukraine: Volhynia*, 2 vols. (Jerusalem: Zalman Shazar Center and Center for Jewish Art, 2017), 75–76.

13. Adam Miłobędzki, "Architecture in Wood: Technology, Symbolic Content, Art," *Artibus et Historiae*, 10/19 (1989): 177–206.

Abrams, Daniel. "From Germany to Spain: Numerology as a Mystical Technique." *Journal of Jewish Studies* 47: 1 (Spring 1996).

Abramsky, Chimen, Maciej Jachimczyk, and Antony Polonsky, eds. *The Jews of Poland*. Oxford, 1988.

Alekandrovich, Volodymyr. "Painters' Circles in Brody" [in Ukrainian]. *Dzvin* 3 (1990).

Alexander, Jonathan J. G. "Jerusalem the Golden: Image and Myth in the Middle Ages in Western Europe." In *The Real and Ideal Jerusalem in Jewish, Christian and Islamic Art*, ed. Bianca Kuhnel. Jerusalem, 1998.

Altman, Richard. *The Making of a Musical: Fiddler on the Roof*. New York, 1971.

Altmann, Alexander. "Eleazar of Worms' Symbol of the Merkabah." In *Studies in Religious Philosophy and Mysticism*. Ithaca, N.Y., 1969.

Amit, David. "Architectural Plans of Synagogues in the Southern Judean Hills and the 'Halakah.'" In *Ancient Synagogues: Historical Analysis and Archaeological Discovery*, ed. Dan Urman and Paul V. M. Flesher. Leiden, 1995.

Anderson, George K. *The Legend of the Wandering Jew*. Providence, R.I., 1965.

Aptowitzer, Victor. "The Celestial Temple as Viewed in the Aggadah." In *Binah: Jewish Intellectual History in the Middle Ages*, vol. 2, ed. Joseph Dan. New York, 1989.

Argan, Giulio Carlo. *The Baroque Age*. New York, 1989.

Avi-Yonah, Michael. "Synagogue." *Encyclopaedia Judaica*, vol. 15. Jerusalem, 1972.

Avrin, Leila. "Micrography as Art." In *La Lettre Hebraique et Sa Signification*. Paris, 1981.

Baile, David. *Power and Powerlessness in Jewish History*. New York, 1986.

Banham, Reyner. *Concrete Atlantis*. Cambridge, Mass., 1986.

Baranowski, Bohdan. *Polska Karczma* (The Polish Inn). Wrocław, 1979.

Bartal, Israel. "The *Porets* and the *Arendar*: The Depiction of Poles in Jewish Literature." *The Polish Review* 22:4 (1987).

Baumgarten, Joseph M. "Art in the Synagogue, Some Talmudic Views." In *The Synagogue: Studies in Origins, Archaeology, and Architecture*, ed. Harry M. Orlinsky. New York, 1975.

Baxandall, Michael. *Patterns of Intention: On the Historical Explanation of Pictures*. New Haven, 1989.

Beauvois, Daniel. "Polish-Jewish Relations in the Territories Annexed by the Russian Empire in the First Half of the Nineteenth Century." In *The Jews in Poland*, ed. Chimen Abramsky, Maciej Jachimczyk, and Antony Polonsky. Oxford, 1986.

Beit-Arie, Malachi. *Perek Shirah*. Ph.D. dissertation, Hebrew University [in Hebrew]. Jerusalem, 1966.

Ben-Sasson, H. H. "The Middle Ages." In *A History of the Jewish People*. Cambridge, Mass., 1976.

———, ed. *A History of the Jewish People*. Cambridge, Mass., 1976.

Benbassa, Esther, and Aron Rodrigue. *Sephardi Jewry: A History of the Judeo-Spanish Community, 14th–20th Centuries*. Berkeley, 1993.

Benin, Stephen D. "A Hen Crowing like a Cock: 'Popular Religion' and Jewish Law." *Journal of Jewish Thought and Philosophy* 8 (1999).

Ber of Bolechow, *The Memoirs of Ber of Bolechow (1723–1805)*. M. Vishnitzer, trans. London, 1922.

Berger, John. *Ways of Seeing*. London, 1972.

Bergman, Eleonora. "Góra Kalwaria: The Impact of a Hasidic Cult on the Urban Landscape of a Small Polish Town." *Polin* 5 (1990).

Bergman, Eleonora, and Jan Jagielski. "The Function of Synagogues in the PPR." *Polin* 5 (1988).

Betlej, Andrzej. "The Church of the Immaculate Conception and the Bernardine Monastery in Gwoździec." In *Kościoły i klasztory rzymskokatolickie dawnego województwa ruskiego* (Roman Catholic Churches and Monasteries of the Old Ruthanian Provinces), ed. Maria Podlodowska-Reklewska. Cracow, 1996.

Beukers, Mariella, and Renee Waale. *Tracing An-sky: Jewish Collections from the State Ethnographic Museum in St. Petersburg*. St. Petersburg, 1992.

Bhabha, Homi. *The Location of Culture*. New York, 1994.

Bialik, Hayim Nahman, and Yehoshua Hana Ravnitzky, eds. *The Book of Legends: Sefer Ha-Aggadah*. New York, 1992.

Biedrońska-Słotowa, Beata. *Kobierce tureckie* (Turkish Carpets), vol. III (Eastern Carpets). Cracow, n.d.

———, ed. *Orient w sztuce Polskiej* (The Orient in Polish Art). Cracow, 1992.

Bland, Kalman P. *The Artless Jew: Medieval and Modern Affirmations and Denials of the Visual*. Princeton, 2000.

Blum, Jerome. *The End of the Old Order in Rural Europe*. Princeton, 1978.

Bonfil, Robert. "Change in the Cultural Patterns of a Jewish

Society in Crisis: Italian Jewry at the Close of the Sixteenth Century." *Jewish History* 3:2 (Fall 1988).

Branham, Joan R. "Sacred Space under Erasure in Ancient Synagogues and Early Churches." *Art Bulletin* 74:3 (September 1992).

———. "Vicarious Sacrality: Temple Space in Ancient Synagogues." In *Ancient Synagogues: Historical Analysis and Archaeological Discovery*, vol. II, ed. Dan Urman and Paul V. M. Flesher. Leiden, 1995.

Brann, M. "Ein Breslauer Grabdenkmal aus dem Jahre 1203." *Schlesische Geschichtsblatter* 1 (1919).

Breier, Alois. "Die Holzernen Synagoen in Galizien und Russisch-Polen aus dem 16, 17 und 18 Jahrhundert." Ph.D. dissertation, Technische Hochshule, Wieden, 1913.

Breier, Alois, Max Eisler, and Max Grunwald. *Holzsynagogen in Polen*. Baden bei Wien, 1934.

Brenner, Robert. "Economic Backwardness in Eastern Europe in Light of Developments in the West." In *The Origins of Backwardness in Eastern Europe*, ed. Daniel Chirot. Berkeley, 1989.

Brodsky, Harold. "A Map of the Shtetl Vinograd." In *Land and Community: Geography in Jewish Studies*, ed. Harold Brodsky. Bethesda, Md., 1997.

Brykowski, Ryszard. *Drewniana Architektura Cerkiewna* (Wooden Architecture of the Orthodox Church). Warsaw, 1995.

———. "Początki drewnianej fary w Tomaszowie Lubelskim" (The Beginnings of the Wooden Parish Church in Tomaszów Lubelski). In *Podług nieba i zwyczaju Polskiego: Studia z historii architektury, sztuki i kultury ofiarowane Adamowi Miłobędzkiemu* (According to the Heavens and Polish Custom: Studies in the History of Art, Architecture and Culture Dedicated to Adam Miłobędzki). Warsaw, 1988.

Buxton, David. *The Wooden Churches of Eastern Europe*. Cambridge, 1981.

Cahn, Walter. "Solomonic Elements in Romanesque Art." In *The Temple of Solomon: Archaeological Fact and Medieval Tradition in Christian, Islamic and Jewish Art*, ed. Joseph Gutmann. Ann Arbor, Mich., 1976.

Camille, Michael. *Gothic Art*. New York, 1996.

———. *Mirror in Parchment: The Luttrell Psalter and the Making of Medieval England*. Chicago, 1998.

Caro, Joseph. *Beit Yosef* (OH 90:4).

———. *Shulhan Arukh* (OH 90:4).

Chanturya, V. A. *A History of Belarusian Architecture* [in Russian]. Minsk, 1985.

Chirot, Daniel, ed. *The Origins of Backwardness in Eastern Europe: Economics and Politics from the Middle Ages until the Early Twentieth Century*. Berkeley, 1989.

Cohen, Gerson. *Messianic Postures of Ashkenazim and Sephardim (Prior to Sabbethai Zevi)*. New York, 1967.

Cohen, Richard I. "'And Your Eyes Shall See Your Teachers': On the Transformation of the Rabbi into an Icon in the Nineteenth Century." Lecture delivered to the Eleventh World Congress of Jewish Studies, Jerusalem, 1993.

———. *Jewish Icons: Art and Society in Modern Europe*. Berkeley, 1998.

Coulton, G. G. *Medieval Faith and Symbolism*. New York, 1928.

Curuk, Cenap and Ersin Cicekciler. *Ornekleriyle Turk Cadirlari* (Tents in the Lives of the Turks). Istanbul, 1983.

Cygielman, A. "The Basic Privileges of the Jews of Great Poland as Reflected in Polish Historiography." *Polin* 2 (1987).

———. *Jewish Autonomy in Poland and Lithuania until 1648 (5408)*. Jerusalem, 1997.

Dan, Joseph, ed. *Binah: Jewish Intellectual History in the Middle Ages*. Westport, Conn., 1994.

———. "The Book of the Divine Name by Rabbi Eleazar of Worms," *Frankfurter Judaistische Beitrage*, 22(1995).

———. "Hokhmath Ha 'Egoz." *Journal of Jewish Studies* 17:1–2 (1966).

———. "Introduction." *The Age of the Zohar*. Jerusalem, 1989.

———. "Prayer as Text and Prayer as Mystical Experience." In *Torah and Wisdom: Studies in Jewish Philosophy*, ed. Ruth Link-Salinger. New York, 1992.

Daston, Lorraine, and Katharine Park. *Wonders and the Order of Nature*. New York, 1998.

Davies, Norman. *God's Playground, A History of Poland*, vol. 1. New York, 1982.

———. *Heart of Europe*. Oxford, 1984.

Davidovitch. David. *The Synagogues in Poland and Their Destruction*. Jerusalem, 1960.

———. *Wall-Paintings of Synagogues in Poland* [in Hebrew]. Jerusalem, 1968.

———. *Wandmalereien in alten Synagogen*. Hammeln und Hannover, 1969.

Dawidowicz, Lucy S., ed. *The Golden Tradition*. New York, 1967.

Demus, Otto. *Byzantine Art and the West*. New York, 1970.

Dinur, Benzion. "The Origins of Hasidism and Its Social and Messianic Foundations." In *Essential Papers On Hasidism*, ed. Gershon David Hundert. New York, 1991.

Dobroszycki, Lucjan, and Barbara Kirshenblatt-Gimblett. *Image Before My Eyes*. New York, 1977.

Dodds, Jerrilynn D. "Mudejar Tradition and the Synagogues of Medieval Spain: Cultural Identity and Cultural Hegemony." In *Convivencia: Jews, Muslims, and Christians in Medieval Spain*, ed. Vivian B. Mann, Thomas F. Glick, and Jerrilynn D. Dodds. New York, 1992.

Dubnow, S. M. *History of the Jews in Russia and Poland*, vol. 1. Philadelphia, 1916.

Eco, Umberto. *Art and Beauty in the Middle Ages*. New Haven, 1989.

———. *Interpretation and Overinterpretation*. New York, 1992.

Efron, Zussia. "Carved Wooden Lecterns and Torah Pointers." In *Treasures of Jewish Galicja*, ed. Sarah Harel Hoshen. Tel Aviv, 1996.

Egbert, Virginia Wylie. *The Medieval Artist at Work*. Princeton, 1967.

Elbaum, Jacob. "Aspects of Hebrew Ethical Literature in Sixteenth-Century Poland." In *Jewish Thought in the 16th Century*, ed. B. D. Cooperman. Cambridge, Mass., 1983.

———. "The Influence of Spanish-Jewish Culture on the Jews of Ashkenaz and Poland in the Fifteenth–Seventeenth Centuries." In *Binah: Jewish Intellectual History in the Middle Ages*, vol. 3, ed. Joseph Dan. Westport, Conn., 1994.

Elbogan, Ismar. *Jewish Liturgy: A Comprehensive History*. Philadelphia, 1993.

Eliach, Yaffa. *There Once Was a World: The Nine-Hundred Year Chronicle of the Shtetl of Eishyshok*. Boston, 1998.

Eliade, Mircea. *The Sacred and the Profane: The Nature of Religion*. New York, 1959.

Elior, Rachel. "The Doctrine of Transmigration in Galya Raza." In *Essential Papers on Kabbalah*, ed. Lawrence Fine. New York, 1995.

———. *The Paradoxical Ascent to God*. Albany, N.Y., 1993.

Epstein, Marc Michael. *Dreams of Subversion in Medieval Jewish Art*. University Park, Penn., 1997.

———. "The Elephant and the Law: The Medieval Jewish Minority Adapts a Christian Motif." *Art Bulletin*, 76:3 (September 1994).

———. "'If lions could carve stones . . .?' Medieval Jewry and the Allegorization of the Animal Kingdom," Ph.D. dissertation, Yale University, 1992. Ann Arbor, 1993.

Ettinger, Shmuel. "The Council of the Four Lands." In *The Jews in Old Poland, 1000–1795*, ed. Antony Polansky, Jakub Basista, and Andrzej Link-Lenczowski. London, 1993.

———. "Jewish Participation in the Settlement of Ukraine in the Sixteenth and Seventeenth Centuries." In *Ukrainian-Jewish Relations in Historical Perspective*, ed. Peter J. Potichnyj and Howard Aster. Edmonton, 1990.

———. "The Modern Period." In *A History of the Jewish People*, ed. H. H. Ben-Sasson. Cambridge, Mass., 1976.

Faber, Alice, and Robert King. "Yiddish and the Settlement of Ashkenazi Jews." In *Approaches to Judaism in Medieval Times*, vol. 2, ed. David R. Blumenthal. Chico, Calif., 1984.

Farber, Shlomo, ed. *Olkienniki in Flames: A Memorial Book*. Tel Aviv, 1962.

Feldman, Louis H. "Diaspora Synagogues: New Light from Inscriptions and Papyri." In *Sacred Realm: The Emergence of the Synagogue in the Ancient World*, ed. Steven Fine. New York, 1996.

Fine, Steven. *The Holy Place: On the Sanctity of the Synagogue during the Greco-Roman Period*. Notre Dame, Ind., 1997.

———, ed. *Sacred Realm: The Emergence of the Synagogue in the Ancient World*. New York, 1996.

Fishof, Iris. "Depictions of Jerusalem by Eliezer Sussman of Brody." *Israel Museum Journal* 14 (Summer 1996).

———. "The Origin of the *Siddur* of the Rabbi of Ruzhin." In *Jewish Art* 12–13 (1986–87).

Foucault, Michel. *Archaeology of Knowledge*. New York, 1982.

Fram, Edward. "Creating a Tale of Martyrdom in Tulczyn, 1648." In *Jewish History and Jewish Memory*, ed. Elisheva Carlebach, John M. Efron, and David N. Myers. Hanover, N.H., 1998.

Franzos, Karl Emil. *The Jews of Barnow*. New York, 1883.

Freehof, Solomon B. "The Chuppah." In *In the Time of Harvest: Essays in Honor of Abba Hillel Silver*, ed. Daniel Jeremy Silver. New York, 1963.

Friesel, Evyatar. *Atlas of Modern Jewish History*. New York, 1990.

Geertz, Clifford. *Interpretation of Culture*. New York, 1973.

George, Wilma. "Sources and Background to Discoveries of New Animals in the Sixteenth and Seventeenth Centuries." *History of Science* 18:40, part 2 (June 1980).

Gieysztor, Aleksander. *History of Poland*. Warsaw, 1968.

Ginsburg, Elliot K. *The Sabbath in Classical Kabbalah*. Albany, 1989.

———. "Zelem 'Elohim: The Image of the Divine and Person in Zoharic Kabbalah." In *In Search of the Divine*, ed. L. Shinn. New York, 1987.

Ginzberg, Louis. *The Legends of the Jews*. Philadelphia, 1947.

Gitelman, Zvi. *A Century of Ambivalence*. New York, 1988.

Glassie, Henry. *Art and Life in Bangladesh*. Bloomington, 1997.

———. *Folk Housing in Middle Virginia*. Knoxville, 1976.

———. *Passing the Time in Ballymenone*. Philadelphia, 1982.

———. *The Spirit of Folk Art*. New York, 1989.

Glick, Leonard B. *Abraham's Heirs: Jews and Christians in Medieval Europe*. Syracuse, 1999.

Gloger, Zygmunt. *Budownictwo drzewne i wyroby z drzewa w dawnej Polsce* (Wooden Building and Wooden Artifacts in Ancient Poland). Warsaw, 1907.

Goitein, S. D. *Jews and Arabs: Their Contacts Through the Ages*. New York, 1974.

Golb, Norman, and Omeljan Pritsak. *Khazarian Hebrew Documents of the Tenth Century*. Ithaca, N.Y., 1982.

Goldberg, Jacob. "The Changes in the Attitude of Polish Society Toward the Jews in the 18th Century." In *Polin* 1 (1986).

———. *Jewish Privileges in the Polish Commonwealth: Charters of Rights Granted to Jewish Communities in Poland-Lithuania in the Sixteenth to Eighteenth Centuries*. Jerusalem, 1985.

———. "The Jewish Sejm: Its Origin and Functions." In *The Jews in Old Poland, 1000–1795*, ed. Antony Polonsky, Jakub Basista, and Andrzej Link-Lenczowski. London, 1993.

———. "The Privileges Granted to Jewish Communities of the Polish Commonwealth as a Stabilizing Factor in Jewish Support." In *The Jews in Poland*, ed. Chimen Abramsky, Maciej Jachimczyk, and Antony Polonsky. Oxford, 1986.

Goldberg, Sylvie-Anne. *Crossing the Jabbok*. Berkeley, 1996.

Goldberg-Mulkiewicz, Olga. *Ethnographic Topics Relating to Jews in Polish Studies*. Jerusalem, 1989.

Goldenberg, Robert. "The Broken Axis." In *Supplement: Journal of the American Academy of Religion* 45:3 (September 1977).

Goldman, Bernard. *The Sacred Portal: A Primary Symbol in Ancient Judaic Art*. Detroit, 1966.

Goldschmidt, Adolph. *German Illumination*, vol. 1. New York, 1970.

Goldsteina, Maksymiljana, Karol Dresdner, and Majer Balaban. *Kultura i sztuka ludu żydowskiego na ziemiach polskich: zbiory Maksymiljana Goldsteina* (Culture and Art of the Jewish People in the Lands of Poland: Collections of Maksymiljan Goldstein). Warsaw, 1991.

Gombrich, E. H. *The Sense of Order*. Ithaca, N.Y., 1979.

Gottlieb, Efraim. "The Meaning of Prayer in Kabbalah." In *Studies in the Kabbalah Literature*, ed. Joseph Hacker. Tel Aviv, 1976.

Grabowski, Józef. *Sztuka Ludowa: formy i regiony w Polsce* (Folk Art: Forms and Regions in Poland). Warsaw, 1967.

Graetz, Heinrich. *History of the Jews*, vol. 5. Philadelphia, 1956.

Grayzel, Solomon. *A History of the Jews*. Philadelphia, 1947.

Green, Arthur. *Keter: The Crown of God in Early Jewish Mysticism*. Princeton, 1997.

———. "Sabbath as Temple: Some Thoughts on Space and Time in Judaism." In *Go and Study*, ed. Raphael Jospe and Samuel Z. Fishman. Washington, D.C., 1980.

———. "The Song of Songs in Early Jewish Mysticism." *Orim: A Jewish Journal at Yale* 11:2 (1987).

———. "The Zaddiq as Axis Mundi in Later Judaism." *Journal of the American Academy of Religion* 45:3 (September 1977).

———. "The *Zohar*: Jewish Mysticism in Medieval Spain." In *An Introduction to the Medieval Mystics of Europe*, ed. Paul E. Szarmach. Albany, N.Y., 1984.

Greenewegs, Martin. Diary, File no. 406-386/90. Biblioteka Gdańska, Gdańsk, Poland.

Gries, Zeev. "Between History and Literature: The Case of Jewish Preaching." *Journal of Jewish Thought and Philosophy* 4 (1994).

———. *The Book in Early Hasidism* [in Hebrew]. Tel Aviv, 1992.

———. *Conduct Literature: Its History and Place in the Life of Beshtian Hasidim* [in Hebrew]. Jerusalem, 1989.

———. "The Copying and Printing of Kabbalistic Books as a Source for the Study of Kabbalah" [in Hebrew]. *Mahanayim* 6 (1993).

———. "From Myth to Ethos: A Portrait of R. Abraham of Kalisk" [in Hebrew]. In *Nation and History: Studies in the History of the Jewish People*, vol. 2, ed. Shmuel Ettinger. Jerusalem, 1984.

Gruber, Samuel D. *Synagogues*. New York, 1999.

Grunwald, Max. "Anhang zur Iconographie der Malerei in unseren Holzsynagogen" (Appendix on Iconography of Paintings in Our Synagogues). In Alois Breier, Max Eisler, and Max Grunwald, *Holzsynagogue in Polen*. Baden bei Wein, 1934.

Guldon, Zenon, and Waldemar Kowalski. "Between Tolerance and Abomination: Jews in Sixteenth-Century Poland." In *The Expulsion of the Jews: 1492 and After*, ed. Raymond B. Waddington and Arthur H. Williamson. New York, 1994.

Guldon, Zenon, and Jacek Wijaczka. "The Accusation of Ritual Murder in Poland, 1500–1800." *Polin* 10 (1997).

Gunst, Peter. "Agrarian Systems of Central and Eastern Europe." In *The Origins of Backwardness in Eastern Europe*, ed. Daniel Chirot. Berkeley, 1989.

Gurevich, Aron. *Categories of Medieval Culture*. London, 1985.

———. *Medieval Popular Culture: Problems of Belief and Perception*. Cambridge, 1988.

Gutmann, Joseph. *Hebrew Manuscript Painting*. New York, 1978.

———. *The Jewish Life Cycle*. Leiden, 1987.

———. "Masorah Figurata: The Origins and Development of a Jewish Art Form" and "Return in Mercy to Zion: A Messianic Dream in Jewish Art." In *Sacred Images: Studies in Jewish Art from Antiquity to the Middle Ages*. Aldershot, U.K., 1989.

———. "The Second Commandment and the Image in Judaism." In *Beauty in Holiness*. New York, 1970.

———, ed. *Beauty in Holiness: Studies in Jewish Customs and Ceremonial Art*. New York, 1970.

Hachlili, Rachel. "Synagogues in the Land of Israel: The Art and Architecture of Ancient Synagogue and Synagogue Archaeology." In *Sacred Realm*, ed. Steven Fine. New York, 1996.

Hallamish, Moshe. "Notes on the Thirteen Gates in Heaven" [in Hebrew]. *Da'at* 22 (1989).

Hallamish, Moshe. "The Influence of the Kabbalah on Jewish Liturgy." In *Priere, Mystique, et Judaisme*, ed. Roland Goetschel. Paris, 1987.

Halperin, David J. *The Faces of the Chariot: Early Jewish Responses to Ezekiel's Vision*. Tubingen, 1988.

Hasan-Rokem, Galit, and Alan Dundes, eds. *The Wandering Jew: Essays in the Interpretation of a Christian Legend*. Bloomington, Ind., 1986.

Heilbronner, Oded. "Introduction: European Jews as a Factor in Multicultural Society." *Jewish Studies* 37 (1997).

Heilman, Samuel C. *Synagogue Life: A Study in Symbolic Interaction*. Chicago, 1976.

Hertz, Aleksander. *The Jews in Polish Culture*. Evanston, Ill., 1988.

Herzog, Marvin. *The Yiddish Language in Northern Poland: Its Geography and History*. Bloomington, Ind., 1965.

Heschel, Abraham Joshua. "The Eastern European Era in Jewish History." In *East European Jews in Two Worlds: Studies From the YIVO Annual*, ed. Deborah Dash Moore. Evanston, Ill., 1990. (Originally published in *Yivo Bleter* 25 [1945]).

Hewryk, Titus D. *Masterpieces in Wood: Houses of Worship in Ukraine*. New York, 1987.

Himmelfarb, Martha. *Ascent to Heaven in Jewish and Christian Apocalypses*. New York, 1993.

Hoshen, Sarah Harel, ed. *Treasures of Jewish Galicja: Judaica from the Museum of Ethnography and Crafts in Lvov, Ukraine*. Tel Aviv, 1996.

Huberman, Ida. *Living Symbols*. Ramat-Gan, 1988.

Hubka, Thomas C. *Big House, Little House, Back House, Barn: The Connected Farm Buildings of New England*. Hanover, N.H., 1984.

———. "Just Folks Designing." In *Common Places*, ed. Dell Upton and John Vlach. Athens, Ga., 1986.

Huizinga, Johan. *Homo Ludens*. London, 1949.

Hundert, Gershon David. "The Implications of Jewish Economic Activities for Christian-Jewish Relations in the Polish Commonwealth." In *The Jews in Poland*, ed. Chimen Abramsky, Maciej Jachimczyk, and Antony Polonsky. New York, 1988.

———. "Jewish Children and Childhood in Early Modern East Central Europe." In *The Jewish Family: Metaphor and Memory*, ed. David Kraemer. New York, 1989.

———. "Jewish Urban Residence in the Polish Commonwealth in the Early Modern Era." *Jewish Journal of Sociology* 26:1 (June 1984).

———. *The Jews in a Polish Private Town*. Baltimore, 1992.

———. "The *Kehilla* and the Municipality in Private Towns at the End of the Early Modern Period." In *The Jews in Old*

Poland, 1000–1795, ed. Antony Polonsky, Jakub Basista, and Andrzej Link-Lenczowski. London, 1993.

——. "Poland: Paradisus Judaeorum." In *Journal of Jewish Studies* 48:2 (Autumn 1997).

——. "The Role of the Jews in Commerce in Early Modern Poland-Lithuania." In *Journal of European Economic History* 16:2 (Fall 1987).

Huss, Boaz. "The Anthological Interpretation: The Emergence of Anthologies of Zohar Commentaries in the Seventeenth Century." *Prooftexts* 19 (1999).

——. "Sefer ha-Zohar as a Canonical, Sacred and Holy Text: Changing Perspectives of the Book of Splendor between the Thirteenth and Eighteenth Centuries." *The Journal of Jewish Thought and Philosophy* 7 (1998).

Idel, Moshe. "Gazing at the Head in Ashkenazi Hasidism." *Journal of Jewish Thought and Philosophy* 6:2 (1997).

——. *Hasidism: Between Ecstasy and Magic.* Albany, N.Y., 1995.

——. *Kabbalah: New Perspectives.* New Haven, 1988.

——. "Kabbalistic Prayer and Colors." In *Approaches to Judaism in Medieval Times,* vol. 3, ed. David R. Blumenthal. Atlanta, 1988.

——. *Messianic Mystics.* New Haven, 1998.

——. "One from a Town, two from a Clan—The Diffusion of Lurianic Kabbalah and Sabbatianism: A Re-Examination." *Jewish History* 7:2 (Fall 1993).

——. "Perceptions of Kabbalah in the Second Half of the 18th Century." *Journal of Jewish Thought and Philosophy* 1:1 (1991).

Idelsohn, A. Z. *Jewish Liturgy and Its Development.* New York, 1995.

Isaievych, Iaroslav. "Naidavnishyi Istorychnyi Opys Lvova." *Zhovten* 10 (1984).

Israel, Jonathan. *European Jewry in the Age of Mercantilism, 1550–1750.* Oxford, 1989.

Israel, R., of Ruzhin. *Knesset Israel.* Warsaw, 1906.

Ittai Tamari. "The Inscriptions Adorning the Synagogue Hall." In *The Synagogue of Samuel Halevy ('El Transito'), Toledo, Spain,* ed. Mordechai Omer. Tel Aviv, 1993.

Jacobs, Louis. *Hasidic Prayer.* London, 1972.

Jaffe, I. and R. Wittkower. *Baroque Art: The Jesuit Contribution.* New York, 1972.

Jellinek, Dr. Ad. *Märtyrer und Memorbuch.* Wein, 1881.

Jick, Leon A. "The Reform Synagogue." In *The American Synagogue: A Sanctuary Transformed,* ed. Jack Wertheimer. Hanover, N.H., 1987.

——. *The Americanization of the Synagogue, 1820–1870.* Hanover, N.H., 1992.

Josephus, Flavius. *The Works of Flavius Josephus, Comprising the Antiquities of the Jews,* vol. 14. Philadelphia, 1896.

Juhasz, Esther. "Synagogues." In *Sephardi Jews in the Ottoman Empire: Aspects of Material Culture,* ed. Esther Juhasz. Jerusalem, 1990.

——. "Textiles for the Home and Synagogue." In *Sephardi Jews in the Ottoman Empire: Aspects of Material Culture,* ed. Esther Juhasz. Jerusalem, 1990.

Kahana, Isaac Ze'ev. *Studies in Responsa Literature.* Jerusalem, 1973.

Kaidanover, Zwi Hirsch. *Kav ha Yashar* (The Honest Measure). Frankfurt, 1705.

Kanarfogel, Ephraim. *"Peering Through the Lattices": Mystical, Magical and Pietistic Dimensions in the Tosafist Period.* Detroit, 2000.

Kanof, Abram. *Jewish Symbolic Art.* Jerusalem, 1990.

Kantsedikas, Alexander. "Semyon An-sky and the Jewish Artistic Heritage." In *Semyon An-sky: The Jewish Artistic Heritage,* ed. Vasilii Rakitin and Andrei Sarabianov. Moscow, 1994.

Kassowski, Witold. "Ze studiów nad detalami zabytkowych konstrukcji ciesielskich" (From Studies on the Details of Historical Carpentry Construction). *Kwartalnik Architektury i Urbanistyki* (Quarterly of Architecture and Urban Planning) 7:1 (1962).

Kastan, Aharon. "Architectural Confrontations in the Old City of Jerusalem." In *L'Architettura a Malta, dalla preistoria all'ottocento; atti del XV congresso di storia dell' architettura, Malta, 11–16 settembre, 1967.* Rome, 1970.

——. "Synagogue Architecture of the Medieval and Pre-Emancipation Periods." In *Jewish Art,* ed. Cecil Roth. Greenwich, Conn., 1971.

Katz, Jacob. *Emancipation and Assimilation.* New York, 1972.

——. *Exclusiveness and Tolerance: Studies in Jewish-Gentile Relations in Medieval and Modern Times.* West Orange, N.J., 1961.

——. "Halakhah and Kabbalah as Competing Disciplines of Study." In *Jewish Spirituality: From the 16th Century Until the Present,* ed. Arthur Green. New York, 1987.

——. "Post-Zoharic Relations Between Halakhah and Kabbalah." In *Jewish Thought in the 16th Century,* ed. Bernard Dov Cooperman. Cambridge, Mass., 1983.

——. *Out of the Ghetto: The Social Background of Jewish Emancipation.* Cambridge, Mass., 1973.

——. *The "Shabbes Goy": A Study in Halakhic Flexibility.* Philadelphia, 1989.

Kaufmann, Thomas DaCosta. *Court, Cloister, and City: The Art and Culture of Central Europe, 1450–1800.* Chicago, 1995.

Kazovsky, Lola Kantor. "Piranesi and Villalpando: The Concept of the Temple in European Architectural Theory." In *The Real and Ideal Jerusalem in Jewish, Christian, and Islamic Art,* ed. Bianca Kuhnel. Jerusalem, 1998.

Kimelman, Reuven. "A Prolegomena to Lekhah Dodi and Qabbalat Shabbat" [in Hebrew]. In *From Rome to Jerusalem,* ed. Aviezer Ravitzki. Jerusalem, 1998.

——. "'Awaken, Awaken, for Your Light has Come': From Garments of Skin to Garments of Light, The Fifth Stanza of Lekha Dodi." *Proceedings of the Rabbinical Assembly* 59 (1997).

Kirshenblatt-Gimblett, Barbara. "Introduction." *Fabric of Jewish Life: Textiles From the Jewish Museum Collection.* New York, 1977.

——. "Introduction." *Life Is with People,* ed. Mark Zborowski and Elizabeth Herzog. New York, 1962.

Kochan, Lionel. *Beyond the Graven Image.* New York, 1997.

Kochanowicz, Jacek. "The Polish Economy and the Evolution of Dependency." In *The Origins of Backwardness in Eastern Europe: Economics and Politics from the Middle Ages until the Early Twentieth Century*, ed. Daniel Chirot. Berkeley, 1989.

Koester, Craig R. *The Dwelling of God*. Washington, D.C., 1989.

Koestler, Arthur. *The Thirteenth Tribe: The Khazar Empire and Its Heritage*. New York, 1976.

Kołodziejczyk, Dariusz. *Podole pod panowaniem tureckim, 1672–1699* (Podolia Under Ottoman Rule, 1672–1699). Warsaw, 1994.

Kopkowicz, Franciszek. *Ciesielstwo Polskie* (Polish Carpentry). Warsaw, 1958.

Kornecki, Marian. "Małopolskie kościoły drewniane doby Baroku" (XVII w) (Wooden Churches in Little Poland during the Period of the Baroque in the 17th Century). *Teka Komisji Urbanistykii Architektury* (Files of the Commission of Urban Planning in Architecture) 13 (1979).

Kostof, Spiro. *A History of Architecture*. New York, 1985.

Kozaczewska-Gołasz, Hanna. "Drewniane kolebki w średniowiecznych kościołach ziemi chełmińskiej i ich wpływ na architekturę" (Wooden Barrel-Vaulting in Medieval Churches of the Chelm Region and their Impact on Architecture). *Kwartalnik Architektury i Urbanistyki* (Quarterly of Architecture and Town Planning) 23:4 (1978).

Kozaczewska-Gołasz, Hanna. "Drewniane kolebki w budownictwie sredniowiecznym" (Wooden roofs in medieval buildings). *Kwartalnik Architektury i Urbanistyki* (Quarterly of Architecture and Town Planning) 24:2 (1979).

Krassowski, Czeslaw and Adam Miłobędzki. "Studia nad zabudową miasteczka Ciężkowice" (Studies in the Building Constructions of the Town of Ciężkowice). *Kwartalnik Architektury i Urbanistyki* (Quarterly of Architecture and Urban Planning) 2:1 (1957).

Kravtsov, Sergei. "On the Genesis of the Nine-Bay Synagogue." *Jewish Art* (in press).

———. "Synagogues of Eastern Galicja." In *Treasures of Jewish Galicja*, ed. Sarah Harel Hoshen. Tel Aviv, 1996.

Kremer, Moses. "Jewish Artisans and Guilds in Former Poland, 16th–18th Centuries." In *Beauty in Holiness: Studies in Jewish Customs and Ceremonial Art*, ed. Joseph Gutmann. New York, 1970.

Krinsky, Carol. *Synagogues of Europe*. Mineola, N.Y., 1985.

Król-Kaczorowska, Barbara. *Teatr Dawnej Polski* (The Theater of Old Poland). Warsaw, 1971.

Kugelmass, Jack, and Jonathan Boyarin. *From a Ruined Garden*. New York, 1983.

Kuhnel, Bianca. "The Use and Abuse of Jerusalem." In *The Real and Ideal Jerusalem in Jewish, Christian, and Islamic Art*. Jerusalem, 1998.

———, ed. *The Real and Ideal Jerusalem in Jewish, Christian, and Islamic Art*. Jerusalem, 1998.

Kuyt, Annelies. *The "Descent" to the Chariot*. Tubingen, 1995.

Landsberger, Franz. "The Illumination of Hebrew Manuscripts in the Middle Ages and Renaissance." In *Jewish Art: An Illustrated History*, ed. Cecil Roth. New York, 1961.

———. "The Sacred Direction in Synagogue and Church." In *The Synagogue: Studies in the Origins, Archaeology and Architecture*, ed. Harry M. Orlinsky. New York, 1975.

Langer, Ruth. "From the Study of Scripture to a Reenactment of Sinai: The Emergence of the Synagogue Torah Service." In *Worship* 72:1 (January 1998).

———. *To Worship God Properly: Tensions Between Liturgical Custom and Halakhah in Judaism*. Cincinnati, 1998.

Lederhendler, Eli. "From Autonomy to Auto-Emancipation." Ph.D. dissertation, The Jewish Theological Seminary of America, 1987.

Leeuw, Gerardus van der. *Sacred and Profane Beauty: The Holy in Art*. London, 1963.

Leśniakowska, Marta. *Polski Dwór: Wzorce Architektoniczne, Mit, Symbol* (Polish Manor House: Architectural Patterns, Myth, and Symbol). Warszawa, 1966.

Levenson, Jon D. "The Jerusalem Temple in Devotional and Visionary Experience." In *Jewish Spirituality*, ed. Arthur Green. New York, 1988.

Levine, Hillel. *Economic Origins of AntiSemitism: Poland and Its Jews in the Early Modern Period*. New Haven, 1991.

Levine, Lee I. *The Ancient Synagogue*. New Haven, 2000.

Levy, Isaac. *The Synagogue: Its History and Function*. London, 1964.

Lichten, Joseph L. "Polish Americans and American Jews: Some Issues Which Unite and Divide." *Polish Review* 18:4 (1973).

Lidov, Alexei. "Heavenly Jerusalem: The Byzantine Approach." In *The Real and Ideal Jerusalem in Jewish, Christian and Islamic Art*, ed. Bianca Kuhnel. Jerusalem, 1998.

Liebes, Yehuda. "How the Zohar Was Written." In *Studies in the Zohar*. Albany, 1993.

———. "Myth vs. Symbol in the Zohar and in Lurianic Kabbalah." In *Essential Papers on Kabbalah*, ed. Lawrence Fine. New York, 1995.

———. "New Trends in the Research of Kabbalah" [in Hebrew]. *Pe'amim* 50 (1992).

———. *Studies in the Zohar*. Albany, 1993.

———. "*Zohar* and Eros" [in Hebrew]. *Alpayim* 9 (1994).

Link-Lenczowski, Andrzej. "The Jewish Population in the Light of the Resolutions of the Dietines in the Sixteenth to the Eighteenth Centuries." In *The Jews in Old Poland 1000–1795*, ed. Antony Polonsky, Jakub Basista, and Andrzej Link-Lenczowski. London, 1993.

Lissitzky, El. "The Synagogue of Mohilev" [in Yiddish]. *Milgroim* 3 (1923).

Litman, Jacob. *The Economic Role of Jews in Medieval Poland: The Contribution of Yitzhak Schipper*. Lanham, Md., 1984.

Logvin, G. N. *Monuments of Art in the Soviet Union, Ukraine, and Moldavia* [in Russian]. Moscow, 1982.

Loukomski, G. K. *L'Art Decoratif Russe*. Paris, 1928.

Lowenthal, David. *The Past Is a Foreign Country*. Cambridge, 1985.

Magocsi, Paul Robert. *Historical Atlas of East Central Europe*. Toronto, 1993.

Mahler, Raphael. *A History of Modern Jewry. 1780–1815*, New York, 1971.

Maldonado, Basilio Pavon. "The Mudejar Elements of the El Transito Synagogue." In *The Synagogue of Samuel Halevy*

('El Transito'), *Toledo, Spain*, ed. Mordechai Omer. Tel Aviv, 1993.

Male, Emile. *The Gothic Image*. New York, 1972.

Malino, Frances, and David Sorkin, eds. *From East and West: Jews in a Changing Europe, 1750–1870*. Oxford, 1990.

Małkiewicz, Adam. *Teoria Architektury w Nowożytnym Piśmiennictwie Polskim* (Theory of Architecture in Polish Writings from the Middle of the Sixteenth Century to the Nineteenth Century). Cracow, 1975.

Mankowski, Tadeusz. *Fabrica Ecclesiae* (Constructions of the Church). Warsaw, 1946.

——. *Orient w Polskiej Kulturze Artystycznej* (The Orient in Polish Artistic Culture). Wrocław, 1959.

Mann, Vivian B. *Jewish Texts on the Visual Arts*. Cambridge, 2000.

Marcus, I. G. "Prayer Gestures in German Hasidim." In *Mysticism, Magic and Kabbalah in Ashkenazi Judaism*, ed. Karl Erich Grozinger and Joseph Dan. Berlin, 1995.

Maszkowski, Karol. Maszkowski letters file, Archiwum Polskiej Akademii Nauk, Krakow.

Mayer, Leo Ary. "Jewish Art in the Moslem World." In *Jewish Art*, ed. Cecil Roth. New York, 1961.

Mayr-Harting, Henry. *Ottonian Book Illumination*, part 1. London, 1999.

Meek, H. A. *The Synagogue*. London, 1995.

Mellinkoff, Ruth. "The Round-Topped Tablet of the Law: Sacred Symbol and Emblem of Evil." *Journal of Jewish Art* 1 (1974).

Menache, Sophia. "Communication in the Jewish Diaspora: A Survey." In *Communications in the Jewish Diaspora*, ed. Sophia Menache. Leiden, 1996.

Mendes-Flohr, Paul. "*Fin-de-Siecle* Orientalism, the *Ostjuden* and the Aesthetics of Jewish Self-Affirmation." In *Studies in Contemporary Jewry*, ed. Jonathan Frankel. Bloomington, Ind., 1984.

Metzger, Mendel. "Style in Jewish Art of the 17th and 18th Centuries in Relation to the Baroque and the Rococo." *Gazette des Beaux-Arts* (November 1976).

Metzger, Therese, and Mendel Metzger. *Jewish Life in the Middle Ages: Illuminated Hebrew Manuscripts of the Thirteenth to the Sixteenth Centuries*. New York, 1982.

Mieszkowski, Zygmunt. *Podstawowe Problemy Architektury w Polskich Traktatach od połowy XVI do początku XIX w* (Basic Problems in Polish Treatises on Architecture from the Mid-Sixteenth to the Early Nineteenth Century). Warsaw, 1970.

Mikoś, Michael J. *Polish Baroque and Enlightenment Literature*. Columbus, Oh., 1996.

Milobędzki, Adam. "Architecture in Wood: Technology, Symbolic Content, Art." *Artibus et Historiae* 19 (1989).

——. *Architektura polska XVII wieku*, t. I–II (Polish Architecture in the seventeenth century, vols. 1–2). Warsaw, 1980.

——. "Medieval Architectural Tradition in the Cultural Landscape of 16th–18th Centuries. Central Europe," *Polish Art Studies* 12 (1990).

——. "The Survival of Gothic in Vernacular and 'Neo-Vernacular' Architecture." In *L'Art et les revolutions* (Actes, XXVIIe Congres International d'histoire de l'Art, Section 6), ed. R. Recht. Strasbourg, 1992.

——. *Zarys dziejów architektury w Polsce* (Outline of Architectural History in Poland). Warsaw, 1988.

Mitchell, Timothy. *Colonizing Egypt*. New York, 1988.

Moore, Deborah Dash, ed. *East European Jews in Two Worlds*. Evanston, Ill., 1990.

Mossakowski, Stanislaw. *Tylman z Gameren: Architekt Polskiego Baroku* (Tilman of Gameren: An Architect of the Polish Baroque). Wrocław, 1973.

Nadav, Mordekhai. "Regional Aspects of the Autonomy of Polish Jews: The History of the Tykocin Kehilla, 1670–1782." In *The Jews in Old Poland, 1000–1795*, ed. Antony Polonsky, Jakub Basista, and Andrzej Link-Lenczowski. London, 1993.

Namenyi, Ernest. *The Essence of Jewish Art*. New York, 1957.

Narkiss, Bezalel. *Hebrew Illuminated Manuscripts*. Jerusalem, 1974.

Natter, G. Tobias, ed. *Bilder des Wiener Malers: Isidor Kaufmann, 1853–1921*. Vienna, 1995.

Nelken, Halina. *Images of a Lost World: Jewish Motifs in Polish Paintings, 1770–1945*. Oxford, 1991.

Newman, Eugene. *Life and Teaching of Isaiah Horowitz*. London, 1972.

Niezabitowska, Małgorzata. *Remnants: The Last Jews in Poland*. New York, 1986.

Norberg-Schulz, Christian. *Late Baroque and Rococo Architecture*. New York, 1974.

Novick, Peter. *That Noble Dream: The "Objectivity Question" and the American Historical Profession*. Cambridge, 1988.

Noy, Dov. "Is There a Jewish Folk Religion?" In *Studies in Jewish Folklore*, ed. Frank Talmage. Cambridge, Mass., 1980.

Ong, Walter J. *Orality and Literacy: The Technologizing of the World*. London, 1995.

Paquada, Bahya. *The Book of Directions to Duties of the Heart*, trans. Menahem Mansoor. London, 1973.

Paszenda, Jerzy. *Kościół Jezuitów w Słucku* (The Jesuit Church in Sluck). In *Kwartalnik Architektury i Urbanistyki* (Quarterly of Architecture and Urban Planning) 23:3 (1978).

Patai, Raphael. *The Hebrew Goddess*. Detroit, 1978.

Pedaya, Haviva. "The Divinity as Place and Time and Holy Place in Jewish Mysticism." In *Sacred Space: Shrine, City, Land*, ed. Benjamin Z. Kedar and R. J. Zwi Werblowsky. New York, 1998.

Perek Shirah (Facsimile Edition of an Illustrated Manuscript). Introduction by Malachi Beit-Arie. The Jewish National and University Library, Jerusalem.

Piechotka, Maria, and Kazimierz Piechotka. *Bramy Nieba: Bóżnice drewniane na ziemiach dawnej Rzeczypospolitej* (Gate of Heaven: Wooden Synagogues in the Territories of the Polish Kingdom). Warsaw, 1996.

——. *Bramy Nieba: Bóżnice murowane na ziemiach dawnej Rzeczypospolitej* (Gate of Heaven: Masonry Synagogues in the Territories of the Polish Kingdom). Warsaw, 1999.

——. "Jewish Districts in the Spatial Structure of Polish Towns." In *Polin* 5 (1990).

———. "Polichromie polskich bóżnic drewnianych" (Wall-paintings in the Polish Wooden Synagogues). In *Polską Sztuka Ludowa* (Polish Folk Art) 43:1–2 (1989).

———. "Polish Synagogues in the Nineteenth Century." *Polin* 2 (1987).

———. *Wooden Synagogues*. Warsaw, 1959.

Pinkas Hakehillot (Encyclopaedia of Jewish Communities, Poland) vol. 2, *Eastern Galicja* [in Hebrew]. Jerusalem, 1980.

Pippal, Martina. "Relations of Time and Space: The Temple of Jerusalem as the *Domus Ecclesiae* in the Carolingian Period." In *The Real and Ideal Jerusalem in Jewish, Christian, and Islamic Art*, ed. Bianca Kuhnel. Jerusalem, 1998.

Piskorski, Jan M. "The Historiography of the So-Called 'East Colonization' and the Current State of Research." In . . . *The Man of Many Devices, Who Wandered Full Many Ways* . . . , *Festschrift in Honor of Janos M. Bak*, ed. Balazs Nagy and Marcell Sebok. Budapest, 1999.

Posner, Raphael. "Synagogues." *Encyclopedia Judaica*, vol. 15. Jerusalem, 1972.

Potocki Family of Radzyń. Files. Old Documents Archives, Warsaw.

Pritsak, Omeljan. "The Pre-Ashkenazic Jews of Eastern Europe." In *Ukrainian-Jewish Relations in Historical Perspective*, ed. Howard Aster and Peter J. Potichnyi. Edmonton, 1990.

Prokopowna, Eugenia. "The Image of the Shtetl in Polish Literature." In *Polin* 4 (1989).

Raczynski, Jerzy. "Przyczynki do Historji Ciesielskich Konstrukcyj Dachowych w Polsce" (Contributions to the History of Carpentry Roof Structures in Poland). In *Studja do Dziejów Sztuki w Polsce* (Studies of the History of Art in Poland), vol. 3. Warsaw, 1930.

Rappoport, Angelo S. *The Folklore of the Jews*. London, 1937.

Ratshabi, Yehuda. "Lekhah Dodi of Rabbi Shlomo Alkabez and Its Sources." *Mahanayim* 6 (1994).

Rechtman, Abraham. *Jewish Ethnography and Folklore* [in Yiddish]. Buenos Aires, 1958.

Reif, Stefan C. *Judaism and Hebrew Prayer*. Cambridge, 1993.

———. *Shabbethai Sofer and His Prayer-book*. Cambridge, 1979.

Reiner, Elchanan. "The Ashkenazi Elite at the Beginning of the Modern Era: Manuscript versus Printed Book." In *Polin* 10 (1997).

Rodrigue, Aron. "The Sephardim in the Ottoman Empire." In *Spain and the Jews: The Sephardi Experience, 1492 and After*, ed. Elie Kedourie. London, 1992.

Rosenberg, Arnold S. *Jewish Liturgy as a Spiritual System*. Northvale, N.J., 1997.

Rosenfeld, Moshe N. "The Development of Hebrew Printing in the Sixteenth and Seventeenth Centuries." *A Sign and a Witness: 2,000 Years of Hebrew Books and Illuminated Manuscripts*. New York, 1988.

Roskies, David G. *The Jewish Search for a Usable Past*. Bloomington, Ind., 1999.

Roskies, Diane K., and David G. Roskies. *The Shtetl Book*. New York, 1979.

Rosman, Moshe [M. J. Rosman, Murray Jay Rosman]. *Founder of Hasidism: A Quest for the Historical Ba'al Shem Tov*. Berkeley, 1996.

———. *The Lords' Jews*. Cambridge, Mass., 1990.

———. "A Minority Views the Majority: Jewish Attitudes Towards the Polish Lithuanian Commonwealth and Interaction with Poles." In *From Shtetl to Socialism*, ed. Antony Polonsky. London, 1993.

———. "The Polish Magnates and the Jews: Jews in the Sieniawski-Czartoryski Territories, 1686–1731." Ph.D. dissertation, The Jewish Theological Seminary of America, 1982.

Roth, Cecil, ed. *Jewish Art*. New York, 1961.

Ruderman, David B. "Unicorns, Great Beasts and the Marvelous Variety of Things in Nature in the Thought of Abraham B. Hananiah Yagel." In *Jewish Thought in the Seventeenth Century*, ed. Isadore Twersky and Bernard Septimus. Cambridge, Mass., 1987.

Ruskin, John. *The Seven Lamps of Architecture*. New York, 1871.

Rutgers, Leonard Victor. "Diaspora Synagogues: Synagogue Archaeology in the Greco-Roman World." In *Sacred Realm: The Emergence of the Synagogue in the Ancient World*, ed. Steven Fine. New York, 1996.

Rydel, Maciej. *Jam Dwór Polski* (I Am a Polish Manor House). Gdańsk, 1993.

Sabar, Shalom. *Mazal Tov*. Jerusalem, 1993.

Sachar, Howard Morley. *The Course of Modern Jewish History*. New York, 1958.

Said, Edward W. *Orientalism*. New York, 1978.

Salisbury, Joyce E. *The Beast Within: Animals in the Middle Ages*. New York, 1994.

Samek, Jan. *Polskie rzemiosło artystyczne* (Polish Artistic Crafts). Warszawa, 1984.

Saminsky, Alexander. "A Reference to Jerusalem in a Georgian Gospel Book." In *The Real and Ideal Jerusalem in Jewish, Christian, and Islamic Art*, ed. Bianca Kuhnel. Jerusalem, 1998.

Samsonowicz, Henryk. "Uwagi o budownictwie w Polsce u schyłku wieków średnich" (Remarks About Building Construction in Poland at the End of the Middle Ages). In *Studia z historii architektury, sztuki i kultury ofiarowane Adamowi Miłobędzkiemu* (Studies in the History of Architecture, Art, and Culture in Honor of Adam Miłobędzki). Warsaw, 1989.

Schafer, Peter. *Synopse zur Hekhalot-Literatur*. Tubingen, 1981.

Schechter, Abraham I. "Cabbalistic Interpolations in the Prayer Book." In *Lectures on Jewish Liturgy*. Philadelphia, 1933.

Scherman, Nosson, and Meir Zlotowitz, eds. *Bircas Kohanim: The Priestly Blessing*, trans. Avie Gold. New York, 1991.

Schiper, Ignacy. *Dzieje handlu żydowskiego na ziemiach polskich* (The History of Jewish Commerce on Polish Lands). Warsaw, 1937.

Schocet, Elijah Judah. *Animal Life in Jewish Tradition*. New York, 1984.

Scholem, Gershom. *Kabbalah*. New York, 1974.

———. *Major Trends in Jewish Mysticism*. New York, 1954.

———. *On the Kabbalah and Its Symbolism*. New York, 1969.

———. *On the Mystical Shape of the Godhead*. New York, 1991.

———. *Sabbatai Sevi; The Mystical Messiah, 1626–1676*. Princeton, 1973.

———. *Zohar: The Book of Splendor*. New York, 1949.

Schreckenberg, Heinz. *The Jews in Christian Art: An Illustrated History*. New York, 1996.

Sed-Rajna, Gabrielle. "Filigree Ornaments in Fourteenth-Century Hebrew Manuscripts of the Upper Rhine." In *Jewish Art* 12–13 (1986–87).

"Sefer Evronot." Ashkenazi, 1664. Hebrew Union College, Cincinnati, file no. 906.

Segal, Eliezer. "The Exegetical Craft of the Zohar: Toward an Appreciation." *AJS Review* 17:1 (Spring 1992).

Segel, Harold B., ed. *Stranger in Our Midst: Images of the Jew in Polish Literature*. Ithaca, N.Y., 1996.

Seltzer, Robert M. *Jewish People, Jewish Thought*. New York, 1980.

Shadur, Joseph, and Yehudit Shadur. *Traditional Jewish Papercuts: An Inner World of Art and Symbol*. Hanover, N.H., 2001.

Shakked, Shlomit. *Poland: Aperture to a World Laid Waste*. Tel Aviv, 1988.

Sherwin, Byron L. *Sparks Amidst the Ashes: The Spiritual Legacy of Polish Jewry*. New York, 1997.

Shulman, Nisson E. *Authority and Community: Polish Jewry in the Sixteenth Century*. New York, 1986.

Shulvass, Moses A. *From East to West: The Westward Migration of Jews from Eastern Europe during the Seventeenth and Eighteenth Centuries*. Detroit, 1971.

Śliwiński, Krzysztof. "Towards a Polish-Jewish Dialogue: The Way Forward." *Polin* 10 (1997).

Słownik Geograficzny Królestwa Polskiego (Geographical Dictionary of the Polish Kingdom), vol. 2. Warsaw, 1881.

Smith, Jonathan Z. *To Take Place: Toward a Theory in Ritual*. Chicago, 1987.

Sokolowa, Alla. "Architecture in the Small Towns of Western Podolia" [in Russian]. In *The History of Jews in the Ukraine and Byelorussia*, ed. V. Dimshitz. St. Petersburg, 1994.

Sokolowa, Alla. "Architectural Space of the Shtetl-Street-House: Jewish Homes in the Shtetls of Eastern-Podolia." In *Trumah* 7 (1998).

Sonne, Isaiah. "Secondary Names for Synagogues" [in Hebrew]. *Tarbiz* 27 (1958).

Sperling, Harry, and Maurice Simon, trans. *The Zohar*, vols. 1–5. London, 1984.

Spira, Roman. *Rabbis and Jewish Scholars in Poland in the 16th, 17th, and 18th Centuries*. Cracow, 1985.

Stampfer, Shaul. "The 1764 Census of Polish Jewry." *Bar-Ilan* 24–25 (1989).

Steinlauf, Michael C. *Bondage to the Dead: Poland and the Memory of the Holocaust*. Syracuse, N.Y., 1997.

———. "Whose Poland? Returning to Aleksander Hertz." *Galed, On the History of the Jews of Poland* 12 (1991).

Stone, Daniel. "Knowledge of Foreign Languages among Eighteenth-Century Polish Jews." *Polin* 10 (1997).

Subtelney, Orest. *Ukraine: A History*. Toronto, 1989.

Sysyn, Frank E. "The Jewish Factor in the Chmielnicki Uprising." In *Ukrainian-Jewish Relations in Historical Perspective*, ed. Peter J. Potichnyj and Howard Aster. Edmonton, 1990.

Szyller, Stefan. *Czy mamy polską architekturę?* (Do We Have a Polish Architecture?). Warsaw, 1916.

Szyszko-Bohusz, Adolf. "Kościoły w Tomaszowie i Mnichowie." (Churches in Tomaszów and Mnichow). In *Sprawozdania komisji do badania historii sztuki w Polsce*. (Reports of the Commission on the Investigation of Art History in Poland) 8:3–4 (1912).

Ta-Shma, Israel M. *The Halachic Residue in the Zohar: A Contribution to the Study of the Zohar* [in Hebrew]. Tel-Aviv, 1995.

———. "On the History of the Jews in Twelfth- and Thirteenth-Century Poland." *Polin* 10 (1997).

"Tabernacle." *Anchor Bible Dictionary*, vol. 6, ed. David Noel Freedman. New York, 1992.

Taitz, Emily. "Women's Voices, Women's Prayers: Women in the European Synagogues of the Middle Ages." *Daughters of the King: Women and the Synagogue*. Philadelphia, 1992.

Talmage, Frank. "Apples of Gold: The Inner Meaning of Sacred Texts in Medieval Judaism." In *Jewish Spirituality: From the Bible to the Middle Ages*, ed. Arthur Green. New York, 1988.

Tazbir, Janusz. "Conspiracy Theories and the Reception of the Protocols of the Elders of Zion in Poland." *Polin* 11 (1998).

———. "Images of the Jew in the Polish Commonwealth." *Polin* 4 (1989).

———. *A State without Stakes: Polish Religious Toleration in the Sixteenth and Seventeenth Centuries*. New York, 1973.

Thompson, E. P. *The Making of the English Working Class*. New York, 1963.

Tishby, Isaiah. *The Wisdom of the Zohar*, 3 vols. Oxford, 1991.

Tollet, Daniel. "The Private Life of Polish Jews in the Vasa Period." In *The Jews in Old Poland, 1000–1795*, ed. Antony Polonsky, Jakub Basista, and Andrzej Link-Lenczowski. London, 1993.

Trzcinski, Andrzej. "Polichromia Nagrobków na Cmentarzach Żydowskich w Polsce Południowo-Wschodniej" (Color Paintings on the Tombstones in Jewish Cemeteries in Southeastern Poland). *Polska Sztuka Ludowa* (Polish Folk Art) 43:1–2 (1989).

Uffenheimer, Rivka Schatz. *Hasidism as Mysticism: Quietistic Elements in Eighteenth-Century Hasidic Thought*. Princeton, 1993.

Ulmer, Rivka. *The Evil Eye in the Bible and in Rabbinic Literature*. Hoboken, N.J., 1994.

Unrau, John. *Looking at Architecture with Ruskin*. London, 1978.

Untermayer-Raymer, Max. "German Synagogue Art: Notes and Drawings." *The Menorah Journal* 25 (1937).

Upton, Dell. "The Power of Things: Recent Studies in American Vernacular Architecture." *American Quarterly* 35:3 (1983).

———. "Outside the Academy: A Century of Vernacular Architecture Studies, 1890–1990." In *The Architectural Historian in America*. Washington, D.C., 1990.

Urbach, E. E. "Heavenly Jerusalem and Earthly Jerusalem" [in

Hebrew]. In *Jerusalem Through the Ages*, ed. Joseph Aviram. Jerusalem, 1968.

Urman, Dan, and Paul V. M. Flesher, eds. *Ancient Synagogues: Historical Analysis and Archaeological Discovery*, vols. 1 and 2. Leiden, 1995.

———. "Ancient Synagogues: A Reader's Guide." In *Ancient Synagogues*, ed. Dan Urman and Paul V. M. Flesher. Leiden, 1995.

Velychenko, Stephen. *National History as Cultural Process*. Edmonton, 1992.

Vinecour, Earl. *Polish Jews: The Final Chapter*. New York, 1977.

Vishniac, Roman. *Polish Jews*. New York, 1965.

Vital, Hayyim. *'Es Hayyim*. Jerusalem, 1910.

Vital, Joseph. *Sefer Ets Hayim*. Podhajce (Ukraine), 1780.

Volavkova, Hana. *The Synagogue Treasures of Bohemia and Moravia*. Prague, 1949.

Volkov, Shulamit. "Minorities and the Nation-State: A Post-Modern Perspective." *Jewish Studies* 37 (1997).

Wandycz, Piotr S. "Historiography of the Countries of Eastern Europe: Poland." *American Historical Review* 97:4 (October 1992).

Weber, Annette. "Ark and Curtain: Monuments for a Jewish Nation in Exile." In *The Real and Ideal Jerusalem in Jewish, Christian and Islamic Art*, ed. Bianca Kuhnel. Jerusalem, 1998.

Weinryb, Bernard D. *The Jews of Poland: A Social and Economic History of the Jewish Community in Poland from 1100 to 1800*. Philadelphia, 1973.

Weiss, Joseph. *Studies in Eastern European Jewish Mysticism*. Oxford, 1985.

Weissler, Chava. "Prayers in Yiddish and the Religious World of Ashkenazi Women." In *Jewish Women in Historical Perspective*, ed. Judith Baskin. Detroit, 1991.

———. *Voices of the Matriarchs: Listening to the Prayers of Early Modern Jewish Women*. Boston, 1998.

Werblowsky, R. J. Zwi. "The Safed Revival and Its Aftermath." In *Jewish Spirituality*, ed. Arthur Green. New York, 1987.

Wertheimer, Jack, ed. *The American Synagogue: A Sanctuary Transformed*. Hanover, N.H., 1987.

White, Hayden V. *Content of Form: Narrative Discourse and Historical Representation*. Baltimore, 1987.

Wierzbicki, Ludwik. (Jabłonów Synagogue drawings) *Sprawozdania Komisji do Badań Historii Sztuki w Polsce*, Polskiej Akademii Umiejętności, t. 1–4, Krakow (Proceedings of the Commission for the Study of the History of Art in Poland, Polish Academy of Science, vols. 1–4). Cracow, 1879–1903.

Wiesel, Elie. *Souls on Fire: Portraits and Legends of the Hasidic Masters*. New York, 1972.

Wiesel, Marion, ed. *To Give Them Light: The Legacy of Roman Vishniac*. New York, 1993.

Wietzmann, Kurt, et al. *The Place of Book Illumination in Byzantine Art*. Princeton, 1975.

Wilensky, Mordecai L. "Hasidic-Mitnaggedic Polemics in the Jewish Communities of Eastern Europe: The Hostile Phase." In *Essential Papers of Hasidism*, ed. Gershon David Hundert. New York, 1991.

Wischnitzer, Mark. *A History of Jewish Crafts and Guilds*. New York, 1965.

Wischnitzer, Rachel. *The Architecture of the European Synagogue*. Phladelphia, 1964.

———. "The Messianic Fox." In *From Dura to Rembrandt: Studies in the History of Art*, ed. Rachel Wischnitzer. Milwaukee, 1990.

———. "Mutual Influences Between Eastern and Western Europe in the Synagogue Architecture from the 12th to the 18th Century." In *YIVO Annual of Jewish Social Science*, vols. 2–3. New York, 1947–48.

Wolf, Larry. *Inventing Eastern Europe: The Map of Civilization on the Mind of the Enlightenment*. Stanford, 1994.

Wolff-Łozińska, Barbara. *Malowidla stropow polskich I połowy XVI w dekoracje roślinne i kasetonowe* (Paintings on Polish Ceilings in the First Half of the 16th Century). Warsaw, 1971.

Wolfson, Elliot R. *Along the Path: Studies in Kabbalistic Myth, Symbolism, and Hermeneutics*. Albany, 1995.

———. *Circle and Square: Studies in the Use of Gender in Kabbalistic Symbolism*. Albany, 1995.

———. "Coronation of the Sabbath Bride: Kabbalistic Myth and the Ritual of Androgynisation." *The Journal of Jewish Thought and Philosophy* 6:2 (1997).

———. "The Face of Jacob in the Moon: Mystical Transformation of an Aggadic Myth." In *The Seductiveness of Jewish Myth*, ed. S. Daniel Breslauer. Albany, 1997.

———. "Forms of Visionary Ascent as Ecstatic Experience in the Zoharic Literature." In *Gershom Scholem's Major Trends in Jewish Mysticism Fifty Years After*, ed. Peter Schafer and Joseph Dan. Tubingen, 1993.

———. "The Hermeneutics of Visionary Experience: Revelation and Interpretation in the Zohar." *Religion* 18 (1988).

———. "Iconic Visualization and the Imaginal Body of God: The Role of Intention in the Rabbinic Conception of Prayer." *Modern Theology* 12:2 (April 1996).

———. "Letter Symbolism and Merkavah Imagery in the Zohar." In *'Alei Shefer: Studies in the Literature of Jewish Thought*, ed. Moshe Hallamish. Tel Aviv, 1990.

———. "The Mystical Significance of Torah Study in German Pietism." *Jewish Quarterly Review* 84:1 (July 1993).

———. *Through a Speculum That Shines: Vision and Imagination in Medieval Jewish Mysticism*. Princeton, 1994.

———. "Yeridah la-Merkavah: Typology of Ecstasy and Enthronement in Ancient Jewish Mysticism." In *Mystics of the Book*, ed. R. A. Herrera. New York, 1993.

Wolitz, Seth. "The Americanization of Tevye or Boarding the Jewish Mayflower." *American Quarterly* 40 (1988).

Yaniv, Bracha. "Ceremonial Textiles for the Synagogue." In *Treasures of Jewish Galicja*, ed. Sarah Harel Hoshen. Tel Aviv, 1996.

———. "The Origins of the 'Two-Column Motif' in European Paroket." *Jewish Art* 15 (1989).

Yargina, Z. *Wooden Synagogues*. Moscow, no date.

Yosef, Rabbi of Dubnow. *Yesod Yosef*. Shklow, Poland, 1785.

Zilbur, Mendel, ed. *The Gwoździec Memory Book* [in Hebrew]. Ramat Gan, Israel, 1974.

Zipperstein, Steven J. *Imagining Russian Jewry: Memory, History, Identity*. Seattle, 1999.

Zoltowskij, H. M. *Monumental Paintings in Ukraine, XVII–XVIII Centuries* [in Russian]. Kiev, 1988.

Żygulski, Zdzislaw, Jr. *Sztuka Islamu w zbiorach polskich* (Islamic Art in Polish Collections). Warsaw, 1989.

INDEX

Page numbers in *italics* represent illustrations.

225

Chodorów Synagogue *(continued)*
207n.61; wall-paintings of, 61–62, *62*, 91, 102; windows of, 207n.65
Chuppah (marriage canopy), 35, 144, 162–63, 212n.49
Churches: Orthodox, *50*, 72, *73*, 75, 199n.91. *See also* Catholic churches
Clasp-like motif, 95, *96*
Clustered-column plan: in masonry synagogues, 67, *67*, 154; in Pińsk Synagogue, *69*; as square synagogue plan, *66*; in Wołpa Synagogue, 63; *Zohar* on, 141, 148–49
Cohanim, 106, 107, 209n.7
Cohen, Gerson, 180n.11
Cohen, Richard, 189n.81
Color, 89–91, 192n.14, 193n.18
Commercial buildings, 4, 71
Conduct literature, 143, 206n.38
Construction: of Gwoździec Synagogue, 48–56; seventeenth- and eighteenth-century practices, 47–48, 185n.48. *See also* Building trades
Council of the Four Lands, 128
Counter-Reformation, 70, 134, 191n.102
Court pageantry, 71
Cracow (Poland): Church of Saints Peter and Paul, *74*; on European trade routes, *120*; Jewish district of, 201n.15; masonry synagogues in, 69; Old Synagogue, *66*
Cupolas: Baroque influences on, 72, 74, 75; of Chodorów Synagogue, 61, 62–63; divergent sources for, 69; Jabłonów Synagogue lacking, 60, 62; precedents for, 75, 191n.103; spatial foreshortening of, 75; as spreading throughout Poland, 59; of Wołpa Synagogue, 63–64, *64*, 75. *See also* Gwoździec Synagogue: cupola

Dan, Joseph, 155
Debno (Poland), *119*
Deer, 100, *100*, 195nn. 39, 40
Deluge, The, 130, *131*
Deutze (Germany), 105
Diaspora synagogues: American Reform synagogues, 151; eastern orientation of worship in, 29; foreign elements in, 18; inscriptions in, 103; interior and exterior contrasted, 23, *56*; material-culture study of, 151; plain exteriors of, 50; size restrictions on, 51, 186n.55. *See also* Masonry synagogues; Polish wooden synagogues
Divine Throne, 149
Dobromil (Ukraine), 125
Donor influences, 107
Donor inscriptions, *91*, 107
Door and window frames, *53*, 53–54, 186n.58
Drohobycz (Ukraine), 72, *73*, 118, *119*, 199n.91

Druja Synagogue (Poland), *52*
Dubnow, S. M., 17, 180n.10

Eastern Europe: building precedents for wooden synagogues, 70–75; construction practices in, 47–48, 185n.48; decorative arts influencing synagogue wall-painting, 117–18; geographic regions of central, *122*; historiography in, 19; map of central, *1*; relations between Jews and Eastern Europeans, 16, 19, 181n.22; statistical tabulation of synagogues in, 187n.65; vernacular buildings, 46–47, 51. *See also* Eastern-European Jewry; Poland
Eastern-European Jewry: Ashkenazi settlement in Poland, 109, 111, 124–26, 198n.73; bias against, 17–18, 180n.10; Chmielnicki massacres, 15, 18, 123, 129–30, *130*, 201n.19; conceptions and misconceptions about, 13–19; and the estates, *134*, 134–37; "golden age" of Polish Jewish culture, 128–29; in historical scholarship, 18–19; impermanence attributed to, 15, 179n.6, 199n.94; the Kahal, 128–29, *129*, 132, 201n.18; magnate support of, 54, 133–34; as middlemen between peasants and serfs, 136–37; population expansion in eastern Poland, 131–32, *132*; poverty of the shtetl, 13–15, 179n.5; pre-Hasidic popular Judaism, 210n.30; privileges granted to, 124–26; relations between Jews and Eastern Europeans, 16, 19, 181n.22; romanticism of the shtetl, 15–17, 179n.7, 185n.36; in trading towns, 126–27, *127*; travel by, 120–21, 199n.94; vernacular building techniques, 20; wall-painting associated with, 84; Western-European Jewry contrasted with, 17; Yiddish, 16, 109, 197n.60. *See also* Gwoździec Jewish community; Hasidism
Eisler, Max, 186n.58
Elbogen, Ismar, 141
Eleazar ben Judah of Worms, 99, 155, 194n.34
Elementary school *(heder)*, 15
Emden, Jacob, 211n.36
Enlightenment, Jewish. *See* Haskalah
Epstein, Marc Michael, 96, 98, 194n.30, 210n.20
Estates, *134*, 134–37
Esther Scrolls, 191n.2
Evening Worship (Hruzik), *84*
Evildoers, prohibition of depiction of, 102, 195n.48
Ezekiel, 145, 149, 182n.12, 207n.58

Farm houses, *135*
Fiddler on the Roof (film and play), 13, 14, 15

Fine, Steven, 182n.9
Floral motif, *117*, *118*, *119*
Frames, door and window, *53*, 53–54, 186n.58
Franzos, Karl Emil, 180n.10

Gameren, Tylman van, 191n.105
Gaon of Vilna, 160
Gate motif, 91, 193n.20
"Gate of Heaven" window, 89, 153–54
Ghettos, 3, 127, 201n.15
Gikatila, Joseph, 144
Ginsburg, Elliot K., 143, 162, 205n.28
Gminna Street (Gwoździec, Ukraine), 2–3, *3*
Goat, 101–2, *102*
Going to Town (Ajdukiewicz), *133*
Goldberg, Jacob, 125, 200n.9
Golden Rose (TaZ) Synagogue (Lviv, Ukraine), 67, *67*, 70
Graetz, Heinrich, 17, 180n.10
Gravestone carving, 111, *112*
Grayzel, Solomon, 180n.10
Green, Arthur, 204n.16, 211n.44
Greenewegs, Martin, 59, *59*
Gries, Zeev, 205n.20, 206n.40
Grodno-Białystok region, 63, 137, 190n.92
Grunwald, Max, 186n.58
Gutmann, Joseph, 162, 180n.12, 211n.43
Gwoździec (Ukraine): aerial diagram of, *2*; agricultural fairs in, 136; Catholics as minority in, 134; early settlement of, 124; ethnic and religious communities of, 1, *45*, 127; on European trade routes, *120*, 123; Gminna Street, 2–3, *3*; history of, 123–24; location of, 1, *1*; log buildings in, 53; noble families owning, 124; plan, c. 1920, *44*; sources of information about, 184n.30; Town Hall, 4, *4*; Town Square, 4, *4*, 43, *46*; as typical trading town, 127; Ukrainian agricultural villages surrounding, 135–36; Ukrainian Orthodox Church, *50*; World War I damage to, 2, 4, *44*. *See also* Bernardine Monastery and Catholic Church; Gwoździec Jewish community
Gwoździec Jewish community: acts of violence against, 203n.33; affluence of, 14–15; becoming majority population, 3, 46, 124; and Chmielnicki massacres, 123; community facilities and buildings, 184n.30; development of, 129–37; expansion of, 46; first mention of, 124; in Gminna Street, 2–3; integration in Polish milieu, 6, 16–17, 19, 46; and Kalinowski/Puzyna family, 4; location of Jewish district, 3, 43–46, *45*, *46*; nonuniform quality of district of, 5; population in 1731, 5, 124, 200n.5; rising aspirations

of, 163; settlement in Gwoździec, 124–29. *See also* Gwoździec Synagogue

Gwoździec Synagogue, 6–11
architecture of, 23–76; ark, 8, *28*, 29–32, *31*, *32*; axis and procession in, 32–33; bimah, 8, *8*, *28*, 29–32, *30*, *31*, *32*, 176; east elevation, *26*; floor plan, *23*; interior informed by Jewish culture, 23, 56–57; north elevation, *27*; organization and function, 29–38; plan organization, *29*; relative size of, *50*, 50–51, 186n.54; section, looking east, *55*, *152*; section, looking south, *28*, *150*, plate 2; section, looking west, *138*; south elevation, *25*; TaZ (Golden Rose) Synagogue ceiling compared with, *70*; unique west wall in, 146, *146*; west elevation, *24*; worship and usage, 36–38
Baal Shem Tov visiting, 185n.43
construction of, 48–56; ceiling remodeling, 57–58, *58*; community support for, 20; history of, 57–59; log walls, 51–54, *53*; remodeling of 1731, *1*, *8*; roof, roof structure, and cupola, 54–57, *55*, *56*; vertical post stiffeners, *49*, 54
cupola, 9, *9*, 33–36; arabesque motif in, 116, *116*; Baroque precedents in, 58, 74, 75, 183n.15; ceiling paintings, 154–61, *156*, *158*, *159*; Chodorów Synagogue's cupola compared with, 61, 62–63; construction of, 54–57; cubic volume created by, 33–34; dating of, 57–59; as first built in region, 1; as making prayer hall appear larger, 29; meaning of, 151–65; pendentives of, 33, *33*; prayers and inscriptions on, 176–77; profile of, *28*; roof shape contrasted with, 56–57; structure and roof framing, *58*; tent motif in, *1*, *9*, 20, 35–36, 47, 54, 72, 93, 117, 157, 161–63; *Zohar* as influence on, 142, 149
dating of, 57–59, 124, 186n.58, 188n.69
design of: architectural specialists in design of, 34–35, 48; Baroque features of, 20, 34, 56, 58, 75, 183n.15; designers of, 46–48; Jewish involvement in design of, 139–49; Jewish style of, 6; *Zohar* influencing design of, 142, 149
destruction of, 137, 203n.33
exterior: east facade, *49*; as informed by non-Jewish culture, 23, 56–57; ornament, 48–51, *49*; west facade, *22*
historical context of, 123–37
interpreting, 19–21
location of, *44*; proximity to Bernardine Catholic Church, 6, *49*, 123, 124, 134

prayer hall, 8, *8*, 29–32; arches behind seats, 37, 183n.23; benches in, 37, *37*; ceiling of, *1*, 8, 20; entrance to, *76*; inscriptions and date on door frame, *53*, 53–54, 186n.58; photographic evidence for, 184n.28; square plan of, 33–34, *34*, 145; as Tent of Heaven, 152, 161–63
support rooms and spaces, 39–46, *39*; courtyard, *5*, *5*, *40*; entrance, *7*, *7*, 39, 76, plate 1; foyer, *7*; house of study (beit midrash), 42–43; religious and community buildings surrounding, *40*; women's section, 10, *10*, 39, 40–41, *41*
unheated, *7*
wall-paintings, 77–121; "All the gates were closed" inscription, 153, 209n.8; animal figures in, *1*, 9, 77, 95–103, *97*, *98*; artists' signatures, *85*, 85–86, 176–77, 192n.8; in Ashkenazi tradition of synagogue art, 85–86, 109–15; Breier's studies of, *79*, plate 3; carpet compared with, 90–91; on central cupola, *78*; Chodorów Synagogue compared with, 61–63; colors in, 89–91, 192n.14, 193n.18; composition of, 87–93, *87*; cosmopolitan sources of, 116–22, 199n.92; documentation of, 85; east elevation, *80*; focal-points of the four walls, 89, *90*; images and inscriptions combined in, *1*, 77; Jabłonów Synagogue compared with, 60; Jewish eschatological figures in, 99; as liturgical art, 20, 191n.4; Menorah, 89, 109, *110*; multicultural influences on, *120*; north elevation, *81*; north wall, plate 4; organization of, 8, 77, 87–91; prayer panels, 91–93, *91*, *92*, 103–9, *104*, *105*, 113, 173–77, 196n.56; as resplendent, *1*; south elevation, *83*; Tablets of Law, 89, *156*; tent symbolism in, 93–95, *93*, *94*, *95*; west elevation, *82*; on west wall, *76*, 87–89, *88*, *89*, 192n.11
windows in, 147–48, *147*; lattice window, *11*, *11*, 152–54, *153*

Halych, 123
Hanhagot, 143
Hasidei Ashkenazi movement, 107–8
Hasidism: acceptance of, 180n.17; decentralized tradition of, 43, 185n.35; and decline of wooden synagogue tradition, 20, 21, 64, 65, 160–61, 210n.33; in Jewish historiography, 18; messianism transformed by, 210n.32; Nusah Sfard liturgy of, 106; opposition to, 160,

210n.31; and popular liturgies, 109; on prayer, 160–61; prosperity and early, 180n.11; and synagogue art and architecture, 189n.81; three Hasidim in Warsaw, *17*
Haskalah (Jewish Enlightenment): and bias against Eastern-European Jewry, 17; and decline of wooden synagogue tradition, 21, 64, 65, 160; in Jewish historiography, 18; and mysticism in popular Jewish culture, 109, 180n.11
Heating, 2, 7, 42, 184n.33
Hebrew script, 107–8, 197n.65
Heder (elementary school), *15*
Heschel, Abraham Joshua, 16
Holy of Holies, 33, 34, 145
Horb Synagogue (Germany), *86*, plate 5
Horowitz, Isaiah, 143
Host desecration, 134
Houses, 2–3, 70–71, *71*, *135*
Hrubieszow (Poland), *128*
Hruzik, Jan Kanty, *84*
Hundert, Gershon, 130, 181n.21, 201n.22
Huss, Boaz, 142

Idel, Moshe: on above/below metaphor, 206n.48; on color, 91, 193n.17; on Divine marriage imagery, 162; on Hasidism, 160–61; on Hebrew letters and words, 197n.65; on Jewish theurgical anthropology, 211n.37; on messianism, 192n.6; on *Zohar*, 142, 204n.16
Illuminated manuscripts, 113–15, *114*, *115*, 198n.78, plate 5
Inns (taverns), 71, *72*, 190n.95
Isaac (son of Judah Leib ha-Cohen), 9, 85, 113, 176–77
Islamic art, 116–17
Israel (son of Mordecai), 9, 85, *85*, 113, 176
Isserles, Moses, 144

Jabłonów Synagogue, 59–60; "All the gates were closed" inscription, 209n.8; arches behind seats in, 183n.23; flat ceiling of, 60, *62*; Kaufmann depicting, 184n.34; Kaufmann's *Rabbi at the wooden synagogue of Jabłonów*, *164*, plate 8; lattice window in, *153*; painted prayers, 108, *108*, 109, 196n.56; prayer stand from, *38*; section, looking north, *61*; wall-paintings in, 60, *60*; west elevation of, *60*
Jacob's ladder, 153
Janów Trembowelski (Ukraine), 207nn. 61, 65
Jarochow (Ukraine), 196n.56
Jarychów (Ukraine), 9, 77, 148, 207n.61, 210n.33
Jellinek, Aaron, 205n.18
Jerusalem, 29, 35, 198n.78, 207n.62

prosperity of, 19, 202n.23; resurgence after Chmielnicki massacres, 130–31, 201n.22; synagogues of, 20, 59, 60, 62

Poland: Ashkenazi settlement in, 109, 111, 124–26, 196n.73; Baroque influence in, 20, 70, 74, 191nn. 102, 105; Chmielnicki massacres, 15, 18, 123, 129–30, 130, 201n.19; contact with Islamic lands, 117; decorative arts imported to, 117–18; The Deluge, 130, 131; eastern expansion of, 124–26, 126; the estates, 134, 134–37; in European trade routes, 120; "golden age" of Polish Jewish culture, 128–29; historiography in, 19, 181nn. 18, 19, 20; Jewish population expansion in eastern, 131–32, 132; Jewish population in 1731, 124; magnates, 54, 124, 127, 133–34, 187n.61; manor houses of, 70–71, 71; partitions of, 136, 137; patterns of Jewish immigration to, 125; privileges granted to Jews in, 124–26; spatial relationship of church and synagogue in, 52; statistical tabulation of synagogues in, 187n.65; tents of the aristocracy, 35; trading towns in, 126–27, 127; as underdeveloped, 200n.6; westernization of eastern provinces, 126–27; Zohar coming to, 143–44. See also Podolia; Polish wooden synagogues

Polin (journal), 181n.21

Polish wooden synagogues: almost-square plans of, 33, 145, 182n.11; axis and procession in, 32–33; Chmielnicki massacres and building of, 130; Christian builders for, 47; cupolas in, 36; dating of, 188n.69; decline of tradition of, 20–21, 64–65, 160–61, 189n.79; design and construction skills required for, 47; destruction by Nazis, 57; Eastern-European building precedents for, 70–75; economic growth and construction of, 132; furnishings of, 38; German influence on, 109, 111; of Grodno-Białystok region, 63, 190n.92; and historical scholarship of Eastern-European Jewry, 18–19; lattice windows in, 154, 208n.4; log walls for, 53; in Lviv, 59, 59; magnates supporting construction of, 54, 133, 187n.61; masonry synagogues compared with, 68–70, 190n.92; masonry synagogues supplanting, 65–66; and misconceptions about Eastern-European Jewry, 13, 14; multicultural design elements in, 20; originality and uniqueness of, 19–20, 132–33, 202n.26; relative size of, 50–51, 186n.54; roof truss systems, 54, 187n.63; typology of, 65; as unheated, 7, 42, 184n.33; unique west walls in, 146, 207n.63; wall-paintings in,

8, 9, 17–18; Zohar in design of, 140–49. See also Chodorów Synagogue; Gwoździec Synagogue; Jabłonów Synagogue; Wolpa Synagogue

Portal of the Rabbis (Kaufmann), 76, plate 1

Posner, Raphael, 141

Potocki family, 124

Poverty, shtetl, 13–15, 179n.5

Prayer: ascent of, 147, 207n.65; ecstatic, 91; Hasidic, 160–61, 211n.36; outdoor, 145, 207n.52. See also Prayers

Prayer books, 38, 105–6, 196n.59

Prayer halls: cupolas and domes generally absent in, 183n.21; of Jabłonów Synagogue, 59–60; used as house of study, 43. See also Gwoździec Synagogue: prayer hall

Prayers: "Al tira mi 'fahad," 106; "Berirkh Shemei," 105, 108, 109; in Chodorów Synagogue wall-paintings, 107, 107; in Gwoździec Synagogue wall-paintings, 91–93, 91, 92, 103–9, 104, 105, 113, 173–77, 196n.56; in Jabłonów Synagogue wall-paintings, 108, 108, 109, 196n.56; "Modim d'Rabbanan," 103, 105, 107, 176; "Ribono shel olam, ani shelakh vehalomatai shelakh," 105; "Ribono shel olam, malei misheloti," 105, 108, 109; "U'v'nuho yomar," 106, 107, 108; "Va'ani b'rov hasdecha," 106, 107, 109. See also "Lekhah Dodi"

Prayer stands, 38, 38

Predator scenes, 101–2, 195nn. 44, 46, 196n.49

Psalm 67, 105, 109, 110

Psalm 130, 140

Puzyna, Zofia, 35, 54, 134, 183n.14

Puzyna family, 4, 124

Rabbi at the wooden synagogue of Jabłonów (Kaufmann), 164, plate 8

Rainbow, 159

Rashbi (Simeon ben Yohai), 141

Rav, 208n.72

Recanati, Menahem, 143, 144

Reform synagogues, American, 151

Renaissance architecture, 145, 207n.62

"Ribono shel olam, ani shelakh vehalomatai shelakh," 105

"Ribono shel olam, malei misheloti," 105, 108, 109

Ritual bathhouses, 46

Romanesque art, 112–13

Roof, 54–57

Rope motif, 94, 94

Rosman, Moshe J., 130–31, 181n.21, 185n.38, 201n.22, 210n.31

Ruderman, David B., 210n.20

Ruskin, John, 187n.64, 193n.18

Sabbatai Sevi, 18, 109, 210n.32

Sabbath worship: Kabbalah influencing, 162, 211n.48; Kabbalat Shabbat, 8, 11, 107, 154, 162; and Tabernacle/Temple imagery, 162

Sachar, Howard Morley, 180n.10

St. George, Church of (Drohobycz, Ukraine), 72, 73, 118, 119, 199n.91

St. Paraskeva, Church of (Krekhiv, Ukraine), 73

Saints Peter and Paul, Church of (Cracow, Poland), 74

"Sarmatian" ideology, 35

Scallop motif, 93, 93, 116

Scholem, Gershom: on above/below metaphor, 206n.48; on ascent of prayer, 207n.65; on Ba'al Shem Tov, 163, 165; on Divine marriage ceremony, 162, 211n.44; on Eleazar of Worms, 99; on Hasidism, 210n.32; on Jewish messianic movements, 192n.6; on Kabbalah in Podolia, 202n.22; on Kabbalistic influence on Jewish life, 211n.48; on Polish Kabbalah, 206nn. 43, 46; on the Zohar, 141–42, 144, 204nn. 14, 15, 16, 17, 205nn. 31, 33

Schor, Rabbi Isaac, 9, 185n.43

Second Commandment, 9, 18

Second Temple, 29, 32, 33, 34

Sefer Evronot, 114, 115, 198n.82, plate 7

Sephardic Jewry, 116–17

Sha'arey 'Orah (Gikatila), 144

Sha'arey Zion (prayer book), 105

Shekhinah: deer representing, 100, 195n.40, 209n.5; and "Lekhah Dodi," 11, 91, 107, 154; as looking through lattice window, 11, 154, 195n.40, 208n.3; Tabernacle as wedding canopy for, 144, 162, 211n.44; weekly exile of, 162, 211n.47; Zohar on, 100, 154, 195n.40, 208n.3, 209n.5

Shenei Luhot ha-Berit (Horowitz), 143

Shmuel, 208n.72

Sholem Aleichem, 13, 16

Shtetl Jewry. See Eastern-European Jewry

Shulhan Arukh (Caro), 143, 204n.7

Shulvass, Moses A., 201n.21

Simeon ben Yohai (Rashbi), 141

Single-vault plan, 67, 67

Smotrich (Ukraine), 196n.56

Snaidowo Synagogue (Poland), 52

Sobieski, Jan, III, 35, 93

Song of Songs, 152, 211n.44

Spytkowice (Poland), 72

Square plan: in Jewish art and architecture, 182n.12; in masonry synagogues, 66–68, 66, 67, 189n.85; Zohar on, 145. See also Clustered-column plan

Stitching motif, 94, 95